I0313887

Travis Zadeh is Assistant Professor of Islamic Studies in the Department of Religious Studies at Yale University, New Haven. Prior to joining Yale, he served as Chair of the Religion Department at Haverford College, Pennsylvania, where he taught Islamic studies and comparative literature for nearly a decade. He received his PhD from Harvard University in Comparative Literature and has published widely on Islamic history. He is also the author of *The Vernacular Qur’an: Translation and the Rise of Persian Exegesis*, which examines early debates over translating the Qurʾān and the development of Persian exegetical literature. In 2013, Zadeh received a multi-year New Directions Mellon Fellowship to conduct research on frontiers and conversion in the formative periods of Islamic religious history.

'A brilliant discussion of the themes of wonder, translation from one medium to another and other major concepts in medieval Islamic writing – both in Persian and in Arabic.'

– Roy Mottahedeh, Gurney Professor of History, Harvard University

'This valuable study allows the reader to better understand not only 'Abbasid culture but also, more broadly, the contemporary Arab World.'

– Jolanda Guardi, *Digest of Middle East Studies*

'Zadeh's approach is refreshing … [and] highly thought-provoking, with new ground broken in many chapters … [and with] novel interpretations of a wide range of topics that touch upon 'Abbasid culture and history.'

– Adam Silverstein, *Journal of the American Oriental Society*

MAPPING FRONTIERS ACROSS MEDIEVAL ISLAM

Geography, Translation, and the ʿAbbāsid Empire

Travis Zadeh

I.B. TAURIS
LONDON · NEW YORK

Paperback edition published in 2017 by
I.B.Tauris & Co. Ltd
London • New York
www.ibtauris.com

Hardback edition first published in 2011 by
I.B.Tauris & Co. Ltd

Copyright © 2011 Travis Zadeh

The right of Travis Zadeh to be identified as the author of this work has been asserted by the author in accordance with the Copyright, Designs and Patent Act 1988.

All rights reserved. Except for brief quotations in a review, this book, or any part thereof, may not be reproduced, stored in or introduced into a retrieval system, or transmitted, in any form or by any means, electronic, mechanical, photocopying, recording or otherwise, without the prior written permission of the publisher.

Every attempt has been made to gain permission for the use of the images in this book. Any omissions will be rectified in future editions.

References to websites were correct at the time of writing.

ISBN: 978 1 78453 739 5
eISBN: 978 1 78672 131 0
ePDF: 978 1 78673 131 9

A full CIP record for this book is available from the British Library
A full CIP record for this book is available from the Library of Congress

Library of Congress Catalog Card Number: available

Edited by Valerie J. Turner, www.valeriejoyturner.com
Typeset by Muhammad I. Hozien, www.scholarlytype.com

Cover image: The Expedition of Alexander the Great in the Encircling Ocean, al-Qazwīnī, *Ajāib al-makhlūqāt* ('The Wonders of Creation'), The John Rylands University Library, The University of Manchester, Persian MS 3, fol. 61a. Reproduced by courtesy of the University Librarian and Director, The John Rylands University Library, The University of Manchester.
Cover design: Positive2

CONTENTS

Plates, Figures, and Maps vii
Note on Conventions ix
Acknowledgments x

Introduction 1

SECTION ONE: GEOGRAPHY, TRANSLATION, AND THE APOCALYPSE
1. Routes and Realms 15
2. Models of Translation 34
3. Al-Wāthiq and the Translators 49

SECTION TWO: MARVELOUS ALTERITY
4. A Geography of Neighbors 67
5. A Wondrous Barrier 97

SECTION THREE: BEYOND THE WALL
6. To Live to Tell 129
7. Beyond the Walls of the Orient 148

Conclusion 179
Postscript: Royal Graffiti 188

Appendix 1: The Dissemination of the Adventure 193
Appendix 2: The Vienna Recension 195
Appendix 3: The Bodleian Recension 201
Appendix 4: The Idrīsī Recension 205
List of Abbreviations 208
Notes 211
Bibliography 262
Index of People 287
Index of Places 296
Index of Subjects and Terms 300
Index of Scriptural Citations 316

PLATES, FIGURES, AND MAPS

Plates

Plate 1: People of Gog and Magog sighted by merchants, Shahmardān b. Abī 'l-Khayr, *Nuzhat-nāma-i ʿalāʾī.*

Plate 2: The expedition of Alexander the Great in the Encircling Ocean, Zakariyyāʾ al-Qazwīnī, *ʿAjāʾib al-makhlūqāt.*

Plate 3: Khusraw Anūshirwān's dream of the creature from the Caspian Sea, Zakariyyāʾ al-Qazwīnī, *ʿAjāʾib al-makhlūqāt.*

Plate 4: *Qibla* map, Zakariyyāʾ al-Qazwīnī, *Āthār al-bilād.*

Plate 5: Iskandar builds a wall against the people of Gog and Magog, Abū 'l-Qāsim al-Firdawsī, *Shāh-nāma.*

Plate 6a: *Mappa mundi,* Abū ʿAbd Allāh al-Idrīsī, *Nuzhat al-mushtāq.*

Plate 6b: Detail of *mappa mundi,* Abū ʿAbd Allāh al-Idrīsī, *Nuzhat al-mushtāq.*

Plate 7: Magnified view of the gate to Dhū 'l-Qarnayn's wall, from Abū ʿAbd Allāh al-Idrīsī's *Nuzhat al-mushtāq.*

Plate 8: Detail of Dhū 'l-Qarnayn's gate in a *mappa mundi,* from an anonymous Egyptian manuscript, entitled *Kitāb gharāʾib al-funūn wa mulaḥ al-ʿuyūn.*

Plate 9: Sallām al-Tarjumān observing a maiden, Zakariyyāʾ al-Qazwīnī, *ʿAjāʾib al-makhlūqāt.*

Plate 10: Sallām al-Tarjumān shown the wall of Gog and Magog in a compilation entitled *ʿAjāʾib al-buldān.*

Plate 11: *Mappa mundi*, with the gate and wall of Gog and Magog, Abū 'l-Qāsim al-Zayyānī, *Riḥlat al-ḥudhdhāq*.

Plate 12: *Mappa mundi* attributed to Abū Yūsuf al-Kindī and Aḥmad b. al-Ṭayyib al-Sarakhsī.

Plate 13: Detail of emended section of Ibn Khurradādhbih, *al-Masālik wa 'l-mamālik*.

Plate 14: Ibn Faḍlān shown a dead giant from the people of Gog and Magog, Muḥammad b. Maḥmūd al-Ṭūsī, *ʿAjāʾib-nāma*.

Figures

Figure 1: The Early ʿAbbāsid Caliphs xiv

Figure 2: *Kishwar* map 85

Figure 3: Recensions of Sallām's Adventure 194

Maps

Map 1: The ʿAbbāsid World circa 225/840 xiii

Map 2: The Khazar and Neighboring Regions 69

Map 3: Transoxiana and Central Asia 122

NOTE ON CONVENTIONS

Arabic and Persian transliterations follow a modified system based on the standard of the *International Journal of Middle East Studies* (*IJMES*). Syriac transliteration largely parallels Gotthelf Bergsträßer, *Einführung in die semitischen Sprachen* (1928); eastern pronunciation is used, with the spirantization marked, but without notation of the schwa. The transcription of Middle Persian follows the system developed by D. N. Mackenzie. Unpointed or otherwise illegible graphemes, such as an undotted tooth (the base for 'b,' 't,' etc.), or an unvocalized consonantal form, are indicated with a period. Chinese characters are Romanized using simplified *pinyin* transcription. Names and toponyms from non-Latin alphabets are transliterated unless common to English. The genealogical sequence Zayd ibn Zayd, etc., is abbreviated with 'b.' for ibn (son); the definite article on the *nisba* and the *laqab* is dropped after its first appearance, i.e., from 'al-Bukhārī' to 'Bukhārī,' or 'al-Jāḥiẓ' to 'Jāḥiẓ,' and so forth. However, definite articles are maintained for honorifics and formal titles, i.e., al-Manṣūr. Dates preceding the start of the Islamic calendar are given according to the common era; dates pertaining to Islamic history are indicated both in *hijrī* and Common Era forms. All translations are mine unless otherwise indicated.

ACKNOWLEDGMENTS

"La Biblioteca es ilimitada y periódica"
— Jorge Luis Borges

The bulge-eyed literary luminary of Basra, Abū ʿUthmān al-Jāḥiẓ was never known to have been much of a traveler, at least according to the geographical authorities, though he clearly enjoyed compiling entertaining anecdotes from far-off lands. In popular legend, he is said to have been crushed to death in old age when his library collapsed upon him. Such has been the fate of bibliophiles. As for their books, in a pattern of seemingly chaotic dispersal, they have traveled along crossroads on camelback, pausing at the remnants of abandoned campsites in the stretching dunes of history; they have been put up for sale in book markets, copied along the way from hand to print to critical editions, translated into, at times, not so willing forms, stacked into archives and libraries, and ultimately lost altogether.

While this is a book for travelers, or at least made up of them, it, too, will undoubtedly share a similar fate of dispersal and loss—though that is another story altogether. For this is a tale not only of the effacement of knowledge, but of its dissemination and re-creation. Much of the groundwork for this tour through the archives was prepared in the service of my doctoral research, which traced the formation of frontiers, as well as their maintenance and dissolution in acts of translation. This current book fits into a larger project on translation and knowledge in medieval Islamic intellectual history. For now, this leads us to the exotic world of geography with its own attachment to imperial archives. The companion to this book follows the problem of mediating alterity, not in the realm of the monstrous and the mundane, but through the sublime word of revelation.

This project has developed through the support of many mentors, friends and librarians. I would like to express particular gratitude to Luis

Girón-Negrón, Wolfhart Heinrichs, Roy Mottehadeh, and Wheeler Thackston, who, during my doctoral research at Harvard University (2007), helped to illuminate this long and tortuous path with their overflowing erudition. Special thanks goes to Katharine Park for introducing me to the wondrous world of Latin paleography; Mary Gaylord for helping me get started on this *quixotic* adventure; the late Mohammad Arkoun for his advice on *ʿajāʾib* literature; Shawkat Toorawa for even more wonders upon wonders; James Montgomery, whose work has been a constant inspiration; Todd Lawson for his input on Islamic apocalyptic; Sidney Griffith and Alexander Treiger for their philological expertise; Susan Halpert at Houghton Library, who made the collection all the more accessible; Mary McWilliams, Curator of the Islamic and Later Indian Art Collection at the Harvard Sackler Museum, for her gracious support during a Mellon fellowship in Islamic art working with the Sackler collection; Jeffrey Spurr and András Riedlmayer from the Aga Khan Program for Islamic Architecture at Harvard's Fine Arts Library; James Gulick, Rob Haley, and the library staff at Haverford College; Betsy Kohut at the Smithsonian Institution; Nicole Fürtig at the Staatsbibliothek of Berlin; Andreas Fingernagel at the Österreichische Nationalbibliothek; Sinéad Ward at the Chester Beatty Library; Dorothy Clayton at the John Rylands Library; Gillian Evison at the Special Collections of the Bodleian Library, as well as Colin Barker and Muhammad Isa Waley in the Arabic and Persian archives of the British Library, all of whom were extremely solicitous and helpful in the course of my research; Christian Lange for the many years of friendship and for our discussion of the *Ḥudūd al-ʿālam* on a Swiss chairlift; Matthew Melvin-Koushki for leading me through the archives of Rabat; Dan Sheffield for his encyclopedic knowledge of pre-Islamic Iran; *shaykh* Isam Eydoo at the University of Damascus; the year-long Humanities Center workshop, "Exploring frontiers in the histories of Islamicate Societies (2005–6)," run by Supriya Gandhi and Aliya Iqbal, which offered a sustained and lasting forum consistently germane to the development of my research. Furthermore, I would also like to acknowledge the invaluable advice and suggestions offered by various colleagues—Blain Auer, Jason Clower, Alexander Key, Luke Leafgren, Elias Muhanna, Martin Nguyen, and Naseem Surhio. Particular gratitude also goes to Valerie Turner for her patient and watchful eye.

My work has benefited from the generous support of a Fulbright-Hays dissertation research grant, a Harvard Sheldon travel grant, a TAARII summer grant for archival work in Europe, as well as a year-long Mellon Humanities Center fellowship at Harvard University. Faculty research grants from the Provost's Office at Haverford College have made possible further research trips to various archives. The Tuttle Grant for visual culture, administered through the Humanities Center at Haverford, has greatly facilitated the reproduction of the manuscript images contained within this book. Over the last three years, the tireless work of my research assistants, Frasat Ahmad, Scott Schnur, Edin Fako, Paul Benjamin, and Maya Bloom, as well as Kay Warner, faculty administrative assistant, has helped see this project to fruition. I would also like to thank my colleagues at Haverford, particularly Deborah Roberts, Aryeh Kosman, Maris Gillette, Tracey Hucks, and Ken Koltun-Fromm for their advice, suggestions, and encouragement. Various sections of this book were read at the Eastern International Regional Meeting of the American Academy of Religion (2005), at the annual conferences of the American Oriental Society (2006), and the Middle East Studies Association (2006). Selections were also presented in my upper level seminar at Haverford College, "Of Monsters and Marvels: Wonder in Islamic Traditions" (2007–8), as well as in the Religion Department symposium at Swarthmore College (2010), and the tenth conference of the School of ʿAbbāsid Studies, Leuven (2010).

My family has been a constant source of inspiration. I would like to express gratitude to my mother, Cynthia Eastman, not only for bringing me into the world, but also for listening to what I had to say once I arrived, and to my father, Mehdi Bahraini Zadeh, for it is through him that my passion for Persian began. My wife's parents, Rajmohan and Usha Gandhi, with their own world adventures, have been role models. This project could not have been done without the continued support of my wife, Supriya Gandhi, who let our many walks along the Charles River and now along the nature trail of this bucolic island drift into questions of translation. She has been the greatest wonder of all.

Haverford College
July 2010

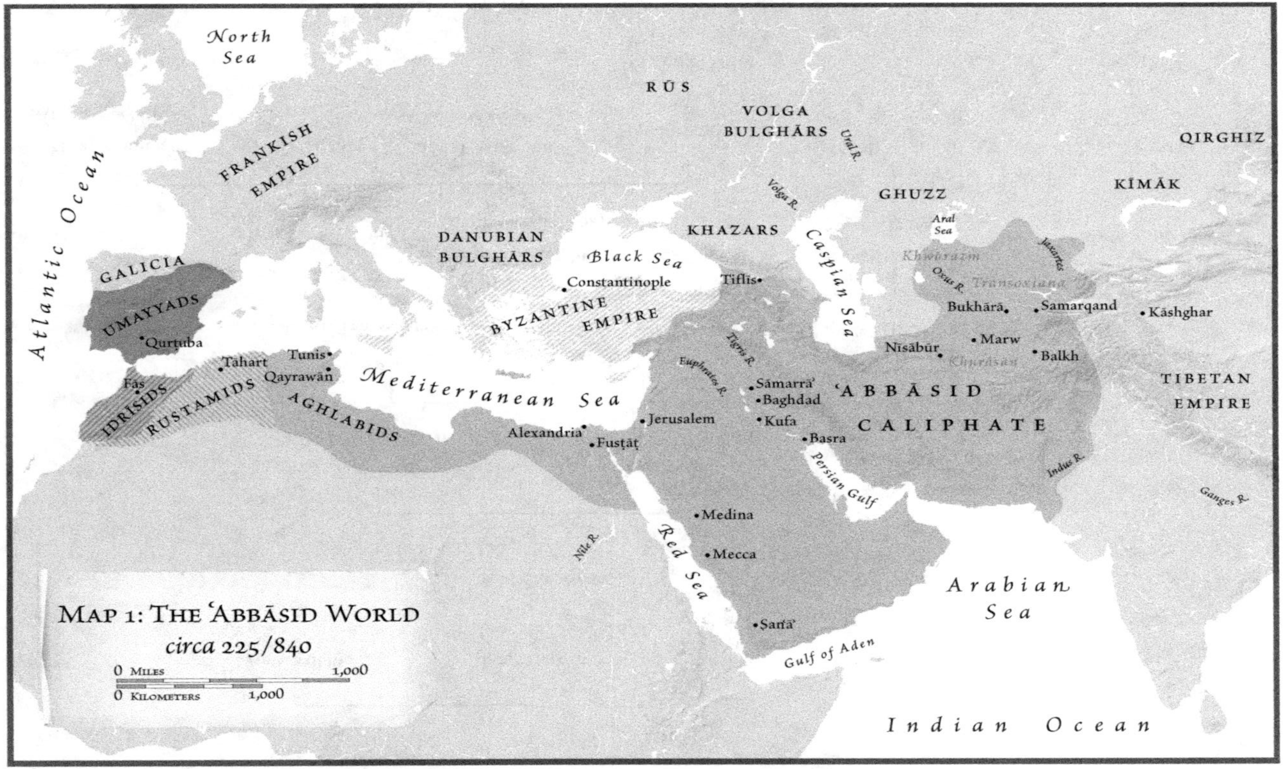

Map 1: The 'Abbāsid World *circa* 225/840

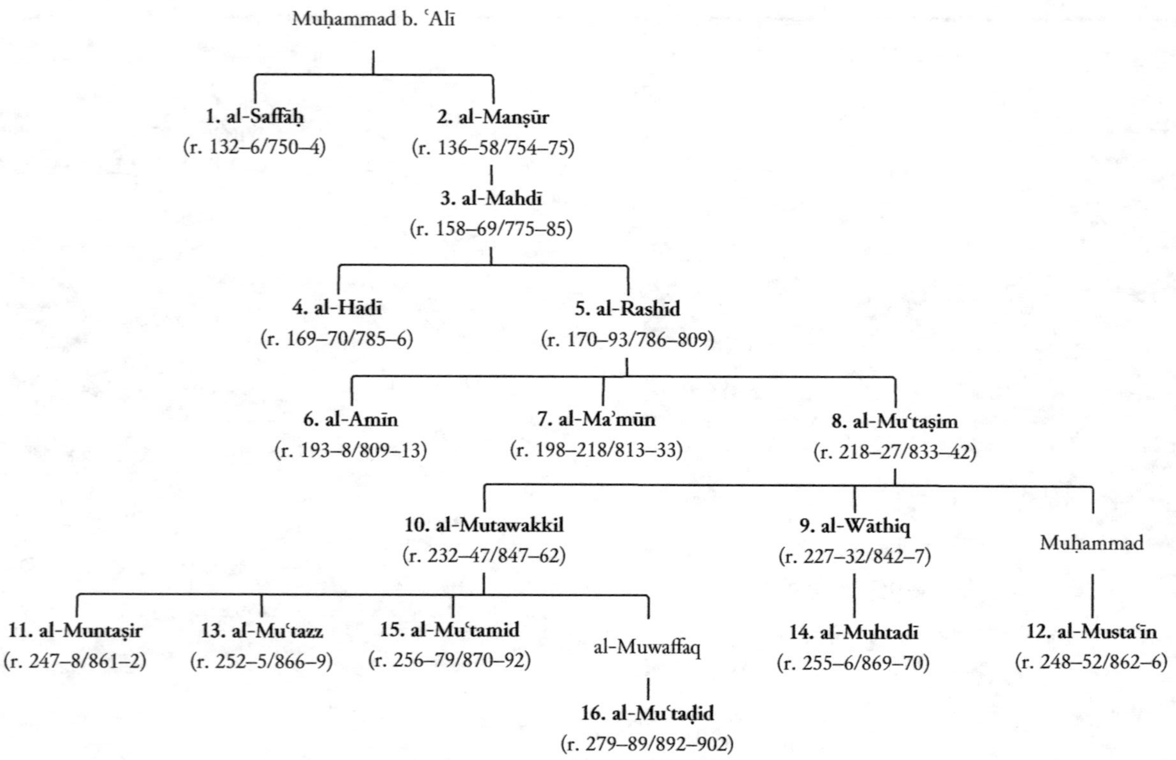

Figure 1: The Early ʿAbbāsid Caliphs

INTRODUCTION

Modes of Translation

The present study examines the role of translation in its hermeneutical capacity and as a basis of epistemology within medieval Arabic and Persian descriptive geography. While geographical writings continued to evolve throughout Islamic intellectual history, the development of the discipline is intimately related to the administration of the ʿAbbāsid empire during the course of the third/ninth century (map 1; fig. 1). The totalizing grandeur of geography, with its imperial illusion of possessing the world, sets out to blanket the horizons of the earth in text and image.

Throughout this field runs a persistent concern with translation and the mediation of difference—in spatial, conceptual, and ethnic terms. This often coalesces around a discourse of the marvelous (*ʿajab*), such that the wonders of the world become a salient feature of Arabic and Persian writings on the nature of existence. This body of literature is infused with the language of the apocalypse, anticipating the annihilation of all human existence in the final hour of judgment, suggesting a paradigmatic intersection of core assumptions and beliefs in the relationship between scripture and geography. The monstrous as a portentous sign is a prominent feature in Islamic apocalyptic literature.

Constructing the 'savage' is arguably a defining characteristic of civilization. The struggles against Humbaba in the Assyrian epic *Gilgamesh*, the Cyclops of Homer's *Odyssey*, Grendel from the Anglo-Saxon *Beowulf*, and Ẓaḥḥāk from the Persian *Shāh-nāma* can all be seen as attempts to mediate and sublimate the danger of the foreign and remote. The monstrous is one of the most palpable demarcations of alterity, and, as wedded to the marvelous and the exotic, dwells most often at the margins of the imagination, pushed from the center toward land's end.

The interpretative act of 'thick description' offers a theoretical model for this project; namely that the individual elements of the particular, of the anecdotal, when constituted or analyzed through their relationship to the broader structures of the universal, may reveal a good deal about culture and ideology.[1] The illusion of the anecdote lies in its simple reduction of ontology into a bounded and closed narrative form. Such sleight of hand is only possible through the interpretive communities that make a given narrative meaningful. Thus the original articulation of any account depends upon the larger context of its production. Yet such original contexts of production do not predetermine meaning across the polysemous expanse of diachronic dissemination, itself animated through a process of interpretation and translation.

Our point of entry into the field of descriptive geography, a discipline concerned with maintaining the semblance of encyclopedic totality, is a single ʿAbbāsid embassy sent beyond the frontiers of Islamic civilization. This narrative has been the subject of an ongoing scholarly debate that has focused primarily on the question of authenticity. Appearing throughout medieval Islamic geography, along with a host of other discursive fields, the anecdote details a mission to the end of the world to discover the land of the monstrous tribes of Yājūj and Mājūj. These tribes, mentioned in the Qurʾān as races set to destroy all of humankind at the end of time, find their place in Christian and Jewish scriptures as Gog and Magog, and thus represent a shared eschatology of final destruction. Here the scriptural is directly fused to the earthly in a landscape of demonic proportions, foretelling the ultimate annihilation of the world. In Islamic geographical discourse, as represented in this particular anecdote and numerous others like it, a pattern of engaging with difference develops, affirming that boundaries themselves are never truly stable, but are, rather, dissolved and erected through acts of translation.[2]

Of Marvels and Monsters

In early ʿAbbāsid geographies we not only see the translation, adaptation, and reconfiguration of marvel-writing from Greek antiquity, often through the medium of Syriac translations, but we also encounter repeated stories of translators and problems of communicating across frontiers. Interpreters populate the frontier as a means of surveilling and articulating imperial dominion, controlling liminal spaces through a construction of knowledge about the other. Here translation serves as a domestication of the foreign and remote, where the translators who appear in geographical writings on marvels and monsters help to bring near and subdue the strange and uncanny.

Recurrent in Islamic philosophical writings is the view that the emotional state of wonder (*ʿajab*) manifests through a confusion that arises from a lack of knowledge about the cause (*sabab*) of a given phenomenon.[3] This definition can be traced back to Aristotle's argument, expressed in the *Metaphysica* (9.82^{b}11–83^{a}23), that in the act of wonder (*θαυμάζειν*) we find the beginning of philosophy. A writer like Zakariyyāʾ al-Qazwīnī (d. 682/1283) constructs his encyclopedia on the marvels of the world, the *ʿAjāʾib al-makhlūqāt* [Wonders of existence], on the basis of this Aristotelian principle that curiosity is the foundation of philosophical speculation (*naẓar*).[4] Much of the material that Qazwīnī and other Arabic and Persian authors draw from can be found in the Greek tradition of pseudo-scientific marvel-writing (*παραδοξογραφία*), a genre populated by dog-headed men (*κυνοκέφαλοι*) and tribes of wild pygmies (*πυγμαῖοι*).[5]

The homiletic force of the Qurʾān serves as a prime source for the concept of the marvelous as it develops within Islamic intellectual history. Repeated in the Qurʾān is the injunction to contemplate the creation of the heavens and the earth. Such homiletic discourse serves to prove God's existence. Accordingly, a teleological argument runs through the entire cosmos, from the stars above to insects below, all reflecting a cosmic order of divine design.[6]

The interconnected relationship between the microcosmic and macrocosmic levels of existence builds upon the notion that every aspect of creation, however minuscule or monstrous, is in concert with this cosmic order. Thus the ʿAbbāsid intellectual and man of letters, Abū ʿUthmān al-Jāḥiẓ (d. 255/868–9), comments in the *Kitāb al-ḥayawān* [Book of the animals] that, in the gnat's wing there is a reflection (*ʿibra*) of this larger divine design, just waiting to be uncovered by those who can discern an "abundance of wonders spread therein" (*min kathrati ʾl-taṣarrufi fī ʾl-aʿājīb*).[7] Jāḥiẓ argues that the small and even the abhorrent all reflect a sublime arrangement:

> [God] leaves nothing without a purpose or without meaning, nothing scattered or unordered, no thread left loose. He makes no errors in His wondrous design (*min ʿajīb taqdīrihi*), and He neglects no detail in His elegant order, not in terms of the beauty of construction, nor magnificence of its power as a proof (*burhān*). All this extends from lice and butterflies to the seven celestial spheres and the seven climes of the earth.[8]

As an ordering principle, such an interconnection between micro- and macrocosms, is, according to Michel Foucault, built upon the logic of "duplicated resemblances," where "nature, like the interplay of signs and resemblances, is closed in upon itself in conformity with the duplicated form of the cosmos."[9] This closure in the context of Islamic theodicy results from a cosmic order that privileges, above all, the principle of divine unity.

In such a configuration, the question of the independent existence of evil apart from God became a theological flash point of debate. For Jāḥiẓ, schooled within Muʿtazilī theology, which promoted unity (*tawḥīd*) and justice (*ʿadl*) as the primary principles of divine nature, the well-being (*maṣlaḥa*) of the world depended upon the balance between good and evil (*imtizāj al-khayr biʾl-sharr*). Without the harmful (*al-ḍārr*), the vile (*al-makrūh*), and the lowly (*al-ḍaʿa*), there could be no way of knowing the good.[10] Such theological articulations were informed by the translation and absorption of material from classical Greek philosophy. With the ʿAbbāsid translation of Galen's *Compendium of Plato's Timaeus*, we have, for instance, a formulation of divine theodicy which came to serve as a source of major contention within the development of Islamic theology: "It is impossible that the world be in any condition more excellent than that in which it is (*lā yumkinu an yakūna ʿalā ḥālin afḍala min ḥālihi ʾllatī huwa ʿalayhā*)."[11]

The Ashʿarī theologian Abū Ḥāmid al-Ghazālī (d. 505/1111) argued along similar lines when he reiterated this formulation as, "It is impossible for the form of this world (*ṣūrat hādhā ʾl-ʿālam*) to be more wondrous (*abdaʿ*) than it is, of a more beautiful arrangement (*aḥsan tartīban*), or of a more complete design (*akmal ṣanʿan*)."[12] Such theological optimism, in the strict sense of the word, proved to be highly contentious, particularly in regard to its perceived limitation of divine omnipotence (*ḥaṣr al-qudra*). However, the argument that there is no substantive quality to evil that could exist as an independent power, apart from God, came to be widely accepted as a normative position within the framework of Islamic theology.[13] The ontological status of the monstrous, of the abhorrent, and of evil was thus shaped within the fabric of salvation history, as part of the marvelous and uncanny design of God's creation. As such, the monstrous, however portentous, was not just a sign of demonic machinations, but also of a sublime and mysterious order.

Epistemes

Generally speaking, medieval Muslim writers, with the notable exception of some philosophers (*falāsifa*), did not question the literalness of the supernatural issues treated in the Qurʾān; *jinn* and angels, talking birds and insects, and people waking up after years of slumber are all part of divine orchestration. The revelation of the Qurʾān is itself viewed as a providential intersection with the course of human history. In such a configuration, the world is full of enchantment, where ruptures with the ordinary (*al-khārij ʿan al-ʿāda*), with normative phenomenological experience, are indications of miraculous workings.

Medieval Arabic and Persian geographical writings form part of a broader ordering of the world within an Islamic cosmographical system, where scripture and salvation enwrap the contours of the globe. The paradigm of the wondrous world of diversity, and with it monstrosity, continues to operate in the early modern transmission of geographical knowledge. Well into the nineteenth century, Islamic cartographical projections circulate that include the land of Gog and Magog, ominously mentioned in the Qurʾānic account of Dhū 'l-Qarnayn (Q. 18:83–100), 'the Possessor of Two-Horns,' who is generally identified with Alexander the Great (356–323 B.C.E.). According to the Qurʾān and sayings of the Prophet Muḥammad, at the end of time these monstrous tribes, which Dhū 'l-Qarnayn bottled up behind a wall at the edge of the earth, will break free from their enclosure and descend upon the world as a scourge to destroy all humanity.

With the authority of the Qurʾān, the existence of this wall, along with questions about its location, has been a field of perennial interest throughout Islamic history. For instance, the Syrian intellectual Rashīd Riḍā (d. 1935) responded in his reformist journal, *al-Manār* (1908), to a letter written by a Muslim from Sudan. The letter inquired whether the barrier mentioned in the Qurʾān as the wall against Gog and Magog corresponded to the Great Wall of China. This particular theory was championed by many western scholars in the eighteenth and nineteenth centuries as a way of demystifying the account of Alexander's barrier and assigning it a historical origin.[14] Rashīd Riḍā replied that these two barriers should not be confused. Rather, he concluded that the wall was most probably located in either the North or South Poles, regions that in his day had yet to be fully explored.[15] Even though the penetration of the earth's farthest frontiers has yet to reveal an invincible barrier, Gog and Magog have continued to stir up the apocalyptic imaginations of the three competing monotheistic faiths; they lurk in the geopolitical landscapes of conspiracy theories and end-time scenarios, now largely reduced to a polysemous language of symbols and portentous signs.[16]

At the most basic level, the wall of Gog and Magog represents for medieval thought the frontiers of knowledge, a semiotic 'No more beyond' (*non plus ultra*), which, like the Pillars of Hercules flanking the Strait of

Gibraltar's egress into the Atlantic Ocean, demarcates the limitations of human capacity. Such conceptual boundaries slowly gave way to a process of competitive mercantile expansion which led, quite accidentally, to the European conquest of the Americas. Charles V (r. 1516–58), the Holy Roman Emperor and ruler of large swaths of newly-conquered American territories, altered the Herculean phrase to suit his imperial motto 'more beyond' (*plus ultra*), and with it claimed an ever-expanding empire. With the Age of Discovery and the rise of the Enlightenment, the limits of knowledge and the systems of thought that governed them underwent radical reformulations the world over.

The putative backwardness of the 'Oriental,' thought to be due, in part, to a childish fixation with superstitions, served as a rationale for European colonialism and its civilizing mission. Just as the enchanted world of European medieval learning and literature was blamed, in large measure, on the disproportionate influence of oriental tales,[17] the category of the medieval itself spoke to a specific Western teleology that led through the Renaissance to the Enlightenment, and concluded with the progress of Modernity. As these were stages of history that oriental peoples did not enjoy, they remained, in some basic sense, in a haze of medieval darkness that could only be illuminated through the rational schooling of European dominion. Or so the discourses of colonialism would have it. Thus the problem with the categories of the marvelous or fabulous, the fictive or imaginary, is that they are still burdened with an epistemic order that attempts to strip the world of mysterious causes and effects through disenchanted, rational explanations of empirical positivism.

As for the limits of our own knowledge, we are restricted, in a fundamental sense, by this legacy of suspicion that has attempted to empty the world of mystery. The significance of the marvelous for the cultures that produced and transmitted such texts and images radically differs from Enlightenment sensibilities, which have sought to sweep away supernatural stories as primitive myths and legends. While we may readily admit that there are no islands populated with dog-headed men, or tribes of women who grow from trees, or nations of savages bottled up behind an ancient barrier at the end of the earth, we need not do so at the expense of understanding the conceptual frameworks that made such stories meaningful.

As a category within medieval Islamic discourse, the marvelous functions in direct relation to its ontological claims about reality. In the context of medieval European epistemology, Caroline Bynum argues that the very function of wonder is predicated on an uncanny reality, for "you can marvel only at something that is, at least in some sense, there."[18] The significance of the marvelous in such contexts emerges through its veridical ontological status, what Bynum calls "the there-ness of the event." Such a configuration highlights the primacy of deixis, of pointing, indicating, and beholding this 'there-ness.' Imbedded within the marvelous of the Latin *mirabilia*, which parallels the Greek *thaumata* (*θαύματα*), is the idea of the spectacle and the ocular perception of something to be seen and to behold (*mirabile visu / θαῦμα ἰδέσθαι*).[19] For Arabic and Persian descriptive geography this is articulated in the privileged position of empirical observation (*ʿiyān*) and eyewitness testimony.[20]

In Islamic illuminated manuscripts the psychological impact of wonder is often translated visually in the expression of the human face confronted with the strange (*gharīb*) or marvelous (*ʿajīb*). It is not hard to identify the iconographic gestures meant to evoke astonishment, demonstrating the power of gesture to negotiate the strange and the remote, in deictic acts of communication, guiding our attention toward the marginal, while simultaneously focusing on the psychological state of the observer, who ultimately serves as the visual intermediary for the phenomenon of the marvelous (plate 1). In Persian, the phrase "the finger of astonishment" (*angusht-i taʿajjub*), in both textual and visual idioms, translates the bizarre, the uncanny, and the savage through the power of gesture. The Arabic lexicographer, Ibn Jinnī (d. 392/1002) describes a theory that the origin of language begins through signing (*īmāʾ*) and pointing (*ishāra*) toward concrete material objects.[21] In this light, gesture is perhaps the most fundamental form of engaging with difference (plate 2).

Much has been said regarding the place of narrative 'fiction' and its role in medieval Islamic writerly culture.[22] I would like to first reiterate the hermeneutic difficulty of using the term fiction when discussing the various traditions of Arabic and Persian storytelling, especially when approaching the genre of marvel-writing. As a category, fiction tends to predetermine for us the place and significance of the marvelous or uncanny, at least in regard to intended reception and the question of entertainment value.[23]

An anxiety for authenticity inflects the presentation and management of the marvelous and can be traced throughout Islamic geographies and cosmographies. As it is the ideal of veracity that animates this material, the issue of assaying the authenticity of marvels becomes a standard feature of geographical discourse. This trope of questioning the accuracy of information concerning the world is fully articulated in Greek geographical writings. Both Strabo (d. ca 23 C.E.) and Ptolemy (fl. 141 C.E.), in their respective geographies, raise eyebrows at the hearsay of travelers' tales.

The account of how Ptolemy gathered information about the earth through informants whom he dispatched around the world became a well-traveled motif in Islamic geographical discussions of measurement and empiricism. The ʿAbbāsid administrator Qudāma b. Jaʿfar (d. 337/948), drawing from the introduction of Ptolemy's *Geographia*, writes that it is impossible to know the conditions of the earth in terms of its form and size, the locations of countries, and the extent of the inhabited regions by way of direct observation (*muʿāyana*), or through eye-witness testimony (*mushāhada*), because of the shortness of human life and the inability to travel to all the locations that one would need to see in order to grasp such knowledge. Qudāma describes how Ptolemy's scouts traveled the world and returned with authentic accounts (*al-akhbār al-ṣaḥīḥa*), which Ptolemy was able to supplement through inference (*istidlāl*), in order to draw further geographical measurements. This stands in marked contrast to Ptolemy's criticism directed toward previous scholars who based their views on the unreliable opinions of merchants (*tujjār*), who were more interested in boasting about the far-flung places they had visited, than in offering an accurate accounting of the world.[24]

The encyclopedist Abū 'l-Ḥasan al-Masʿūdī (d. 345/956) picks up the same anecdote describing the danger of relying on information collected from merchants, who are prone to lies, exaggerations, and omissions with respect to distant locations and the extremity of inhabitable lands.[25] Tangled in the yarns of merchants is not just the misinformation of geographical distances, but stories of fabulous creatures and wondrous tales of riches and spices waiting to be negotiated on the world's edge. A prime example lies in the journeys of Sulaymān the Merchant (fl. 237/851), which make their way into the geography of Ibn al-Faqīh (fl. 289/902) and the encyclopedia of Masʿūdī. These accounts of the exotic lands of the east and the strange customs of their inhabitants are supplemented with the even more fantastic merchant tales collected by Abū Zayd al-Baṣrī (fl. 303/915).[26]

The authenticity of the strange accounts conveyed in such writings was, indeed, an ongoing concern. Ibn al-Nadīm (d. ca 385/995), in his bio-bibliographical compendium, situates books on the marvels of the world after the Persian stories of Shahrāzād in the *Hazār afsān* [The thousand fables] and accounts of sexual encounters between *jinn* and humans. This comes in a section on evening tales and fables (*al-asmār wa 'l-khurāfāt*), suggesting not only an awareness of the less than factual nature of much of the material, but also an appreciation for the entertainment value undergirding the narrative production of marvel literature.[27]

As a discrete field within ʿAbbāsid letters, writing on marvels also reflected a broad mercantile network through which traveled the exotica of precious metals, jewels, perfumes, textiles, strange animals, rare foods and spices. The *Kitāb al-tabaṣṣur biʾl-tijāra* [An inquiry into commerce], ascribed to Jāḥiẓ, offers an early example of a geographical system ordered around a mercantile economy that privileged specialities (*khawāʾiṣṣ*) of the various regions of the world, indulging in the sandalwood, coconuts, and elephants of India; the silk, paper, and ink of China; and the brocades, medicaments, and singing-girls of Byzantium.[28]

This economic geography of luxury was used in the service of imperial projections of power; it was not only indicative of economic networks, but also literary courtly practices. ʿAbd al-Malik al-Thaʿālibī (d. 429/1038) relates the deft linguistic showmanship of the courtier and traveler Abū Dulaf (fl. 375/985) in an audience before ʿAḍud al-Dawla (r. 338–72/949–83), the Būyid ruler over the ʿAbbāsid caliphate. Abū Dulaf described, in literary jest, the exotic wonders of the various regions of the world: sable marten furs of the Bulghār, mink of the Kāshghar, quinces of Nīsābūr, and camphor of Sumatra.[29] For the geography of Abū ʿAbd Allāh al-Muqaddasī (fl. 375/985), this modality of fashioning the world through exotic specialties is consistently matched with an attention to the imperfections of a given region. In this pairing, the exotic is circumscribed by the dangerous and the liminal.

In a discursive economy that privileged such rare commodities, an epistemological structure developed to give authenticity to what was a growing body of marvels, inherited from an international network of travelers, textually and orally crossing frontiers. The foremost illusion of the marvelous is its ability to collapse being—what is out there—into a coded system of writing. This emplotment of ontology into language is one of the great acts of translation upon which geography is predicated.

A variety of remedies were proposed to assay the veracity of any given account. The geographer Ibn Ḥawqal (fl. 378/988) details how he obtained knowledge from his own journeys, consulted other travelers and merchants, and read earlier geographical literature. In order to test the authenticity of the material collected during his travels, Ibn Ḥawqal would attempt to corroborate it through multiple sources.[30] Needless to say, the most privileged mode of knowledge was direct observation. In the preface to his geography, Muqaddasī outlines a three-staged hierarchy of acquiring knowledge about the world and inquiring into the unseen (*al-naẓar fī ʾl-ghayb*):

> We have divided our book into three sections: the first, concerning that which we saw with our very eyes (*mā ʿāyannāhu*); the second, that which we heard (*samiʿnāhu*) from trustworthy sources (*thiqāt*); and the third, that which we have found in books composed on this subject (*al-kutub al-muṣannafa fī hādhā 'l-bāb*); no royal library has remained unexamined, nor are there any scattered writings I have not leafed through.[31]

The problem for most geographers was that the truly marvelous and rare, of the order of dog-headed creatures and flying monsters, were usually not seen but heard or read from others.

On the knowledge of the unseen (*ʿilm al-ghayb*), Jāḥiẓ offers a similar three-tiered system for attempting to establish the veracity of that which cannot be verified through direct sight or contact. At the highest level are accounts that are so widely transmitted and universally accepted that there is no need to question their accuracy. Next are traditions that have been related by several different transmitters whose accounts can be tested against each other. Finally, there is information passed on from only one or two people, who are equally likely to be lying or telling the truth, in which case some degree of doubt must remain.[32]

A central component in the transmission of the marvelous is this question of doubt, which in large measure activates the pleasure of entertaining the strange and uncanny. Medieval Muslim authorities privileged an empirical system of beholding reality and then translating that ocular perception of intelligiblia (*maḥsūsāt*) into writing. One of the central modalities of this geographical discourse is the ekphrastic display of the world and its wonders in the reconstruction of being into language. The sacred Kaʿba of Mecca, the pyramids of Giza, and the wall of Gog and Magog are all sites to be erected linguistically through the illusion of direct ocular perception captured in language. This textual medium of display within the world of manuscripts is also translated visually in maps and miniature paintings that further highlight the power of geographical discourse to collapse the vast distance of space and time before the eyes of readers and viewers who behold the wonders of the world in the highly transportable capital of mimetic reproduction.[33]

For us the limits of knowledge are very much the product of archives and the historical transmission of information. The site for our knowledge of the unseen, however, is the past, which can only be verified indirectly through a process of textual archeology which, as James Montgomery argues, is in large measure shaped by the serendipity of what survives, itself by no means indicative of what was.[34] As a field, Islamic geographical writing reflects a cumulative process of adaptation and transformation, such that what is preserved of the earliest strata of material is often embedded in the reception history of later generations.

The radical transformation of texts in the age of mechanical reproduction has entirely reconstituted our own access to the royal archives that Muqaddasī so studiously leafed through for his research. As with all forms of display and presentation, the texts of today, often expressed through binary bits of information, shape our entrance into the material and greatly determine the kinds of questions we ask of our sources. While the atomistic configuration of word searches has allowed for an incredible collation of information, unseen in ages past, it has also resulted in a further closing off of the polysemous reality of the archive. In large part, this closure was produced through the gains of print technology, which saw the rise of critical editions brought forth by generations of Orientalists. These editions developed out of an epistemic system that attempted to recover an original authorial design and intention, and to cull away spurious accretions that made their way into the porous medium of manuscripts.

Implicit in this process of textual criticism is the judgment, and thus in some part creation, of the authentic and the authorial. The messy reality of multiple recensions that inhabit medieval manuscripts as testaments to the collaborative process of textual production and the formulation of meaning may be, in part, preserved in the form of a critical apparatus within an edition. This apparatus, in turn, collates the meaningful variants of a given text within the space of the margins in a process of redaction that inevitably produces a text that never existed in the course of its medieval reception, but is supposed to reflect a kind of platonic ideal of what the original text would have been. In the process of mechanical reproduction, this multivalent record of dissemination is displaced largely into the space of the margins. However, as with acts of translation, what is gained is the ability to telegraph this information to an even broader audience. In this ever-iterated process of loss and recovery, or deficit and surplus, to use a mercantile metaphor, we have today, with most of the digitally searchable forms of Arabic and Persian medieval material, the complete removal of the critical apparatus, if one ever existed, and with it any semblance of this cacophonous reception history. Likewise, what is available either digitally, or in print, is usually based on the narrow selection of what has been edited.

Significant parts of this reception history have been effaced in the nineteenth- and early twentieth-century constructions of ʿAbbāsid geography. What has been reconstructed in printed and digital forms, as a mechanical reproduction, only partially accounts for the codicological record. We have found it necessary to return to the royal archives in an attempt to reconsider the value of this cacophony and what it may tell us about our modern reconstruction of the past. Yet, like all historical knowledge, so many stages removed from the veritable there-ness of the event, it is perhaps enough to leave room not just for the felicity of recovery but also for the uncertainty over what has been lost.

SECTION ONE

GEOGRAPHY, TRANSLATION, AND THE APOCALYPSE

1

ROUTES AND REALMS

The caliph al-Wāthiq bi'llāh awoke after a night filled with bad dreams. So begins the story that will begin our story. This tale serves as an anecdote of a larger tale, a kind of metaphor for a metaphor. It is one of adventure and peril, a geography of action and conception that questions who we are, where we come from, and where we are going. Our adventure will flirt with the monstrous and the apocalyptic, take us to the world's farthest extreme and back again. There will be loss; some of our companions will die as we skirt the edge of the known world and peer into that crack of oblivion, into a projection of desire that ebbs and flows from generation to generation. Foremost, this is a tale of translation, of the acquisition and transference of knowledge, of communicating the unseen, the unknowable, the demonic and the divine through the porous medium of language.

We begin this journey in the setting of its original production, with the ʿAbbāsid imperial administration of the third/ninth century. Our guide is himself the translator, ever present, yet never seen, veiled in words that are both his and not his own. His name reduces to a word that has entered into our language, transliterated through other tales of transmission: *turchemannus*, *trujamán*, *truchement*, *turcimanno*, *dragoman*, and *dragomen*, a plural formed by specious analogy. He is an interpreter who travels in both political and scholarly domains. The importance of this figure for understanding the world will anchor our telling from the beginning to epistemology, while the dynamism of crossing frontiers will pin our trajectory across maps of seas, deserts, and high mountains. The caliphal interpreter was sent on an embassy to the edge of the world to bring back an account of the unseen, beyond the territorial limits of state and empire, past the settled cities, and into the landscape of ominous nomads.

We know him merely as Sallām al-Tarjumān—the interpreter, the translator, the dragoman. His identity, for the most part, has escaped us. We know nothing of where he came from, when he was born, when he died, or if he really existed at all. His name, however, is linked to almost every Arabic geography written for over six hundred years, and his tale has entered into Persian, Turkish, Latin, French, Spanish, Russian, Hungarian, Polish, Dutch, German, and English, to name but a few. The various international incarnations that our translator adopts, both in the sources and in the scholarship, play in concert as a meta-narrative of uncovering stories hidden by the perfidious hands of history and the treacherous slippage of language.

Administrative Geography

The guide for our journey, Sallām al-Tarjumān, first appears in a work entitled *Kitāb al-masālik wa 'l-mamālik* [The book of routes and realms],[1] composed by Ibn Khurradādhbih (fl. 269/882) sometime during the latter half of the third/ninth century.[2] This geography received its modern debut with an edition prepared by Charles Barbier de Meynard in 1865. De Meynard, who acknowledged that his publication of the geography represented a significantly redacted form of what the original must have been, based his edition on two manuscripts, one housed in the Bodleian Library (MS Hunt 433, dated 631/1232), and a nineteenth-century copy obtained in Istanbul, with corrections made by a certain Arabic instructor, ʿAbd al-Raḥmān Efendī, now held in the Bibliothèque nationale of France (Supplément arabe 895). This manuscript parallels the Bodleian recension.[3]

With the discovery of another manuscript, now housed in the Österreichische Nationalbibliothek of Vienna (MS Mixt. 783), Michael Jan de Goeje was able to present a re-edited version of the *Masālik*; this appeared in 1889 as the sixth volume in his series of edited Arabic geographical texts, the *Bibliotheca geographorum Arabicorum* (1870–94). While these two editions share the same general contours and are clearly based upon a corpus of common material, there are several significant points of divergence. The problem of the reception history, as reflected in these manuscripts, comes into sharper relief as Sallām approaches his goal. The extent to which the manuscripts known to survive and the editions based upon them reflect the original form, or forms, of the geography is a question that may never be fully resolved.

In order to understand Sallām al-Tarjumān more fully, we must first explain the textual world from which he steps forth. As our anecdote is first preserved in the administrative geography of Ibn Khurradādhbih, we choose to start our journey with him. A Persian by origin, Ibn Khurradādhbih descended from an illustrious family. His father was the governor of Ṭabaristān during the caliphate of al-Maʾmūn (r. 198–218/813–33) and helped to expand the ʿAbbāsid territories throughout Daylam and into the mountainous strongholds of the region.[4] Ibn Khurradādhbih received historical material on the lives of Sāsānian kings from his father.[5] His grandfather was a Zoroastrian who is said to have converted to Islam through the influence of the powerful Barmakids, a family of high-ranking ʿAbbāsid officials, whose ancestor was a hereditary priest of a Buddhist temple in the region of Balkh.[6]

Given the frequency with which later writers, across a wide range of fields, rely on Ibn Khurradādhbih's geography, it is clear that this work enjoyed a great deal of popularity from its inception. Though not the first work on world geography produced in Arabic, the *Masālik* exerted a considerable influence on later writers, to such an extent that Ibn Khurradādhbih has been heralded by some modern scholars as the "father of Arab-Islamic geography."[7] From Ibn al-Nadīm's *al-Fihrist* [The index], we may glean that a body of writings, all entitled *al-Masālik wa 'l-mamālik*, began to coalesce in the second half of the third/ninth century.[8] While Ibn Khurradādhbih's work is not the first, it is certainly the earliest Arabic descriptive geography to come to us in a somewhat complete form.[9]

Ibn Khurradādhbih served as the master of post and information (*ṣāḥib al-barīd wa 'l-khabar*) for the district of the Jabal, in modern-day Iran. Given his intimate knowledge of imperial administrative records,[10] several scholars have hypothesized, though without any textual basis, that he may also have served as the primary director of the ministry of communications in either Baghdad or the palatine city of Sāmarrāʾ.[11] While this is merely conjecture, it is certainly compelling to imagine Ibn Khurradādhbih composing his administrative geography while in the direct service of the state bureaucracy, particularly as much of the information contained in his work draws on a close association with the ruling elite. This association is crystallized in Ibn Khurradādhbih's formal status as a court companion (*nadīm*) of the caliph al-Muʿtamid (r. 255–79/870–92), a position that formed part of the routinized composition of the ʿAbbāsid court in this period,[12] and was stylized, in part, to reflect Sāsānian courtly practice.[13]

In Muqaddasī's estimation, Ibn Khurradādhbih was a minister (*wazīr*) responsible for the deposits of scholarly material in the caliphal library.[14]

The diverse list of works attributed to Ibn Khurradādhbih—including such topics as the culinary arts, court companionship, musical instruments, and genealogies of Persians—suggests a high-society littérateur, a connoisseur of good taste, associated with the ruling elite,[15] with a wide array of scholarly and bureaucratic resources. All of these characteristics form an image of perfect urbanity, molded around the archetypal figure of the *adīb*, multifaceted, skilled in the etiquette of a variety of subjects and connected to a wider universe of ʿAbbāsid literary culture.[16] As a courtier he frequented caliphal assemblies and attended drinking sessions of notables.[17] The Arab court poet Abū ʿUbāda al-Buḥturī (d. 284/897) composed verses honoring his friendship, describing him as a descendent of noble kings, and highlighting his Persian aristocratic lineage.[18]

While his geography became one of the most influential in the field, several medieval authorities questioned his accuracy and reliability. Yāqūt al-Rūmī (d. 626/1229), known both for his geographical dictionary and his biographical account of littérateurs (*udabāʾ*), mentions that Ibn Khurradādhbih's writings contained so many accounts of questionable authority (*gharāʾib*) that several scholars who copied from him would comment that this was merely Ibn Khurradādhbih's opinion, adding, "if it turns out to be untrue then it is he who is responsible for the lie."[19] This assessment is articulated by the literary historian Abū ʾl-Faraj al-Iṣfahānī (d. 356/967), who deemed Ibn Khurradādhbih's work on poetry and music to be of little merit and of a highly dubious pedigree. Despite its popularity, similar attacks were made against his geography, parts of which were drawn into question by succeeding generations of geographers.

Nonetheless, according to Masʿūdī, the geography was one of the most famous and valuable in the field, for specialists and non-specialists alike.[20] The Persian geographer Ibn Ḥawqal describes how, in his own travels, he made sure that he kept the writings of Ibn Khurradādhbih, along with those of the ʿAbbāsid administrator Qudāma b. Jaʿfar and the Sāmānid *wazīr* Abū ʿAbd Allāh al-Jayhānī (fl. 309/922), always by his side.[21] Needless to say, both Masʿūdī and Ibn Ḥawqal find room to criticize Ibn Khurradādhbih in the course of situating the importance and uniqueness of their respective writings.[22] Yet his close association with the ʿAbbāsid administration and the encyclopedic range of information that he was able to gather gave his work a lasting air of authority.

The administrative elements of Ibn Khurradādhbih's career are foregrounded in his geography, which includes a detailed account of the economic and agricultural administration of the ʿAbbāsid empire. The work opens with an inventory of the monetary value of the production of lands under the dominion of the caliphate, a calculation of the assets of given tax districts, and a description of the primary stage routes of communication between various regions. These interests, along with such details as the proper titles used for addressing various rulers of the world and a description of the major commercial trade routes, highlight a set of administrative and bureaucratic concerns. The geography thus suggests an audience of caliphal secretaries (*kuttab*) responsible for overseeing various institutional bureaus (*dawāwīn*). Ibn Khurradādhbih showcases information bearing directly on the office of taxation (*dīwān al-kharāj*) and the office of communication (*dīwān al-barīd*),[23] two governmental agencies that benefited from geographical information applicable to the oversight of their respective institutional functions.

Though the addressee of the opening dedication remains unknown, as redacted in the Vienna manuscript,[24] the proposition that a high official to the caliph, or even the caliph himself, would commission such a work is not entirely far-fetched. The opening highlights Ibn Khurradādhbih's special status as a client (*mawlā*) to the caliph and thus a protected member of the ruling family's household.[25] Through his own expertise as a provincial postmaster and through any later administrative positions he might have held at the court, it is reasonable to believe that Ibn Khurradādhbih would feel encouraged, or even compelled, to write such a geographical description of the ʿAbbāsid territories and the surrounding regions of the world.

We can also discern that the political and cultural roles of the secretary (*kātib*) and the man of letters (*adīb*) appear to be linked in the production of these works.[26] In administrative geography, this fusion is perhaps best illustrated in the figure of Qudāma b. Jaʿfar, the author of both a seminal work on Arabic literary poetics and a descriptive geography that appears in a broader study on the fiscal administration of the ʿAbbāsid empire. Qudāma's *Kitāb al-kharāj wa ṣināʿat al-kitāba* [Book of land-tax and craft of writing] bears the hallmark of a seasoned state secretary instructing up-and-coming bureaucrats in the etiquette of state administration.[27]

According to Qudāma, secretaries in the administration had to possess a thorough knowledge of geography in order to perform the duties of their post.[28] This is most clearly the case in Qudāma's description of the responsibilities incumbent upon the minister of communication (*ṣāḥib dīwān al-barīd*).[29] Qudāma describes how the minister was responsible for overseeing all missives sent from the ministry to any given destination, and for presenting to the caliph the dispatches of other postmasters and agents of information from the outlying regions, or making a summary of such reports:

> It is necessary for the chief minister of this ministry to have at his immediate disposal, without the need for further research, [information concerning the roads and routes of all regions] so that, when the caliph calls on him and sends out an army to [deal with] some pressing affair, or some other situation where the knowledge of routes is necessary, thanks to this previous work, the chief minister will find himself already prepared for the caliph, with accurate information at hand.[30]

According to Qudāma the ministry of communication was to be run by someone of great integrity and honesty, on whom the caliph could place the highest esteem and trust.[31] In this light, Ibn Khurradādhbih's own personal relationship with the caliph al-Muʿtamid, as a learned court companion who served within the administration, speaks to the bureaucratic and cultural contexts that frame his geography.

ʿAbbāsid Contexts for Translation

One of the most pronounced paradigms in the intellectual history of the ʿAbbāsid empire is expressed in the translation movement as it developed in the second/eighth and third/ninth centuries, flourishing under caliphal and individual patronage. The study of foreign material became a mainstay in the administrative and intellectual horizons of the period. The phenomenon of translation as it existed in the early stages, from the reign of al-Manṣūr (r. 136–58/754–75) onwards, demonstrates a remarkable interest in and respect for the achievements of other civilizations. While there are accounts of translations from Syriac, Greek, Middle Persian, and even Sanskrit during the Umayyad caliphate,[32] the extent to which translation as an epistemological paradigm flourished under ʿAbbāsid patronage remains unparalleled in the early development of medieval Islamic intellectual history.

A brief historical sketch of the ʿAbbāsid rise to power takes us back to the setting of the initial Arab conquests of Mesopotamia. The Sāsānian empire (r. 224–651 C.E.), the great antagonist of the Byzantines, stretched across the Fertile Crescent beyond the Oxus, until it fell dramatically in a series of key battles to invading armies of Arab converts to Islam.[33] By 93/711, Arab-led armies had conquered a vast territory that stretched from southern Iberia to western India. In the period immediately following this monumental expansion, the various conquered peoples did not immediately embrace Islam *en masse*.[34]

Rather than bring entirely new administrative systems of governance to these territories, the Umayyads adopted and transformed the administrative structures of their predecessors. In the case of the lands captured from Byzantium and the former Sāsānian empire, the new ruling class made only slight modifications.[35] With the continuation of such diverse, local traditions of administration and taxation, the bureaucratic system that arose was highly heterogeneous and idiosyncratic, often dependent upon the character of various treaties drawn on the submission of a given territory to an Arab army. The garrison cities of Basra, Kufa, and Wāsiṭ were built, for all intents and purposes, *ex nihilo* in the heartland of Sāsānian Mesopotamia; the new settlements of conquering Arab armies served as emblems of what was, at times, an isolated disjunction between the Arab ruling elite and their non-Arab subjects.[36]

The ʿAbbāsid revolution, which culminated with the overthrow of the Umayyad caliphate in 132/750, outwardly brought Persian culture and previous Sāsānian models back to center stage. The transference of the caliphate from Damascus to the heart of what was, in Sāsānian times, referred to as Īrānshahr, came to mark a departure from the preferential status enjoyed by Arabs in the Umayyad ruling elite. As the Banū ʾl-ʿAbbās rose to power, so too did their base of supporters, represented by Persian clients (*mawālī*).

The ʿAbbāsid administration actively drew on Persian cultural elements, envisioned in large measure through Sāsānian imperial ideology, in the formation of their new state. To appeal to Arab Muslim factions, the ʿAbbāsids presented themselves as descendants of the Prophet Muḥammad. All the while they adopted Persian ideals of good governance and regal customs of state, thus speaking to their Persian supporters, wherein they claimed to be legitimate inheritors of the ancient imperial dynasty of the Sāsānians.[37] When the second ʿAbbāsid caliph, al-Manṣūr, founded his caliphal city of Baghdad, officially Madīnat al-Salām (the City of Peace), near the ruins of what was once Ctesiphon, a capital city of the Sāsānians, he consciously united the ʿAbbāsid regime with the long tradition of cosmopolitan empires of Mesopotamia.

This period witnessed the dramatic rise to power of Persian officials. The vizierate and the secretarial administration, to whom the *wazīr* was connected, were occupied, from the very early period of ʿAbbāsid rule, almost entirely by non-Arabs.[38] The administrative language took on an outwardly Persian flavor, as many technical terms were adopted from Sāsānian governmental practices into Arabic. The imitation of so-called 'ancient Persian' traditions was, rather than an unbroken continuum, more a reflection of historical revisionism.[39] Persian etymologies for administrative structures, such as the communication service (*barīd*), circulated, evidently to align the ʿAbbāsids, in a self-conscious refashioning, with a glorified Sāsānian past.[40]

The multi-ethnic dimensions of Mesopotamia can be seen in the mixed population of Armenians, Greeks, Jews, Persians, Turks, and Syrians, who all came to reside in the region. Baghdad, the city of al-Manṣūr, transformed into a political and intellectual center of gravity. Jāḥiẓ describes the capital as the most noble and grand city he had ever seen.[41] Iraq and the caliphal city of Baghdad figure in many ʿAbbāsid geographical writings as the 'navel of the world' (*surrat al-arḍ*), a phrase often reserved for the sacred Kaʿba in Mecca.[42] As a cosmopolis, Baghdad naturally attracted scholars, diplomats, and merchants from the surrounding regions and from beyond the administrative frontiers. For successive generations, the ʿAbbāsid caliphs and their entourage drew upon this diverse population to sponsor an ambitious and sustained project of translation that continued for over two hundred years.

This intellectual movement built upon an array of foreign philosophical, political, and scientific material. By the end of the fourth/tenth century an encyclopedic range of mainly Greek writing from classical antiquity was introduced into Arabic.[43] However, this movement did not focus solely on Hellenistic learning and the translation of Aristotelian philosophy, Galenic medicine, and Ptolemaic geography, but also included significant studies and translations of Middle Persian and Sanskrit sources. Sponsored by lucrative patronage, non-Arab translators brought forth an astonishing breadth of material that effectively transformed the Arabic language into a highly developed and efficient means of communicating abstract scientific and philosophical thought. The ethos of this age figures as one in which cross-pollination and multicultural interactions were encouraged by synthesizing disparate traditions of learning within a polyphonic cultural matrix, eventually legitimized through an imperial process of appropriation and naturalization.[44]

Shaping and Orienting

In the opening dedication to his unnamed patron, Ibn Khurradādhbih positions the *Masālik* in concord with the tradition of translation characteristic of the period. Immediately following the various customary invocations to God, the author announces that he has made a translation from Ptolemy for his patron's consideration:

> I have comprehended what you have requested. . . [namely that you desire] an outline (*rasm*) that would elucidate the routes and realms of the earth, and their description, along with how distant and how near they are, with information concerning the parts of the earth cultivated, versus those that are wasteland, and the distances between such areas, including the way stations that lead to the remote ends of the world, and depictions (*rusūm*) of the ways (*ṭuruq*) and forms of cantons (*ṭassūj*) in these lands, [all] according to how the ancients used to describe such affairs. I have found that Ptolemy had distinguished the regions [of the earth] and given an authoritative account of [the earth's] description (*ṣifa*) in a foreign language (*bi'lughatin aʿjamiyyatin*), so I translated this from his language into an understandable language (*bi'l-lughati 'l-ṣaḥīḥati*), so that you might examine it.[45]

Ibn Khurradādhbih mentions that this work of Ptolemy was written in a foreign language (*lugha aʿjamiyya*), but does not specify as to whether it was in Greek, Syriac, or Middle Persian. As we comb the *Masālik* for traces of Ptolemy's writing on geography, we find the text to be a secretarial manual on geographic elements of administration spiced with poetic flourishes and highlighted by entire sections dedicated to the wonders (*ʿajāʾib*) of the world. Passing over this opening dedication, other references to Ptolemy prove to be not just superficial, but also misguided. At one point, Ibn Khurradādhbih claims that during Ptolemy's age there were 4,200 cities in the world.[46] This estimate, which Ibn Khurradādhbih attributes to a work of Ptolemy, is not to be found in any of Ptolemy's known writings.[47] Ibn Khurradādhbih also makes the common error of confusing Claudius (al-Kalūdhī) Ptolemy, the astronomer and geographer, with one of the Greek Ptolemaic kings of Egypt.[48] However, though never stated, there are clear indications in the *Masālik* that Ibn Khurradādhbih draws upon the cosmographical system outlined in Ptolemy's *Tetrabiblos*, a work of geographical astrology.[49]

Additionally, Ibn Khurradādhbih makes reference to the Ptolemaic system of dividing the inhabited world from south to north into seven latitudinal climes (*aqālīm*), a system developed most fully in Ptolemy's *Geography*. However, rather than adhering to this climatic model, the *Masālik* essentially follows an Iranian four-part division, based on the cardinal directions. According to Qudāma, ancient Iranian kings conceptually divided the world into four sections and believed that the region of Mesopotamia corresponded to the navel of the earth (*surrat al-arḍ*), a practice which Ibn al-Faqīh traces back to the Iranian king Ardashīr I (d. 242 C.E.), the founder of the Sāsānian dynasty.[50] While Ibn Khurradādhbih applies Greek geographical terminology to his four-part division of the world,[51] the central location of Iraq within the structure of his geography appears to be based on an older Sāsānian conceptual model,[52] which is deployed here to position the ʿAbbāsid empire at the cosmic center of the world. Ibn Khurradādhbih's reference to the translation of this unspecified Ptolemaic work is evidently aimed at contemporary values, which found ancient science in general, and Greek learning in particular, to be authoritative.

The geography was composed during the height of the translation movement of Greek into Arabic, and specifically during the Arabic absorption of Ptolemy's geographic and astronomical writings. Muḥammad b. Mūsā ʿl-Khwārazmī (d. ca 232/847), famous mathematician and court astrologer for the caliph al-Wāthiq (r. 227–32/842–7), is said to have composed a descriptive geography, entitled *Ṣūrat al-arḍ* [Image of the earth], in which he drew on, and, in some cases, revised Ptolemy's geographical calculations and projections of co-ordinates. The title of this work, "Image of the earth," itself serves as the general Arabic translation for Ptolemy's *Geography*, which is often left in the Arabic sources transliterated from the Greek as *jughrāfiyā*.[53]

Khwārazmī's work is believed to be part of a larger project commissioned by the caliph al-Maʾmūn to create a *mappa mundi* based on the Ptolemaic projection of the earth and the surrounding cosmos.[54] The philosopher and scientist Abū Yūsuf Yaʿqūb al-Kindī (d. ca 260/874) is credited with a geographical work entitled *Rasm al-maʿmūr min al-arḍ* [Description of the inhabited section of the earth], which he is said to have based on Ptolemy's *Geography*.[55] In the third/ninth century, Ptolemy's work received considerable attention, as manifested in several adaptations and translations into Arabic. In this vein, the polymath Thābit b. Qurra (d. 288/901) made a revision of what were, until his time, unsatisfactory Arabic translations of Ptolemy's *Geography* and *Almagest*.[56]

In the opening dedication, Ibn Khurradādhbih does more than just demonstrate the importance of Greek science to the field of descriptive geography; he also highlights the bureaucratic elements of land management. The administrative culture of the ʿAbbāsid empire evolved out of real, or imagined, Sāsānian traditions. This is articulated, for instance, in the Persian terminology repeatedly employed in the discourse of state bureaucracy.

Of note in this regard are the administrative units of land and taxation. Ibn Khurradādhbih describes how his geography outlines the customs and forms of taxation throughout the various regions of the world. He uses here a Persian loanword, *ṭassūj* (canton),[57] which he explains as an administrative district or region drawn from a Sāsānian model of land management.[58] Persian vocabulary, from the administrative to the architectural, echoes throughout the geography as a testament to the hybrid linguistic and political cultures of third/ninth-century Mesopotamia. Reference to Sāsānian bureaucratic land divisions serves as a mainstay of ʿAbbāsid administrative geography,[59] a genre of writing with antecedents in Sāsānian administration.[60]

Though Ibn Khurradādhbih often relies on pre-Islamic Persian models, he also gives ample voice to Islamic conceptions of space. The opening pages offer an example of how he brings together two projections of geography. Immediately following the proemium, he briefly situates the various regions of the world with respect to their orientation (*qibla*) to the Kaʿba, the sacred shrine in Mecca.[61] He then transitions into an administrative account, casting Mesopotamia through the lens of Sāsānian tradition: "Now I begin with the mention of the Sawād [i.e., Iraq and more generally Mesopotamia], since the Persian kings would call it *dil-i Īrānshahr*, that is the heart of Iraq."[62] The term *dil-i Īrānshahr* calls to mind the Sāsānian view that the Persian empire, "best in every art" (*buzurgwār-tar ast bi-har hunarī*), commanded the center of the world, and all other regions, inferior by nature, revolved around it.[63]

After a detailed account of Mesopotamia and its administration, Ibn Khurradādhbih positions the regions of the world in relation to ʿAbbāsid rule: the east (*mashriq*) stretches past the lands of Khurāsān to China and the far-flung islands of the Indian Ocean;[64] the west (*maghrib*) is circumscribed by the lands of Byzantium, the Levant, North Africa and Iberia, along with various Mediterranean islands;[65] the north (*jarbī*) accounts for Azerbaijan, Armenia, the Khazar, and, according to the Bodleian recension, the lands of Gog and Magog;[66] while the south (*tayman*) covers the Arabian Peninsula and the various pilgrimage routes to Mecca.[67]

Although the center of gravity lies in Mesopotamia and ʿAbbāsid imperial power, the description of sites attendant to the course of Islamic salvation history also promotes a sacred conception of space that intersects with the life of the Prophet and the centrality of the Qurʾān. References to holy relics and sacred history are scattered throughout the geography. Adam's expulsion from the celestial garden of Eden, for instance, is mapped onto a mountain in the island of Sri Lanka (Sarandīb), where Adam is believed to have landed on earth. His footprint, which is set in stone, is said to measure nearly seventy cubits, a reference to the long-standing belief in the gigantic stature of the first inhabitants of the earth.[68] In the description of the Sacred Mosque of Mecca (*al-masjid al-ḥarām*), the narrative relates how Adam took up residence in Mecca, which became a sanctuary for all the nations of the world; it was here that God chose the ground for Ibrāhīm and his son Ismāʿīl to build the Kaʿba.[69]

In the course of outlining various routes and networks, Ibn Khurradādhbih adumbrates such details as the itinerary of the Prophet on his migration (*hijra*) from Mecca to Medina,[70] the tombs of notable figures in Islamic history, and a range of events mentioned in the Qurʾān.[71] As part of prophetic history, which represents the miraculous intersection of divine will in the course of human affairs, marvelous phenomena resonate throughout the geography. The marriage between the prophet Sulaymān and Bilqīs, the Queen of Sheba, is juxtaposed with an account of various palaces built by demons (*shayāṭīn*) in the region of Yemen. This architectural grandeur serves as an allusion to Sulaymān's power over the *jinn*, who are prominent players in the Qurʾānic and exegetical narratives of his encounter with Bilqīs.[72] The land of the eastern Caucasus witnesses the stories (*qiṣaṣ*) of Moses searching for the spring of immortality and his adventures with the enigmatic figure known in exegetical traditions as Khiḍr. The rock that contains the mysterious spring (Q. 18:63), believed by many to be the fountain of life, is located in the region of Sharwān, and the reference to the meeting place of the two seas (*majmaʿ al-baḥrayn*, Q. 18:60) is situated past Armenia.[73] It is in such a world, pregnant with the wondrous signs of God's creation, that the wall of Gog and Magog is erected. This barrier, which intersects with Qurʾānic eschatology and the development of early Islamic salvation history, marks a conceptual boundary against which the religious and political authority of the Arabian Peninsula and Mesopotamia are projected.

Within this articulation of what is a specifically Islamic geography, Ibn Khurradādhbih presents Persian cultural and linguistic elements as naturally integrated dimensions in this broad progression of salvation. By drawing on pre-Islamic Persian traditions, Ibn Khurradādhbih's work fits into a pattern of Persian scholars who graft Iranian history onto an explicitly Islamic narrative of time.[74]

One example of this is Ibn Khurradādhbih's use of Persian administrative vocabulary. When treating the bureaucratic division of Mesopotamia, he presents pre-Islamic Persian categories and then glosses them with Arabic words. As for the Sawād, it consists of ten districts (*kūra*); each *kūra* is comprised of a municipality (*ustān*) and sixty cantons (*ṭassūj*). He translates the Persian word *ustān* into Arabic as *iḥāza*, land taken over by the state, and the Persian word *ṭassūj* into Arabic as *nāḥiya*, a region or district.[75]

As Ibn Khurradādhbih squares Arabic with Persian administrative terminology, he approaches his subject matter from a perspective in which Persian may claim a historical precedence over Arabic. The term *ṭassūj* from the Middle Persian *tasūg*, meaning one quarter, is a case in point, as it is linked to the administrative and geographical practices of the Sāsānians during the reign of Qubādh I (r. 488–531 C.E.).[76] The translation of this Persian administrative lexicon into Arabic foregrounds the historical reality that, long before the Arab conquest of the Sāsānian empire, there existed in Persian a fully developed manner of commanding the world in language.

Ibn Khurradādhbih casts his eye on these bureaucratic antecedents, projecting a configuration of geography that follows the contours of a pre-existing conception of the world. He relates that the districts (*kuwar*) in the region of Fārs are five: Iṣṭakhr, Shābūr, Ardashīr-Khurra, Dārābjird, and Arrajān.[77] While this division, and others like it, speak directly to Sāsānian administrative models,[78] the degree of overlap with such Sāsānian traditions is in large measure a projection of continuity with ancient Persian precedent.

The terminology Ibn Khurradādhbih employs when making evaluations of the agricultural and monetary assets of regions under ʿAbbāsid control also reflects Sāsānian administrative practices. For instance, he writes that the canton (*ṭassūj*) of al-Anbār, a town on the Euphrates, whose name in Persian means 'storehouse' or 'granary,' possesses five village districts (*rustāq*), 250 threshing-floors (*baydar*), with a tax revenue in wheat of 2,300 *kurr*, and in barley of 1,400 *kurr*, a dry measurement equal to six ass-loads,[79] in addition to 150,000 *dirhams* in currency. Apart from *dirham*, which derives from the Greek *δραχμή*, the rest of these terms are of Near Eastern origin, and can be traced back to earlier Sāsānian bureaucratic models.[80]

Ibn Khurradādhbih draws on Sāsānian history in order to contextualize later land management by subsequent Arab conquerors. Thus he outlines how the second caliph, ʿUmar b. al-Khaṭṭāb (r. 13–23/634–44), made a cadastral land survey (*misāḥa*) of Mesopotamia for taxation purposes and compares it to the taxes that would have been collected from the Sawād for the Sāsānian ruler Qubādh.[81] Such comparisons fit into a specific historiographical pattern of remembering a pre-Islamic imperial legacy. This is the case with Abū ʿAbd Allāh al-Jahshiyārī (d. 331/942), who describes in his administrative history, *Kitāb al-wuzarāʾ wa 'l-kuttāb* [The book of ministers and secretaries], how Sāsānian kings used the bureaucratic apparatus of the secretariat to conduct land surveys with the aim of leveling taxes, suggesting how geographical measurement could serve as a form of imperial knowledge and possession.[82]

The *Masālik* at times reads as an account of geography projected through the lens of pre-Islamic Persian history. For example, Ibn Khurradādhbih uses a Persian creation myth as a vehicle to describe the division of the world into different peoples and kingdoms. He describes how the ancient Persian king of the world, Farīdūn (Afīdhūn), divided the earth into thirds, between his son Salm, Ṭūj, and Īrān. Ibn Khurradādhbih highlights this foundational moment in Persian history with Arabic verses, which he says were originally sung by one the poets of the Persian kings:

وَقَسَمْنا مُلْكَنا فِي دَهْرِنا   قِسْمَةَ ٱللَّحْمِ عَلَى ظَهْرِ ٱلْوَضَمْ
فَجَعَلْنا ٱلشَّامَ وَٱلرُّومَ إلى   مَغْرِبِ ٱلشَّمسِ إلى ٱلْغِطْرِيفْ سَلَمْ
وَلِطُوجٍ جُعِلَ ٱلتُّرْكُ لَهُ   وَبِلادُ ٱلصِّينِ يَحْوِيها ٱبن عَمٌّ
وَلإيرانَ جَعَلْنا عَنْوَةً   فارِسَ ٱلْمُلْكَ وَفُزْنا بِٱلنِّعَمْ

We divided our kingdom during our age,
like a piece of meat on the butcher's block.
Thus we gave the Levant and Byzantium
up to the setting of the sun to the noble Salm.
And to Ṭūj was given reign over the Turks
and the region of China which his progeny inherits.
For Īrān we have reserved by might the Kingdom of Persia
and we have triumphed with blessings.[83]

The story of how the mythic Persian hero Farīdūn divided his kingdom between his three sons recurs throughout Persian literature, drawn from an ancient legend that appears throughout Zoroastrian tradition, and is taken up in various Sāsānian sources.[84] This mythical division of the world, out of which Iran is born, figures prominently in the opening of the Persian epic, the *Shāh-nāma* [Book of kings], composed by Abū 'l-Qāsim al-Firdawsī (d. 411/1020) in 400/1010.[85] Ibn Khurradādhbih showcases these verses, attributed to an unnamed Persian court poet, as part of his project of inscribing Persian history into the geographic order of the world.[86]

As for this broader historiographical projection, Ibn Khurradādhbih is known to have composed a text devoted, in some measure, to the history of pre-Islamic Persian kings, *Kitāb al-kabīr fī 'l-taʾrīkh* [Major compendium of history], which Masʿūdī extols as one of the most valuable works of its kind.[87] Though Ibn Khurradādhbih's historical writings no longer survive today, we may glean from the fragments that have been preserved through other sources that he took particular interest in Persian history. The history of pre-Islamic Persian kings credited to the anthologist ʿAbd al-Malik al-Thaʿālibī draws heavily on Ibn Khurradādhbih's compendium,[88] which is treated as an authoritative source.[89] Through the filter of Thaʿālibī's narrative, Ibn Khurradādhbih speaks on such sundry figures as the religious leader Zoroaster, the military hero Alexander the Great, and the heretic Mazdak.[90] Ibn Khurradādhbih's material on pre-Islamic Iran proves indispensable for Thaʿālibī, who ranks it alongside such a monumental text as Muḥammad b. Jarīr al-Ṭabarī's (d. 310/923) universal history, *Taʾrīkh al-rusūl wa 'l-mulūk wa 'l-khulafāʾ* [History of the prophets, the kings, and the caliphs].

After the conquests, Arabic eclipsed Persian as the privileged medium of communication in all forms of writing, from the literary to the official. Broadly speaking, Middle Persian, known as Pahlavi, was used during the Sāsānian period as an official, administrative, and liturgical language, and existed side-by-side with Dari, a language spoken at the Sāsānian court.[91] After three centuries of Arab rule, a dialectical form of Persian developed into a full written language in the Arabic script; this language is today referred to by scholars as early New Persian.[92] Ibn Khurradādhbih gives us a glimpse into the development of Persian literature in the Arabic script when he describes in his geography the northern quarter of the ancient Sāsānian empire. He states that the Sāsānian king Bahrām V (r. 420–38 c.e.), whose sobriquet was the Onager (Gūr), recited the following verse in Persian about the township in Damāwand, named Shalanba:

منم شير شلنبه ومنم ببر تله

I am the lion of Shalanba, I am the tiger ready to attack.[93]

When treating the life of Bahrām Gūr in his history of Persian kings, Thaʿālibī recites a slightly longer variant of this verse. He quotes Ibn Khurradādhbih as saying, "This verse is among that which my companions have related of [Bahrām Gūr's] poetry."[94] Such information suggests the oral transmission of Persian poetry in the ʿAbbāsid court. The life of Bahrām Gūr, as an epic hero and model king, continues through various New Persian literary endeavors, as represented in such poetic renditions as the *Shāh-nāma* of Firdawsī, the *Haft paykar* of Niẓāmī Ganjawī (d. ca 600/1203) and the *Hasht bihisht* of Amīr Khusraw (d. 725/1325).[95]

The *Masālik* unfolds a landscape inflected with Persian literary culture. Such is the case with the quotation of the following Persian verse from the ʿAbbāsid poet Abū 'l-Yanbaghī 'l-ʿAbbās b. Ṭarkhān (fl. 225/840), who describes the Central Asian city of Samarqand:

سمرقند گندمند   بذینت کی افگند
از شاش نه بهي   همشـــه نه جهي

Stinking Samarqand
    Who has thrown you into such a state?
No better than Shāsh
    Never will you escape![96]

While the presence of Persian verse within the geography is overshadowed by the dominance of Arabic, its appearance nonetheless reflects a set of courtly practices and linguistic exchanges. According to the literary historian Abū 'l-Faraj al-Iṣfahānī, Persian verse and song were already features of court life by the time of Hārūn al-Rashīd (r. 140–93/786–809).[97] Al-Wāthiq, for instance, found great pleasure in singers from Khurāsān who could recite in both Arabic and Persian.[98] Such literary contacts between languages gave rise to the use of macaronic poetry, which alternated between Arabic and Persian, often with a range of puns and word plays.[99] More broadly, the countless loanwords and calques, which each language took and transformed from the other, point to what were deep and lasting cultural and linguistic exchanges.

Apart from the *Masālik*, the fragments of Ibn Khurradādhbih's writings that survive in other sources, along with various references to him, fill out our portrait of this cultured son of Khurāsān, who took great interest in the preservation of Persian history and the cultivation of poetry. Ibn Khurradādhbih appears as an insider in the caliphal court in Masʿūdī's world history, *Murūj al-dhahab* [Fields of gold], and Iṣfahānī's encyclopedia of Arabic poetry and poets, *Kitāb al-aghānī* [Book of songs].[100] The surviving excerpts of Ibn Khurradādhbih's *Kitāb al-lahw wa 'l-malāhī* [The book of playing and of musical instruments] further highlight his literary and artistic pursuits. In addition to serving as a source of information for the origins of musical instruments and musical techniques as understood and employed in the ʿAbbāsid period, this treatise also preserves a piece of Persian poetry ascribed to Bārbad, the famous court minstrel of the Sāsānian king Khusraw II Parwīz (r. 591–628 c.e.):

قیصر ماه مانذ وخاقان خرشید

آن من خذای ابر مانذ کامغاران

کخاهذ ماه پوشد کخاهذ خرشید

The Caesar resembles the moon, the Khāqān the sun.
My lord is powerful like the cloud:
At will he covers the moon and at will the sun.[101]

These Persian verses, which hearken back to a pre-Islamic period, are written down in the Arabic script, and supplemented with an interlinear translation in Arabic. Their authenticity and their relationship with Bārbad remain to be seen, a question that need not concern us here.[102] Regardless of whether or not they truly belong to the Sāsānian minstrel, the verses speak to the broader cultural mosaic of Ibn Khurradādhbih's universe and its role in the preservation of Persian history and literature through the larger vehicle of Arabic belles-lettres.

When compared to the over eighty quotations of Arabic poetry in the geography, it is clear that Persian, as a literary medium, does not possess the same privileged position. Nonetheless, Ibn Khurradādhbih showcases a poetic universe that is very much the product of cultural interactions among cosmopolitan elites.[103] Thus while the poetry sings of the feats of pre-Islamic Arab poets and the legendary battle days (*ayyām*) of the Arabs, it also praises, in Arabic, the grandeur of Sāsānian history, memorialized, for instance, in the imperial city of Ctesiphon and in Bahrām Gūr's palace of Khawarnaq, near Kufa.[104]

The weight given to Arabic poetry in Ibn Khurradādhbih's projection of space speaks to the manner in which the Persian elite adapted and transformed Arabic literary culture. Ibn Khurradādhbih weaves into his writing a colorful display of quintessential Arabic verse, representing a poetical canon as constructed within ʿAbbāsid court culture at the end of third/ninth century. From the paragon of pre-Islamic (*jāhiliyya*) poets, Imruʾ al-Qays b. Ḥujr (d. ca 550 c.e.), to the so-called poet laureate of the Prophet, Ḥassān b. Thābit (d. ca 40/659), Ibn Khurradādhbih landscapes his geography with a broad repertoire of Arabic verse.

One of the basic semiotic structures of the geography involves stringing together lines of poetry in order to accentuate the various routes of the world. When describing the route from Mecca to Yemen, for example, Ibn Khurradādhbih cites a verse from Abū Nuwās (d. ca 198/813), who was, perhaps, the best known poet of the ʿAbbāsid period, and a chief representative of a new style of poetry ushered in by poets known as 'the moderns' (*muḥdathūn*):

نَحْنُ أَرْبابُ ناعِطٍ وَلَنا   صَنْعاءُ وَٱلْمِسْكُ فِي مَحارِبِها

We are the lords over Nāʿiṭ,
And ours are Ṣanʿāʾ and the musk of its princely chambers.[105]

Nāʿiṭ, a remote fortress in Yemen, is thus imbricated through the logic of the geography, within a larger discursive network of literary history. Ibn Khurradādhbih uses poetry as a way of glossing specific toponyms, often in an effort to localize obscure literary references. As, for instance, is the case of the renowned opening lament (*naṣīb*) for the departed beloved in the *Muʿallaqa* of Imruʾ al-Qays:

فَتُوضِحَ فَٱلْمِقْرَاةِ لَمْ يَعْفُ رَسْمُها   لِمَا نَسَجَتْها مِنْ جَنُوبٍ وَشَمْأَلِ

Then Tūḍiḥ, then al-Miqrāt, the traces [of her campsite] not effaced,
by what the winds, south and north, wove across them.[106]

Ibn Khurradādhbih situates Tūḍiḥ and al-Miqrāt, two watering holes made famous by these opening verses, in his description of the outskirts of Yamāma in the Arabian Peninsula; by doing so he positions the discipline of geography as a central means of understanding the larger belletristic cultures of the urban elite.

The geography opens a window on the literary tastes cultivated by a court culture that promoted the production and performance of poetry in the articulation of its own identity and power. Thus, when reaching the strongholds of Anqira (Ankara) and ʿAmmūriya (Amorium), in the marchlands (*thughūr*) with Byzantium, the narrative turns to a verse composed by the ʿAbbāsid court poet Ḥusayn b. al-Ḍaḥḥāk (d. ca 250/864), in honor of al-Muʿtaṣim's (r. 218–27/833–42) conquests of these two cities in 223/838:

لَمْ تُبْقِ مِنْ أَنْقِرَةٍ نَقْرَةً وَٱجْتَحْتَ عَمُّورِيَةَ ٱلْكُبْرَى

The heart of Anqira ceased to beat
And you annihilated Greater ʿAmmūriya.[107]

References to conquest, rivalry, pilgrimage, and loss echo throughout Ibn Khurradādhbih's poetic landscape, which is populated by well-known cities and obscure way stations. These poetical moments of digression privilege the place of literary pleasure in the organization of geographical knowledge. The encyclopedic range of poetic material takes discursive dominion over the world through the core unit of verse, which, like graffiti, both inscribes and appropriates. These poetic citations are predicated on the logic of intertextuality. All of this is enacted through the illusion of the anecdote (the name of a town which triggers the quotation of a verse, which alludes to a certain moment in time) to collapse the heterogeneity of existence into the intelligible, and thus manageable, structure of narrative.

These moments of intertextuality, which are oriented around a hybrid literary culture, are thus acts of transposition that are set to interpret the world as much as to shape it. Interestingly, the continued allusion to poetry, which serves as a projection of an imagined, cosmopolitan community, falls silent precisely as the geography moves further towards land's end, along the savage frontiers of the world.[108] Such a pattern suggests how the citation of verse in Ibn Khurradādhbih's geography functions as a discursive demarcation of imperial dominion, marking the lands that have been incorporated into the literary fabric of ʿAbbāsid power.

2

MODELS OF TRANSLATION

Considerations on Wonders and Frontiers

Anecdotes of marvels and monsters offer a means of engaging with the foreign and liminal spaces of the frontier. While Ibn Khurradādhbih focuses on the ʿAbbāsid sphere of influence politically, culturally, and geographically, he also journeys deep into remote lands, removed from the religious and political centers of Islam. A geography with a running interest in the wonders of the world, the *Masālik* has many antecedents in classical antiquity.[1] The barbarous nature of the frontier and the space beyond the *oecumene* has been a continual preoccupation throughout the ages. Both the Greeks and the Persians confronted lands beyond civilization; from the Scythians to the Mazandārān, the margins of the earth were in a constant state of flux.

The relation of the *Masālik* with the ʿAbbāsid court foregrounds its conception of the world. The recurring mention of postal routes of communication between various stages (*sikāk*) gives it an administrative perspective. The central administration used these networks of communication to spy on outlying territories, an administrative tradition of surveillance with a variety of antecedents shrouded in imperial garb.[2] The master of the communication and information (*ṣāḥib al-barīd wa 'l-khabar*) was charged with communicating to the caliph the state of affairs across the empire. Likewise, the office of communication (*dīwān al-barīd*) functioned much like a ministry of intelligence. The world pictured in the *Masālik* speaks to adventures of reconnaissance and espionage, of embassies and expeditions with caliphal orders to report about the lands beyond the frontier. To the west, the ongoing conflicts with neighboring Byzantium mark a conceptual border, as do the conquered territories of Sind to the east. The desert stretch through the Arabian Peninsula to the south leads to Yemen and then to the ocean, while north, beyond the Caspian Sea, lie the lands of the Khazar, and then, somewhere beyond them, the civilized world (*al-arḍ al-maʿmūra*) ends.

In the vicissitudes of war and peace, the Byzantine empire functions as a mirror image for the ʿAbbāsids. The *Masālik* gives a description of the Byzantine administration, offering a picture of the bureaucratic system of a neighboring empire. Much of the information on the region is taken from Muslim b. Abī Muslim al-Jarmī, a captive along the Byzantine marchlands (*thughūr*), who, with some four thousand others, was released in a prisoner exchange negotiated during the reign of al-Wāthiq in 231/845. Masʿūdī describes how Jarmī's writings (*muṣannafāt*) contain details on the main routes through the region, accounts of the neighboring kingdoms, as well information relevant for making military incursions into Byzantium, highlighting the strategic importance of such material.[3]

Just as Jarmī's firsthand experience helps open up the Byzantine empire, so, too, those with a mastery of different languages appear as intermediaries in the facilitation of trade and communication between the regions of the world. The *Masālik* famously describes a network of Jewish merchants (*rādhāniyya*) who traveled and traded around the world, selling an array of goods, from slave girls and boys to furs and spices.[4] Their command of Arabic, Persian, and Greek, as well as the languages spoken by the Franks, Andalusians, and Slavs no doubt helped them on their international itineraries, traveling from China to Iberia and back.[5] The description of the itinerary of the Rūs merchants,[6] also featured in the *Masālik*, echoes that of the *rādhāniyya*. However, their need for interpreters stands in marked contrast to the linguistic prowess of the Jewish merchants. We learn that when these Rūs traders, who are identified with the Slavs (*hum jinsun min al-ṣaqāliba*), and who claimed to be Christians, reached Baghdad by way of the Caspian Sea to sell their beaver pelts and swords, the ʿAbbāsid court called in Slav servants to help translate for them.[7]

In geographical writing, the translator often serves as the guide to local knowledge. Such a figure is alluded to in Ibn Khurradādhbih's account concerning the caliphal expedition sent to uncover the 'People of the Cave' (*aṣḥāb al-kahf*) who are described in the opening of the Qurʾānic chapter "The Cave" (*Sūrat al-Kahf*, 18:9–26). The story's center of gravity, and, arguably, that of the whole chapter, lies in the question of the unknown (*ghayb*) and the limits of human knowledge (cf. Q. 18:22, 26).[8] The episode in the

Qurʾān is in dialogue with the Christian hagiographic story of the 'Seven Sleepers of Ephesus.' According to this legend, a group of Christians, variously numbering seven or eight, escaped the persecutions of the Emperor Decius (r. 249–51 C.E.) by fleeing to a cave near Ephesus, where they fell asleep. Miraculously, they remained in a state of sleep for centuries, not awaking until the reign of the Christian Emperor Theodosius (d. 395 C.E.).[9] In the diverse traditions of Qurʾānic exegesis, considerable speculation arose concerning the details of this narrative, referred to invariably as an edifying tale (*qiṣṣa*). Such speculation, also a theme in the Qurʾānic account, sparked a desire to locate the Cave of the Sleepers. According to Ibn Khurradādhbih, the caliph al-Wāthiq, apparently always curious to learn more of the world's wonders, took up this account and resolved to send the astrologer (*munajjim*) Muḥammad b. Mūsā as an emissary to Byzantium in order to find out more about the state of the cave.[10] In a letter to the emperor of Byzantium (*ʿaẓīm al-rūm*), al-Wāthiq asks that Muḥammad b. Mūsā be provided with a guide who would lead him to the cave. Ibn Khurradādhbih goes on to narrate this story, basing himself on the eyewitness testimony of Muḥammad b. Mūsā, who describes the events to him (*ḥaddathanī*).

The emperor of Byzantium sent a guide with the expedition to take them to the cave. There they found a deep well dug into the base of the mountain, at the bottom of which they were able to discern water. Their group descended into the cave until they arrived at the gate of the burrow; walking along the cavern for about three hundred paces, they reached an overlook where they spotted below a colonnade formed out of the mountain, raised on columns carved from rock. Located on the top of this were a number of chambers, one with an elevated doorstep. In this chamber were dead bodies (*mawtā*) and a man responsible for standing guard over them. We learn of the remarkably beautiful eunuchs that accompanied the guard. Muḥammad b. Mūsā goes on to complete the anecdote:

> The guard was not inclined that we see [the bodies]. Wanting to deceive us so that his charge over them would continue, [he said that] he considered it was not safe, for whoever touched them would be plagued by misfortune. I said to him, "Let me see them and you are free from any responsibility." So I climbed with a large torch with my slave until I saw them, in coarse woolen fabric. In order to preserve them, their bodies were enwrapped in aloe, myrrh, and camphor. Their skin stuck to their bones. I only had to brush my hand over one of their chests to discover the hair to be coarse and to have been

> forcibly implanted. The overseer had prepared food for them. He invited us to eat with him. When we tried his food, it disagreed with us and immediately we threw it up. In effect, he wanted to either kill or choke us, with the aim of perpetuating that which he had claimed to the king of Byzantium, [namely,] that these bodies were those of the People of the Cave. So we said to him, "We believed that you would show us bodies that would resemble the living, but these are nothing like that."[11]

Abruptly, the journey to discover the People of the Cave ends; the effect of which is to debunk any Byzantine claim of propriety over the relics and, by extension, over the Qurʾānic account. The adventure to the cave condenses complex diplomatic relations with Byzantium into an anecdote of competing teleologies of scriptural authority and geopolitical dominion. After consuming a poisoned meal, the astrologer Muḥammad b. Mūsā escaped with his life and with an account (*khabar*), which circulated widely, to discredit the authenticity of the Byzantine shrine.[12]

For the most part the role of the one who silently guides the astrologer to what turns out to be a mishap in the cave escapes the attention of later sources that transmit this tale. Perhaps it is not surprising that, when other writers turn to this story, the figure of the guide collapses into the background, for he does not seem to play a prominent role in the outward trajectory of the anecdote; he is ancillary to the figures of al-Wāthiq, the astrologer, the emperor of Byzantium, the guard of the cave, his beautiful eunuchs, and the dead bodies themselves. Even Ibn Khurradādhbih's narrative only refers elliptically to the guide as the "one who led him" (*man sāra bihi*). To the extent that later sources are bound to the textual blueprint of the account, they are unable to fill out further details. That said, the *Jahān-nāma* of Muḥammad b. Najīb Bakrān (fl. 604/1208), a Persian geographical work based primarily on Arabic sources, is freed, through translation, from following *verbatim* Ibn Khurradādhbih's description of the embassy. Bakrān relates that al-Wāthiq "wrote a letter to the emperor of Byzantium (*qayṣar-i rūm*) asking that [the emperor] supply daily provisions and a road guide (*qalawūz*) and whatever might be necessary for this expedition."[13]

Centuries later and in a foreign language, the Turkish word *qalawūz* offers some insight into the profession of this character—the guide who disappears into the margins, unnoticed and unobtrusive, upstaged by the other players who enact the performance of discovery. We may contemplate how much the guide knew as he led these foreign visitors through the treacherous turns of the cavern; but the very structure of such anecdotes—the seemingly innocuous building blocks of history—defies this kind of speculation. We have barely a reference to the guide, let alone information about what motivates him. Nonetheless, as much as history effaces these go-betweens, preferring the illusion of immediacy to the filters of mediation, the role of such informants in shaping the transmission of local knowledge cannot be underestimated. Both the guide and the translator, who are, after all, variations on the same theme, slip by silently, unnoticed, while shaping the course of the trajectory and the outcome of the tale.

In the logic of descriptive geography, translators serve as guides and there is sufficient documentation to sketch such figures. The ʿAbbāsid geographer Ibn al-Faqīh records a case in which the Umayyad caliph Hishām b. ʿAbd al-Malik (r. 105–25/724–43) sent to the Turks an envoy who communicated with the population by way of an interpreter (*tarjumān*), with the goal of converting them to Islam.[14] The role of translation in the process of conversion is woven into the memory of the early spread of Islam, reflected in the well-known tradition that the Prophet Muḥammad, toward the end of his life, sent messengers to the rulers of the world, translating verses from the Qurʾān into multiple languages, calling them to embrace Islam.[15]

One of the most vivid depictions of the *tarjumān* in this proselytizing capacity is showcased in the epistle of Ibn Faḍlān (fl. 310/922), in which he describes his journey as part of the caliphal embassy sent north to the king of the Turkish Bulghārs along the Volga River. Ibn Faḍlān is charged with reading a letter from the ʿAbbāsid caliph al-Muqtadir (r. 295–320/908–32) to the Bulghār king, in addition to presenting gifts to him and his court. Along with building a fortress to protect the Bulghār king, who had recently converted to Islam, from attack by the neighboring Jewish Khazar, the caliphal embassy was sent to help construct a mosque and to instruct the newly converted Muslims in the proper ways of Islamic law (*sharīʿa*).[16] During his adventure, Ibn Faḍlān describes how he could only communicate with the local people through the aid of his Turkish translators, who are named Takīn and Bāris.[17] He understands the wondrous and often savage world around him through the filter of his translators' explanations, and with their aid he makes inroads in his broader mission of converting pagans to Islam:

> A severe cold spell struck us for some days. Takīn was guiding me and beside him was a man from among the Turks. This man began to speak in Turkish. Takīn started to laugh and he said, "This Turk asks you, 'What is it that our Lord wants from us, for he is killing us with this cold weather, if we knew what it was that he wanted, we would

> bring it to him.'" I said to Takīn, "Tell him that the Lord wants from you that you say, 'There is no deity but God.'" The man laughed and replied, "If we had know that [was all], then we would have done it."[18]

Ibn Faḍlān experiences others through the mediation of translation (*ʿalā lisān al-tarjumān*), not directly, but through someone else's interpretation.[19] From conversing with peasants to addressing the king of the Bulghārs, the translators are always present, opening for Ibn Faḍlān a universe on the margins of Islam. As he continues his journey along the Volga, encountering beardless Ghuzz Turks and tattooed Rūs traders, the translators act as ethnographic informants displaying a dazzling spectrum of customs and beliefs that range from mundane curiosities to orgiastic funeral rites of human sacrifice.[20]

Following a discursive pattern set in the marvel-writing of classical antiquity, Ibn Khurradādhbih serves as a guide to the foreign and remote, giving a taste of the innumerable wonders found in the distant islands of the Indian Ocean; he describes cannibals who eat people alive, serpents large enough to devour elephants, and boundless jewels and spices ready for the taking. Here are pygmies, who, in their savagery shun people (*yastawḥishūn min al-nās*); they dwell in trees swinging from branch to branch; their speech is incomprehensible because of their small stature.[21] Yet there are other cases, such as the Nicobar Islands, where the inhabitants seem to be rather friendly: they go about naked and eat bananas, fresh fish and coconuts; they have a currency based in iron and are in commerce with merchants.[22] While Ibn Khurradādhbih's itinerary along the far-flung islands of the east is populated with idol worshipers, tribal kings bedecked in gold, and ravenous cannibals, it is also filled with such exotic commodities as sandalwood, cloves, and highly sought-after camphor.[23] This suggests not only well-established mercantile networks leading back to the centers of ʿAbbāsid power, but also a literary shaping of the exotic frontiers, balanced between horror and pleasure.

At the edges of the inhabited world, past the cities and the villages into the wastelands and islands, at the furthest extreme of the known earth, mediation through language fails; in those encounters between what could be called the civilized and the savage, where the interpreters themselves will go no further, communication breaks down into signs and gestures. Ṭāhir al-Marwazī (fl. 483/1090) examines the various customs of indigenous peoples while trading with foreign merchants. In his natural history, *Ṭabāʾiʿ al-ḥayawān* [The natural properties of animals], he describes the Kīmāk, a Turkish tribe of Siberia, who trade with foreigners (*ghurabāʾ*) by signs (*bi'l-ishārāt*), and without speech.[24] Rather, the foreigner brings his goods for trade and sets them on a plank of wood, and then leaves. A Kīmāk then comes and places an offering in exchange for the goods. If the owner of the goods returns and is pleased, he takes the offering, leaving behind what was on the plank; and if he is not pleased, he leaves the offering alone.[25] Marwazī describes what is known today as 'silent trade' or 'dumb barter,' a practice of trading without direct contact or speech.[26] Here communication and exchange continue through a sophisticated performance that effaces both speech and presence. Important to this exchange is the fact that the two parties never come in direct contact; this form of barter insures both the exchange of goods and the protection of each side from the other.

Following the same track, Marwazī relates how the Bulghār travel to the far north across high packed snows in sleighs drawn by dogs, in order to trade with the Yūra, a Siberian tribe of savages (*mutawaḥḥishūn*) who live in forests (*ghiyāḍ*) and are hostile to outsiders, not associating with others for fear of being harmed.[27] The Bulghār merchants take goods such as clothes and salt to barter for sable pelts. The entire exchange of merchandise between the Bulghār and Yūra, however, is enacted in the absence of the other, without direct communication but through a mediated process of absent trade (*mughāyaba*).

We get a fuller picture of this activity of absent exchange when Marwazī moves into warmer territory and describes the economic barter activity of islanders off the coast of India. On one such island, inhabited by cannibals believed to be *jinn*, merchants barter with the savages (*mutawaḥḥishūn*) without making direct contact and thus insuring the safety of the two sides.[28] The maritime trade of clove in the islands of the Indian Ocean is likewise described. There, because of the hostility of the islanders, the clove is bought by absent trading (*mughāyabatan*).[29]

This dance of the merchants with the savages suggests its own form of communication, filtered through an elaborate system of signs. The mutual absence (*mughāyaba*) is paralleled morphologically, but is opposed conceptually, with the privileged act of direct observation (*muʿāyana*), which functions as the dominant epistemological paradigm of descriptive geography. The implied oppositional relationship highlights how subversive and exotic this particular economic practice must have seemed. Such an economy of exchange based on values of absence and presence captures how two sides mediate their own frontiers. In these liminal spaces, on the edge of the forest and on the shore of the island, direct contact is never made but exchange, and with it description, take place nonetheless. For such texts, the category of 'the savage' serves as a foil to legitimate the normative position of 'the civilized,' enacted through the mimetic power of language to control and fashion the other within the reducible and sublimated form of the anecdote, readily transmitted and translated. Within the context of the marvelous, which serves explicitly as the backdrop for this material, the question of relative veracity should not be ignored, as these accounts are not neutral descriptions of reality, but are deployed as a means of defining the self in negative dialectic with an imagined and highly formalized other. Rather than reflecting discrete events, such anecdotes serve as descriptive *topoi* of the process of exchange across frontiers.

From globe-trotting Jewish merchants who speak multiple languages to guides who serve as translators across foreign lands, and then, finally, to an exchange of goods through the mutual absence of both parties, we can trace various levels of detachment from immediate experience. What emerges from this partially reconstructed mosaic is the fact that the textual world of the wondrous, of crossing the frontier and coming back, has always been the space of translation, separated by degrees from the thing itself. It is the translator, the intermediary between worlds and a supplement for presence, who, hidden in a textual chain of transmission, makes contact to negotiate the space of the frontier.

An Approach to the Story of Sallām al-Tarjumān

As a discipline, geography promises a description of the earth and its features presented through word and image. Translation, rather than an end—such as geography, which is an entire field within itself—suggests a process; the movement and transference, be it linguistically or physically, from one register to another. The Greek word geography (*γεωγραφία*) derives from the compound of *geo*, earth, coupled with *graphia*, which signifies writing and maintains a representational element, thus pointing to a semantic charge that hearkens back to the act of carving. Ptolemy, in the introduction to his *Geography*, links the projection of the earth through maps and words with imitation (*μίμησις*) and pictorial representation, suggesting in the first instance what we today take to be cartography.[30]

The Arabic translation of this Greek term, 'image of the earth' (*ṣūrat al-arḍ*), highlights the mimetic quality of the discipline; it is an encyclopedic branch of knowledge whose horizons blanket the entire earth, following coastlines and mountains, harbors and settlements, telescoping out to view the contours of countries and continents, and finally the globe itself. All this is enacted through the magic of mimesis, in the imitative capacity of word and image to capture the impossible: the space outside us and our position in it.

Translation serves as the *modus operandi* of geography, first by gathering knowledge of the world and its inhabitants across frontiers, and second by transmitting that knowledge and projecting it in a meaningful way. The anecdote of Sallām al-Tarjumān's journey to the edge of the inhabited world serves as an emblem of the relationship between geography and translation. From the third/ninth century, when his story first circulated in the caliphal court, to the thirteenth/nineteenth century, when Orientalists tried to determine the trajectory of his expedition, and today, as we rehearse his tale, Sallām the translator continues his journey through uncharted territory, alive in the minds of admirers and detractors.

Sallām's narrative is predicated on the Qurʾānic treatment of the nations of Yājūj and Mājūj and the wall built by Dhū 'l-Qarnayn, as outlined in *Sūrat al-Kahf*.[31] According to the Qurʾān, Dhū 'l-Qarnayn traveled to the land of the rising sun, where he encountered a people who were plagued by Yājūj and Mājūj; they beseeched him to protect them from the ravaging of these nations. Thereupon, Dhū 'l-Qarnayn erected a wall between two mountains to protect humankind. Dhū 'l-Qarnayn figures in the Qurʾān as the heroic model of piety and ultimate instrument of God's will. The story of Yājūj and Mājūj plays a central role in Islamic eschatology, where, according to the Qurʾān, the Lord will allow these nations to break forth from the barrier to descend across the world and surge against humankind. Their destruction of the earth represents one of the signs of the Hour (*āyāt al-sāʿa*), signifying the advent of the apocalypse and ultimately the Day of Resurrection (*yawm al-qiyāma*).[32]

The tale of Yājūj and Mājūj, along with the wall built by Dhū 'l-Qarnayn, has a pedigree that predates the Islamic configuration, with its roots in Jewish and Christian eschatological traditions tied to the figures of Gog and Magog, who appear, either individually or together, in Genesis 10:2, 1 Chronicles 1:5, 5:4, Ezekiel 38–9, and Revelation 20:7–10. In Christian apocalyptic scenarios, the hordes of Gog and Magog, whose number is as the sand of the sea (*ὡς ἡ ἄμμος τῆς θαλάσσης*), will come as an army to spread destruction over the earth. In a process of transposition that occurs already with the Jewish historian Flavius Josephus (fl. 93 C.E.), the savage Scythians of the Greek *imaginaire* are identified with Magog, who are connected to the apocalyptic races that Alexander the Great bottled up behind a barrier near the Caspian Sea.[33] In Syriac writings by Eastern Christians in the early seventh century, this barrier was a well-established motif, expressed, for instance, in the anonymous *Neṣḥānā d'Aleksandrōs* [The triumph of Alexander] and in a homily (*mēmrā*) on Alexander attributed to Jacob of Sarug, in which Gog and Magog are fused with the

Romance cycle of Alexander and the building of the wall.[34] Demonstrating the fluidity of this narrative, with the rapid series of Arab conquests later in the seventh century, Syriac apocalyptic writings, such as the homily by Pseudo-Ephraem and the *Apocalypse* of Pseudo-Methodius, incorporate the rise of Islam as part of an eschatological narrative in which Gog and Magog are accorded significant roles.[35]

Early Muslim exegetes were quick to associate Alexander the Great with the epithet Dhū 'l-Qarnayn, meaning *bicornis*, the possessor of two horns, a name that reflects an iconographic pattern, established in antiquity, of representing an apotheosized Alexander with horns.[36] These horns are a feature of the seventh-century Syriac adventure, the *Neṣḥānā d'Aleksandrōs*, in which Alexander, explicitly configured as an archetypal Christian hero, is endowed by God with horns (*qarnāṯā*) upon his head.[37] In early Qur'ānic exegesis, the figure of Dhū 'l-Qarnayn takes on a saintly air, often placed on a par with the divinely-inspired prophets who precede Muḥammad.[38] His Arabic and Persian adventures lead him around the world, where he appears as a heroic champion of monotheism and a protector of humankind.[39]

The ravaging meted out by Gog and Magog is a story shared among religious traditions, enwrapped variously in Jewish, Christian, and Muslim retellings. As the tale of Gog and Magog disseminated through these three monotheistic faiths, the interpretations concerning who, and where, these monstrous races were multiplied and grew ever more heterogeneous over time. Gog and Magog have been identified variously as Scythians, Huns, Celts, Goths, Alāns, Khazars, Arabs, Turks, Magyars, Mongols, and the Ten Tribes of Israel.[40] An apocalyptic story for every generation, they are the quintessential illustration of fluid and ever-changing notions of the margin.

When the caliph al-Wāthiq awoke after dreaming that the barrier holding back Gog and Magog had burst open, he did not take his vision lightly. This anecdote stands as a showpiece to Ibn Khurradādhbih's geography of the world and the wonders therein. The journey to Dhū 'l-Qarnayn's rampart may be read as a moment of translation set against a culture of translators. Ibn Khurradādhbih is such a translator, standing on the cusp of two arcs of culture, beholding Persian and Arabic traditions, retelling Islamic and pre-Islamic tales. Sallām, the emissary chosen by al-Wāthiq to head his mission to the wall and to bring back eyewitness testimony (*ʿāyinhu wa jiʾnī bi-khabarihi*),[41] is also a translator, mediating between the civilized and the savage.

Possessing the Marvelous

In the Vienna redaction of Ibn Khurradādhbih's geography, Sallām's journey to the wall appears in a section treating the marvelous buildings of the world (*ʿajāʾib al-bunyān*). In fact, the opening of the *Masālik* promises a description of architectural wonders.[42] The first series of structures described under this rubric, the pyramids of Giza, are notable as they position al-Wāthiq's mission in dialogue with issues of salvation history, royal patronage, and adventurous confrontations with the grotesque.

As with Muḥammad b. Mūsā's encounter with the preserved corpses disguised as the People of the Cave, the description of the pyramids enters into the subterranean world of crypts and mummified remains. Ibn Khurradādhbih starts with an account, which appears to either share a common source with, or be directly based on, the *Kitāb al-ulūf* [The book of the thousands] of the famed Persian astrologer Abū Maʿshar (d. 272/886). According to Masʿūdī, Abū Maʿshar dedicated an entire section of his astrological history to a description of the marvelous temples and buildings of the world.[43] Abū Maʿshar held that the pyramids were part of a Hermetic astrological design, erected, according to his mythological conception of history, by the original Hermes, who was the first to learn the science of the stars and to build temples.[44] This broader cosmographical pattern informs Ibn Khurradādhbih's description of how the two largest pyramids of Giza, said to tower four hundred cubits above the ground, were engraved with hieroglyphics (*musnad*) and talismanic symbols (*taʿāwīdh*), containing every secret (*sirr*) and marvel (*ʿajīb*) of medicine and astrology. These inscriptions, which, according to Ibn al-Faqīh were translated for an unnamed caliph, read, "I have built these two pyramids, so whoever claims to be powerful in his dominion, try to destroy them, for destruction is easier than building."[45] Ibn Khurradādhbih relates how all the wealth of the world (*kharāj al-dunyā*) could not accomplish such a task.

The narrative of the exterior, with its majestic, yet cryptic aura, leads to an underground adventure into the belly of one of the smaller adjoining pyramids. As with the missions of Sallām and Mūsā, the following account is based on the direct testimony of one of the participants, Ismāʿīl b. Yazīd al-Muhallabī. In all three accounts, the narrators are tied to the ruling elite, as emissaries who interpret the wonders of existence. Muhallabī, our guide on this adventure, served as a secretary (*kātib*) to Luʾluʾ (d. 304/916–7), a commander in the service of Ibn Ṭūlūn (d. 270/884), the ʿAbbāsid Turkish general and *de facto* ruler of Egypt and Syria.[46] Luʾluʾ and his entourage broke off with Ibn Ṭūlūn and joined the service of the ʿAbbāsid prince al-Muwaffaq (d. 278/891), the effective administrator of the empire,[47] to fight the Zanj revolt in 269/883.[48] This would be a likely *terminus ante quem* for the relation of the account to Ibn Khurradādhbih.[49]

Accompanied by Abū ʿAbd Allāh al-Wāsiṭī, the secretary (*kātib*) of Ibn Ṭūlūn, and a group of laborers, Muhallabī details how they entered the pyramid by pulling away three layers of stone blocks, each separated by fine sand. Beneath the third layer led a passageway to an open courtyard measuring forty cubits squared; this was filled with three hundred and sixty statues (*timthāl*) in the form of people making offerings. At each side of the courtyard were separate chambers (*nīmkhānjāt*), closed by high stone doors, facing the cardinal directions; Muhallabī relates these directions with respect to the *qibla* orientation toward Mecca.

Within the chambers lay onyx urns, the lids of which were shaped in the form of different animals. Cracking open the urns they discovered mummies (*mūmiyāʾī*). In the north chamber was a sarcophagus (*jurn*) made of a massive black stone, sealed tight with lead. Unable to open the lid by force, they lit a fire so the lead cementing the tomb would melt:

> We found in the sarcophagus the corpse of a ruler (*shaykh*); under his head was a tablet of white onyx that had cracked from the fire we had set, just as the clothing covering the corpse had burned. We took the tablet, and joining it together, found on one side two images (*ṣūratān*) of gold. One of the images was of a man, in his hand was a serpent, the other was the image of a man on a donkey, holding a staff, on the other side of the tablet was a third image of a man mounted on a camel bearing a rod. So we took all of this to Aḥmad b. Ṭūlūn, who called for an artisan to join together the tablet. We collectively came to the consensus that the three images corresponded to Mūsā, ʿĪsā, and Muḥammad.[50]

This rather destructive treasure-hunting foray is predicated on the power of eyewitness observation (*ʿiyān*), which leads deeper beneath the surface, like one of the many subterranean encounters in the cycle of *The Thousand and One Nights*, into the symmetrical labyrinth of the crypt, replicating itself within a mirrored pattern of increasingly smaller stages of unveiling. The royal audience, represented in the figure of Ibn Ṭūlūn, not only legitimates this act of ekphrastic recovery, but animates it with a scriptural hermeneutic that unlocks the cosmic design hidden within the monuments of pharaonic Egypt. The Muslim ruling elite reads the hieroglyphs through a teleology of prophetic history, positioning themselves as the rightful inheritors of these mysterious treasures. As with the *translatio* of relics, highlighted in the medieval Christian practice of the sacred theft (*furta sacra*),[51] the transferral of the human remains from the crypt justifies a broader cosmological narrative affirming the salvific power of Islam as prophesied in the monumental wonder of the pyramids.

The opening up of the pyramids serves as an established pattern for the articulation of political power and dominion, manifest in the famed account of how the caliph al-Maʾmūn sought to unlock the hidden treasures contained within the pyramids, in a project that appears to have been inspired by the desire for both monetary and intellectual gain.[52] Muhallabī's adventure through the pyramids fits into a pattern in Ibn Khurradādhbih's geography of highlighting the divine order of Muslim rule in the course of human history.

The description of marvelous buildings shares part in a mosaic of wonders and curiosities showcased throughout the geography. Shortly before the description of the pyramids, Ibn Khurradādhbih devotes a section to the wonders of the world (*ʿajāʾib al-arḍ*), and includes the portentous discoveries in Toledo preceding the Umayyad conquest of the Iberian Peninsula in 93/711. The account of how the last Visigoth king, Roderick (Ludhrīq), broke an ancient taboo and with it brought on the Muslim invasion of Iberia, forms part of a historiography shared by medieval Christians and Muslims.[53] After relating that Muslim armies, during the conquest of Toledo, came into possession of Solomon's bejeweled table (*māʾida*), Ibn Khurradādhbih describes how the invasion of the peninsula was precipitated by Roderick breaking into an enchanted, sealed temple (*bayt*) in the city. According to custom, each Visigoth king would place a lock upon the temple to ensure the safety of their reign. Despite the many admonishments from his counselors, who warned of the taboo barring any king from setting foot in the temple, Roderick broke into the inner chamber, only to discover talismanic statues of Arabs on horseback wearing turbans and bearing swords. Ibn Khurradādhbih's account concludes with the year that Roderick forced open (*fataḥa*) the temple gate—exactly the year when the Arab armies invaded the Visigoth kingdom.[54] The dangers of such exploration and curiosity are circumscribed by a providential order that legitimates the expansive territory gained in the course of the early Muslim conquests (*futūḥāt*).

The wonders of the world in Ibn Khurradādhbih's geography are framed by the logic of imperial acts of discovery and possession, in part constructed through a pre-existing Umayyad ideology of expansion. The intimate relationship between the early Arab conquests and geography itself points to a developed discourse of territorial description.[55] Turning from the wonderous enchantment that preordained the collapse of the Visigoth state, Ibn Khurradādhbih relates that the Umayyad general Qutayba b. Muslim (d. 96/715) uncovered during his conquests of the Sogdian city of Paykand in Transoxiana (87–90/706–9) a giant skeleton, the top of which could only be reached with the aid of ladders.[56] This early form of paleontology could position what were evidently the bones of prehistoric creatures, not only as proof of an ancient race of giants, but also as trophies acquired through conquest.

Ibn Khurradādhbih's list of wondrous buildings, mountains, bodies of water, and natural dispositions crescendos in a discursive display of mimetic possession. Symbolically, marvels of relics, bones, strange customs, and bizarre phenomena are controlled and possessed in the capital of textual production. Much of the marvelous material displayed in the geography builds upon earlier paradigms of conquest and dominion that inform the ʿAbbāsid interest in curiosities. As Ibn Khurradādhbih draws on examples of marvels from Umayyad conquests, he positions the ʿAbbāsid caliphate as not only continuing in a tradition of marvelous possessions, but also surpassing it.

Such is the case with Ibn Khurradādhbih's inclusion of the four wonders of the world enumerated by ʿAbd Allāh, the son of ʿAmr b. al-ʿĀṣ (d. 42/663), the conquerer of Egypt. ʿAbd Allāh's list situates marvels as trophies of imperial control that accompanied the vast territory conquered by the Umayyads.[57] Topping ʿAbd Allāh's list of wonders is the lighthouse (*manāra*) of Alexandria, from which, it was said, one could see across the stretch of the Mediterranean to Constantinople. His account resonates with the belief that the mirror of Alexandria was capable of burning enemy ships by way of concentrating the sun's rays. Thus, as part of Umayyad dominion, the lighthouse, long thought to have been built by Alexander the Great, served as a symbol of imperial power.

As for the lighthouse, it was a major attraction for medieval travelers and formed an established *topos* for geographers, who offered detailed descriptions of the ancient structure, which, in turn, further fed the curiosity surrounding the marvel itself. Abū 'l-Faraj al-Iṣfahānī, in his *Adab al-ghurabā*ʾ [The etiquette of strangers] relates an account of a traveler who visited the lighthouse in 303/915. Inside he found verses dated 270/883–4, written by a certain Muḥammad b. ʿAbd al-Ṣamad, who desired to leave a record of the pain, fatigue, and hardship he endured in the course of reaching the marvel. Iṣfahānī goes on to describe how these poetic inscriptions inspired a series of verses that were later carved onto the monument, continuing the motif of the fragility and temporality of life.[58] This graffiti encoding the marvel is itself shaped by a discourse of beholding the wonders of the world, and like descriptive geography, represents a means of re-inscribing and appropriating the monument.

Yet even this marvel, which Ibn Khurradādhbih domesticates by likening it to the minaret of Sāmarrāʾ, seems parochial in the context of the geography, eclipsed by a dazzling orchestration of strange and morbid adventures. As with the logic of storytelling, reiterated throughout the marvels of *The Thousand and One Nights*, in which each story attempts to surpass that which precedes it, Ibn Khurradādhbih's encyclopedic display of wonders showcases ever-increasing levels of astonishment. The courtly production and reception of these curiosities are part of a caliphal conception of imperial management and control over the diversity of existence.

Illustrative of this caliphal interest in possessing such curiosities is Masʿūdī's claim regarding the purported mission of al-Mutawakkil (r. 232–47/847–61), who succeeded al-Wāthiq. He is said to have sent the famed translator and physician Ḥunayn b. Isḥāq (d. 260/873) to procure vipers, as well as a specimen from the Nasnās.[59] The Nasnās, monstrous creatures thought to be related to apes, were said to possess only half a head, one arm, and one leg, upon which they hopped. Al-Wāthiq's earlier adventure to the wall of Gog and Magog, its own form of imperial trophy also requiring the aid of a translator, may have been a model for al-Mutawakkil's request. In such imperial dispatches, or at least in the anecdotal form of imagining them, the translator is called upon to manage the liminal spaces of the map's edge.

3

AL-WĀTHIQ AND THE TRANSLATORS

Generally speaking, the sources paint al-Wāthiq biʿllāh, the ninth ʿAbbāsid caliph, as a profligate, given over to song, dance, and the sensuality of singing-girls (*jawārī*). For all intents and purposes, al-Wāthiq's own power was dependant on the Turkish military elite whom his father, al-Muʿtaṣim, had instated.[1] The Turkish guard came to exercise a considerable control over the caliphate within the palatine city of Sāmarrāʾ, which was founded by al-Muʿtaṣim and continued to be the seat of ʿAbbāsid rule through the reign of al-Muʿtamid.[2]

Al-Wāthiq pursued the monumental development of Sāmarrāʾ initiated by his father.[3] The capital city continued to expand into a cosmopolitan center surrounded by cantonments of an international military corps that consisted of Central Asian Turks, Khazars, Sogdians, and Arab tribesmen.[4] Ibn Khurradādhbih's geographical awareness of the various Turkish tribal confederations of Central Asia, many of which were replicated in the social universe of Sāmarrāʾ, highlights the strategic importance of the region.[5] Beyond the Khazar kingdom and returning through the heartlands of Transoxiana, Sallām's own itinerary, which originated in the ʿAbbāsid capital, included travels among non-Muslim populations who inhabited lands beyond the frontiers, but were interconnected with the center of the empire. With this mixed population, Sāmarrāʾ was a site for both the cross-pollination and the demarcation of religious and cultural practices.[6]

As for the religious climate of the period, al-Wāthiq is said to have continued the inquisition (*miḥna*), started by al-Maʾmūn, instituting the

Muʿtazilī doctrine of the createdness of the Qurʾān as official state policy. Though at the end of his life it is reported that al-Wāthiq changed his stance on this issue, the sources depict, often with gruesome detail, his bloody implementation of the doctrine, and how at times he oversaw and even participated in the execution of those who affirmed the uncreatedness of the Qurʾān.

Taken by the pleasures of food, poetry, and music, his brief and undistinguished reign as caliph came to an abrupt end with his death, at approximately thirty-six, only five years after assuming the caliphate.[7] While there is a significant corpus of historical detail on the life of al-Wāthiq, the sources are, inevitably, composite and perspectival. Ibn Khurradādhbih, who was a member of al-Muʿtamid's court a generation later, records the stories of Muḥammad b. Mūsā's journey to the cave of the Seven Sleepers of Ephesus and Sallām al-Tarjumān's adventure to the wall of Gog and Magog. Here al-Wāthiq appears as a distant, and perhaps even idealized, figure of caliphal authority. In contrast, the image presented by the historian and exegete Ṭabarī has no pretenses of ideal grandeur; in his history, the various events of al-Wāthiq's reign fit into the larger geopolitical realities facing the ʿAbbāsid ruling elite. The political uprisings and frontier skirmishes, however, are removed from Abū 'l-Faraj al-Iṣfahānī's version of al-Wāthiq, who is presented as the first ʿAbbāsid caliph to not only express a passion for poetry and singing, but to be a practiced performer himself.[8] Al-Wāthiq can be thanked in part for Iṣfahānī's *Kitāb al-aghānī*, as he ordered Isḥāq al-Mawṣilī (d. 235/850), one of the most prominent singers of the court, to compile a list of the best one hundred songs, said to have followed a model laid out by Hārūn al-Rashīd; this collection, in turn, served as a major source for Iṣfahānī's literary history.[9]

Despite all the details which remain, we cannot determine with certainty the age of the caliph when he died, much less make a full account of his reign. While the sources mention that al-Wāthiq's mother was of Greek origin, named Qarāṭīs, that he was handsome, of white complexion, had a fleck in his left eye, and savored, above all, eggplant, the details that survive cannot fill out his life as it really was (*wie es eigentlich gewesen war*).[10] Although we may picture al-Wāthiq reclining on a jewel-encrusted couch, wearing a gold embroidered robe, listening to Farīda, his favorite singing-girl,[11] the biographical details do not fully complete this picture, or shed light on the psychological or historical motivations which might have precipitated a far-flung mission across the Caucasus.

Details on the life and identity of the caliphal envoy to the wall are even more obscure. Other than Ibn Khurradādhbih, none of the contemporary sources mention a man referred to as Sallām al-Tarjumān. The Persian geographer Ibn Rusta (fl. 300/912), a keen reader of Ibn Khurradādhbih, does make the comment that Sallām translated Turkish dispatches for al-Wāthiq; this might help us to delineate Sallām's relationship to the Turkish general Abū Jaʿfar Ashinās (d. 230/844) who recommended him for the adventure. It may also situate Sallām within the social world of the Turkish military guard of Sāmarrāʾ. Yet it is unclear where Ibn Rusta derives this added information, as he bases the rest of Sallām's account of the rampart, which he views with great suspicion, explicitly on Ibn Khurradādhbih.[12] Notably, every subsequent continuation of al-Wāthiq's embassy finds its origin in Ibn Khurradādhbih's geography. Other than conjecture, we cannot speak of the translator's identity, his relationship to the author, or to the caliph.

We may, however, turn our attention to other more prominent translators of the period, in order to adumbrate the figure of Sallām al-Tarjumān. The Nestorian Christian Ḥunayn b. Isḥāq, undoubtedly the most famous ʿAbbāsid translator, frequented al-Wāthiq's court. In addition to his command of both Syriac and Arabic, Ḥunayn had reached such a mastery of classical Greek that he is said to have been able to recite Homer from memory.[13] A prolific translator, Ḥunayn introduced an encyclopedic range of Greek material into Arabic and Syriac, from the oneiromancy of Artemidorus (fl. second century C.E.) to a translation of the Septuagint.[14] In addition to expanding the holdings of the caliphal library (*bayt al-ḥikma*), his work as a translator attracted wealthy individual patrons. Ḥunayn's interest in such diverse fields as astronomy, belles-lettres, history, magic, mathematics, and philosophy comes to light in his extensive translations and through his own writings. However, Ḥunayn made his greatest contribution to the advancement of science in the field of medicine, through his translations of Galen and Hippocrates, which served as foundational Arabic texts for generations of physicians. Well before Ḥunayn reached the position of court physician during the reign of al-Mutawakkil, he had established himself as a leading intellectual of ʿAbbāsid society.

Masʿūdī describes formal assemblies of doctors and intellectuals over which al-Wāthiq presided and where Ḥunayn figured as a leading authority. The caliph prompted Ḥunayn and the assembly members to illuminate various matters ranging from natural sciences to theological speculations. As an idealized textual projection of al-Wāthiq and Ḥunayn, Masʿūdī's description shares part in a broader articulation of ʿAbbāsid imperial authority as rooted in the promotion and cultivation of learning. Far from the extravagance of decadent detachment, Masʿūdī pictures al-Wāthiq as actively involved in the promotion of scientific investigation (*naẓar*). Favoring intellectual curiosity, the caliph is said to have detested following tradition blindly (*taqlīd*) and all those who did so.

In addition to Ḥunayn, such prominent translators and physicians as the Nestorian Christians Bukhtīshūʿ (d. 256/870) and Ibn Māsawayh (d. 243/857) attended this assembly,[15] which al-Wāthiq commenced by asking how the knowledge of medicine was achieved; what was the source for its principles; was this knowledge obtained by perception, through deduction by analogy (*qiyās*), by tradition, through principles of reason; or were the principles of medicine reached through an oral tradition of transmitted knowledge (*samʿ*), as is the case with the religious scholars.[16] This line of questioning speaks to the broader intellectual climate of the period, which continued a scholastic tradition of classifying knowledge into principles (*uṣūl*) and branches (*furūʿ*) of sciences (*ʿulūm*). It also suggests the authority of the caliph privileging observation, experimentation, and independent reason in a routinized projection of power.

The anecdote continues with a detailed description of the scientific laws (*qānūn*) of investigation used for the development of medicine through trial and experimentation (*tajriba*). The conversation addresses the scientific practices of Hippocrates and Galen, such as deduction by means of analytical analogy as a technique for determining illness or discovering remedies. The didactic format of questions and answers moves freely from the general to the specific, as al-Wāthiq directs the discussion toward an exposition of the elements of the body that aid in digestion. In a seamless digression into the details of dentistry, the narrative displays Ḥunayn as a master physician, as he describes with precision the anatomy of the mouth and the concomitant field of dentistry, drawn largely from Greek models and vocabulary.[17]

Inspired by the assembly, Ḥunayn completed for al-Wāthiq a monograph entitled *Kitāb al-masāʾil al-ṭabīʿiyya* [Issues of natural science], wherein he outlined the differences between food, medicine, laxatives, and the digestive functions of the body.[18] The caliphal sponsorship of scientific learning underscores the role of the state in the production of knowledge. From this anecdote of the translator and the caliph we may perceive how Ḥunayn emulates the ideal of the sage (*ḥakīm*) as a master of an encyclopedic horizon of knowledge. Likewise, a specific ideal of caliphal authority emerges. The caliph was more than a vice-regent to the Prophet; as the second ʿAbbāsid caliph, al-Manṣūr is said to have argued, the caliph represented "the power of God over His land" (*sulṭān Allāh fī arḍihi*).[19] As God's potentates on earth, the intellectual interest of various caliphs and their role in the transmission of learning took on sacred and ritualized dimensions.[20]

The Anxiety of Translation

The third/ninth century emerges as the zenith of the translation movement, a time when the authority and influence of professional translators of classical material reached an unprecedented level. Many of the prominent translators were non-Arab Christians who had originally learned Syriac and/or Greek for liturgical purposes. The lucrative sums paid for translations encouraged the development and refinement of the profession, sustaining generations of translators. Despite the value placed on the transmission of Greek, Persian, and Sanskrit works into Arabic, there existed simultaneously an anxiety concerning the act of translation.

The grand littérateur Jāḥiẓ puts this unease into words in a now famous passage from his anthology of animals, the *Kitāb al-ḥayawān*.[21] Taking zoology as a unifying theme, Jāḥiẓ weaves into his study topics ranging from Qurʾānic exegesis and metaphysical speculations to fables, poetry, and literary criticism. In the beginning of this encyclopedia, he turns to the subject of translation, discussing the difficulties and dangers that surface in the intermediation of languages and cultures. The difference between poetry and prose serves as his entry into this excursus. Jāḥiẓ affirms that poetry cannot be translated, as it is impossible to render verse into another language. Whenever poetry is translated, he argues, its form (*naẓm*) is cut up, its meter is lost, its aesthetic value disappears, its sublime quality evaporates, and its ability to cause astonishment (*taʿajjub*) falls away. Poetry, he maintains, is not like prose, which is more suitable for translation, as it does not contain the same formal and thus untranslatable qualities.[22]

Keenly aware of the role of translation in the dissemination of knowledge, Jāḥiẓ traces how the science of the Indians, the philosophy of the Greeks, and the literary traditions of the Persians all passed into Arabic; in the process, some works increased in excellence, while some diminished in quality. Thus he describes the way works of learning were translated (*nuqilat*), crossing nations and languages, until finally reaching Arabic, the latest inheritor of classical knowledge.[23] The danger, however, that nuances of meaning could be lost in this process remains quite real for Jāḥiẓ. Such is the case with the translation of Greek philosophy into Arabic. The Arabic translator of Aristotle, he argues, does not fully express what the philosopher said in the particularities of meanings and in the precision of technical vocabulary. Jāḥiẓ concludes that a translator would have to equal the actual writer and composer of the work to fully comprehend the meaning of the original text.[24] In the case of highly specialized writing, this is held as an untenable position. Jāḥiẓ argues that the Arabic translators of Greek philosophy never reached the same level as Aristotle or Plato. In such a configuration, translation portends miscommunication and imperfect understanding; it is a supplement that only approximates the original that it tries to replace.

For Jāḥiẓ a good translator must be the most learned of people in both the source and target languages, so that no damage may suffer either one of them. Complete bilingualism is, however, put into question, as Jāḥiẓ doubts that one could possess equal competence in two languages, without the faculty to communicate in one being stronger and thus influencing the other. He stresses that the more specialized the work being translated, the smaller the number of learned scholars in the field, and thus all the more difficult for the translator, as it becomes more likely that the translation will misrepresent the original text.

The problems of translating scientific and philosophical discourse come as a prelude to a deeper misgiving; Jāḥiẓ warns of the dangers of translating scriptural material, where erring in matters of religion is more egregious than mistranslating Greek philosophy. By touching on the theological implications raised in the act of translation, Jāḥiẓ moves from general doubts to a specific charge against the translation of sacred texts. This uneasiness toward the possibly perfidious turns of linguistic mediation sounds as a counter voice to the authoritative position of translation as promoted by a significant portion of the ʿAbbāsid elite.

Jāḥiẓ's comments on the dangers of translation fit into a larger debate concerning the ontological and linguistic status of the Qurʾān. The doctrine of the inimitability of the Qurʾān (*iʿjāz al-Qurʾān*) in Islamic dialectical theology (*kalām*) developed as a proof (*ḥujja*) that the scriptural revelation to Muḥammad was a miracle (*muʿjiza*) proving his prophethood. The extent to which this inimitability was defined in linguistic terms, through the unique Arabic character of the Qurʾān, was itself a point of contention. On this subject, the jurist, Muḥammad b. Idrīs al-Shāfiʿī (d. 204/820), in his epistle on jurisprudence, the *Risāla*, stresses, "the Qurʾān indicates that there is nothing in the book of God which is not in the tongue of the Arabs."[25] In such a configuration the Qurʾān is defined as an immutable Arabic linguistic expression, a point that is arguably part of the Qurʾān's own image of itself as scripture.[26] This focus on the vessel of revelation led theologians and legal scholars to raise the question of the translatability of the Qurʾān.[27] The remarks of Jāḥiẓ on translation can be seen, in addition to their references to the translation of Greek science, in the light of broader philosophical and theological debates over the status of revelation and language.[28]

Though the translation movement emerged as a prominent feature in the intellectual climate of the first centuries of ʿAbbāsid society, the quality of the translations was not always of the highest standard. This may help to explain, in part, such anxieties concerning the distorting effects of translation. Ḥunayn b. Isḥāq, in his account of the works that he translated of Galen, laments the poor state of many Syriac and Arabic translations of original Greek source material. He repeatedly finds himself having to re-translate works that had been poorly translated.[29] In a similar vein, the polymath Ibn Sīnā (d. 428/1037) complains of the difficulty he had grasping Aristotle's *Metaphysics* (*Mā baʿd al-ṭabīʿa*)—a translation he felt to be utterly incomprehensible (*lā sabīla ilā fahmihi*).[30] He made this judgment after reading the work over forty times, and ultimately memorizing it. Not until Ibn Sīnā had read the commentary of Abū Naṣr al-Fārābī (d. 339/950) was he able to begin to understand Aristotle's work.[31] The critique leveled by Jāḥiẓ speaks directly to the difficulty of rendering complicated terms and expressions into comprehensible Arabic.[32] The opacity of many translations led Jāḥiẓ to conclude that a text that has circulated through multiple languages, been marked by different pens, and changed into the different scripts of the various creeds and nations, moves further from its original meaning.

In a famous debate recorded by Abū Ḥayyān al-Tawḥīdī (d. ca 414/1023) in his *Kitāb al-imtāʿ wa 'l-muʾānasa* [The book of delight and conviviality], the philologist Abū Saʿīd al-Sīrāfī (d. 368/979) casts such a charge against the Nestorian translator of Syriac works into Arabic, Abū Bishr Mattā b. Yūnus (d. 328/940).[33] The broad scope of this debate explores the relationship between logic and language. According to Tawḥīdī, a certain Qudāma b. Jaʿfar attended the disputation.[34] Assuming this is the same Qudāma as the author of the administrative geography, *Kitāb al-kharāj*,[35] then we have another example of how the ʿAbbāsid administrative class found points of entry into the broader theoretical debates of translation occurring in the period.

As outlined by Tawḥīdī, the outcome of this assembly, held by the *wazīr* Abū 'l-Fatḥ b. Furāt (d. 327/938), colorfully favors the philologist Sīrāfī, who adroitly mentions each instance in which he believes his interlocutor errs. Abū Bishr Mattā takes as a starting point the premise that the underlying signification of words is the same for all languages, and that the structures of logic and philosophy exist independent of language. With this position, he claims that the intentions and aims of a given text can be faithfully reproduced into another language, for, just as the concept that four plus four equals eight is the same in any language, so, too, the structures of meaning are the same across linguistic expressions. Even though, for instance, the ancient Greek of Aristotle is no longer spoken, Abū Bishr Mattā believed that translation can preserve the argumentation, convey the meanings, and be faithful to the conclusions of Aristotle's work.

The grammarian Sīrāfī argues, to the contrary, that the significations (*maʿānin*) are themselves bound to the signs of a given language (*alfāẓ*) and, as such, translation ultimately distorts and corrupts the intentions of any original text. Attacking Abū Bishr Mattā for not even knowing ancient Greek, but relying on Syriac intermediaries, Sīrāfī contends that, in the various stages of mediation, from Greek into Syriac and then Syriac into Arabic, the original meanings are transformed through translation.[36]

The distorting effects of translation pose a particular problem for the interpretation and reception of ancient learning into Arabic. This difficulty is fully highlighted in the notoriously confusing Arabic translation of Aristotle's *Poetics* made by Abū Bishr Mattā himself. Based on a Syriac intermediary, not the original Greek, this translation, mediated through the filter of yet another language, must convey concepts and terminology utterly foreign to Arabic. With the continual use of transliterations of Greek words, along with blatant mistranslations, Abū Bishr Mattā often obfuscated the meaning of Aristotle's highly specialized literary terminology.[37] For example, rather than explaining *poesis* (*ποίησις*), our translator leaves us wondering what is meant by his Arabic transliteration *fawāsīs*.[38] We also lose other important details in Abū Bishr Mattā's version, where, for instance, the original meanings of tragedy (*τραγῳδία*) and comedy (*κωμῳδία*) are collapsed into the Arabic words for praise (*madīḥ*) and ridicule (*hijāʾ*).[39] The terms *madīḥ* and *hijāʾ* are taken from genres of Arabic poetry, and do not adequately account for the original Greek theatrical forms that are largely alien to the Arabic literary culture of the period.

Translations of highly specialized and complex material were often supplemented with commentaries by other writers who sought to elucidate what, at times, could be the perplexing language of a given translation. The philosopher Fārābī wrote commentaries on the translated works of Aristotle not only to add his own voice to various philosophical issues, but also to explain foreign terminology that remained unclear in Arabic. His minor commentary on Aristotle's *Poetics*, the *Risāla fī qawānīn ṣināʿat al-shuʿarāʾ* [Epistle on the canons of the poets' craft], speaks to the opaque transliterations and poorly presented concepts that Arabic readers were often confronted with when approaching this text.[40] Yet, even his glosses of Greek literary terms leave much to be desired and highlight the challenge of comprehending such translations.[41]

The debate over the ill effects of translation, however, did not arrest the translation movement, which came to an almost organic end when practically all of the available works of Greek antiquity had been translated. The transmission of classical learning in the intellectual development of ʿAbbāsid society cannot be underestimated. The advent of Plato and Aristotle, now shrouded in new forms, had a tremendous influence on the intellectual horizons of the period. A writer such as Jāḥiẓ did not escape the effects of this movement; his *Kitāb al-ḥayawān*, the very work in which he lambastes the poor quality of translations, speaks directly to the Arabic reception of Aristotle's *History of Animals*. The work of such philologically trained scholars as Ḥunayn b. Isḥāq demonstrates the prevalent desire for accuracy in translation. Even more, a figure like Ḥunayn openly acknowledged the challenges of translating foreign terms and concepts into Arabic.[42] The effort to incorporate remote traditions of learning into Arabic far outweighed any objections over translation, and however distorted the transmission might have been, in the final analysis, foreign material and modes of thinking became fully integrated into the variegated fields of ʿAbbāsid learning.

Al-Tarjumān, al-Turjumān, al-Tarjamān

There are a variety of ways in Arabic to express the idea of translation, although the verb *tarjama* stands out, taking as its primary signification to interpret, to explain speech or language in another language, to translate from one language into another. While there exists a certain amount of debate in the classical Arabic lexicons over the origin of the word, the connection between the verb *tarjama* and the expression *rajama biʾl-ghayb*, to conjecture or speak about something of which one knows nothing, is attested in classical dictionaries.[43] The semantic link between translation and speaking about the unknown has interesting epistemological implications as to the role of the translator or interpreter in any given act of communication. It follows that from *tarjama* is born the *tarjumān*, a word whose correct vocalization has been the subject of dispute, read variously as *turjumān* and *tarjamān*. Ibn Manẓūr (d. 711/1311–12), in his encyclopedic lexicon, *Lisān al-ʿArab*, glosses *tarjumān* as an interpreter (*mufassir*), who translates speech (*yutarjimu ʾl-kalām*), moving it (*yanqaluhu*) from one language to another. Modern philologists have long viewed the Arabic *tarjumān* to be a loanword from the Aramaic *targəmānā*, 'an interpreter,' thus linked with the word for the Aramaic translation of the Hebrew Bible, the

Targum, though the link with the Akkadian verb to speak, *ragāmu*, has been largely discredited.[44] The term *tarjumān* has entered Latin, Greek, French, Italian, and Spanish, taking on a variety of forms and significations, fully crystallized in *dragoman*, the English word for a native informant or guide.

From the gnostic to the mundane, a spectrum of figurative significations are reflected in the profession of the *tarjumān*. The word stands out in such common expressions as 'the tongue is the interpreter of the heart' (*al-lisānu tarjumānu 'l-qalb*),[45] one moment honest and the next mendacious.[46] Such a sentiment views translation with a certain level of ambivalence. The *tarjumān* signifies the negotiation of presence, forever filtering the immediate. As the degrees of separation amplify in the mediation of increasing levels of interpretation, so does the potential for distortion. This metaphoric reflection on the figure of the *tarjumān* gains further authority through a saying (*ḥadīth*) attributed to the Prophet, which states that on the Day of Resurrection no veil (*ḥijāb*) will conceal those to be judged before God, just as no interpreter (*tarjumān*) will come to intercede on their behalf.[47] Here the acts of intercession, interpretation, and translation all turn together in this image of veiled communication, seen as both derivative and suspect.

Just as the figurative picture casts the *tarjumān* negatively into the intricate notions of intercession (*shafāʿa*) recurrent in Islamic eschatological discourse, there also exists a positive theological configuration concerning the acts of mediation and translation. The mystic and scholar, Muḥyī 'l-Dīn Ibn al-ʿArabī (d. 638/1240), in his *al-Futūḥāt al-Makkiyya* [The Meccan revelations], uses the expression 'interpreter of divine truth' (*tarjumān al-ḥaqq*) as a descriptive designation for the manner in which the Prophet communicated revelation.[48] The prophetic dissemination of the divine message offers a hermeneutic intermediary between God and humankind. Perhaps only when elevated to such a unique prophetic position can interpretation and translation be seen as unadulterated forms of communication. The variegated hues of these figurative uses all silhouette the hermeneutic role of the *tarjumān* in communication, imagining both the dangerous and simultaneously divine potential that lies residually in the various substrata of significations buttressing this term.

The sources join together the professional roles of the translator and interpreter in this one word. We can imagine a difference between the translator of scientific texts and the interpreter, standing at a caliphal court, who translates diplomatic messages in foreign languages. Though *tarjumān* can refer to both figures, Arabic sources are just as inclined to describe a translator of scientific works as a *nāqil*, one who transposes from one language into another, or as a *mutarjim*, the active participle of the verb *tarjama*, meaning one who makes a translation.

The highly developed culture of translation surrounding Ḥunayn's circle appears to have cultivated a technical vocabulary to refer to the various personages and stages of the profession. In an anecdote concerning the translation of Dioscorides' *Materia medica*, made into Arabic during the third/ninth century, the physician and biographer Ibn Abī Uṣaybiʿa (d. 668/1270) sheds light on the evolutionary process of the translation and redaction of a given text. Ibn Abī Uṣaybiʿa bases his information on the authority of an earlier account made by the physician and biographer Ibn Juljul of Córdoba (d. ca 384/994), which prefaces the introduction to Ibn Juljul's own *Tafsīr anwāʿ al-adwiya 'l-mufrada min Kitāb Diyusqūrīdūs* [Explanation of the names of simples according to the treatise of Dioscorides], a work that survives today only in fragments.[49] Ibn Juljul states that Dioscorides' text was originally translated in Baghdad during the reign of al-Mutawakkil. Here Ibn Juljul describes a two-tiered process of translation: Iṣṭifan b. Basīl is referred to as the translator (*tarjumān*) from Greek into Arabic, while Ḥunayn b. Isḥāq is addressed as the *mutarjim*, signifying 'head translator,' for he is said to have examined (*taṣaffaḥa*) Iṣṭifan b. Basīl's translation of Dioscorides, corrected the parts he saw fit, and then, finally, approved it (*ajāzahu*). The difference in nomenclature in this account is clear enough, as the *tarjumān* refers to a kind of apprentice translator, in contrast to the title *mutarjim*, which is reserved for the master of the craft.[50]

This distinction seems convincing, as the fully developed translation movement in Ḥunayn's day could easily support such differentiation. Yet, matters are confused by the fact that many sources also refer to Ḥunayn as a *tarjumān*. On this issue, Ḥunayn himself remains silent, though in one instance he refers to translators as *mutarjimūn*.[51] In an autobiographical account of questionable origin, Ḥunayn describes himself as a *nāqil*, a term that was frequently used to designate the translators of scientific material.[52] The etymology of this word is connected to the verb *naqala*, signifying to move; this speaks directly to a spatial dimension imagined in the act of translation. Furthermore, the semantic resonance of this word evokes a degree of estrangement, as with the adjective, *naqīl*, which signifies a stranger (*gharīb*) who comes to reside among a tribe or a people.[53] In this fashion, the *nāqil* evokes an importation and grafting of the foreign, moved across both physical and conceptual space.

In his *Risāla*, a bibliographical index of his translations of Galen's work, Ḥunayn illuminates the translation movement and its surrounding cultural milieu. Many details, however, remain only lightly sketched. From this index we know that translations often went through several stages of correction in the process of a final recension. Such is the case with Ḥunayn's translation of Galen's *De motu musculorum*, in which he relates, "I translated this work into Syriac, and no one had preceded me in translating it. Then Iṣṭifan [b. Basīl] translated it into Arabic. Muḥammad b. Mūsā asked that I review the translation against the original Greek and correct any errors, which I then did."[54] This, along with many other similar instances recorded in the *Risāla*, reveals a highly developed, professional process of translation at work. Through the various stages of emendation and correction, we may conjecture a space in the translation movement for a semantic differentiation between the roles of the *tarjumān*, who would make a first draft, and the *mutarjim* who would oversee the final corrected version.

The semantic valence of the *tarjumān* could fit the diverse activities of scholarly, professional translators as well court interpreters chosen by a caliphal court to journey to the edge of the known world. In the most basic sense, the *tarjumān* communicates across frontiers, whether conceptual or physical. Although the outward form of their translations diverges, both Ḥunayn and Sallām are pioneers of uncharted territory, transmitting remote knowledge across linguistic boundaries. With the entire translation movement brought together through the official sponsorship of the ʿAbbāsid state, both Ḥunayn and Sallām are in dialogue with caliphal audiences.

As Sallām sets off on his way through the world of signs, we may pause to contemplate how he himself is but a sign, inflected with all the positive and negative charges of translation. Just as the *tarjumān* may both veil and reveal, Sallām's story conceals as much as it discovers. What separates Sallām from his contemporary Ḥunayn is that the original text of Sallām's translation no longer survives. Nor, for that matter, could it ever survive. Sallām's quest for knowledge represents a phenomenological, first-person engagement with existence. Unlike Ḥunayn, Sallām claims to translate signs through experience and not through texts. Yet the tautology plays out, as we perceive that Sallām's ocular testament of the world out there is very much a product of a textual universe, linked intertextually with the inner world of books. However, in contrast to Ḥunayn, there is no single text against which we can cast Sallām's story to analyze the quality of his translation.

The Interpretation of Dreams

The narrative logic that moves the story of Sallām's journey to the edge of the world starts with a dream. Al-Wāthiq's apocalyptic vision fits into a pronounced strain of messianic discourse undergirding ʿAbbāsid political legitimacy.[55] Stories of caliphal dreams and their interpretations form a recurring theme in the writing of the period.[56] The interpretation of dreams developed into an all-encompassing hermeneutic strategy of reading the past movement of history and the future trajectory of time.[57]

The practice of interpreting dreams to reveal unperceived designs in the world took shape on a canvas much older than the stage of ʿAbbāsid politics. Throughout antiquity, the divination of dreams served as a vehicle to understand the relationship between humankind and the divine. Those learned in the art of divination often emerged as prominent figures in the social networks of pre-Islamic Arab tribes. The figure of the soothsayer or the diviner (*kāhin*, pl. *kuhhān* and *kahana*) formed a central part of the religious landscape of pre-Islamic Arabic society. The interpretation of dreams was a prominent feature of the *kuhhān* in their prophetic leadership capacity, as they drew on esoteric knowledge to reveal the mysteries of nature (*asrār al-ṭabīʿa*).[58]

The tradition of discovering prophetic messages in dreams and events (*taʾwīl al-aḥādīth*) finds authority in the Qurʾān and in the biographical construction of the life of the Prophet.[59] The reverence accorded to dreams gave rise to the sustained development of dream interpretation (*taʿbīr al-ruʾyā*), considered to be a legitimate field of learning in the sciences of religious law (*al-ʿulūm al-sharʿiyya*).[60] Among the early community of religious scholars and *ḥadīth* transmitters, the art of oneiromancy was an established discipline, as evidenced in the corpus of interpretations associated with Muḥammad b. Sīrīn (d. 110/728), referred to by the ʿAbbāsid polymath Ibn Qutayba (b. 276/889) as the leading authority in the field.[61]

Ibn Qutayba's *Kitāb taʿbīr al-ruʾyā* [Book of interpreting the dream vision] approaches dreams within the framework of a pre-existing hermeneutical praxis, constituted as a field of religious learning and authenticated by the model of the Prophet and the early Companions. A driving concern in this work is not only the afterlife, but also apocalyptic signs of the Day of Judgment.[62] The Prophet is consistently positioned as the supreme reader of dreams, offering interpretations that are often inflected with eschatological significance.[63]

From the early stages of ʿAbbāsid rule, the caliphate promoted the activity of oneiromancy, in concord with a greater repertoire of techniques for divining the future. In this broader context of divination, the figure of the astrologer (*munajjim*) and the practice of judicial astrology through the study of the decrees of the stars (*aḥkām al-nujūm*) in the determination of human destiny were prominent features in the ʿAbbāsid court. Within Ibn Khurradādhbih's geography the astrologer parallels the translator in caliphal quests beyond the frontiers. The promotion of astrology, as well as the translation of Zoroastrian astrological material, played a part in the larger imperial ideology that linked the ʿAbbāsid state to their Persian predecessors, the Sāsānians.[64]

The cultural value placed on divination suggests the political potential of dreams, which could be positioned as a readily discernible means of comprehending and often justifying the course of human events. The signification of dreams as divine portents of the destiny of the state forms a marked theme in the historiographical documentation of the vicissitudes of the ʿAbbāsid elite.[65] Anecdotes of interpreting dreams often serve as a method of perceiving a divine architecture, buttressing the various causes and effects of history.[66]

In the course of the third/ninth century, what could be called autochthonous Arabic practices of dream interpretation, as advanced, for instance, in Ibn Qutayba's formulation, are shaped ever more by foreign influences.[67] From Brahmans to Zoroastrians, Muslims turned to an international milieu of practitioners, skilled in variegated forms of interpreting dreams.[68] One of the sources to have had a lasting influence on Islamic dream interpretation is the *Oneirocritica* of Artemidorus. Ibn al-Nadīm attributes the translation of this work, entitled *Kitāb taʿbīr al-ruʾyā,* to Ḥunayn b. Isḥāq.[69]

Al-Wāthiq's vision that the wall of Gog and Magog had broken open and, by implication, the Day of Resurrection was drawing near, took place within a cultural matrix in which the divination of dreams held a significant value. The Prophet himself is said to have dreamt of these monstrous creatures, indicating that the final hour was at hand.[70] Dreams about the wall and the Prophet's confirmation of their validity also form an established trope in the *ḥadīth* corpus and the exegetical tradition on Gog and Magog.[71]

The hermeneutic dimension of oneiromancy is central to the Arabic expression for dream interpretation, known as *taʿbīr al-ruʾyā*. The word *taʿbīr* is the verbal noun of the causative second form verb, *ʿabbara*, and expresses the specific practice of interpreting dream-visions. Just as the Arabic verb, *naqala,* to move, comes to signify the practice of translation, so, too, does the notion of movement resonate with the act of dream interpretation; for crossing from one space to another is an essential element in the etymology of this word, which finds root in the first form verb, *ʿabara*, 'to cross, ford, pass over.'

The interpreter of dreams, known as the *muʿabbir,* reads signs of dreams or psychic visions (*al-takhayyulāt al-nafsāniyya*), so as to draw out (*li-yantaqila*) the hidden affairs of the world (*al-umūr al-ghaybiyya*).[72] Early Arabic oneirocritic writing frames dream interpretation as an activity of translation, in which, for example, a vision of coarse bread could signify wealth, or a dream of writing could suggest artifice.[73] The interpreter renders the signs of dreams comprehensible to the human mind, translated into a coherent narrative. Al-Wāthiq's dream frames the anecdote of the journey to the wall of Gog and Magog, foregrounding the entire narrative movement as encoded inside a broader landscape of interpretation and translation.

The destruction of the barrier that holds back the monstrous races of Gog and Magog stands, in Islamic eschatological discourse, as one of the signs of the end of time, signifying the annihilation of all living things, the advent of the Day of Resurrection, and, ultimately, the enactment of the Final Accounting. When God flattens the wall, Gog and Magog will spread through the earth, destroying everything in their path.

These monstrous tribes are thought to be so numerous that they will stretch from their front line in Damascus to their rearguard in Balkh; when they reach the ocean they will drink all of the water and devour everything in it.[74] As suggested in Ibn Qutayba's study, the interpretation of dreams concerning the apocalypse figures as a recurrent theme in Islamic oneirocritic writing, so much so that a section treating the Day of Resurrection was seamlessly inserted into the Arabic translation of Artemidorus' dream-book.[75] Such recontextualization within an explicitly Islamic teleology of salvation is indicative of a broader pattern of absorption into Arabic classical learning.[76]

Visions of the apocalypse, or of the signs relating to the end of the world, such as Gog and Magog, are interpreted uniformly as a blessing for faithful believers and a warning for sinners.[77] Where al-Wāthiq's soul stands is altogether a separate matter. His proclivity, however, for dreaming about the world beyond, particularly heaven, is a theme that finds resonance in the sources.[78] Such other-worldly dreams serve as an established motif in the literature of the ʿAbbāsid court and, as such, should be viewed, when set against Sallām's anecdote, in light of the broader social and political context, suggesting a well-trodden path of discursive conventions and literary *topoi*.

SECTION TWO

MARVELOUS ALTERITY

4

A GEOGRAPHY OF NEIGHBORS

Historical Landscapes

Sallām's anecdote begins with the ethereal realm of dreams, only to move quickly into the terrestrial world of economics and geopolitics. Ibn Khurradādhbih relates that al-Wāthiq, intent on sending a mission to discover the state of the wall, asked his Turkish general, Abū Jaʿfar Ashinās, to recommend someone capable of undertaking such an adventure.[1] This piece of information is of particular importance, for it suggests a political backdrop shaped by the power dynamics of the Turkish military guard of Sāmarrāʾ and their growing influence over the caliphate. Ashinās figures prominently during the reign of al-Muʿtaṣim, who granted him a palace in Sāmarrāʾ, along with administrative rule over the Arabian Peninsula, Greater Syria, and Egypt.[2] As a military commander, Ashinās led battles on the outer frontiers (*thughūr*) between Byzantium and the ʿAbbāsid empire.[3] One of the first administrative appointments al-Wāthiq made on assuming the caliphate, in Ramaḍān of 229/843, was to bestow a crown upon Ashinās and adorn him with ornamental belts. This inaugural ceremony is said to have signified the beginning of Ashinās' rule over the western portion of the ʿAbbāsid territories, which stretched from Iraq to North Africa.[4]

Sallām, who is said to speak thirty languages, is called upon to venture to the world outside, to bring back information of the unknown, and to communicate this information to the caliph. As we set Ashinās next to Sallām, we move from the register of historiographic specificity into the extraordinary space of legends. For though it is not impossible for someone to speak thirty languages, it is surely exceptional. The number itself is inconsequential and serves as a projection of Sallām's skill as a translator. Indeed, exactitude in the number of languages spoken is not what is at hand, for the discourse of the marvelous always flirts with specificity, in a dialectic that keeps the marvelous continually present, yet somehow just beyond reach.

After the short introductory frame that sets the journey in motion, Ibn Khurradādhbih transfers diegetic control of the narrative to Sallām, who relates the account through the authority of his own direct experience. Admittedly, this immediacy of the first person is interrupted on several occasions, wherein the authorial voice of Ibn Khurradādhbih, as the direct transmitter (*rāwī*) of the narrative, repeats the phrase 'Sallām reported.' These interruptions, though meant to confirm the authenticity of the transmission, also suggest a process of redaction. The two voices point to distinct authorial planes, creating a space wherein Ibn Khurradādhbih, as the transmitter, serves also as the redactor of an original report. As a narrative technique, the diegetic form of a directly related report strengthens the appearance of factuality.

Sallām relates how the caliph equipped him with fifty strong, young men for the expedition. Provisions were prepared for the cold weather that the entourage would face and included felt coats, lined with leather and fur-covered saddlecloths (*kushtubānāt bi'l-firā*ʾ, from the Persian *gustuwān*, horse-armor).[5] Here, as in other parts of the journey, Sallām's language is imbued with Persian vocabulary. In addition to the two hundred mules packed with supplies, the embassy is outfitted with enough hard currency to last an entire year. Describing the various preparations, Sallām's narrative speaks to a course of concrete pragmatism.

Caliphal embassies sent across the expansive territory of the ʿAbbāsid lands, which stretched from North Africa to India, helped maintain the stability of the empire. The broader foreground of Ibn Khurradādhbih's descriptive geography addresses the concerns of empire, tracing postal routes and stages, the itineraries of merchants, and the networks of communication set in place to sustain political rule over vast and disparate territories. As Ibn Khurradādhbih follows the course of Sallām's trajectory to the farthest end of the known world, we see theory put into practice. The various routes and stages minutely described in the beginning of the geography come to life under Sallām's feet, as the lists of towns, cities, and districts transform into the backdrop of a larger narrative progression.

Leaving the caliphal capital of Sāmarrāʾ behind, Sallām heads north into the heart of the tightly-knit territories of the Caucasus (map 2). Through the mountainous regions that form the isthmus between the

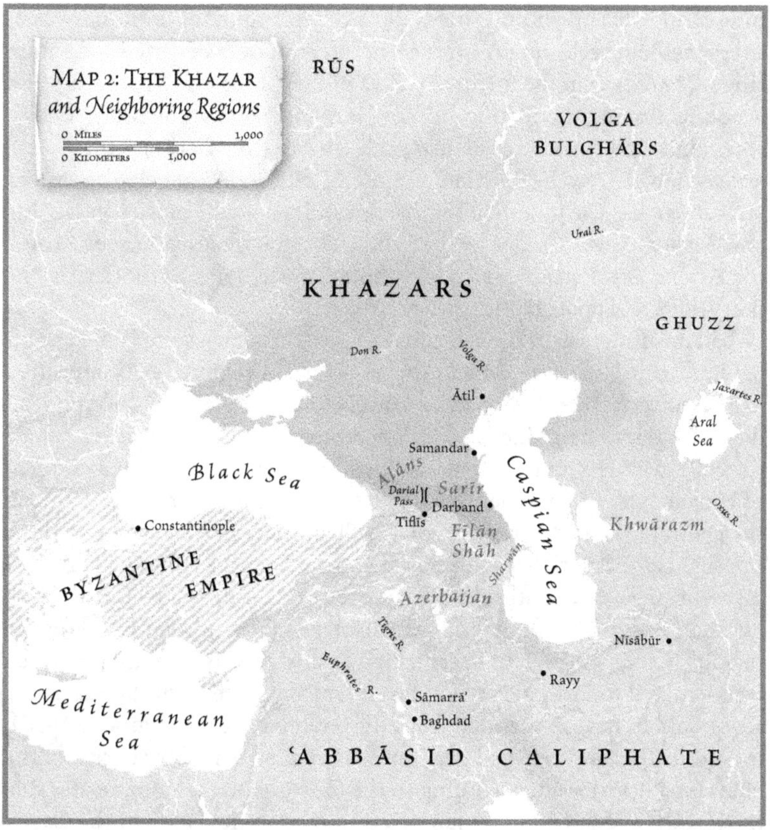

MAP 2: THE KHAZAR *and Neighboring Regions*

Black Sea to the west and the Caspian Sea to the east, Sallām crosses a well-trodden literary landscape. The Caucasus mountain range is associated with the mythical mountain of Qāf, which figures prominently in Islamic cosmographical configurations of the universe.[6] When describing the Caucasus earlier in his geography, Ibn Khurradādhbih mentions several fortified mountain passes (*abwāb*) that block access to the various kingdoms of the region. Here he makes reference to the mysterious fountain of life as being located next to the Caspian Sea.[7] This tradition is carried on by the geographer Ibn al-Faqīh, who also sees in the Caucasus a site for the Qurʾānic passage in *Sūrat al-Kahf* that narrates the story of Moses and Khiḍr and alludes to their quest for immortality.[8]

This chapter of the Qurʾān, which Ibn Khurradādhbih quotes in regard to the miraculous fountain, culminates with a description of how Dhū 'l-Qarnayn built his wall to protect humankind. Many early exegetes believed this rampart to be located between two mountain ridges (*saddayn*) in the fortified passes of the Caucasus.[9] There were also accounts linking the fortification of Darband (Persian, literally, 'barred gate'), known in Arabic as al-Bāb wa 'l-Abwāb (the 'Gate and the Gates') and as Bāb al-Abwāb (the 'Gate of Gates'), positioned next to the eastern stretch of the Caspian Sea, with Alexander's wall holding back Gog and Magog.[10] At the edge of the ʿAbbāsid state, this region represented, for Arabic and Persian writers, a liminal space, on the frontiers of the marvelous and apocalyptic.

Sallām's itinerary in the Caucasus weaves through a complicated political landscape that was critical to the ʿAbbāsid regime. With a written dispatch from the caliph, Sallām travels to the city of Tiflīs, in modern-day Georgia, to meet the Muslim governor of Armenia, Isḥāq b. Ismāʿīl (d. 238/852).[11] His journey through the Caucasus takes place at a moment of considerable tension between the frontier provinces in the region and the central ʿAbbāsid administration. Sallām makes no reference to these internal conflicts related to ʿAbbāsid control over the frontier; rather, he gives only a skeletal outline of his journey to the ruler of Tiflīs.

Isḥāq b. Ismāʿīl emerges as a prominent figure in the history of the region largely as a result of his rebellion against ʿAbbāsid control, in which he attempted to form his own independent state free from caliphal suzerainty. Said to have descended from the Arab tribe of the Quraysh, Isḥāq is described as an Umayyad partisan who challenged ʿAbbāsid rule.[12] The encyclopedist Masʿūdī, narrating in the fourth/tenth century, relates that the history of Isḥāq became famous throughout the region of the Caucasus and beyond.[13] The ʿAbbāsid administrator Yaʿqūbī (fl. 278/891), who had personal experience on the Armenian frontier, writes in his universal history that during the reign of al-Wāthiq, state control over the region weakened. This is an issue that had plagued earlier caliphs. According to Yaʿqūbī, Armenian patricians, along with the local Arab elite, revolted against the yoke of ʿAbbāsid control. In response, al-Wāthiq sent a military expedition to the region to put down the uprising. This military force was able to bring about the submission of some of the rebelling factions; however, despite the mounting pressure, Isḥāq b. Ismāʿīl remained defiant. He refused to capitulate to the caliph's demands and successfully repelled the ʿAbbāsid military force.[14]

An anonymous Arabic work known as the *Taʾrīkh Bāb al-Abwāb* [History of Darband], which is thought to have been written around 500/1106, documents in detail the historical developments of the region under Muslim rule.[15] This history exposes a problem of chronology when it mentions a discrepancy in the sources over the date of the military expedition sent by al-Wāthiq against Isḥāq, offering one account that positions the campaign in 230/844, as Yaʿqūbī suggests, and another claim that the campaign had occurred two years earlier, in 228/842–3.[16] The *Taʾrīkh Bāb al-Abwāb* mentions that, after the failure of the first military campaign against Isḥāq and the sudden death of the ʿAbbāsid general overseeing the expedition, al-Wāthiq sent another force in 230/844 to wage war against the rebel leader.[17] This second attempt, nonetheless, also ended in failure. Effectively, Isḥāq remained free from caliphal rule, until the reign of al-Mutawakkil, who sent the Turkish general Bughā al-Kabīr al-Sharābī (d. 248/862) to Armenia in 238/852 in order to bring a final end to the rebellion. After numerous battles, Bughā succeeded in setting the city of Tiflīs to flames. Isḥāq was captured and decapitated, and his revolt, which lasted thirty-five years, came to an end.[18]

This outline of events is a curious backdrop for Sallām's journey to Tiflīs. Al-Wāthiq must have dispatched Sallām sometime during his reign, which lasted from 227/842 to 232/847. From Yaʿqūbī, we know that Ashinās, the Turkish general who recommended Sallām, died in 230/844. In the same year, al-Wāthiq ordered a military campaign against the rebel Isḥāq in Tiflīs. Moreover, there is the indication, as the *Taʾrīkh Bāb al-Abwāb* suggests, that al-Wāthiq's first campaign against Isḥāq was sent two years earlier. Assuming that Sallām would not travel to Tiflīs at the very moment that caliphal forces were trying to besiege it, we would have to date the expedition to the wall of Gog and Magog sometime in the first year of al-Wāthiq's reign. Yet, if we are to take seriously the statement in the *Taʾrīkh Bāb al-Abwāb* that Isḥāq's rebellion lasted for over thirty-five years, it would seem odd that Sallām, a caliphal envoy, would have met with such a mutinous figure. Unfortunately, the historiographical sources cannot fully illuminate Sallām's narrative, for none of them speak independently of his expedition. We could contemplate Sallām's stay in Tiflīs as a secret caliphal reconnaissance mission to discover the strength of Isḥāq's rebel forces; the anecdote both resists and encourages such speculation.

Ṭabarī relates that Isḥāq, a stocky man covered with tattoos, was married to the daughter of the ruler of the neighboring province of the Qoy-su river valley in southern Dāghistān, a region in the western Caucasus that borders the Caspian Sea.[19] After his stay in Tiflīs, Sallām headed with a dispatch from Isḥāq to this neighboring ruler, referred to as the 'Lord of the Throne' (*ṣāḥib al-sarīr*). For details and information concerning the region and this sobriquet, we must look outside Sallām's narrative. Early in the *Masālik,* Ibn Khurradādhbih mentions the Lord of the Throne when describing the fortified mountain passes of the Caucasus.[20]

This region gives Ibn Khurradādhbih cause to return to the recurrent theme of the splendid days of Sāsānian rule. He outlines how King Qubādh, followed by his son Khusraw I Anūshirwān (r. 531–78 C.E.), built fortresses along the mountain passes of the Caucasus in order to stave off the hordes of invading northern tribes.[21] The historian Aḥmad b. Yaḥyā 'l-Balādhurī (d. ca 279/892), a contemporary of Ibn Khurradādhbih, describes in his *Futūḥ al-buldān* [Conquests of the regions] a systematic program undertaken by the Sāsānian kings of settling and fortifying the region. Continuing the tradition established by his father, Anūshirwān conferred governorship on the rulers of the Caucasus, making them pledge loyalty and pay tribute to the Sāsānian state. Among these rulers was the 'Chief of the Mountain' (*khāqān al-jabal*), named the king of Wahrārzān, who bore the title the Lord of the Throne.[22]

A mantel of Persian history shrouds the region. The geographer Abū Isḥāq al-Iṣṭakhrī (fl. 324/936) writes that the 'People of the Throne' were Christians and that the name of the territory finds its provenance in a throne made of gold, which originally belonged to the Sāsānian kings.[23] In addition to mentioning that there existed a peace treatise between the People of the Throne and the ʿAbbāsid state, Iṣṭakhrī explains that their ruler descended from the heroic Persian ruler Bahrām Gūr.[24] According to Masʿūdī, the last Sāsānian king, Yazdagird III (d. 31/651), while retreating from invading Muslim forces, sent his golden throne and his royal effects to one of Bahrām Gūr's descendents who was in the region, and then ordered that this man await his arrival. Before Yazdagird could return for his royal belongings, he was caught and killed by the invading Muslims. This descendant of Bahrām Gūr settled in the region and took authority from the symbol of the throne, establishing himself as king over the people.[25]

The sources describe the incredible power that the Lord of the Throne possessed, with fortified positions across the mountains, from which he made forays into the territory of his northern neighbors, the Khazars. Referencing the Persian heritage of the kingdom, the geographer Ibn Rusta mentions that this ruler received his royal treasury from the Sāsānian king Anūshirwān. Ibn Rusta takes particular interest in the peculiar customs practiced in the region. The inhabitants of the palace were said to be Christians, while the rest of the subjects were pagans (*kuffār*) who performed strange funerary rights and worshipped dried heads.[26] Beyond the realm of ʿAbbāsid control and outside the reach of Islam, the Lord of the Throne and his kingdom invoke a landscape of the foreign and remote.

With a dispatch from the Lord of the Throne, Sallām continued his travels to the king of the Alāns (al-Lān).[27] Though he gives no further details concerning this part of his itinerary, we can suppose that between the two kingdoms there existed cordial relations during the period. This idea is supported by Masʿūdī, who, writing nearly a hundred years after Sallām's journey, mentions that between the Lord of the Throne and the king of the Alāns were bonds of marriage.[28] As with the Lord of the Throne, the king of the Alāns is said to have converted to Christianity, though Ibn Rusta describes the people of this kingdom as pagans (*kuffār*) who worship idols (*aṣnām*).[29] The Alāns, descendants of Iranian tribes, were a powerful force in the central part of the northern Caucasus; this was due in part to their control over the Darial pass (Bāb al-Lān). The Alāns also appear in the pre-Islamic Persian history of fortifying the region. Legend holds that the castle of the Alāns (*qalʿat al-Lān*) was originally built by one of the ancient mythical Iranian kings, Isfandiyār, the son of Bishtāsb.[30] This fortress, perched at an inaccessible point in the Darial pass, was designed to stave off attacks from the very Alāns who later came to possess it. Masʿūdī mentions that the exploits of Isfandiyār, along with the story of his castle, not only formed a recurrent theme in Persian literature, but also featured prominently in the Persian *Paykār-nāma* [Book of battles] that was translated into Arabic by Ibn al-Muqaffaʿ (d. ca 142/759).[31]

The ruler of the Alāns directs Sallām to the king of Fīlān (Fīlān Shāh), whose title also invokes pre-Islamic Persian history. Balādhurī includes Fīlān Shāh in a list of honorary titles bestowed by the Sāsānian king Anūshirwān on the rulers of the Caucasus.[32] In the sources, reference is made to the Fīlān Shāh as a ruler near the fortified city of Darband.

The philologist and historian Ḥamza al-Iṣfahānī (d. ca 350/961), in his history of the pre-Islamic Persian kings, gives an etiology of this title that harkens back to the Sāsānian period and describes how Anūshirwān, after building the barrier of Darband, dispatched captains to defend the frontier, investing each of them with a brocade robe of honor. These brocade robes were decorated with images of animals. Each captain was then named after the brocade designs on his robe, thus the names of 'Bughrān Shāh,' from *baghrā*, the boar, 'Sharwān Shāh,' from *shīr*, the lion, and 'Fīlān Shāh,' from *pīl*, the elephant.[33] For this account, Ḥamza al-Iṣfahānī draws his work from Arabic translations of pre-Islamic Persian sources. This story offers a conceptual link between the defensive wall of Darband and the placement of governors, such as the Fīlān Shāh, along the Sāsānian frontier in the Caucasus.[34]

The Fīlān Shāh sends Sallām to the king of the Khazars, where he stays for only one day and one night, which, given the distance covered and the political importance of the Khazars, is quite remarkable.[35] As a narrative device, such a short stay serves to highlight the apocalyptic barrier as the primary object of the mission. While we may wish to see in al-Wāthiq's delegation to the wall a historical core of actual diplomatic engagements along the frontier, the account suggests international relations and imperial diplomatic activities, but only superficially and in a rather confused way. In the opening to his recension of Sallām's adventure, Muqaddasī relates that al-Wāthiq also sent the court astrologer Muḥammad b. Mūsā 'l-Khwārazmī to the ruler (*ṭarkhān*) of the Khazar.[36] However, the relationship between this mission and that of Sallām's is not elucidated. The idea that these adventures were part of the same caliphal dispatch is likewise not developed. It could well be that Muqaddasī has confused Khwārazmī's mission to the People of the Cave with Sallām's adventure, as this is the only reference to Khwārazmī's journey to the Khazar in the early sources. Yet in Muqaddasī's account is the suggestion of ongoing caliphal relations with the Khazar through the figure of the astrologer, geographer, and caliphal go-between.

Unlike the Fīlān Shāh, there is a considerable body of information detailing the history of the Khazar state, which, centered along the Volga River, flourished for over three hundred years, from the seventh to tenth century C.E. By the time Sallām visits the region, the ruling elite of the Khazar had already converted to Judaism.[37] The peculiar political structure of the double kingship of the khaqanate,[38] along with the strange religious practices and rites of the Khazar, make this a site of continual interest for Arabic and Persian writers.[39] Outlining an exotic syncretism of tribal, autochthonous rituals, and Judaic traditions, the sources describe how the Khazar state consisted of a minority of Jews, Christians, and Muslims, and a majority population of heathens who followed ancient traditions (*rusūm qadīma*) of worshipping graven images (*awthān*).[40]

Sallām's journey to the Volga Basin speaks to a well-established network of trade during the period. According to Masʿūdī there was a sizable population of Muslim mercenaries, merchants, and artisans living in Ātil, the Khazar capital on the Volga.[41] The numismatic record of hoards of ʿAbbāsid coins that survived in northeastern Europe demonstrates that, in the course of the third/ninth century, the Caucasus was one of the major arteries of trade between Mesopotamia and the Central Asian steppe.[42]

Yet Sallām's trajectory, crisscrossing the Caucasus mountains into the Khazar territory on the Volga, represents an erratic and embroiled itinerary.[43] The geographical place names he references consistently correspond to historical kingdoms and peoples. However, his course from Tiflīs to Sarīr, Sarīr to the Alāns, the Alāns to Fīlān Shāh, and finally, from Fīlān Shāh to the Khazar, has him backtracking at various points. We could produce any number of extra-textual hypotheses to speculate why Sallām followed this particular route: the political situation of the region could have demanded it; the caliph could have given him specific orders to spy on these kingdoms; or bad weather could have blocked certain passes.

Though the narrative gives the most general sketch of Sallām's itinerary, the journey itself takes place in a textual landscape fully foregrounded in Arabic and Persian sources. After two wars against the Khazar in the first/seventh and second/eighth centuries, the Arab conquests of the region were brought in check. As with the Pyrenees in the west, the mountains of the Caucasus came to serve as a frontier and border zone, halting the initial Arab military expansion. The ʿAbbāsids inherited from the Umayyads the challenge of fortifying themselves against incursions from the region. The Arabic and Persian geographic accounts draw parallels between the ancient Sāsānian program of establishing fortifications and settlements and the more recent confrontations between Muslims and the heathen tribes of the Caucasus.

In the description of this region, two themes consistently resurface in the Arabic and Persian sources: first, the vast number of languages spoken by the different nations; and second, the defensive wall built by the Sāsānians at Darband to keep these very nations at bay. The linguistic diversity of the Caucasus was proverbial; a tangled expanse of inaccessible mountains, hidden valleys, steep ravines, dense forests, and raging rivers, all of which served as a refuge to various isolated tribes.[44] Described as a virtual "mountain of languages" (*jabal al-alsun*),[45] the linguistic situation in the Caucasus suggests a confused and incomprehensible babble of heathens, with each village isolated and unable to understand the next.

The number of languages spoken in the Caucasus is usually placed between seventy and seventy-two; however, the seemingly exaggerated figure of three hundred also appears.[46] Ibn Ḥawqal states that originally he could not imagine that three hundred languages were spoken in such a small area, until he traveled through the region and saw that each small village he visited had its own distinct language.[47] A similar sentiment is expressed by the ʿAbbāsid geographer Ibn al-Faqīh, who explains that the people of the Caucasus can only understand the language of their rulers (*lughat ṣāḥibihi*) through the aid of an interpreter (*tarjumān*).[48]

Though this may seem to verge on hyperbole, the linguistic and ethnic diversity plays an important role in shaping the cultural and political landscape. The mutual incomprehensibility of the languages says nothing of the difficulties that foreign travelers would have had traversing the region. Against such linguistic variance it seems clear why Sallām, an interpreter said to be proficient in thirty languages, was chosen to head al-Wāthiq's expedition. This region, pitched in the unintelligible speech of heathens who cannot even understand each other, represented a noisome threat, poised just beyond the frontiers of the ʿAbbāsid empire.

The danger that the Caucasus posed for pre-Islamic Persian kings was a motivating force in their establishment of fortifications and settlements along their northwestern frontier. Yāqūt views the vast number of these uncontrollable tribes as a cause for the anxiety of Sāsānian emperors toward this frontier; the threat meant that the Sāsānians could never divert their attention from the constant maintenance of their defenses.[49] Erecting the wall at Darband symbolically condensed this anxiety into a single act. Tradition held that the wall built by Anūshirwān was one of the amazing architectural feats of the Sāsānian dynasty.[50]

Concomitant with the accounts of Darband is the tale of Anūshirwān's fabled stratagem of deceiving the king of the Khazar in order to build the various defenses of the barrier. Masʿūdī senses a divine hand in the architecture, remarking, that had God not aided his servants, the kings of Persia (*mulūk al-furs*), as they built the defensive walls around Darband, then surely the kings of the Khazar, the Alāns, the Avars, the Turks, and all the other nations of the region would have overrun them.[51] Detailed descriptions outlining the dimensions of Anūshirwān's rampart (*sadd*) recur in the geographical and historiographical writings. Ibn al-Faqīh describes various statues and images that were located on the wall; these represented human, animal, and vegetal forms, all considered to be talismans used to protect the defenses of Darband.[52]

One widely circulated tale related by Qazwīnī, in his encyclopedia of natural wonders, details how Anūshirwān, after building the bulwark along Darband against the Turks and the Khazars, sat on the top of it wondering if indeed his wall would stand the test of time. He then fell asleep, whereupon he had a vision of a creature (*sākin min sukkān*) from the Caspian Sea. The creature recounted that God had informed him that while all other such fortifications would not withstand the vicissitudes of time, Anūshirwān's wall would last forever (plate 3).[53] Various elements from this anecdote clearly relate to Dhū 'l-Qarnayn's rampart, and are perhaps indicative of an older Sāsānian parallel to the wall of Gog and Magog, suggesting a broader historical motif of bottling up nomadic tribes against incursions at the edge of civilization.[54]

The heroism of Anūshirwān, one of the most glorified Sāsānian emperors, known by the sobriquet the 'Just' (*ʿādil*), is central to the lionized history of the fortifications. It is Anūshirwān who, in the words of the historian Thaʿālibī, "civilized the world, subdued its petty kings and established noble customs."[55] Following the architectural monuments of Persian kings, Ibn Khurradādhbih lists the great audience hall (*īwān kisrā*) built in the Sāsānian capital Ctesiphon, and often associated with Anūshirwān, as one of the marvels of the world. On this subject, he quotes from the famous ekphrastic ode by his associate, Buḥturī, composed in 270/883–4. Buḥturī's nostalgic *qaṣīda* marvels at the supernatural design of the ruined edifice:

لَيْسَ يُدرَى أَصُنْعُ إِنْسٍ لِجِنٍّ   سَكَنُوهُ أَمْ صُنْعُ جِنٍّ لِإِنْسِ

No one knows whether it is a creation of man for the *jinn*
to inhabit, or a creation of the *jinn* for man.[56]

In addition to monumental works of architecture, and the demarcating of civilization, Anūshirwān represents the cultivation and promotion of intellectual and cultural pursuits. His entourage included the famed advisor Buzurgmihr, who is said to have had a command of all languages and alphabets.[57] From flirtations with Greek philosophy to sponsoring the translation of the Indian 'mirror of princes' known as the *Pañcatantra*, or *Kalīla wa Dimna*, Anūshirwān embodies imperial majesty and sophistication, a symbol of Persian high culture and past glory. This splendor serves as a contrast to the disordered and chaotic tribes that threaten the existence of the state.

Throughout late antiquity, Greek and Latin writers associated the bulwark at Darband with Alexander's wall against Gog and Magog.[58] The identification was known to Arabic and Persian writers. Yet practical experience showed that Darband could not be the site of Alexandar's wall. Although the Sarīr, the Alāns, and the Khazars dwelled beyond Darband, and lurked as foreign threats, they were also known entities, and, as such, were generally not seen to correspond to the peoples of Gog and Magog mentioned in the Qurʾān. The anonymous author of the Persian world history *Mujmal al-tawārīkh wa 'l-qiṣaṣ* [Compendium of histories and narratives], written in 519/1126, outlines this issue when he argues that there is no justification to the claim that the fortifications at Darband built by Anūshirwān represent the wall of Alexander the Great.[59] Though Darband might evoke the rampart of Alexander, with its ancient, imperial history, Gog and Magog had to be located farther afield. As geographical information on the frontier spread and knowledge of the world developed, this barrier holding back the apocalypse was itself pushed farther away, to some remote, septentrional land.

Of Archetypes and Precedents

The story of the Arab conquest of the Sāsānian forces at Darband in 22/643 during the reign of ʿUmar b. al-Khaṭṭāb shares in the long tradition of searching for Alexander's wall. In his universal history, Ṭabarī relates how the Persian general at Darband, Shahrbarāz, finding himself surrounded by the invading Arabs to the south, and blocked by hostile tribes of the Caucasus to the north, chose to convert to Islam and accept Arab suzerainty. One night, while Shahrbarāz was holding audience with the Arab general ʿAbd al-Raḥmān b. Rabīʿa and a retinue of Arabs, an envoy appeared before them in a state of fatigue and emaciation. Two years earlier Shahrbarāz had sent this very scout to examine Alexander's wall, so as to learn about the people on the other side.

Shahrbarāz had equipped the unnamed envoy with great wealth for the purpose of completing the journey, writing on his behalf to the rulers of the adjoining territories, giving each a gift, and requesting that they, in turn, send his envoy on to the next ruler, such that he would eventually reach the wall. The last ruler, whose land ended at the wall, sent with the envoy a falconer (*bāzyār*) to serve as a guide. The envoy gifted the guide a piece of silk, in gratitude for his service. Finally, they reached two mountains, closed off by a large fortified wall (*sadd masdūd*) that rose up to the height of the ridge. Beneath the wall was a vast chasm.

The envoy looked at the entire edifice, examining it in great detail. As he set out to return, the guide stopped him, explaining that generations of kings had come before this wall and had offered God the best that they had of this material world, throwing their offerings into this abyss. Then the guide cut up a piece of meat and threw it into the chasm; thereupon his eagle immediately dove down after it. The guide turned to the envoy and said that if the eagle were able to catch the meat before it hit bottom then this truly was an abyss. Whereupon the eagle returned with the meat in its mouth; in the meat they uncovered a precious gem (*yāqūt*), which the guide then gifted to the envoy.

Upon returning, the envoy presented this invaluable stone to Shahrbarāz. The Arab general ʿAbd al-Raḥmān turned to the envoy, asking him what the rampart was like. The envoy gave a description, which the Arabs at the assembly immediately identified with the wall of Dhū 'l-Qarnayn, as described in the Qurʾān. Thus with this equivalence—placed in the context of the early Muslim expansions—the entire account is situated within the broad arc of Islamic eschatology.[60]

Shahrbarāz's conversion and his submission of Darband to the Muslim armies serves as an opening frame onto the narrative of the mission to the wall. Moreover, the matter of conversion is further highlighted when the Arabs transform the envoy's story into an account that corresponds to the Qurʾānic description of the barrier that holds back Gog and Magog. This story, positioned on the frontier, pushes the rampart built by Alexander past Darband to some distant land beyond the Caucasus.[61] The tale of Shahrbarāz's envoy speaks to a continuity between Sāsānian power in the region and the advent of Islam. The Sāsānian governor not only hands over power to the Arab general, but he also offers this story and the idea that out there, somewhere beyond the horizon, exists this marvelous and strange world, waiting to be uncovered.

The anecdote of the Sāsānian emissary has many obvious parallels with Sallām's journey. Both are official missions to discover the wall, and both move from kingdom to kingdom, returning after successfully reaching the wall in the space of roughly two years. There are, however, elements of the anecdote laid forth by Shahrbarāz's envoy that do not correspond to Sallām's narrative. The falconer's story of kings making offerings to God at the abyss before the wall, along with the eagle, and the precious gem it retrieves, relates to the widespread belief in the wondrous qualities of the *aetites* (ἀετίτης), or the eagle-stone, which was thought to have magical powers and could only be found in the nests of eagles. The story of precious stones retrieved from the bottom of a deep ravine by eagles forms part of an international web of tales on powerful gems.

St. Epiphanius (d. 403 C.E.), bishop of Constantia in Cyprus, in a treatise on gemstones, transmits an account similar to the story related by Shahrbarāz's envoy. He describes a series of mountains in the deserts of Scythia that stretch up like walls over a seemingly bottomless ravine. Here kings would search for precious stones by throwing the meat of sheep down into the chasm; gemstones located at the bottom would then adhere to the meat, which was, in turn, retrieved by eagles that inhabited the high peaks and would dive after the carcasses and return with the gems to their mountain nests. According to St. Epiphanius, these stones had a range of mysterious powers, including the ability to aid women during parturition.[62] This account, which appears also in early Chinese sources,[63] makes its way into Arabic and Persian versions of the exploits of Alexander the Great, where it is transformed into a ruse for recovering diamonds in a valley of giant snakes, itself the basis for an adventure of Sindbad the Sailor.[64]

Shahrbarāz's mission transposes the wall of Gog and Magog with that of a gem-filled chasm, as this is apparently a coordinate already fixed to the adventures of Alexander. In contrast to the tale of the Sāsānian envoy, Sallām does not veer into the romances of gems uncovered in remote lands with ancient rituals. Yet despite the obvious divergences, the overwhelming similarities between the separate missions of Shahrbarāz and al-Wāthiq suggest an established *topos* of following Alexander to the end of the world.

Ostensibly, the tale of the Sāsānian envoy precedes Sallām's journey by nearly two hundred years. The chain of transmitters, which Ṭabarī lists as relating this account, date back to the original event of Shahrbarāz's audience with ʿAbd al-Raḥmān in 22/643. The authenticity of this chain of transmission, however, may be called into question. Ṭabarī narrates the anecdote on the authority of ʿAmr b. Maʿdī Karib, who in turn bases it on Maṭar b. Thalj al-Tamīmī, who was present when the envoy of Shahrbarāz arrived, and thus listened firsthand to the story as it unfolded before him. Little is known of Maṭar b. Thalj, whose name means 'Rain the son of Snow,' the original narrator of this story.[65]

However, we have much more information on the second transmitter, ʿAmr b. Maʿdī Karib. A famous Arab warrior and pre-Islamic poet who converted to Islam, he participated in many key battles during the initial days of the Arab conquests. As for the date of his death, the sources disagree. There are accounts of his exceptional longevity, with some claiming that he died during the reign of the caliphate of Muʿāwiya b. Abī Sufyān (r. 41–60/661–80). However, it is quite possible that ʿAmr b. Maʿdī Karib died during the battle of al-Qādisiyya (ca. 16/637), which would, in turn, make him an unlikely transmitter of a tale that is said to have taken place several years later.[66]

It is noteworthy that Ṭabarī, infamous for including long chains of transmitters in his history, relies here on only one intermediary who lived nearly two hundred and fifty years before him. That this anecdote is ascribed to Amr b. Maʿdī Karib evokes, to some degree, the yarns of the idealized warrior poet of the early days of the Arab conquests. Yet the parallels with the Alexander Romance also suggest further degrees of elaboration in the formation and dissemination of the account.

The uncertain line of transmission, along with the central anecdote surrounding the wondrous eagle-stone, raises the question of the historicity of the mission. There is, however, no good reason to suspect or suggest, given Ṭabarī's eye for authenticity, that he either invented this narrative or that he considered it to be anything other than genuine. Without other earlier sources to substantiate the account, it is difficult to determine whether or not the story of Shahrbarāz's envoy to the wall predates Sallām's journey, given that Ṭabarī is a younger contemporary of Ibn Khurradādhbih. However, all outward appearances suggest that it does. If, indeed, the tale of the Persian expedition from Darband to Alexander's wall circulated before al-Wāthiq's expedition, then we have a clear tradition that anticipates and foregrounds Sallām's narrative.

After Ṭabarī, the Sāsānian mission from Darband to the wall of Dhū 'l-Qarnayn continues to circulate and develop in Persian and Arabic sources. Abū ʿAlī Balʿamī (d. 363/974), the Persian historian and translator of Ṭabarī's history, focuses his attention on the marvelous tale of the precious stone in which Shahrbarāz set his ring.[67] Other writers do not fail to find similarities between the mission sent by Shahrbarāz and the story of Sallām al-Tarjumān. For example, the exegete Fakhr al-Dīn al-Rāzī (d. 606/1209), the historian Shams al-Dīn al-Dhahabī (d. 748/1348), and the geographer Ibn ʿAbd al-Munʿim al-Ḥimyarī (d. 900/1494) all relate these two narratives side-by-side as historical accounts of the wall against Gog and Magog, and consider the expedition sent by Shahrbarāz as a genuine Sāsānian undertaking that preceded al-Wāthiq's mission.[68]

The Andalusian geographer Abū ʿUbayd al-Bakrī (d. 487/1094) relates a similar royal quest for the wall of Gog and Magog, based on the account of the distinguished Egyptian historian, genealogist, and jurist, Saʿīd b. ʿUfayr (d. 226/840), who appears as an authority in both Andalusian historiography and Arabic descriptive geography.[69] In this anecdote, as with Shahrbarāz's quest, the wall is imagined to lie beyond the Caucasus. According to Ibn ʿUfayr, Muʿāwiya b. Abī Sufyān, the founder of the Umayyad dynasty, sent twenty-five men to uncover the location of Alexander's rampart. Muʿāwiya dispatched his embassy with a letter and gifts to the king of the Khazar, seeking permission to travel beyond the Khazar kingdom.

On their northern journey, the party reached two mountain ridges (*jabalayn*), where they saw the iron wall shining lustrously. Beyond, they could hear the uproar (*jalaba*) of Gog and Magog. On the wall was a staircase ascending to the top of the barrier, which a man from among the group attempted to climb. However, as he reached the middle of the wall he suddenly panicked (*taḥayyara*), whereupon he fell and died. Before returning, the delegation took as evidence of their journey a piece (*qiṭʿa*) of an iron shovel, apparently because it had been used by Alexander when he first built the wall. The account ends with Muʿāwiya's astonishment (*fa-taʿajjaba*) over the entire affair.[70]

Whether Ibn ʿUfayr's narrative reflects a historical embassy sent by Muʿāwiya remains to be seen. However, taken broadly, the anecdote offers a glimpse, even if imagined, into Umayyad–Khazar relations, themselves in large measure defined by a struggle for hegemony in the Caucasus.[71] As part of the larger discursive *imaginaire*, this account connects the salvation history of the Qurʾān, represented through the enclosed nations of Gog and Magog, with the geopolitical landscape of Umayyad legitimacy and power.

Against this highly developed literary landscape, the missions of Shahrbarāz and Muʿāwiya push the frontier beyond the Caucasus. For our purposes, the authenticity of these two quest narratives is not as significant as the memory of them, both of which, according to the sources, significantly predate al-Wāthiq's expedition to discover the fabled barrier. It is thus possible to argue that when Ibn Khurradādhbih composed his geography, adventures to the wall of Gog and Magog already formed a discrete trope in the articulation of imperial dominion.[72] Such narratives endured because they circumscribed what were complex historical encounters beyond imperial frontiers within a discernible teleological pattern of sacred geography.

These three expeditions to the wall depend upon the ability of rulers to send exploratory delegations across the far reaches of the earth. Such quests are not only semiotic adventures in the pursuit of knowledge, but also projections of authority in the expansive demarcation of political and geographical boundaries. Each of these accounts uses an idiom of apocalyptic thought to shape the significance of historical interactions between Muslims and their northern neighbors.

In a similar vein, the figure of Dhū ʿl-Qarnayn offers a standard archetype of the devout and pious king who enacts God's will on earth. Drawing similarities between Muslim rulers and the world-conquering hero was a common motif in panegyric poetry. Ibn al-Faqīh, for instance, relates how the many conquests (*futūḥāt*) of al-Muʿtaṣim, the father of al-Wāthiq, were celebrated in verse,[73] as in the following line, which likens the ʿAbbāsid caliph to Dhū ʿl-Qarnayn in search of the mysterious Khiḍr, who had attained immortality from the fountain of life:

تَنَاوَلْتَ أَطْرَافَ ٱلْبِلَادِ بِقُدْرَةٍ كَأَنَّكَ فِيهَا تَبْتَغِي أَثَرَ ٱلْخِضْرِ

With power you acquired regions of the world,
as though you were following Khiḍr's trail.[74]

In Ibn al-Faqīh's geographical compendium, the ʿAbbāsid conquests are mapped out onto a poetic landscape:

وَمَا كَانَ ذو ٱلْقَرْنَيْنِ يَبْلُغُ سَعْيَه   وَلا غَزْوُ كِسْرَىٰ لِلْهَياطِلَةِ ٱلْجُرْدِ

Dhū 'l-Qarnayn did not reach his goal,
nor did Khusraw invade the hairless Huns.[75]

These verses were sung in honor of Hārūn al-Rashīd's victories in Khurāsān. In the poetic expanse, the caliph surpasses the models of Greek and Sānānian kingship; where Dhū 'l-Qarnayn fails to reach the waters of life and Khusraw makes no incursions against the Huns, the caliph is imagined, in contrast, at the height of imperial power.

When Ibn Khurradādhbih relates the account of al-Wāthiq's mission to the wall, he does so within a discursive universe in which the might of caliphs is measured against the legendary prowess of Dhū 'l-Qarnayn. Al-Wāthiq's reign, unlike those of his forefathers, was not distinguished by territorial expanse. By encoding an embassy to the Caucasus within an established paradigm of following the traces of Dhū 'l-Qarnayn, Ibn Khurradādhbih's geography amplifies the dominion of ʿAbbāsid power and circumscribes al-Wāthiq and his legacy within pre-existing models of caliphal authority.

On Frontiers and Dispositions

The Bodleian manuscript of Ibn Khurradādhbih's geography, which has a different ordering than the Vienna recension, situates al-Wāthiq's embassy directly after a description of the fortifications of Darband and the Khazar city of Samandar. In the stage-route logic of the work, this would locate the wall north beyond the lands of the Khazar.[76] As Sallām travels past the Caucasus on his way to discover this remote land, he does so against an imagined landscape of both Sāsānian and Umayyad forays into the region. Sallām conspicuously bypasses any mention of the defensive walls at Darband—long identified with Alexander's rampart against Gog and Magog and considered the standard *locus in quo* for passage through the Caucasus. That the trajectory of Sallām's narrative avoids such an important site suggests an almost conscious distancing from the tradition itself.

The association of the Caucasus with the peoples of Gog and Magog draws on the historical reality that, since antiquity, this region formed a central artery through which tribes from the Eurasian steppes descended into the fertile crescent of Anatolia and Mesopotamia. As Sallām makes his way through a landscape marked by ancient fortifications, he moves across a geography of differentiation, where kingdoms are defined against their neighbors, tribes against tribes.

After describing the various regions of the world, along with the outer frontiers and the fortifications (*ribāṭāt*) that separate nations from each other, the encyclopedist al-Muṭahhar b. Ṭāhir al-Maqdisī (fl. 355/966), in his universal history *Kitāb al-badʾ wa ʿl-taʾrīkh* [The book of creation and history], explains that every nation (*qawm*) faces enemies that threaten its existence. Thus Byzantium and Armenia make war against Greater Syria, Azerbaijan, and Mesopotamia; Byzantium threatens western regions (*maghārib*); India stands against the people of Balkh; and the Turks are enemies of Khurāsān.[77] This world of hostility informs the social logic behind tales of bottling up hostile nations behind defensive barriers.

The Shāfiʿī jurist Ibn al-Qāṣṣ (d. 335/946), who served as a judge in Tarsus along the frontier with Byzantium, writes, in a geographical treatise marking the coordinates for the *qibla*, that the ancient Persians divided the world into seven climes, with Iran situated in the center. He adds that they further divided these seven parts into four sections that paired the Arabs with Indians, the Chinese with Turks, the Byzantines with Africans, and the Persians in the center by themselves.[78] Such a system suggests a way of linking two major geographical models both associated with ancient Persian traditions.

In his geographical–mathematical study treating the determination of latitudes and longitudinal differentiation, *Taḥdīd nihāyāt al-amākin li-taṣḥīḥ masāfāt al-masākin* [The determination of the coordinates of positions for the correction of distances between inhabited areas], Abū ʿl-Rayḥān al-Bīrūnī (d. ca 442/1050) outlines a similar tension inherent in geographical divisions of space and territory. He explains how the ancient Persian kings, for the sake of governance (*siyāsa*) and to demarcate land, divided the inhabited world into seven circular sections, in the form of six circles rotating around a seventh circle with each circle being equal in size.

According to Bīrūnī, ancient Persian kings devised the seven-part *kishwar* division to better determine the distances of other kingdoms from their own territory.[79] The word *kishwar* is derived from the Avestan stem form *karshuuar-*, the noun from the Iranian root *karsh*, which has the basic meaning 'to make furrows.'[80] The term itself evokes demarcations that highlight one region as distinguishable from the next, just as something that is delineated by lines is readily perceived (fig. 2).

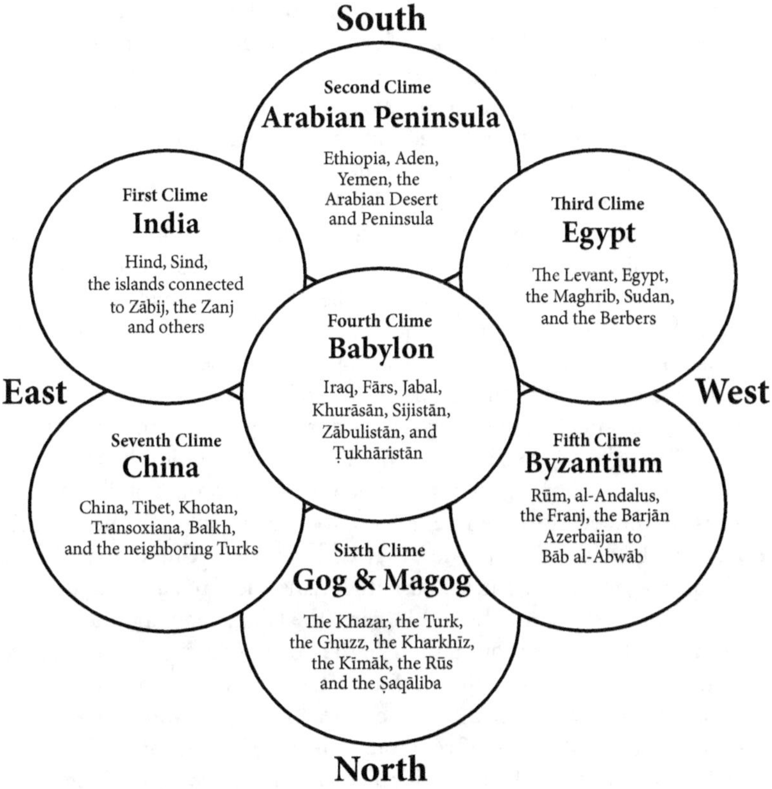

Figure 2: *Kishwar* map based on Abū 'l-Rayḥān al-Bīrūnī, *Taḥdīd nihāyāt al-amākin*, 61.

Concluding his explanation of this ancient Persian geographical system, Bīrūnī comments that there exists no connection between these seven divisions and the natural order of things, nor does this geographical system have any link with the phenomena of astronomy. Rather, he adds, these divisions are made arbitrarily, according to the diverse kingdoms, the difference in features of their peoples, along with their different morals, customs, languages, and religions.[81]

Here Bīrūnī differentiates the natural divisions of the world from political and cultural ones. There existed, however, a widespread notion, which Bīrūnī himself held,[82] that the external, natural cosmos influenced the formation of ethnic, cultural, and geographical identities. Drawing specifically from the Galenic division of the four humors and their effects on a person's character, Arabic and Persian geographers continued a long tradition of viewing the balance of temperature and moisture as a cause for the temperamental differences between peoples.[83] These Galenic concepts entered directly into geography and cosmography through the writing of Ptolemy, who strongly influenced Arabic and Persian writers with his climatic division of the world. The extremities of heat and cold were viewed as natural factors that defined where civilization could take root. Accordingly, the severe temperatures in the farthest extremes of the north and south made these regions of the earth uninhabitable.[84]

It was taken for granted that climate and geography influenced the innate disposition of people; those who lived either too close to, or too far from, the sun were thought to suffer a deficiency of the intellect and were often considered to border on the savage. Following this principle, the Andalusian scholar Ibn Ṣāʿid (d. 462/1070), in his *Ṭabaqāt al-umam* [The classes of nations], outlines how nations living too far north or south of the equator, because of the severity of temperature, have been unable to achieve much intellectually; of these people he lists, to the north, the Chinese, the Turks, Gog and Magog, the Khazar, the Sarīr, the Alāns, the Slavs, the Bulghār, and the Rūs; and to the south, the Ethiopians, the Ghanaians, and the Zanj.[85]

Similarly, the anonymous author of the Persian descriptive geography, the *Ḥudūd al-ʿālam*, posits that each country differs from another in four respects (*rūy*): first, by the difference of water, air, soil, and temperature; second, by the difference of religions (*dīn-hā*), laws (*sharīʿat-hā*), and beliefs (*kīsh-hā*); third, by the difference of words (*lughāt*) and languages (*zabān-hā*); and fourth, by the difference of kingdoms (*padhshāhī-hā*).[86] This description of the world echoes a notion that the external natural universe influences temperament and character, determined by the climatic balance of the four humors.

The link between climate and disposition also forms part of a cosmographical conception of the earth in relation to the universe. The field of astrology engages with the diversity of temperament, moving from the climatic influence on innate dispositions to address the role of the stars in determining the characteristics of people. In his geography the scholar and geographer al-Ḥasan b. Aḥmad al-Hamdānī (d. 334/945) explains how both the variations of climate and the astrological movements of the zodiac influence the different regions and peoples of the world. He adheres to a division of the world into quadrants that are each subdivided into three smaller sections, with a total of twelve divisions that correspond to the twelve signs of the zodiac, such that, over each subdivision move a combination of heavenly bodies, all of which operate in concord over the world below.[87]

Such geographical and cosmographical demarcations attempt to account for and manage the incredible diversity of creation. By the middle of the second/eighth century, as territorial expansion slowed, the new Islamic state went through a process of consolidating power and defining boundaries. A technical vocabulary evolved to account for the intricate configuration of the frontiers. Against the Byzantines, a two-tiered system of frontiers developed in Syria and in Mesopotamia: an outer series of breaches, or strongholds (*thughūr*) was defended by an inner level of fortifications (*ʿawāṣim*), where the people of the frontier could retreat in times of war. These two levels served as a buffer zone against enemy incursions into the heart of the state. As the political landscape of the Islamic community fragmented during the ʿAbbāsid period into autonomous or semi-autonomous kingdoms, such as the Umayyads of al-Andalus, the Idrīsids of the Maghrib, and the Sāmānids of Transoxiana, a variegated nomenclature (*ākhir*, *tukhūm*, *ḥāshiya*) to describe an internal system of borders between Islamic states also emerged.[88]

Yet, in the face of this fragmentation there existed a fully expressed notion of the Muslim lands as distinct from the territories beyond the reach of Islam. As a category, Islam is often imagined by medieval Muslim geographers as a nominal, reified site of political dominion.[89] The terminology used to describe the division between the realm of Islam (*dār al-islām*) and the realm of strife (*dār al-ḥarb*) was evidently a feature of Umayyad legal discourse.[90] These categories of identity find further expression in the third/ninth century, with imperial law codes composed for the early ʿAbbāsid caliphate by state-sponsored jurists. Juridical writings, such as the *Kitāb al-siyar* [Book on military campaigns] by the Ḥanafī jurist Muḥammad b. al-Ḥasan al-Shaybānī (d. 189/805), addressed the legal complexity of interactions with lands beyond the territory of Islam.[91] As deictic demarcation, the categories of *dār al-islām* and *dār al-ḥarb* underscore an important connection between religious and geographical identities. These two realms, divided between the lands of peace and the lands of war, stand as mirror images of each other; binary opposites, separated, nonetheless, by ever-changing, porous boundaries, where the outer frontiers (*thughūr*) are never drawn as firm lines, but represent rough points of contact between two sides that are unstable, and always transforming. Both the Umayyads and the ʿAbbāsids enacted a variety of peace treaties (*hudna* / *ṣulḥ*) with Byzantium; these guaranteed safe conduct (*aman*), facilitating trade and travel. Prolonged periods of peace often served as moments of great cultural and intellectual exchange, as, for example, was demonstrated with the various caliphal missions undertaken to procure ancient Greek works to be translated into Syriac and Arabic.[92]

Arabic and Persian geographical writings, indebted to ancient Greek models, generally reflect a perspective on the frontier that is not predetermined by juridical considerations of religious law. Not once in the surviving sections of the *Masālik* does Ibn Khurradādhbih make reference to either the *dār al-islām* or the *dār al-ḥarb*, two terms which come to be fully determined within juridical discourse. His work rather showcases diverse tales of travelers interacting with various people from around the world. In his geography, *Kitāb al-buldān*, the historian and geographer Yaʿqūbī, a contemporary of Ibn Khurradādhbih, refers to the land of Islam (*arḍ al-islām*) with Baghdad as the center of the universe and the navel of the earth (*surrat al-arḍ*),[93] thus orienting the world around a political and religious power of Islam.[94] Nonetheless, Yaʿqūbī does not make reference to either the *dār al-islām* or the *dār al-ḥarb*, nor, for that matter, does Balādhurī, whose history is very much focused on relations with non-Muslims, deploy these particular binary oppositions.

This should not suggest, however, that early geographers did not engage with such terminology in their construction of space. Iṣṭakhrī, followed by Ibn Ḥawqal, refers a handful of times to both terms when describing the political formations of the world.[95] Likewise, Masʿūdī on occasion mentions Muslim territories as the *dār al-islām*.[96] Muqaddasī focuses his work primarily on the 'kingdom of Islam' (*mamlakat al-islām*) and chooses to ignore altogether the 'kingdoms of the infidels' (*mamālik al-kuffār*), for, as he explains, he has neither traveled to those regions, nor does he believe that there is much benefit to be gained by discussing them.[97] The ʿAbbāsid secretary Qudāma b. Jaʿfar, who, in his administrative geography, does not limit himself to the lands of Islam, employs the term 'kingdom of Islam' (*mamlakat al-islām*), and refers to the territorial limit of Islam (*ḥadd al-islām*).[98] When surveying the traditions of geographical writing, we find that though there is a clear projection of the category of Islam spatially, the terminology used to describe the regions inhabited by Muslims and their place in the world is neither monolithic nor anchored solely to the concerns of jurists.

With regard to the geographical tradition, the division of the world into the realms of war and peace has been overstated, for though the early geographers often treat in detail the societies and customs of the nations outside the territory of Islam, they use the polarizing oppositions of *dār al-islām* and *dār al-ḥarb / kufr* to describe their relations to foreign regions much less than might be expected, given the subject matter.[99] Generally Muslim geographers do not address commerce and travel across the diverse kingdoms of the earth by dividing the world into a single legal partition between two monolithic realms. In the discourse of geographical writing—from descriptions of the magnificent capital of Byzantium to the mysterious inhabitants of the Wāqwāq islands—the foreign comes into view not only in its capacity to threaten, but also as a wondrous sign of how the strange and exotic is spread throughout creation. Though the narratives travel across kingdoms of unbelievers and islands of savage cannibals, the writing itself serves to mediate such dangerous elements. In the form of narration, through the power of discourse, the monstrous and illicit can be managed and controlled by description itself.

The geographical techniques for grasping and projecting natural and political formations offer highly idiosyncratic visions, employing a variety of often contradictory models to fathom the shape of the world and the political formations therein. In general, geographers draw, in some fashion, on what they viewed to be the Ptolemaic division of the world into climes (*aqālīm*), divisions that follow various parallel latitudes running from the equator to the North Pole. However, in the literature, there is no consensus on how many climes existed; numbers range from seven to twenty.[100] The Arabic and Persian geographers also make use of the Sāsānian model of dividing the world into seven territories.[101] This model held that the Sāsānian territory of Īrānshahr was the center of the universe, a tradition that was emulated by ʿAbbāsid geographers.[102]

There are striking resemblances between the *kishwar* model of concentric satellites orbiting around one centered territory and the Islamic tradition of *qibla* maps that orient the world around Mecca. The *qibla* marks the correct position to which Muslims, relative to their given location in the world, turn during prayer so that their faces and prayers align with the sacred Kaʿba in Mecca (plate 4). As a result, *qibla* maps order the cosmos as rotating around a sacred geography. Yāqūt details all three of these systems, along with a variety of cosmographical accounts concerning the position of the earth relative to the universe, in the introduction to his geographical dictionary *Muʿjam al-buldān*. He concludes that, with all the divergence of opinions concerning the shape, position, and composition of the earth, it is God alone who knows the truth of the entire matter.[103]

Despite these varying viewpoints, a widespread belief existed that the earth was divided into a section of inhabitable regions, existing only in the northern hemisphere, and that these regions were surrounded by an encircling ocean (*al-baḥr al-muḥīṭ*/Ὠκεανός).[104] A range of opinions developed concerning what shape these land masses took, many of which appear to be informed by ancient Persian traditions, such as the belief that the inhabited lands look like a hooded garment.[105] Another theory was that the land masses of the world took the shape of a bird, with disparaging remarks made of those who inhabited the west, i.e., the part that represented the bird's tail.[106]

In large measure, Arabic and Persian geographers drew their idea of the inhabitable territories of the earth from the ancient Greek concept of the *oecumene* (οἰκουμένη), often translated into Arabic as *al-arḍ al-maʿmūra* and into Persian as *ābādhānī*. As for Ibn Khurradādhbih, he divides the inhabited world into four land masses or continents (*aqsām*), consisting of Europe (*arūfā*), Libya (*lūbiya*), Ethiopia (*ityūfiyā*), and Scythia (*isqūtiyā*).[107] Ibn al-Faqīh follows this same tradition,[108] as does Hamdānī, who assigns this particular quadripartite division an astrological significance by describing how each of these regions are subsequently subdivided into thirds, with a total of twelve sections, each corresponding to a sign of the zodiac.[109] The transliterated form of the place names used to describe these four continents—Europe (*Εὐρώπη*), Libya (*Λιβύα*), Ethiopia (*Αἰθιοπία*), and Scythia (*Σκυθία*)—does little to disguise the Greek origin of this tradition, which entered into Arabic through the various translations of Greek scientific material.

Of the aforementioned authors, only Hamdānī consciously acknowledges Ptolemy as the source of this astrological conception of the earth. Yet the division of the *oecumene* into quarters is not to be found in either Ptolemy's *Geographia* or his star-catalog, the *Almagest*. In his geography, Ptolemy follows a tradition of dividing the earth into not four, but three continents.[110] The anonymous author of the Persian geographical work, the *Ḥudūd al-ʿālam*, draws on this tripartite Greek tradition when partitioning the earth into the three sections, and refers to them accordingly, as Libya (*lūbiya*), Europe (*arūfā*), and Asia (*āsiyā*).[111] Outlining this ancient Greek tradition, Bīrūnī, followed by Yāqūt, explains how Greek writers further subdivided Asia into two smaller sections, known as Asia Major (*āsiyā 'l-kubrā*) and Asia Minor (*āsiyā 'l-ṣughrā*).[112]

This subdivision of Asia into two categories harmoniously echoes the four continents set forth by Ibn Khurradādhbih, where the last two sections of Ethiopia and Scythia correspond respectively to these two divisions of Asia. However, all indications suggest that Ibn Khurradādhbih, along with Ibn al-Faqīh, who copies him *verbatim*, do not draw their information from the three-continent division of the inhabited world as set forth in Ptolemy's *Geography*. Rather, we may surmise from Hamdānī's exposition on the astrological influences upon the characteristics of the inhabitants of the world, that Ptolemy's *Tetrabiblos*, a short treatise on astrological geography, served as the source for this particular classification of the inhabited earth into four continents.[113] In this work, which was translated several times into Arabic under the title *Kitāb al-arbaʿa*,[114] Ptolemy explains the effects of the astral bodies on the characteristics of the various regions of the *oecumene*. He quarters up the world into the divisions of Europe, Libya, Ethiopia, and Scythia, which appear centuries later as transliterations in Ibn Khurradādhbih's *Masālik*.[115] Moreover, in this exposition, Ptolemy mentions that Ethiopia and Scythia are sections of Greater Asia, a term that encompasses both Asia Minor and Asia Major; for Ptolemy this rationale dovetails seamlessly with the more common tripartite division of the inhabited earth, as outlined clearly in his *Geography*.

The path of transmission and translation of such Greek geographical categories highlights the unique and heterogeneous manner in which the traditions of Arabic and Persian geography developed. When Ibn Khurradādhbih describes the inhabitable lands of the earth as partitioned into these four sections, he does so in dialogue with Ptolemy's *Tetrabiblos*, the source for this division, and a pillar in the pantheon of Greek astrological works translated into Arabic. Ibn Khurradādhbih demonstrates how this division of the earth into quadrants corresponds to the four natural elements, the humors of the body, and the twelve signs of the zodiac.[116] In the Bodleian manuscript a diagram is given of the earth shaped as a circle with four mixtures of humors grafted onto the cardinal directions.[117] Ibn Khurradādhbih states that the sages (*ḥukamāʾ*) have mapped out these humors on the earth so that the subtlety of God's divine design (*luṭf tadbīrihi*) could be ocularly observed (*li'l-ʿiyān*).[118] Similarly, as Ibn Rusta explains, the diversity found in the various communities (*milal*) of the world is based upon humoral composition, which varies with respect to the four geographical regions of the earth and their relationship to the influence of the stars. According to Ibn Rusta, this natural variation is something that can be verified through direct observation (*ʿiyān*), just as its interconnection with the broad system of astral influence is readily supported by reason (*ʿaql*).[119]

One obvious effect of this theory of astral influences and humoral dispositions is the promotion of rather chauvinistic ideologies of naturally ordained superiority. Marwazī, whose natural history follows this theory of humoral geography, situates Īrānshahr in the middle of the seven climes and claims that because this region is governed by the sign of the Sun it is associated with more special qualities (*faḍāʾil*) than other parts of the world. Accordingly, the inhabitants of Iran possess the perfect expression of ethics, beauty, natural temperament, and overall greatness, just as the kings of this land are the ornament of dominion and power, because of their maintenance of order and justice.[120] As for those who live at the far extremes of civilization, their natures and dispositions are shaped in relation to their lack of humoral balance (*iʿtidāl*). According to Marwazī this can be observed notably in the Turks, who suffer from an the excess of cold the farther north they dwell, especially in the country of Gog, where their "stature shortens, their eyes become small, their nostrils and mouths narrow, their souls compress, and their joy diminishes."[121]

Such natural and geographical demarcations were emploted into ʿAbbāsid ideology. The very constitution of the palatine city of Sāmarrāʾ was founded, according to legend, on the site where Sām the son of Noah was born.[122] Considered the ancestor of the Arabs and the Persians, Sām (Shem) is thought to have inherited the middle of the earth; this is in contrast with Noah's other two sons; Ḥām is the progenitor of the Africans, while the Turks and Gog and Magog are descended from Yāfith (Japheth).[123]

The elaborate ethnographical discourse that frames Ptolemy's astrological geography translates directly into later Arabic and Persian geographical traditions. The *Tetrabiblos* points to a quarry of ancient Greek anxieties about the world. Drawing on long-established xenophobic and ethnocentric stereotypes, Ptolemy details how the influence of the zodiac predetermines the natural disposition of the various nations that inhabit the four regions of the world. What are at times grotesque caricatures find their way into Arabic practically unaltered.[124]

The division of the earth evoked by Ibn Khurradādhbih speaks explicitly to an epistemology in which natural dispositions are assigned to the various peoples of the world.[125] This brings us to the final region of the *oecumene*, known to Ibn Khurradādhbih as *isqūtya*. Greek authors invariably located Scythia in the Caucasus and around the Caspian Sea.[126] Ibn Khurradādhbih identifies the same region with toponyms familiar to Arabic readers; accordingly, Scythia consists of Armenia, Khurāsān, the Turks, and the Khazars. For ancient Greek writers, Scythia stood as a symbol of the barbaric and monstrous on the edges of civilization. Herodotus describes how the Scythian warriors, after drinking the blood of their victims, would fashion clothing out of their skins and carve goblets out of their skulls.[127] Such descriptions of their gruesome customs and the horrific burial rites of their kings serve as common motifs in the geographical literature on the region.[128]

For classical Greek literature, Scythia is synonymous with exotic barbarism. In the *Tetrabiblos*, Ptolemy situates in this region the mythical, martial tribes of Amazon women, who cut off their right breasts in order to better wield swords and bows during combat.[129] On this section, Hamdānī adds to Ptolemy's description, stating that the peoples of Gog and Magog reside in this quarter of the world.[130] The invasion of the Huns across Central Asia and through the Caucasus in 396 C.E. encouraged Christians, writing in Greek and Syriac, to identify Gog and Magog with the Scythians.[131] This pre-Islamic tradition continued not only with Hamdānī, but with other Muslim writers who saw in the Greek toponym of Scythia the apocalyptic tribes of Gog and Magog.

It is logical that, just as the figure of Dhū 'l-Qarnayn in the Qur'ān corresponds to Alexander the Great of Macedonia, so too should the peoples Alexander bottles up at the end of the earth appear in ancient Greek writings. The Andalusian religious scholar and *adīb*, Ibn Ḥazm (d. 456/1064), writing in his doxography on the various religions and philosophies of the world, *Faṣl fī 'l-milal wa 'l-ahwā' wa 'l-niḥal* [The division on the religious communities, sects, and creeds] argues for the existence of Gog and Magog. He states that Aristotle made reference to Gog and Magog in his *Kitāb al-ḥayawān* (*Historia animalium*), in a section on the natural characteristics of cranes (*gharānīq*).[132] As for Aristotle, this anachronism could not be further from the truth, for nowhere does he make mention of these scriptural monsters. The section in question is Aristotle's treatment of the migratory patterns of cranes (*γέρανοι*), which, according to him, take these birds to Scythia. In this region, Aristotle says that pygmies dwell in caves with their equally small horses. Aristotle is quick to affirm that this account is not a myth (*μῦθος*).[133] Just as Aristotle's work on the classifications of animals inspired Greek traditions of marvel-writing, so, too, his influence was felt in the later *ʿajāʾib* discourse in Arabic and Persian.[134] Though the Arabic translation of the *Kitāb al-ḥayawān* made by Yūḥannā b. al-Baṭrīq (d. ca 200/815) does not explicitly identify the pygmies with Gog and Magog, it is perfectly reasonable for Ibn Ḥazm to see in the description of the people from Scythia (*iskūthiyā*), who are the height of one cubit (*dhirāʿ*), the apocalyptic figures mentioned in the Qur'ān, often characterized by their small stature.[135] The transposition of Gog and Magog onto the race of pygmies from classical Greek sources, who are attacked by cranes, finds full expression in Arabic and Persian letters.[136]

Between the Arabic translation of Aristotle's *Historia animalium* and Ibn Ḥazm's notion that Aristotle references Gog and Magog, we observe in Hamdānī a tradition of identifying the Scythia of ancient Greece with the region of Gog and Magog. Ibn Ḥazm further states that Ptolemy, in his *Geography*, mentions the wall of Gog and Magog and gives the length and width of the region they inhabit.[137] Such a statement offers insight into how Muslim writers viewed Greek geographical and scientific authorities as corresponding to pre-existing scriptural notions of the universe. In the case of Ibn Ḥazm, he uses ancient Greek sources as proof of the existence of Alexander's wall against Gog and Magog. The association in early Christian writings, first in Greek, then in Syriac, of Scythia with Gog and Magog, aided Muslim writers in their identification of these apocalyptic peoples.

The influence of Ptolemy's *Tetrabiblos* on Ibn Khurradādhbih's conception of geography speaks to the central place of astrology in the development of geographical thought and highlights how the notion that astrological influences predetermine human temperaments, forming ready-made types and characteristics, is implicit to this division of the inhabited world. The narratives surrounding Gog and Magog also play a part in this astrological ethnography, for these two tribes, trapped at the farthest edge of the world, represent the most brutal savages on the earth. As a result of the severity of the climate, the lands beyond them are believed uninhabitable. Although Ibn Khurradādhbih does not explicitly identify Scythia with Gog and Magog, the nations through which Sallām al-Tarjumān journeys readily recall the delineations of Scythia's boundaries.

By the time Sallām undertakes his adventure, early Arabic geographical tradition had already established that the lands of Gog and Magog lie beyond the Khazar, situated between the sixth and seventh climes, stretching across the farthest edge of the inhabited world.[138] As Sallām crosses the Caucasus, he meets the Khazar king, who dispatches five guides to take him to the wall.

At this point in his narrative Sallām leaves all traces of the known world behind and enters *terra incognita*.[139] As the expedition veers off the map, he keeps a steady account of the days traveled. The demarcation of time now serves as the primary means of charting the terrain covered. After having traveled away from the Khazar in an unspecified direction for a period of twenty-six days, the party enters a putrid black smelling land (*arḍ sūdāʾ muntinat al-rāʾiḥa*).[140] Abū ʿAbd Allāh al-Idrīsī (d. 560/1165), in his world geography, *Nuzhat al-mushtāq fī ikhtirāq al-āfāq* [Pleasant journeys into faraway lands], refers to Sallām's description of traveling through the black stinking land for ten days when he describes the region as a completely savage land, where no plant grows or living thing dwells. He further adds that navigating through it is torturous (*sālikuhā karbun*), as it gives off a wretched stench, there is no water to survive, and there is no path to enable anyone heading out across the land to find his way.[141]

Sallām describes how his delegation prepared themselves for this odoriferous onslaught by taking along vinegar; this they applied to rags to cover their noses, in an effort to protect themselves from the rancid odors. After traveling through this land for a period of ten days, they finally reached the ruins of cities upon cities, laid to waste long ago by Gog and Magog, before Alexander the Great finally shut them behind the wall. The image of ruined cities reflects a Qurʾānic theme of traveling across the earth to witness the destruction of past civilizations; a proof of the wrath of God and confirmation of the final judgment to come:

أَفَلَمْ يَسِيرُوا۟ فِى ٱلْأَرْضِ فَيَنظُرُوا۟ كَيْفَ كَانَ عَـٰقِبَةُ ٱلَّذِينَ مِن قَبْلِهِمْ ۚ كَانُوٓا۟
أَكْثَرَ مِنْهُمْ وَأَشَدَّ قُوَّةً وَءَاثَارًا فِى ٱلْأَرْضِ فَمَآ أَغْنَىٰ عَنْهُم مَّا كَانُوا۟
يَكْسِبُونَ ﴿٨٢﴾

> Have they not traveled across the land to see what was the end of those before them? They were more numerous than them, superior in strength, and in their monuments [left] on the land; yet all they accomplished was of no profit to them. (Q. 40:82)[142]

In its eschatological treatment of the end of time, the Qurʾān makes a cryptic allusion to a town (*qariya*) that was laid to waste, the inhabitants of which will only be able to return when Gog and Magog break out from the barrier (Q. 21:95–6). In these ruins, Sallām offers ocular confirmation of the broader course of Qurʾānic history, as he witnesses a vast apocalyptic landscape inscribed within a scriptural projection of the destruction of past civilizations.

The expedition travels through these destroyed cities for twenty days, then finally reaches a series of fortified outposts. Throughout the narrative Sallām balances the specific with the vague, revealing enough information to maintain an almost scientific engagement with the material world. Unlike the territories of Armenia, the Alān, the Fīlān Shāh, and the Khazar, these lands that Sallām now crosses do not correspond to any known location that could be assigned to specific peoples and places.

For nearly a month Sallām treks through this black putrid region, crossing a no-man's land hostile to life and civilization. Though he keeps a steady account of the time that transpires, rationally ordering the world into segments of distance, the initial pattern of identifying in language the locations through which he travels ends. The exactitude of his account, so intimately linked to the belief that the world can be described in language, begins to loosen and finally dissolves across this sinister landscape. As the specificity of the cartographer's coordinates breaks down we lose track of Sallām's exact location in this apocalyptic land.

5

A WONDROUS BARRIER

Ut Pictura Poesis

As Sallām draws near the wall, he follows the trail of Alexander the Great, laid out in the body of writing surrounding the Pseudo-Callisthenes tradition. Originally believed by early western scholars to be the work of Callisthenes, the Greek historian and contemporary to Alexander, the Romance cycle developed well after Alexander's historical exploits. It transformed over the years as it spread through various translations and adaptations, including Greek, Syriac, Arabic, Persian, Coptic, Ethiopic, Armenian, Latin, and all the major European vernaculars.[1]

In the early history of Islam there was a lively debate over the true identity of Dhū 'l-Qarnayn.[2] One prominent identification was with an ancient South Arabian Ḥimyarī king, generally referred to in the sources as al-Ṣaʿb b. Dhī Marāthid. Ibn Hishām (d. ca 218/833) in his *Kitāb al-tījān fī mulūk Ḥimyar wa 'l-Yaman* [The book of crowns on the kings of Ḥimyar and Yemen] traces the controversy back to the earliest scenes of Qurʾānic exegesis, in which Wahb b. Munabbih (d. ca 102/720) asks the Companion of the Prophet, Ibn ʿAbbās (d. 68/687–8), about the identity of Dhū 'l-Qarnayn. Ibn ʿAbbās responds that the hero mentioned in the Qurʾān corresponds to al-Ṣaʿb b. Dhī Marāthid, to whom God gave dominion over the earth, as a means for all of his conquests. This Ḥimyarī king traveled to the lands where the sun rises and sets, and built the wall against Gog and Magog. Wahb inquires about Iskandar the Greek (al-Rūmī), to which Ibn ʿAbbās replies that he was merely a pious wise man who built two lighthouses on the Mediterranean.[3] Ibn Hishām, who also relates the adventures of searching for the fountain of life, traveling around the world with Khiḍr, and the building of the barrier in the north, is of the opinion that Dhū 'l-Qarnayn was indeed a Ḥimyarī king. Ironically, the life of Dhū 'l-Qarnayn, as represented in Ibn Hishām's *Kitāb al-tījān*, is substantially shaped through the adventures of Alexander the Great, as developed within the Pseudo-Callisthenes cycle.

Pointing to the evidently archaic contours of this debate, Ibn Hishām draws support for his claim by turning to a range of citations from poetry and speeches that the Arab Bedouins had marshaled forth as proof of Dhū 'l-Qarnayn's Yemeni origins. Quoted as an authority is the paragon of pre-Islamic Arabic poets, Imruʾ al-Qays b. Ḥujr, who is said to have sung of the exploits of Dhū 'l-Qarnayn al-Ṣaʿd b. Dhī Marāthid, the Ḥimyarī king:

وَسَدَّ بِحَيْثُ تَرقَى ٱلشَّمْسُ سَدّاً   لِيَأْجُـوجَ وَمَأْجُـوجَ ٱلْجِـبَالا

And he built a barrier where the sun rises
against Gog and Magog among the mountains.[4]

Indeed the association of Dhū 'l-Qarnayn with the South Arabian ruler can be traced in many early Arabic sources. Ḥassān b. Thābit, famed poet of the Prophet, is said to have composed a poem that turns to the victories of the South Arabian Dhū 'l-Qarnayn as an inspiration for the ensuing Arab conquests.[5] Here the Ḥimyarī ruler climbs the heavens through divine cords (*awtār / asbāb*),[6] stares down the sun, and forces Gog and Magog into submission behind a barrier. This *qaṣīda*, like much of the poetry ascribed to Ḥassān b. Thābit, was most likely composed in a later Umayyad context.[7] It is of note that, in the course of the early Arab conquests, the figure of Dhū 'l-Qarnayn was positioned, at least metaphorically, as a source of emulation for military expansion.[8]

For the Arab philologist and expert on South Arabian genealogies, Nashwān b. Saʿīd al-Ḥimyarī (d. 573/1178), the question over the true identity of Dhū 'l-Qarnayn continued to be an issue worth debating. Ḥimyarī argued that non-Arabs (*ʿajam*) were responsible for promoting the belief that Dhū 'l-Qarnayn, who was truly a South Arabian king, was, rather, Alexander the Great, the Macedonian conqueror.[9] At play within these debates is the question of ownership. Early Muslims undoubtedly wondered why a pagan Greek ruler, who was lionized in Byzantine propaganda as a Christian hero,[10] would appear in the Qurʾān.

Rejecting Greek origins was one means of avoiding this problem. Absorbing and appropriating them was another. This is the framework that informs a prophetic *ḥadīth* preserved in the *Futūḥ Miṣr wa 'l-Maghrib* [The conquests of Egypt and the West] by the Egyptian scholar Ibn ʿAbd al-Ḥakam (d. 257/871). He traces this particular account back through several transmitters to the Egyptian traditionist ʿUqba b. ʿĀmir (fl. first/seventh century), who later transmitted the *ḥadīth* from his home in Alexandria. ʿUqba b. ʿĀmir relates that he was with the Prophet when a group from the People of the Book came bearing their scriptures (*maṣāḥif / kutub*) to test Muḥammad, which they did by asking him about Dhū 'l-Qarnayn. This is in keeping with the Qurʾānic passage in which the very name of Dhū 'l-Qarnayn is posed as a kind of riddle to the Prophet (Q. 18:83).

Muḥammad, proving his status as the messenger of God, gives the group an account fully in accord with the Alexander Romance. This *ḥadīth* describes how Dhū 'l-Qarnayn, who was a Greek, was given a kingdom and traveled to the edge of the ocean in the land of Egypt, where he established a city called Iskandariyya (Alexandria). The Prophet then relates how Dhū 'l-Qarnayn built a barrier against Gog and Magog; here Dhū 'l-Qarnayn encountered a nation (*umma*) whose faces were like those of dogs (*wujūh al-kilāb*, i.e., *κυνοκέφαλοι*), and who fought against Gog and Magog. Beyond them were a race of pygmies (*ummat qiṣār*, i.e., *πυγμαῖοι*), who battled with the dog-headed monsters, and were, in turn, at war with a nation of cranes (*gharānīq*, i.e., *γέρανοι*), much akin to Aristotle's account of pygmies in his zoology. Dhū 'l-Qarnayn continued traveling until he reached a valley of serpents, finally arriving at the encircling ocean (*al-baḥr al-mudīr*).[11] In Ibn ʿAbd al-Ḥakam's history, the Prophet's speech to the People of the Book is placed as an authoritative response to the exegetical claim that Dhū 'l-Qarnayn was from Yemen.[12] The account, a version of which is preserved in Ṭabarī's exegesis,[13] draws from the marvels long associated with the adventures of Alexander in the monstrous lands of the east. Recounted in the shadow of the lighthouse of Alexandria, this *ḥadīth* not only identifies Dhū 'l-Qarnayn with the Alexander of Greek antiquity, but also situates the newly conquered territory of Alexandria, and by extension Egypt, within the framework of Islamic eschatology.

While Ibn Hishām's *Kitāb al-tījān* and Ibn ʿAbd al-Ḥakam's *Futūḥ Miṣr* diverge radically over their identification of Dhū 'l-Qarnayn, each suggesting regional appropriations of the Qurʾānic hero, they share an engagement with the general outlines of the Alexander Romance. This speaks to the fact that the adventures of Alexander were well known in some form in Arabic, most likely transmitted orally by early preachers (*quṣṣāṣ*) through the vehicle of prophetic tales (*qiṣaṣ*), which built upon material available regionally. As attested by the Qurʾānic adventure of

Dhū 'l-Qarnayn, many of these accounts were in circulation during the earliest periods of Islamic history.

Despite the early link between Dhū 'l-Qarnayn and the Ḥimyarī king of Yemen, the identification with Alexander the Great was already a feature of Umayyad exegetical writing.[14] The Qurʾānic commentary associated with Muqātil b. Sulaymān (d. 150/767) refers to him as Iskandar, the emperor (*qayṣar*) who reached the mountain of Qāf that surrounds the earth, suggesting the broad influence of the Alexander cycle upon early exegetical traditions.[15] This is a pattern continued in ʿAbbāsid letters, as with Ibn Qutayba and Abū Ḥanīfa al-Dīnawarī (d. ca 282/895), who, during the generation of Ibn Khurradādhbih, followed prevailing wisdom when they identified Dhū 'l-Qarnayn with Alexander the Great, the world-conquering hero.[16]

As represented in Arabic and Persian continuations, the adventures of Alexander served as a wellspring of material, immortalized in such poetic creations as Firdawsī's *Shāh-nāma* and Niẓāmī's *Iskandar-nāma* (plate 5). Throughout this process of adaptation, the general framework of the Pseudo-Callisthenes cycle remains discernible, as in Masʿūdī's description of historical accounts (*akhbār*) concerning Alexander's adventures, which consist of "his travels in the eastern and western regions of the world, the kingdoms he conquered, and the kings he encountered, the cities he built, the wonders (*ʿajāʾib*) he saw, the barrier he erected against Gog and Magog, and his communications with his teacher, Aristotle."[17]

Sallām's narrative of traversing a black putrid region conjures up Alexander's journey through the land of darkness, already a fixture within early Islamic configurations.[18] When Sallām approaches the wall, passing through cities laid to waste by Gog and Magog, he bears witness to the veracity of Dhū 'l-Qarnayn's heroic exploits. The adventure not only confirms the Alexandrian origin of the barrier, but also reinforces the notion that the Qurʾānic account of the wall corresponds to the reality of the world; that a physical barrier exists, holding back beasts, who, with their voracious appetite, are set to devour all of God's living creatures on earth.[19]

After roughly two months of traveling, first through a rancid black land, and then past the destruction of ruined cities, Sallām finally reaches a series of fortifications at the last mountain range before the wall. Amazingly, the people Sallām encounters here speak Arabic and Persian. They are Muslims who recite the Qurʾān and have Qurʾānic schools for learning, along with mosques; yet they are completely cut off from the broader Muslim community. The inhabitants, inquisitive, look upon their visitors utterly astonished (*yataʿajjabūn*), as they learn for the first time about the caliph, the region of Iraq, and the caliphal city of Sāmarrāʾ. The conversion of these people, conversant in both Arabic and Persian, yet isolated from the rest of Islamic civilization, comes to Sallām and his retinue both as a surprise and as a testament to how Islam has spread around the world, to the farthest edges of the inhabitable earth.

Though Sallām does not give us any more information concerning this group of Muslims, his account readily suggests the presence of Muslim merchants and missionaries among Turkic tribes along the Volga and in parts of the Central Asian steppe.[20] Another variant of Sallām's narrative, not present in the redaction of Ibn Khurradādhbih's geography, but recorded by Idrīsī,[21] gives a short narrative of how these people, explicitly identified as the Adhkish Turks, converted to Islam years before, when a man on a camel appeared to them bearing a copy of the Qurʾān. This man taught them religious precepts (*sharāʾiʿ*) and communicated to them the meanings of the Qurʾān in a language they could understand; they converted, and memorized the Qurʾān. Such accounts of conversion, while stylized, nonetheless echo historical missions beyond the frontiers. Early in the *Masālik*, Ibn Khurradādhbih alludes to the report by the intrepid adventurer Tamīm b. Baḥr, who appears to have traveled around 206/821 to the Uyghur (Tughuzghuz) capital on the Orkhon River, in modern-day Mongolia.[22] Tamīm b. Baḥr's sobriquet, *al-muṭṭawwiʿī*, identifies him with a class of volunteer fighters who occupied forward posts against the borders of the Turks and other infidels. This further suggests how inroads were made into the territories beyond the frontiers of Islam, both in the north and to the east. Ibn Khurradādhbih refers to communities of Muslims settled at the farthest reaches of China; other early sources describe isolated populations of Muslims not only living in China, but also in Tibet, and among the Uyghur.[23] In contrast to such examples of far-flung Muslim populations, Sallām's depiction of this community, situated beyond the Khazar before the wall of Gog and Magog, who are so cut off from the religious and political centers of Islamic civilization that they had never heard of a caliph in Iraq, speaks to a remote landscape, imbued with an uncanny sense of the familiar.

Moreover, the description itself evokes a widely circulating *ḥadīth*, contained, for instance, in the *Muṣannaf* of ʿAbd al-Razzāq (d. 211/827) and the canonical collection of Muḥammad b. Ismāʿīl al-Bukhārī (d. 256/870); it describes, as one of the signs of the end of time, the emergence from the east (*min qibali ʾl-mashriq*) of a people, unknown to the rest of Muslims, who recite the Qurʾān.[24] Sallām's account of this Qurʾān-reciting community at the edge of the known world is deployed not only to resonate with Islamic apocalyptic imagery, but to concretize, both historically and geographically, the reality of these scriptural teachings, in concert with a broader projection of salvation.

According to the Vienna recension of Ibn Khurradādhbih's geography, the expedition moves from this isolated community of Muslims to a series of closely situated fortifications, each one to two *farsakhs* from the other. Here is located a large fortified city that lies a distance of three days journey from the wall. Sallām names this city, which has gates with iron doors, mills, and cultivated fields, though the vocalization of this name, as represented in the manuscript, remains unclear.[25] The parameter, at ten *farsakh*s, or roughly sixty kilometers,[26] makes the city enormous; the description suggests colossal dimensions.[27] Sallām explains that here Dhū 'l-Qarnayn set up camp when he came to build the wall. The precision of the description and measurement do not belie the wondrous world surrounding the fortifications.

The Vienna manuscript situates the barrier as the last and most spectacular in a list of marvelous buildings around the world. The genre of writing about man-made marvels has a long pedigree; the idea of a canon of seven man-made wonders of the world was itself a popular conceit in classical antiquity.[28] The rampart crowns Ibn Khurradādhbih's list of amazing architectural achievements, which include the pyramids of Giza, the ruins of Palmyra, and the pavilion at Ctesiphon.[29] The story of Sallām's expedition, however, takes up the largest portion of this section, such that all of these great structures collapse under the weight of the rampart.

While maintaining the greater significance of the edifice, Sallām delves into an architectural description of the wall that draws upon an established discourse of measuring buildings. Through his description, Sallām builds with pictorial vividness (*evidentia* / *ἐνάργεια*) an image to be imprinted on the mind's eye—*ut pictura poesis*, 'as is painting so is poetry'—inflected through an ekphrastic register to capture in language a mimetic representation.[30] This act of observation and description is presented as a form of empirical and evidentiary knowledge, such that readers are able to imagine themselves beholding the wall (*mirabile visu* / *θαῦμα ἰδέσθαι*). Sallām renders the dimensions of the rampart into linguistic form with the same scientific rigor that characterizes the entire narrative, itself predicated on the value of individual ocular proof (*ʿiyān*) as an epistemic modality for fathoming the frontiers of the world.[31] Idrīsī's recension of the adventure explicitly mentions that Sallām took descriptive notes (*ṣifāt*) while standing before the wall, and these were used in the redaction of the adventure submitted to the caliph.[32] Al-Wāthiq's command to survey, inspect, and observe (*muʿāyana*) the wall is part of a process of controlling and regulating, under the watchful authority of the caliphal eye, the anxieties about the apocalypse associated with frontiers and the limits of knowledge.

Sallām describes how Dhū ʿl-Qarnayn dug the foundation thirty cubits into the ground, which he filled with iron (*ḥadīd*) and copper (*nuḥās*) until it reached the surface of the earth. Then Dhū ʿl-Qarnayn set up two doorposts framing the mountain sides that stretched above the pass. This description echoes the Qurʾānic account:

ثُمَّ أَتْبَعَ سَبَبًا ﴿٩٢﴾ حَتَّىٰٓ إِذَا بَلَغَ بَيْنَ ٱلسَّدَّيْنِ وَجَدَ مِن دُونِهِمَا قَوْمًا لَّا
يَكَادُونَ يَفْقَهُونَ قَوْلًا ﴿٩٣﴾ قَالُوا۟ يَٰذَا ٱلْقَرْنَيْنِ إِنَّ يَأْجُوجَ وَمَأْجُوجَ
مُفْسِدُونَ فِى ٱلْأَرْضِ فَهَلْ نَجْعَلُ لَكَ خَرْجًا عَلَىٰٓ أَن تَجْعَلَ بَيْنَنَا وَبَيْنَهُمْ
سَدًّا ﴿٩٤﴾ قَالَ مَا مَكَّنِّى فِيهِ رَبِّى خَيْرٌ فَأَعِينُونِى بِقُوَّةٍ أَجْعَلْ بَيْنَكُمْ
وَبَيْنَهُمْ رَدْمًا ﴿٩٥﴾ ءَاتُونِى زُبَرَ ٱلْحَدِيدِ ۖ حَتَّىٰٓ إِذَا سَاوَىٰ بَيْنَ ٱلصَّدَفَيْنِ
قَالَ ٱنفُخُوا۟ ۖ حَتَّىٰٓ إِذَا جَعَلَهُۥ نَارًا قَالَ ءَاتُونِىٓ أُفْرِغْ عَلَيْهِ قِطْرًا ﴿٩٦﴾ فَمَا
ٱسْطَٰعُوٓا۟ أَن يَظْهَرُوهُ وَمَا ٱسْتَطَٰعُوا۟ لَهُۥ نَقْبًا ﴿٩٧﴾

> Then [Dhū ʿl-Qarnayn] followed a path until he reached two mountains, and found at their base a people who could hardly understand a word. They said, "O! Dhū ʿl-Qarnayn, behold Gog and Magog are destroying the land! Could we pay tribute to you on the condition that you erect between us and them a barrier?" He said, "That which my Lord has granted me is better [than your tribute]. But do help me by [your] strength, I will erect between you and between them a rampart. Bring me pieces of iron." Then, when he made level the pass with the two cliffs, he said, "Blow!" Then, when he had made it a fire, he said, "Bring me molten copper that I will pour on this." So then [Gog and Magog] were unable to surmount it, nor could they pierce it. (Q. 18:92–7)

Sallām situates his testimony in dialogue with this scriptural tradition, affirming that the rampart that he presents corresponds to the description immortalized in the Qurʾān.

Sallām's account catalogs the dimensions of the gate: an iron lintel (*darwand*) one hundred and twenty cubits long, and doorposts (*ʿiḍādān*) fifty cubits high and twenty-five cubits wide, framing a locked paneled gate, through which no wind can pass. Both the doorposts and the lintel stretch out from the wall for a distance of ten cubits, like a barbican at the entrance to a fortress. Above the lintel extends the wall, flanking the skirt of the mountain pass, rising higher than sixty cubits, farther than the eye can see.

Lining the rampart stretches a crenelated parapet of thirty-seven iron battlements or merlons (*shurfa*, pl. *shuraf*), five cubits high and four cubits long. The top of each merlon is armed with two angled points (*qurnatān*) that face each other, a detail that appears to echo the two horns in Dhū 'l-Qarnayn's name.[33] Each of the two door panels (*miṣrāʿān*) is fifty cubits wide, sixty cubits high, and five cubits thick. The two panels hang on thick vertical pivot bars set into the sides of the lintel.

Sallām turns from the expansive reach of the rampart to the fine details that compose each element of the structure. Narrowing down to the infinitesimal, he focuses his attention on a description of the key to the gate:

> On the lock is attached a key, which is a cubit and a half long; it has twelve teeth (*dandānka*), each tooth is in the form of a pestle used in mortars (*dastaj al-hawāwīn*). The key's circumference is four hand spans; it is connected to a chain welded to the gate, which is eight cubits long and four fingers thick in circumference. Each ring on the chain is like the ring of a ballista (*manjanīq*).[34]

The description moves from the looming structure down to the bolt of the lock and the key for the bolt, and the teeth on the key. With the description of the twelve teeth on the key, the passage suggests that each element in the variegated material world of existence can be rendered into language.

The display of such empirical measurements forms part of a broader discourse in descriptive geography, in which descriptions of wondrous buildings take on a generic quality, defined by certain tacit conventions. Accounts of architectural formations fit within a cosmographic framework as articulations of civilization and demarcations of territory. The astrologer Abū Maʿshar includes in his astrological history, the *Kitāb al-ulūf* [The book of the thousands], a section on temples and monumental structures (*al-hayākil wa 'l-bunyān al-ʿaẓīm*) erected over the ages.[35] Though only fragments of this study survive, we may gather from the many quotations made by later authors that it enjoyed a fair amount of popularity. Demonstrating the importance of this genre, Masʿūdī dedicates an entire chapter of his encyclopedia to the great buildings and temples of various nations. He mentions that many authors over the course of history have written on the subject of the marvelous buildings and the wonders of the world, for which he says the wall built by Dhū 'l-Qarnayn stands as an emblem.[36]

This ekphrastic attention to producing, through language, an image in the mind's eye was an object of literary inquiry. In the discourse of Arabic poetics and rhetoric a technical vocabulary developed to discuss literary techniques and tropes, theorizing the descriptive power of language. The literary critic Abū Hilāl al-ʿAskarī (fl. 395/1005), in his study on poetry and prose, *Kitāb al-ṣināʿatayn* [Book of the two arts], posits that the best description (*waṣf*) "is that which consists of the most signifying elements (*maʿānī*) of the object described, to such a point that it is as though the description represents before you an image of the object, so that you see it as if it were before your very eyes."[37]

This notion of the visual quality of descriptive language has a long genealogy. The philosopher Fārābī, in his general commentary on Aristotle's *Poetics*, draws an explicit parallel between the art of poetry and the art of painting, for though the two may differ in the media used, both arts produce a likeness (*tashbīh*) with the aim of "impressing imitations (*muḥākayāt*) on peoples' imaginations and senses."[38] Fārābī presents the notion that mimetic qualities of language parallel other representational arts; a view expressed in Abū Bishr Mattā's Arabic translation of the *Poetics*.[39] Despite the various peccadilloes in Abū Bishr Mattā's redaction, such a line of argumentation comes across clearly as he follows Aristotle, paralleling imitations produced by sound and speech with those of color and form.

In addition to the concept of vivid description (*waṣf*), the category of *bayān*—clarity, exposition, elucidation, manifestation—is another site for the configuration of visuality in language. The variegated notions of *bayān* are interconnected to the self-image of the Qurʾān as a linguistic articulation; *bayān* is deployed as a synonym for the Qurʾān, as is the word *mubīn*, from the same root, signifying that which makes manifest. A motif repeated numerous times in the Qurʾān is the revelatory power of signs:

كَذَٰلِكَ يُبَيِّنُ ٱللَّهُ لَكُمۡ ءَايَٰتِهِۦ لَعَلَّكُمۡ تَعۡقِلُونَ ٢٤٢

Thus God makes manifest His signs so that you may understand. (Q. 2:242)

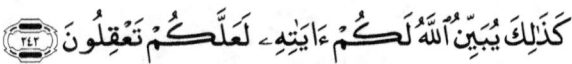

The notion that God created man and then taught him *bayān* (Q. 55:2–3), a term that may be rendered as utterance, speech, or even reason, in the sense of *logos*, adds a further dimension to the visual and linguistic elements implicit to this concept, echoing the scene in Q. 2:31, in which God creates Adam and then teaches him all the names (*ʿallama Ādama ʾl-asmāʾa kullahā*).

The revelatory power of communication is woven into the development of philosophical exploration on the nature of language. Jāḥiẓ writes that meanings residing in the hearts of humans, imagined in their minds, are veiled and hidden, and only come to life when they are mentioned and spoken to others. For him, this act of communication is *bayān*, the signification that makes a hidden meaning manifest, clearly, and unequivocally.[40] Jāḥiẓ equates clear expression (*bayān*) with sight, and inarticulateness with blindness, just as knowledge (*ʿilm*) is sight and ignorance is blindness, a notion that underscores the visual element tied to knowledge and the concepts of *bayān* and *faṣāḥa* (eloquence); for to be eloquent is to be intelligible and clear in speech (*faṣīḥ*).[41]

Jāḥiẓ describes how signs (*dalālāt*), producing meanings, are expressed either through words or through non-linguistic elements, as the act of signification can be effected through gesture and sound, in addition to the written word and visual representation. These acts all possess the potential to communicate meaning. Jāḥiẓ punctuates this point with a quote by the Persian administrator of the caliphal library, Sahl b. Hārūn (d. 215/830), who states that *bayān*, here communication, or elucidation, is the interpreter of knowledge (*al-bayānu tarjumānu ʾl-ʿilm*).[42]

Sallām's description not only presents an image of the wall, translating material existence through the illusory quality of sight into language, but it also engages in a long tradition of imagining the physical dimensions of this particular marvelous edifice. The expedition to the rampart, from its very outset, is in dialogue with a set of expectations and conventions. As Sallām opens before our eyes an image of the barrier, he translates into Arabic the very patterns used over centuries to describe the physical reality of the wall, producing what appears to be an architecturally coherent structure.[43]

Even More Walls

The striking parallels between Sallām's adventure and the Syriac tradition of casting the wall against Gog and Magog—drawn in part from, and elaborated significantly on, the Greek Pseudo-Callisthenes cycle—suggest that Sallām forms his narrative around certain generic expectations. Of particular interest is an apocalyptic homily (*mēmrā*) on the adventures of

Alexander, ascribed to the bishop Jacob of Sarug (d. 521 C.E.), but likely composed around 630 C.E.[44] This sermon in verse, which details Alexander's quest for the eternal waters of life and the barrier he constructs against Gog and Magog, fits into a corpus of apocalyptic Syriac literature from the seventh century that focuses on the heroic life of Alexander. The description of the barrier follows an ekphrastic paradigm of imagining the wall:

ܥܒܕ ܐܣܟܘܦܬܐ ܠܟܠ ܡܢ ܬܪܥܐ ܠܟܠܗ ܫܘܩܐ
ܥܒܕ ܫܬ ܦܬܘܗ ܐܦ ܪܘܡܗ ܫܬ ܒܐܘܡܢܘܬܐ
ܢܚܫܐ ܘܦܪܙܠܐ ܥܒܕܐ ܬܡܝܗܐ ܕܠܝܬ ܐܝܟܘܬܗ

. . .

ܐܢܥܨ ܡܘ̈ܟܠܐ ܒܟܠ ܐܣܟܘܦܬܐ ܘܒܟܠ ܬܪܥܐ
ܘܪܨܦ ܐܢܘܢ ܕܠܐ ܐܢܫ ܝܕܥ ܕܘ̈ܟܝܬܗܘܢ
ܒܟܠ ܐܣܟܘܦܬܐ ܒܐܦ̈ܝ ܪܘܚܐ ܠܒܪ ܡܢ ܬܪܥܐ
ܩܝ̈ܡܐ ܕܚܝܠܐ ܢܚܫܐ ܘܦܪܙܠܐ ܥܒܕ ܗܘܐ ܡܠܟܐ

[Alexander] made a lintel (*eskuppṯā*) over the gate (*tarʿā*)
for the entire pass (*shūqā*),
He made it skillfully six [cubits] wide and also six [cubits] high
of copper (*nḥāshā*) and iron (*parzlā*),
a marvelous construction (*ʿḇāḏā tmīhā*) beyond compare.

. . .

He drove bolts (*muḵlē*) into the lintel and into the gate,
and fortified them such that no one knew where their junctions were.
For the entire lintel, over the gate against the wind,
The king made formidable posts (*qāymē*) of copper and iron.[45]

The lintel, the iron and copper, the wind blocked out, the exacting precision of the measurements, all speak to the established *topoi* against which Sallām positions his own narrative. Other elements beyond the wall suggest parallels between Sallām's tale and the details of the Syriac homily. The distant land and the mountainous surroundings are echoed in both narratives, as is the region of noxious odor adjacent to the lands of Gog and Magog. In the Syriac poem this is a great fetid sea (*yammā saryā*) producing the deadliest smells, which is itself a reference to the surrounding ocean (*ūqiyanōs* / Ὠκεανός).[46] How a putrid sea and the land of darkness, scenes central to this *mēmrā* ascribed to Jacob of Sarug, are transformed in Sallām's account into a black putrid land, is likely the product of textual residue, which is both lost and gained through the various stages of transmission and adaptation.

While the physical dimensions change with each telling, the convention of projecting in language such precise details remains a fixed trope. This is certainly the case with what is considered to be a slightly earlier Syriac version, the *Neṣḥānā d'Aleksandrōs* [The triumph of Alexander], which was most likely produced in Mesopotamia and formed part of pro-Byzantine propaganda under the reign of Heraclius (r. 610–41 C.E.).[47] This text emplots the ancient hero within an explicitly Christian framework. The *Neṣḥānā* depicts Alexander traveling through the north to build a wall against the Huns, whose leaders are named Gog and Magog.[48] The association with the Huns illustrates how Syriac accounts consistently locate the barrier in the frontiers of the north (*sawpay garbyā*),[49] an identification set to echo the Biblical prophecy of Jeremiah that predicts how disaster will issue forth across the land from the north (Jer. 1:14).[50]

The *Neṣḥānā* treats the dimensions of this northern wall with precision, picturing with detailed measurements the physical space of the edifice. Of particular interest is the treatment of the way Alexander built the gate:

> ܘܩܒܥ ܠܬܪܥܐ ܘܠܡܘܟ̈ܠܐ. ܘܐܪܡܝ ܣܟ̈ܐ ܕܦܪܙܠܐ ܘܪܦܣ
> ܐܢܝܢ ܚܕܐ ܒܚܕܐ. ܕܐܢ ܐܬܝܢ ܗܘ̈ܢܝܐ ܘܚܦܪܝܢ ܫܘܥܐ
> ܕܠܬܚܬ ܡܢ ܐܣܩܘܦܬܐ ܕܦܪܙܠܐ. ܐܢ ܓܒܪ̈ܐ ܪ̈ܓܠܝܐ
> ܥܒܪܝܢ. ܣܘܣܝܐ ܕܪܟܝܒ ܠܐ ܡܫܟܚ ܕܢܥܒܪ. ܟܡܐ ܕܬܪܥܐ
> ܕܪܦܝܣ ܒܡܘܟ̈ܠܐ ܩܐܡ. ܘܐܝܬܝ ܘܢܩܒ ܐܣܩܘܦܬܐ
> ܬܚܝܬܝܐ ܘܨܝܪܬܐ ܠܬܪܥܐ. ܘܥܒܕܐ ܒܗܝܢ ܡܘܟ̈ܠܐ
> ܕܦܪܙܠܐ... ܘܐܝܬܝܘ ܘܠܒܟܘ ܒܢ̈ܝܐ ܦܪܙܠܐ ܘܢܚܫܐ ܘܥܒܕܗ
> ܠܬܪܥܐ ܘܠܡܟܬܒܐ ܚܕ ܒܚܕ ܐܝܟ ܒܢ̈ܝܐ ܗܟܢܐ ܕܒܢܝܢ
> ܠܫܘܪܐ. ܘܒܢܐ ܫܟܬܐ ܕܦܪܙܠܐ ܒܢ̈ܚܫܬܐ. ܘܢܩܒ ܘܠܒܫܐ
> ܕܦܪܙܠܐ ܕܐܬܪܟܣܪܐ ܒ̈ܢܚܫܬܐ. ܘܐܪܒܥ ܠܒܘܗܝ ܒ̈ܠܘܬܐ
> ܕܢܚܫܐ.

He fixed the gate and the bolts, and he placed nails of iron and beat them down one by one, so that if the Huns came and dug out the rock which was under the lintel (*eskuppṯā*) of iron, even if footmen were able to pass through, a horse with its rider would be unable to, so long as the gate stood hammered down with bolts (*mukḇlē*). And

> he brought and hammered down a lower lintel and hinge for the gate, and he cast on it bolts of iron, and made it swing round one side... And the men brought and kneaded iron and copper and covered with it the gate and its posts one by one, like one molding clay. And he made a bar (*sekkṯā*) of iron teeth with grooves, and hammered out an iron key (*qlīḏā*) which had twelve grooves (*shnānāṯā*), and he attached onto the gate locks (*ʿalqāṯā*) made of copper.[51]

Alexander is depicted as the master builder, as he erects the barrier against barbarous tribes linked to the Huns. The strong parallels between this description of the wall and the Qurʾānic account of the adventure of Dhū ʾl-Qarnayn have, since the nineteenth century, drawn considerable scholarly attention.[52] In the *Neṣḥānā*, as with the homily attributed to Jacob of Sarug, the wall built to stave off the hordes of savages from the north has an explicit eschatological message framed through a Christian vision of the apocalypse. Already with the Qurʾānic episode, the overtly Christian theological significance of Alexander's wall is entirely missing, suggesting multivalency in the staging of the account throughout the sectarian milieu of the seventh century.[53]

In addition to the vivid description of the wall with its foundation, the threshold, and the hinges for the gate, there exists another striking parallel between the *Neṣḥānā* and Sallām's account, namely the detail of the key (*qlīḏā*). In this Syriac projection of the apocalypse, the figure of the twelve grooves (*shnānāṯā*) to the key that unlocks the door resonates as part of a broader numerical Christian symbolism. While this stratum of signification is absent, the detail of the twelve teeth remains firmly tied to Sallām's version of the wall.

As is the nature of such tales, the wide dissemination of the Alexander cycle, reconfigured in a dizzying range of linguistic and cultural avatars, impedes a clear delineation of transmission. It would be tempting to argue that Sallām's account is drawn directly from the Christian Syriac tradition; that, for instance, he came in contact with a Syriac-speaking Christian who could have informed him of the shape of the wall. Several notable Christians and Christian converts were active participants in ʿAbbāsid administration and cultural life.[54] Likewise, the ʿAbbāsid court was enriched by translators, such as the Christian scholar Ḥunayn, suggesting the broader fecundity of transmission and dissemination across religious and cultural boundaries. Yet these lines of argumentation that seek to establish origins often only obfuscate a historical record that was neither linear nor reductive, but polyvalent and multidimensional. Rather than a direct line of influence, it seems more probable that the account of the wall and its key of twelve teeth was already part of the broader absorption of the legend, shaped both orally and textually.

That said, the Syriac expansion of the Alexander cycle had a tremendous influence on framing the reception of Alexander throughout late antiquity. For instance, a North African Arabic account of the life of Dhū 'l-Qarnayn also prominently features twelve teeth, and follows quite closely the description of the wall presented in the *Neṣḥ̣ānā*.[55] Likewise the *Sīrat al-Iskandar* [The life of Alexander] cluster of Arabic manuscripts, which dates from the sixteenth and seventeenth centuries but appears to draw upon more archaic Arabic material, describes the same key with twelve teeth. Based on the vocabulary and imagery used, these later Arabic tellings of Dhū 'l-Qarnayn appear not to be directly under Sallām's sphere of influence.[56] This later cluster and Sallām's account engage with the Alexander cycle at very distinct points of entry, shaped by distinct cultural and linguistic fields.

Sallām's choice of language to describe the wall speaks to a circuitous path through various layers of translation. His repeated use of Persian words to outline the architectural dimensions suggests another venue for the transmission of such details as the lintel (*darwand*) of the gate and the teeth (*dandānka*) of the key, which he likens to pestles of mortars (*dastaj al-hawāwīn*). The Arabic tradition of the Pseudo-Callisthenes cycle as it survives for us today, unlike Sallām's narrative, is devoid of such Persianate flourishes.

In contrast to the Syriac and Arabic tellings, Sallām, as an eyewitness, places the focus of his narrative onto his own perspective. All around him lie signs that speak to the past age of Dhū 'l-Qarnayn. Sallām describes the traces that remain of the epic project, indicating an area dug out of the mountain in which the gates were cast, along with the location where cauldrons were used to mix the copper, and where the lead and copper were poured out. On each cauldron were handles on which hung chains with prongs. Referencing the traces left behind, Sallām brings to light a textual universe rich in detail, fully conversant with what it would mean to actually build such a monumental structure:

> Near the gate are two fortifications, each one with a perimeter of two hundred cubits by one hundred cubits. By the gate of these two fortifications are two trees. Between the fortifications is a fountain with drinking water. Located in one of these fortifications are the construction tools with which the barrier was built, including iron cauldrons and iron mixing rods. On each trivet (*dīgdān*, Persian)

are four cauldrons, similar to cauldrons for making soap. Here the remaining iron bricks have all clumped together with rust.[57]

The artistry of erecting the edifice, so central to the Syriac tradition, figures as a sign of the miraculous feat.

The residue of Persian lexical items recurrent in Sallām's account suggests several issues. Foremost, we have seen the role of Persian bureaucrats and men of letters in shaping the contours of ʿAbbāsid literary society. This is the case with Ibn Khurradādhbih's *Masālik*, which frames Sallām's tale through a geographical narrative intercalated with stories of ancient Persian kings. The extent to which Ibn Khurradādhbih himself had a hand in the redaction of Sallām's account, when weaving this narrative into the larger fabric of his geography, remains unseen. We could, however, imagine a Middle Persian intermediary to the Syriac tradition, from which Sallām might have drawn so many of his striking parallels. Though we may find a certain amount of satisfaction positing that Sallām's unique choice of vocabulary originates from some earlier Persian tradition, the extent to which the exploits of Alexander were developed in Middle Persian remains a matter of some debate.[58]

Possible support for such a formulation is offered in Ibn al-Jawzī's (d. 597/1200) universal history, in which he draws his description of the adventure from Muḥammad b. ʿUbayd Allāh b. al-Munādī (d. 333/944), a religious scholar from Baghdad who specialized in the study of the Qurʾān and had an interest in apocalyptic writings and the history of Persian kings.[59] According to Ibn al-Munādī, the Persians (al-Furs) were in possession of writings that they had inherited (*kutub mawrūtha*) concerning the wall built by Alexander. These writings described the process of constructing the barrier and gave an account of its physical appearance, detailing how groups of four cauldrons (*qudūr*) of iron were hung on trivets (*dīgdān*); these were used by Alexander to forge the bricks for the wall.[60] The entire edifice, including the door panels, the lock and the key, was measured in greater cubits (*al-dhirāʿ al-aʿẓam*). Ibn al-Munādī concludes his description of the Persian account with the full narrative of Sallām's adventure, which he had received via Ibn Khurradādhbih.[61]

The similarities between the purportedly ancient Persian record of the wall related by Ibn al-Munādī and Sallām's description are striking. According to Ibn al-Munādī this ancient account included such elements as the stinking black land, the door panels, the key, the Persian word for trivet (*dīgdān*), and even the number of cauldrons on each trivet. These details, ascribed to ancient Persians, are deployed as a confirmation of Sallām's narrative, just as Sallām's eyewitness testimony offers ocular proof of this earlier Persian tradition. Such tautology makes it difficult to affirm whether or not there existed a Middle Persian or early Arabic version of the Alexander cycle containing such details that would have served as an established intertext for Sallām's adventure. This is very much the suggestion made by Ibn al-Munādī's arrangement; a point that is no less important, as it underscores how Sallām's narrative, from its earliest reception within ʿAbbāsid society, was set to confirm what were seen as ancient Persian accounts of the wall. Such a line of analysis is further supported through the early association of Sallām's adventure with Shahrbarāz's mission to the barrier.

The Syriac versions of the Alexander cycle contain many similar details, lending credence to the notion that Sallām's text was in dialogue with pre-existing material in Arabic and Persian that was evidently shaped by early Syriac sources on Alexander's barrier. In such a formulation it is also possible that the *Neṣḥānā*, most likely produced in Mesopotamia, could have drawn out these details of the wall from a body of oral and textual traditions that also circulated in Middle Persian. While Alexander's conquests of Darius and his destruction of Persepolis represent traumatic events in the arc of Persian history,[62] the Greek hero had long been absorbed into the imagined pantheon of Persian kings. The ʿAbbāsid scholar Abū Ḥanīfa al-Dīnawarī relates that the Persians believed that Alexander was actually the son of the Kayanid king Dārāb, thus giving Alexander a full royal Persian genealogy—an association that continues throughout Persian letters.[63]

Another point of similarity with Ibn al-Munādī's Persian description is the question of the greater cubit, which appears to echo the 'Alexandrian' cubit alluded to in Sallām's account.[64] When giving the dimensions of the wall, Sallām states that he based his calculations on the 'black' cubit (*sūdāʾ*), a standard measurement used during the ʿAbbāsid period; it corresponds to slightly more than half a meter.[65] This added piece of information enables us to reconstruct with precision Sallām's account of the wall's dimensions, thus offering an architectural blueprint in which every detail is accounted for, bringing the magnificence of the design into full relief. The description outlines a massive structure whose dimensions appear to present a coherent picture. It stretches over eighty meters (266 feet) between the mountain pass, rising more than sixty-five meters (213 feet) into the air, with each doorpost extending twenty-seven meters high (87 feet). The key itself is a formidable object at eighty-one centimeters (32 inches).

Inquiring as to whether the locals had ever seen Gog and Magog, Sallām hears that on occasion they had reached the top of the wall only to be helplessly blown back down by a providential black wind. Sallām learns that

Gog and Magog do not measure more than a cubit and a half, underscoring a subhuman alterity. Their minuscule stature stands in stark juxtaposition to the colossal size of the barrier. Eager to uncover the condition of the edifice itself, Sallām asks if the gate has suffered any harm:

> They said, "Nothing has ever occurred except for this crack (*shaqq*)." The crack was the width of a thin thread.
>
> I then replied, "Are you nervous at all about [this crack]?"
>
> They responded, "No. For this gate is five cubits wide using the Alexandrian cubit." This cubit measures a cubit and a half according to the black cubit. Each cubit was the length of Alexander's forearm.
>
> Sallām stated: I drew close and I took out from my leggings a knife and I scraped the spot of the crack, and there broke off a piece the size of half a dirham. So I packed it securely into a cloth in order to show it to al-Wāthiq bi'llāh.[66]

As Sallām peers into this thin fissure, he edges nearer the great frontier of existence, between the ordered world of daily events and the eschatological expanse of the final destruction. As with Shahrbarāz's envoy and Muʿāwiya's mission to the wall, Sallām also takes back with him a testament of his journey, in the form of this small chip of iron, a token from the seemingly impregnable rampart, which, one day, too must fall.

With the passing mention of the conversion of the 'Alexandrian' cubit to the 'black' cubit, the narrative explicitly draws attention to Alexander the Great, the epic hero identified in early Qurʾānic exegetical traditions with the figure of Dhū 'l-Qarnayn. The cubit, fixed to the length of a forearm (*dhirāʿ*), suggests the relativity of measuring, dependent upon the body as the frame of reference. Alexander's arm stands as the rubric for every detail of the structure, which in each corner and turn corresponds to the physical size of the hero, a point also suggested in Ibn al-Munādī's account.

Moving beyond the traditions that fix the building of the wall in some remote moment of history, Sallām stands before a living community of caretakers who man the fortifications. According to the Bodleian recension, a guardian (*raʾīs*) rides in every Friday with a group of knights each bearing an iron mallet (*mirzabba*, Persian) in order to inspect the wall.[67] The choice of Friday, the day of the congregational prayer, further sets this ritualized praxis within a larger religious symbolism. During the day, the guardian strikes the bolt of the gate, once in the morning, once at noon, and again at the start of the afternoon. Each time he strikes the wall, he puts his ear to the gate, listening to Gog and Magog clamor on the other side like a nest of hornets. At sunset, the guardian raps the bolt one last time, in order that Gog and Magog may hear and understand that on the other side there are guards watching over the gate. From this elaborate ritual set to protect humankind, we learn that no damage has befallen the gate, and that though Gog and Magog clamor to escape, they have never been able to damage the wall.

While the Vienna recension relates a similar account, it places the ritual of inspecting the wall on every Monday and Thursday. This falls on the days of the supererogatory fast (*ṣawm al-taṭawwuᶜ*), which, according to a *ḥadīth* of the Prophet, are when human actions are presented to God.[68] Furthermore, the choice of these two days parallels ᶜAbbāsid ceremonial in Sāmarrāʾ, where the caliph held open sessions on Mondays and Thursdays in the great public audience chamber (*dār al-ᶜāmma*). Here the caliph would address visitors and supplicants, make rulings and dispense justice, often in a spectacle of public punishment through a performance meant to echo divine judgment and arbitration.[69] The similarities between the ceremonial practices before the wall and those of the caliphal palace are further highlighted in the Vienna recension, which explicitly likens the inheritance of the post of overseer from generation to generation to the way in which the caliphs inherit the caliphate from each other.

The description of the caretakers who guard over the barrier in ritualized processions suggests not only a military order, but also a religious obligation poised on the precipice of the apocalypse. By commanding the fortifications with key in hand, the guardians manage the inviolate gates. In the Vienna manuscript, the inheritance of the guardianship over the barrier evokes the succession of the caliphate. The ᶜAbbāsid caliphs, through their descent from ᶜAbbās b. ᶜAbd al-Muṭṭalib (d. ca 32/653), the uncle of the Prophet, had special ancestral rights to the guardianship of the sanctuary in Mecca. After the conquest of the city, the Prophet is to have bestowed upon ᶜAbbās custodianship of the *siqāya*, a hereditary right of giving drink to pilgrims.[70] This right itself is connected to the providential dream that led ᶜAbbās' father, ᶜAbd al-Muṭṭalib, in the previous generation, to discover the long hidden Zamzam spring; a discovery which further strengthened ᶜAbbāsid hereditary claims over the sanctuary and the ritual performance of the pilgrimage rite (*ḥajj*).[71]

As the *Masālik* itself highlights, control of the shrines at Mecca and Medina was directly tied to caliphal legitimacy.[72] The importance of Mecca for the early ᶜAbbāsid caliphs is further expressed in the architectural refashioning of the sanctuary complex undertaken by al-Manṣūr and al-Mahdī (r. 158–69/775–85).[73] Al-Wāthiq, too, joined in this symbolic articulation of religious authority with renovations of the sacred mosque (*al-masjid al-ḥarām*) and by rebuilding the *siqāya* enclosure next to the Zamzam well, an edifice connected to ritual libations and symbolically associated with ʿAbbāsid rule.[74] As *ex officio* guardians of the sanctuary, the caliphs appointed the leader of the pilgrimage and the governor of Mecca; many caliphs performed pilgrimages to the sanctuary. The practice of leaving offerings at the Kaʿba, often associated with military conquest and the spread of Islam, is a further feature of ʿAbbāsid ceremonial.[75] Al-Maʾmūn sent rare jewels to adorn the Kaʿba on an annual basis, just as al-Muʿtaṣim gifted a precious lock, highlighting his role as legitimate guardian of the sanctuary.[76] The keys of the Kaʿba themselves became a feature of caliphal investiture.[77]

The connection between the Kaʿba and the wall of Gog and Magog is further expressed in the ekphrastic traditions of measuring the Meccan sanctuary. The mathematical specificity of the barrier's dimensions echoes the descriptions of sacred sites characteristic of Near Eastern temple registers, such as the description of the Jerusalem temple in Ezekiel 40:5–42:20.[78] As with the measurement of the wall, mathematical descriptions of the holy sites of Mecca are a fully developed feature in ʿAbbāsid letters.[79] The sanctuary and the wall represent the arc of Islamic civilization, both are under the guardianship of ʿAbbāsid control and both are connected to the eschatological unfolding of the end of time.[80] Just as Gog and Magog will ultimately destroy Dhū ʿl-Qarnayn's barrier, according to several prophetic *ḥadīth*, so, too, will the Kaʿba be leveled by a foreign army, in a kind of apocalyptic symmetry of portentous destruction.[81] The link between these two structures is accentuated in accounts that circulated in the early ʿAbbāsid period; these describe how Dhū ʿl-Qarnayn, the architect of the ominous barrier, undertook a pilgrimage to the Kaʿba on his course to conquer the world.[82]

Linguistic Cacophony

Sallām's last spectacular act of translation turns to one particular feature of the wall: the inscription in iron, written high above the right doorpost, in what Sallām calls the first language (*biʾl-lisāni ʾl-awwal*). He translates this ancient inscription into Arabic, which corresponds, word for word, to the Qurʾānic verse that concludes the account of the barrier:

فَإِذَا جَآءَ وَعْدُ رَبِّي جَعَلَهُۥ دَكَّآءَ ۖ وَكَانَ وَعْدُ رَبِّي حَقًّا ﴿٩٨﴾

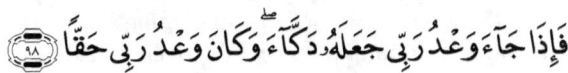

> When the promise of my Lord comes to pass, He will flatten [the rampart], the promise of my Lord is true (18:98).

As with the Qurʾānic episode, prophecy figures centrally in the Syriac traditions of imagining the wall,[83] where Alexander is pictured having left an inscription, predicting the end of the world. A consistent feature in the Arabic treatment of the Alexander cycle is the convention of describing Alexander's prophecy and dating the advent of the world's demise.[84] In the Arabic Romance cycle, Dhū 'l-Qarnayn begins a prophetic speech quoting this very Qurʾānic verse, which concludes the account of the barrier. In turn, Dhū 'l-Qarnayn's words serve as a gloss to the Qurʾānic passage, as the prophecy signifies the final act of the wall's construction, while simultaneously gesturing toward its destruction. This is a widely accepted reading in exegetical circles, where the verse is understood to correspond to what Dhū 'l-Qarnayn proclaimed upon completing the wall.[85] What makes Sallām's account unique is his discovery of Dhū 'l-Qarnayn's words written in the first language, engraved on the wall.

By evoking this original language, the narrative engages with a long tradition of imagining an idyllic time of unity when all humankind spoke in one tongue with perfect, mutual understanding, before the advent of linguistic fragmentation and cacophonous discord. The destruction of the tower of Babel signifies the instance when the one tongue divides into many. While the Qurʾān appears to allude to the account (cf. Q. 16:26), it is greatly expanded upon in the exegetical literature, in large measure through the dissemination of historical narratives drawn from Jewish and Christian sources. God's destruction of the tower of Babel (Gen. 11:1–9), an *aggadic* motif in Rabbinic *midrashim*,[86] signifies for Muslim writers the birth of linguistic multiplicity and the necessity of translation.

Ibn Qutayba, basing himself on the famous transmitter, Wahb b. Munabbih, notes that after Nimrod constructed the tower of Babel, God fragmented the one tongue, which had been spoken by the progeny of Noah, into seventy-two.[87] Ṭabarī, in his Qurʾān commentary, describes the crumbling of the tower's foundations as the point when God sowed discord among humankind, dividing the one original language into many—a mutually incomprehensible babble (*fa-tabalbalat alsunu 'l-nās*).[88] Ṭabarī claims that the city was called Babel because of this etiological link to the verb *tabalbala*.

There was considerable debate concerning the original language or languages of humankind. Agreeing with one commonly held opinion, Masʿūdī states that *suryāniyya*, perhaps something akin to Assyrian, was the first language (*al-lisān al-awwal*), as spoken by Adam and his descendants before the destruction of the tower.[89] We can only speculate about whether Sallām means *suryāniyya* when he describes this inscription written on the wall. What remains clear is that by mentioning the first language of humankind, Sallām evokes an ancient and remote script placed in some primeval landscape, before the unity of language was divided. This foundational articulation of scripture thus attests to the great antiquity of the barrier. As Sallām translates Dhū 'l-Qarnayn's inscription into Arabic, he confirms the Qurʾānic prophecy while affirming the efficacy of translation. For these words, written in this ancient script, represent the very verse that centuries later would be revealed to Muḥammad in Arabic.

The exact nature of the speech (*kalām*) of God was a pressing issue during the time in which Sallām made his journey to the wall. Al-Wāthiq is said to have brutally continued the inquisition (*miḥna*) instating the Muʿtazila doctrine of the createdness of the Qurʾān.[90] The theory of the created Qurʾān held that speech presupposes both articulation and movement, and thus would contradict the divine immutable nature attributed to God. The Muʿtazila argued that the speech of God was, rather, created in the articulations of prophets, and through the pages on which revelation was inscribed. This theory served as the official doctrine of the ʿAbbāsid court during the reigns of al-Maʾmūn, al-Muʿtaṣim, and al-Wāthiq, and was used as a justification to strengthen the power of the caliphate as a source of religious authority.[91] Ṭabarī records a letter ascribed to the caliph al-Maʾmūn, in which he bolstered his case for the establishment of the doctrine. Quoting the Qurʾānic verse, "We have made it an Arabic recitation" (Q. 43:3), al-Maʾmūn argued that everything God has made (*jaʿala*), He has created (*khalaqa*).[92] This argument held the Arabic nature of the Qurʾān to be an indication of its createdness, as it was revealed through the temporal and contingent vehicle of language. Similarly, one could imagine that the prophetic inscription of Dhū 'l-Qarnayn is recorded through the temporal medium of an ancient language. Perhaps, for the theologically minded and for the purposes of state propaganda, Sallām's translation of words written in the first language, which correspond directly to the Qurʾān itself, might have suggested that the revelation was created through a temporal linguistic vehicle. However, the idea that the ʿAbbāsid regime could put to use this dimension of Sallām's story for political or theological ends is questionable, considering how far removed the adventure is from the explicit theological debates concerning the createdness of the Qurʾān. While the eternality of revelation may well not be implicated here, the Qurʾān itself serves as the gravitational center for the entire adventure. Both the Qurʾānic inscription on the barrier and the community of Qurʾān-reciting

Muslim converts before the wall highlight the centrality of scripture in the definition of territory and community.

Irrespective of the implications for language and revelation that this ancient inscription might evoke, Sallām's adventure is consistently framed by a course of concrete pragmatism. The envoy acquires warm clothes, supplies, ready hard cash, diplomatic letters that allow free movement from kingdom to kingdom, guides who serve as go-betweens, and uses standard measurements that account for it all. In his detail of the prophetic inscription, he mentions how this was written in the first language of man, as it would be hard to suggest that Dhū 'l-Qarnayn would have written these words in Arabic, considering the antiquity of the barrier. All these details are in dialogue with the universe of actualization and causality, in which signs are enveloped in an *ordo rerum*, in the semiotics of existence.

Despite this ordered chain of signs and significations, the mention of the first language—evoking the ancient linguistic unity before fragmentation—distances Sallām's narrative from earlier traditions of imagining the wall and from the concomitant anxieties which bespeak its construction. The variance of languages around the world serves as an established convention in the many reenactments. The *Neṣḥānā* foregrounds this anxiety when Alexander inquires about the people of Gog and Magog, "what do they look like (*demwāṯhōn*), what are their tongues (*leshshānayhōn*) and what are their clothes (*lḇūshayhōn*)?"[93]

The Qur'ānic treatment of Dhū 'l-Qarnayn's mission to confine Gog and Magog highlights the issue of communication and linguistic diversity; before reaching the land of these savage tribes, Dhū 'l-Qarnayn faces difficulties in communicating with the people who beseech his help against Gog and Magog:

حَتَّىٰٓ إِذَا بَلَغَ بَيْنَ ٱلسَّدَّيْنِ وَجَدَ مِن دُونِهِمَا قَوْمًا لَّا يَكَادُونَ يَفْقَهُونَ قَوْلًا ﴿٩٣﴾

> Until he reached two mountains, and found at their base a people who could hardly understand a word. (Q. 18:93)[94]

Several exegetes locate a translator (*mutarjim*) at the scene who aids this community in their dialogue with Dhū 'l-Qarnayn, highlighting how central the problem of communication is to the narrative logic of the Qur'ānic passage.[95] The question of comprehending the nations of the world stands as a central motif to the prophetic tales on the life of Dhū 'l-Qarnayn. As outlined in Ibn Hishām's *Kitāb al-tījān*, Wahb b. Munabbih describes how God sent Dhū 'l-Qarnayn around the world to call the various nations to the true faith. To enable this, God gave Dhū 'l-Qarnayn the power to speak in every language of the world.[96] This added dimension is further highlighted in Ṭabarī's transmission of Wahb b. Munabbih's account, which strongly echoes the trope of the reluctant prophet, established in the paradigm of Moses' hesitation when called to undertake his prophetic mission (Exodus 3:11–21; 4:1–14). Addressed directly by God, Dhū 'l-Qarnayn is commanded to convert the unbelieving nations of the world, all of whom speak different languages. When he hears this, he asks how he could possibly complete such a task:

> You have described to me, O Lord!, a great thing. There is no one capable of such an affair but You. So tell me about these nations to whom You have sent me. With what strength am I to overpower them? With what group am I to outnumber them? With what ruse will I plan a stratagem against them? With what endurance will I stand strong against them? With what language will I speak to them, and how will I understand their words, with what ear will I be able to hear their speech?[97]

God replies that He will expand Dhū 'l-Qarnayn's mind to deepen his understanding, "I will stretch out your tongue so that you may utter everything, I will open up your ear so you can hear everything."[98] Granted super-human abilities, with the power of tongues and with light and darkness under his command, Dhū 'l-Qarnayn conquers nations of varying customs and languages with darkness, and then, with light, he calls them to the one true faith. Only Gog and Magog remain beyond his reach.

After the episode of the wall, in Wahb's account, the narrative turns toward a remote, utopian society that knows no crime. This community, we are told, is not in need of judges, upholds the laws of God, and has neither rich nor poor. Dhū 'l-Qarnayn, amazed by these people, asks them a series of questions. The version of Wahb's tale as recorded by Ibn Hishām places this mysterious group of people in India and refers to them as the *tarjumāniyyūn*, the translators. The etiological justification given for their name is that they had translated the revealed scrolls (*ṣuḥuf*) of Abraham into their own language, and they agreed to follow the precepts contained in these works.[99]

There is a striking similarity between this story of the translators of India and the Pseudo-Callisthenes cycle. Both the Greek and Syriac traditions outline a series of philosophical questions and answers between Alexander and the sagacious Brahmans of India (*brāhmaṇa*, *βραχμάνοι*, *brakmānē*).[100] Starting with the Greek redaction, the Brahmans are cast in an idealized light, representing the apogee of wisdom. They walk around naked and are totally disengaged from the material trappings of this world. Wahb's treatment of the Indians and Dhū 'l-Qarnayn directly parallels the Pseudo-Callisthenes episode of Alexander and the Brahmans. Through a process of mistranslation and transposition, the word for Brahman (بَرْهَمَن) was transformed into the word Tarjumān (تَرْجُمان), suggesting primarily a textual line of transmission.[101]

The anxieties over linguistic diversity inflected in the accounts of Dhū 'l-Qarnayn play out metatextually in their own dissemination. As Dhū 'l-Qarnayn crosses the mutually incomprehensible speech of the world, Brahmans transform into translators, and the chain of transmission takes the adventure in often unexpected directions. These continuations transform across time and space, so that centuries later the *tarjumāniyyūn* appear in a version of the life of Dhū 'l-Qarnayn translated into *aljamiado*, i.e., Spanish written in the Arabic script.[102]

Sallām's mention of the primal language sidesteps altogether the linguistic anxieties so palpable in the various narrative approaches to Alexander. Sallām does not need to engage in a past world of linguistic cacophony, for he inhabits one. Just as the narratives that cycle through the adventures of Dhū 'l-Qarnayn accentuate the interrelation between geography and language, so, too, does Sallām move through various linguistic fields to make his way to the promise of the Lord, of the day when the pitched cacophony will stop. The wall signifies the destruction that awaits the nations of the earth and stands as a reminder of the greater promise of everlasting paradise, where such linguistic veils of difference will be dissolved.

Re-entries

From the wall—at the crossroads of scripture and geography—Sallām makes his way back into the world of fixed coordinates. Leaving behind the well-imagined fields of the *terra incognita,* he is led by his guides into the region of Khurāsān, having disappeared off the map somewhere beyond the Caspian Sea. As with the journey through the Caucasus, Sallām gives an outline of his itinerary through Transoxiana (*mā warāʾ al-nahr*). It is of note that many details of his return journey are not included in the Bodleian manuscript,[103] or the later reception history as preserved in the successive Arabic and Persian recensions of the adventure,[104] which give a streamlined account of Sallām's re-entry into the orbit of ʿAbbāsid dominion. According to the Bodleian version, guides lead the exhibition back to the region of Khurāsān until reaching Samarqand. They stay with the famous ʿAbbāsid governor of Khurāsān, ʿAbd Allāh b. Ṭāhir (d. 230/844), before returning to the caliphal capital of Sāmarrāʾ.

While the Vienna recension gives much more detail, it also raises several problems. Foremost, parts of the sections in question are illegible in the manuscript, which has been emended in the process of its medieval restoration.[105] Based on this account, the party first make their way to a ruler (*malik*), who appears to be named al-Lub, al-Labb, or some variant thereof. Then they set off toward another ruler, whose name is partly illegible and left without vowel or consonant markers. De Goeje, in his edition, offers Tabānūyan as a reading, however, this is conjecture, as the name is unknown to other sources.[106] The expedition remained several days with this ruler, who is said to have served as the head tax collector of the region (*ṣāḥib al-kharāj*). Eight months after leaving the wall, they finally reach Samarqand, whereupon they head to the city of Isbījāb and then cross the Oxus River at Balkh, then onto Ushrūsana, followed by Bukhārā, Tirmidh, and then finally Nīsābūr (map 3).

Though the names of these two rulers remain obscure, the toponyms mentioned correspond perfectly with the region described; all are well-known place names appearing in Arabic and Persian geographies. Yet, the itinerary appears to be quite erratic, as it requires the expedition to crisscross back and forth several times: from Samarqand they return to Isbījāb, from Balkh they backtrack to Ushrūsana at the western borders of Samarqand, only to cross back past Samarqand, to Bukhārā. From Bukhārā they return, back in the direction of Balkh, in order to reach Tirmidh.

As in Sallām's itinerary through the Caucasus, the trajectory through Transoxiana is confused and suggests, rather than an actual journey, a list of famous toponyms mixed together. Sallām identifies this region as part of the administrative rule of Khurāsān, the northeastern province of the ʿAbbāsid empire. No reason is given for the erratic trajectory, nor is any suggestion made, such as we had in the Caucasus, that Sallām was directed from one ruler to the next, which could perhaps explain the several backward steps on the way home.

Even a textual error in the transmission of the narrative would not readily explain the movement of the expedition across the region.[107] As with his journey through the Caucasus, we could speculate as to what led Sallām down this particular path. Or we could assign the inconsistencies in the

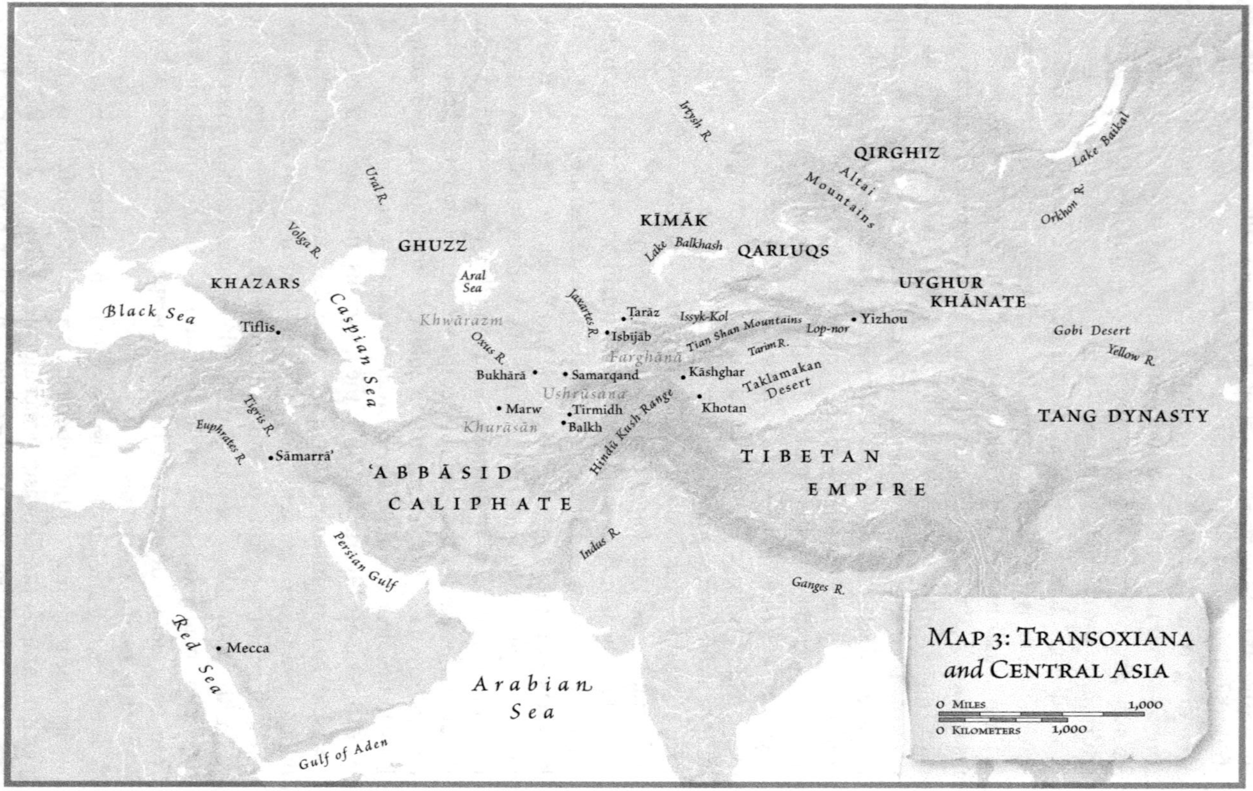
Map 3: Transoxiana and Central Asia
0 Miles 1,000
0 Kilometers 1,000
QIRGHIZ
Lake Baikal
Orkhon R.
Altai Mountains
Irtysh R.
Ural R.
Volga R.
KĪMĀK
Lake Balkhash
QARLUQS
GHUZZ
Aral Sea
KHAZARS
Black Sea
Caspian Sea
Tiflīs
Khwārazm
Jaxartes R.
Tarāz
Isbījāb
Issyk-Kol
Tian Shan Mountains
Lop-nor
Yizhou
UYGHUR KHĀNATE
Gobi Desert
Yellow R.
Oxus R.
Farghānā
Tarim R.
Bukhārā
Samarqand
Kāshghar
Taklamakan Desert
Ushrūsana
Marw
Tirmidh
Khotan
Khurāsān
Balkh
Hindū Kush Range
TANG DYNASTY
Tigris R.
Euphrates R.
Sāmarrā'
'ABBĀSID CALIPHATE
TIBETAN EMPIRE
Indus R.
Persian Gulf
Ganges R.
Red Sea
Mecca
Arabian Sea
Gulf of Aden

order of the toponyms to a broader issue, namely that both Transoxiana and the Caucasus were remote regions at the edge of ʿAbbāsid territory, and that it was enough for Sallām to mention a list of well-known place names for his tale to engage with established geographical discourse. It is also of note that there circulated within ʿAbbāsid letters an account of how Alexander traveled through Transoxiana and Khurāsān after having built the wall against Gog and Magog.[108] Sallām's itinerary upon returning from the barrier thus could, itself, be meant to evoke Alexander's travels through Central Asia.

The question of Sallām's re-entry into the domain of the ʿAbbāsid empire is complicated by a further recension of his itinerary as preserved by Idrīsī, which he explicitly states is based upon the account as preserved by Ibn Khurradādhbih and the no longer extant redaction of the adventure by the Sāmānid *wazīr* Jayhānī.[109] According to this itinerary, after leaving the wall, Sallām traveled through Barskhān and Ṭarāz,[110] territory of the Qarluq Turks, a confederation of western Turkish groups who lived across the Central Asian steppe, between Lake Balkhash and Lake Issyk-Kol, in the Seven Rivers region of modern-day Kazakhstan and Kyrgyzstan.[111] Based on this recension, Sallām traveled on from Ṭarāz to Samarqand. According to Idrīsī, the region located north beyond the Qarluq Turks was laid to waste by Gog and Magog before Alexander had erected the wall. Idrīsī admits, however, drawing from the direct experience of a Turkish informant, that during his own day these lands, once destroyed, had been re-inhabited.[112]

Idrīsī's recension would thus situate the wall beyond the Qarluq, bordering the Adhkish Turks, who appear to have been located in the region of the Altai Mountains of Mongolia.[113] Yet, even this itinerary, which Idrīsī plots through the toponyms of his world map, leaves much ambiguity in terms of exactly where Sallām entered into the Qarluq territory.[114] It is noteworthy that Idrīsī's trajectory most explicitly engages with the heartland of what was the Uyghur Khanate (744–840 C.E.) in the Orkhon Valley of Mongolia, which had been the seat of an imperial power until it was overrun in 840 C.E. by Qirghiz Turks.[115] The Uyghurs, known to Arabic and Persian sources of the period as the Tughuzghuz, represented a powerful imperial force beyond the ʿAbbāsid frontiers.[116] The collapse of the Uyghur Khanate precipitated a significant shift in the geopolitics of the day. It could well be the case that al-Wāthiq's dream in 227/842 of Gog and Magog, long identified with Turks, offers an eschatological projection of the political disturbances in the Central Asian steppe.

While the three major variants, expressed in the Bodleian and Vienna manuscripts and Idrīsī's account of the adventure, detail radically different trajectories for Sallām's re-entry into the ʿAbbāsid empire, they all follow him through the region of Transoxiana and Khurāsān. Sallām journeys past the Caspian on his outward journey to return on the eastern side of the Aral Sea. Traveling through Transoxiana, the adventure skirts along the northeastern frontier of ʿAbbāsid dominion, through regions that were very much present in the ʿAbbāsid political imagination. It is in Samarqand that al-Wāthiq's father, al-Muʿtaṣim, had begun acquiring the Turkish slaves who later came to serve an important function in the military composition of the caliphal capital of Sāmarrāʾ.[117]

During this period, the caliphate in Sāmarrāʾ was politically intertwined with the region in the form of the Sogdian and Turkish guard, who played a central role in governing and protecting the empire.[118] The established trade routes of goods and slaves from the Central Asian steppe into the ʿAbbāsid heartland was facilitated by economic networks of Sogdian merchants whose itineraries, centuries old, stretched across Central Asia and the western frontiers of China.[119] However obliquely, all three of the major recensions suggest historical interconnections between the ʿAbbāsids and the lands beyond Transoxiana, suggesting, but never fully delineating, a broader political and economic backdrop to the adventure.

Even more pressing to the historical reality is Sallām's mention of the casualties suffered over the course of the journey. While traveling to the rampart, twenty-two men perished, all of whom were buried along the way. On the return from the wall, another fourteen died, leaving Sallām, from the original group of fifty who began the expedition, with only fourteen. We learn also that of the two hundred mules that started the expedition only twenty-three survived. The difficulties of traveling such long distances over challenging terrain comes to the fore in this passing mention that the majority of the expedition perished. The journey is framed as a religious mission across a sacred geography, a point suggested with the mention that all the men who died were buried in their clothes. This is a direct reference to the practice of burying martyrs in the garments they wore when they died, to serve as proof on the Day of Judgment of their martyrdom.[120]

Bringing the narrative ever closer to the historical contingencies of the period, Sallām details how they reached ʿAbd Allāh b. Ṭāhir, governor of Khurāsān. Just as the historical figure of Ashinās, the Turkish general in al-Wāthiq's retinue, frames the opening of the tale, so, too, does ʿAbd Allāh b. Ṭāhir signify a full return to the established world of ʿAbbāsid politics. Poet, statesman, and forefather of the Ṭāhirid dynasty of Khurāsān, ʿAbd Allāh b. Ṭāhir is a famous figure in the political history of the ʿAbbāsid state. We are told that he granted everyone in the expedition a lofty sum, for which Sallām gives an exacting account.

This reference helps situate the narrative in historical space, for Sallām must have met with ʿAbd Allāh b. Ṭāhir before he died on 11 Rabīʿ al-Awwal 230/26 November 844.[121] Sallām explains that, from the time he left Sāmarrāʾ to the day he returned, over twenty-eight months had passed—sixteen months to reach the wall, twelve months and some days to return. This permits us a *terminus post quem* for the start of the expedition as having occurred during the first nine months of al-Wāthiq's reign, between Rabīʿ al-Awwal and Dhū 'l-Qaʿda of 227 / January and August of 842.

The details that frame the narrative, the dates recorded, the historical figures met, the places crossed, the sums of money given, the provisions made, the numerous deaths along the way, are all in dialogue with an external world that is used to support the veracity of the expedition. Just as Sallām's description of the rampart engages with this enveloping discourse, so, too, the framing elements that lead toward and away from the wall, the cities crossed and the people met, suggest a world fully actualized.

The inconsistencies of the irregular routes traveled through the Caucasus and Transoxiana would be hard to detect without a firm understanding of these two regions on the edge of the ʿAbbāsid empire. The variants in the different recensions suggest a real confusion and even disagreement as to where exactly Sallām traveled. However, the details maintained throughout Sallām's adventure appear to bring together a narrative consistent with the pragmatic necessities required by such an undertaking. This is the ultimate aim of the tale, for its value lies in the claim that this expedition not only took place, but that it succeeded in reaching the wall, thereby serving as the ultimate gloss on the Qurʾānic passage. For those who survived its perils, the expedition paid off. At the caliphal reception in Sāmarrāʾ, when al-Wāthiq saw the chip of iron that Sallām had taken from the wall and heard the tale (*qiṣṣa*) of the expedition, he praised God, ordered that alms (*ṣadaqa*) be distributed, and granted all those who returned generous sums of money.[122]

Here the anecdote to the wall ends, as Ibn Khurradādhbih relates that Sallām the Interpreter narrated the account in its entirety directly to him. Sallām confirmed his transmission of the adventure with the formal report (*kitāb*), which he had written outlining the events for al-Wāthiq. The narrative thus has the authority of both oral and textual transmission. This suggests, through the immediacy of presence, that Sallām, in direct contact with Ibn Khurradādhbih, would have had the opportunity to correct any errors or mistakes in the transmission of the report. It is from this account, preserved first in Ibn Khurradādhbih's geography, that later generations of writers have come to imagine al-Wāthiq's mission. Despite these textual guarantees, the question of the truth claims made consistently throughout the narrative surfaces as a major issue for successive generations who seek out the location of the wall.

SECTION THREE

BEYOND THE WALL

6

TO LIVE TO TELL

Storytelling

At the opening of the mission, al-Wāthiq seeks a report (*khabar*) on the condition of the wall. While the word *khabar* has the sense of a factual testimony, it also carries the meaning of a story or anecdote. As a crafted, generic form within the broader sphere of belletristic discourse, there are several common techniques which *khabar*-narratives deploy to convey the impression of factuality, such as direct speech, dialogue, and ekphrastic attention to detail.[1] Idrīsī, for instance, describes Sallām's report as consisting of factual descriptions (*akhbār*) of the journey and the sights seen, as well as an account of the conversations (*khiṭāb*) with people he met along the way.[2] The dramatic character of the report, with its focus on both description and dialogue, speaks to a discrete set of discursive expectations. The framework of the *khabar*-narrative, with its diegetic attention to detail and emphasis on eyewitness authority, offers a window onto the past; it is designed to maintain an intrinsic truth value.[3] However, as a discursive form bound to an established body of literary strategies and conventions, the *khabar*-narrative affirms its own authenticity, while continually flirting with the tension it produces between the factual and the fictional.[4]

According to the Vienna recension, Sallām concludes his adventure by referring to the entire account as a *qiṣṣa*. The respective semantic layers of both *khabar* and *qiṣṣa* shape the reception history of the adventure. As for *qiṣṣa*, it immediately suggests an "edifying account," in the sense that the writings on the lives of the prophets came to be known as *qiṣaṣ al-anbiyā*ʾ (stories of the prophets).

Likewise, preachers who narrated sermons based on edifying tales would be called, from the same etymological root, *quṣṣāṣ*. Though the noun *qiṣṣa* never appears in the Qurʾān, the word *qaṣaṣ* does, signifying something close to narrative, explanation, or story, as in Q. 12:3, where God informs Muḥammad, upon commencing the story of the prophet Yūsuf, "We will relate in detail unto you the most edifying narrative" (*naḥnu naquṣṣu ʿalaykum aḥsana 'l-qaṣaṣ*).

In this context, the verb *qaṣṣa, yaquṣṣu* signifies to narrate an event giving all the details, in its proper manner (*ʿalā wajhihi*). As for *qaṣaṣ*, it appears with another sense of the root '*q-ṣ-ṣ*,' meaning to follow the tracks of an animal or a man, as in the Qurʾānic account, in *Sūrat al-Kahf* (18:64), of Moses, his servant, and the lost fish, "following after their tracks they retraced their footsteps" (*fa-'rtaddā ʿalā āthārihimā qaṣaṣan*). The semantic valence of interpreting and following tracks and marks on the ground resonates with the hermeneutic frame with which Sallām's tale opens, as he crosses the world following the traces of Dhū 'l-Qarnayn.

However, by the time Sallām undertook his journey, the semantic valence of *qiṣṣa* had also grown to include not only edifying tales, but also explanations of strange and peculiar phenomena.[5] Such is the case when Jāḥiẓ, in his *Kitāb al-tarbīʿ wa 'l-tadwīr* [The book of the square and the circle], poses a series of questions concerning the causes and explanations for an encyclopedic range of issues, pondering, for example, how marble is formed (*mā qiṣṣatu 'l-rukhām*), or the account of the planet Venus (*mā qiṣṣatu 'l-zuhara*).[6] Sallām's narrative of the wall of Gog and Magog represents an intersection between these various nuances that resonates with the word *qiṣṣa*. His tale details a journey that tracks and traces its course, just as it offers an edifying narrative which, above all, gives an explanation of a wondrous phenomenon.

As for the question of storytelling, Sallām's narrative enjoyed a broad reenactment over time, and thus offers an indication of the wide dispersal and reconfiguration of knowledge throughout Islamic intellectual history. Almost all of the major Arabic geographies relate Ibn Khurradādhbih's account of Sallām al-Tarjumān. The list of geographers who draw on Sallām's tale is quite impressive: Sarakhsī (d. 285/899),[7] Ibn al-Faqīh,[8] Ibn Rusta,[9] Jayhānī,[10] Ibn al-Qāṣṣ,[11] Muqaddasī,[12] Abū ʿUbayd al-Bakrī,[13] Idrīsī,[14] Yāqūt,[15] Qazwīnī,[16] and Ibn ʿAbd al-Munʿim Ḥimyarī.[17] Likewise, Sallām's anecdote appears in Persian geographical literature, with the *Jahān-nāma* [The book of the world] of Muḥammad b. Najīb Bakrān,[18] and the *Nuzhat al-qulūb* [Stroll of the intellects] of the Īlkhānid historian and geographer Ḥamd Allāh al-Mustawfī of Qazwīn (d. ca 741/1340).[19] As part of a broader absorption of Arabic and Persian geographies, the account also makes its way into several geographical works in Ottoman Turkish, as attested in Ḥājjī Khalīfa's (d. 1067/1657) dubious assessment of the adventure in his world geography *Kitāb-i jahān-numā* [The world-revealing book], where he draws into question the authenticity of Sallām's description.[20]

The inclusion of the narrative within the succeeding generation of ʿAbbāsid geographies suggests not only the popularity of the anecdote, but also the way in which geographical discourse developed through the adaptation and incorporation of previous authorities. This wide transmission speaks to the authoritative position that the anecdote enjoyed in the discursive fashioning of geographic space, marking out the extent to which later geographical writing drew upon previous generations, reconfiguring older sources into new discursive molds. Tracing the frontiers of Islam, this body of geographical writing returned to Sallām's mission to map out the earth's end. From climatic models to alphabetized dictionaries, the wall against Gog and Magog and the journey to it is recontextualized with new meaning in each telling.

Notably absent from this early reception is Ibn Ḥawqāl's Sāmānid geography, which directly incorporated the writings of Abū Zayd al-Balkhī (d. 322/934) and Iṣṭakhrī. Ibn Ḥawqāl, who traveled extensively in the course of compiling his geography, drew widely from his own direct empirical observation. For his treatment of Gog and Magog, he incorporates an anecdote that he received from a Sāmānid chamberlain. Like Ibn Khurradādhbih's description, Ibn Ḥawqal's account of Gog and Magog highlights the role of the state in the knowledge and maintenance of frontiers.[21]

This desire for empirical evidence based upon eyewitness accounts shapes the way Muqaddasī introduces his geography. Yet even Muqaddasī, who prided himself on firsthand experience, relates Sallām's tale as copied from authoritative sources. His justification for incorporating such material is quite revealing:

> Whenever it was necessary that I myself should go to a place and make inquires there, I did so; whatever I found unsatisfactory, that my reasoning would not accept, I have ascribed to the person who related it, or I have simply written, "it has been asserted." I have supplemented my work, too, with materials I came across in the royal archives. . . The scope of [geography] is, in our opinion, so wide that we need not repeat, copy from a book, or purloin the work of another, except where the nature of the matter compels, or some

difficulty makes such action imperative. This is what we have done in the account. . . of [Dhū 'l-Qarnayn's] wall.[22]

Beyond his own reach, Muqaddasī mentions how he read (*qaraʾtu*) from the work of Ibn Khurradādhbih and others the account of the barrier (*qiṣṣat al-sadd*). He relates that the geographical authorities on this issue agree (*ʿalā nasaqin wāḥidin*), and that the subsequent transmission (*isnād*) of this anecdote is based solely on Ibn Khurradādhbih, who, according to Muqaddasī, had access to the caliphal library.[23] In his geography, Muqaddasī stresses the authority of state archives and takes pride in his own access to the bibliographic holdings of various royal libraries.[24] In Muqaddasī's estimation, Ibn Khurradādhbih's proximity to the caliphal library serves as an authoritative mark attesting to the authenticity of the anecdote.

Reception History

The early transmission of the account across a broad range of geographical writings is reflected by the Shāfiʿī jurist Ibn al-Qāṣṣ in the *Dalāʾil al-qibla*, a treatise for determining the direction of prayer, popular among medieval Muslim travelers.[25] Mixing mathematical geography with descriptive narratives and studies on the calendric systems of Iranians, Indians, Byzantines, and Arabs, Ibn al-Qāṣṣ, who wrote during the reign of the ʿAbbāsid caliph al-Rāḍī (r. 322–9/934–40),[26] promoted the field of geography as indispensable for religious knowledge and praxis. By studying the movements of astral bodies and their relation to the earth, one is able to determine not only the direction of the *qibla*, but the times for prayer, fasting, and performing the pilgrimage. According to Ibn al-Qāṣṣ, the disciplines of geography and astronomy form part of the scholarly pursuit of religious learning (*ṭalibat al-ʿilm al-sharīf*).[27]

It is in the domain of sacred geography, oriented around the holy site of the Kaʿba, that Ibn al-Qāṣṣ deals with the barrier of Gog and Magog, which he locates as seventy-two days past the Khazars. For his description he draws on the account of Sallām's journey to the barrier; in the structure of the treatise this account serves as a means of demarcating the authority of scripture within the expanse of geography. Ibn al-Qāṣṣ, who, according to ʿAbd al-Karīm al-Samʿānī (d. 562/1166), was so named because of his penchant for relating prophetic tales (*qiṣaṣ*),[28] offers a direct transmission for the account, "Ibrāhīm b. ʿAlī related to me (*ḥaddathanī*) that he read directly under (*qaraʾa ʿalā*) Muḥammad b. ʿAbd Allāh [from ʿUbayd Allāh] b. Khurradādh[bih], who said, 'Sallām al-Tarjumān related to me. . . .'"[29] The oral and written lines of transmission (*isnād*) serve as formal conventions in *ḥadīth* scholarship, exegetical and juridical discourses, and a host of other belletristic writings of the period. The *isnād* represents an idealized process through which knowledge was transmitted in early Islamic intellectual history. Ibn al-Qāṣṣ's description imagines a written form of the geography in the course of the transmission, adumbrating the process of learning, by which students studied directly under an author or transmitter in a routinized and idealized communicative performance.[30] This pattern of dissemination points to a broad social and intellectual network, reflected in the other transmitters of Ibn Khurradādhbih's work, such as Abū ʿAlī 'l-Kawkabī 'l-Kātib (d. 327/939) and Abū ʿAbd Allāh al-Kātib al-Ḥakīmī (d. 336/948), both of whom were connected to the secretariat in Baghdad.[31]

Such a structure of transmission, in which teachers would read to students, often from informal lecture notes and personal copies, akin to the *hypomnemata* of classical antiquity,[32] underscores the opportunity for a multiplicity of redactions that often evolved over time. As for Ibn Khurradādhbih's geography, it is evident, based upon the codicological evidence, that a good deal of the material was reworked and updated during a process of what was most likely multiple stages of composition, redaction, and publication (appendix 1; fig. 3). The case of Sallām's story bears witness to this, as the manuscript copies of Ibn Khurradādhbih's geography preserve significantly different accounts, and the reception of the adventure suggests noticeable variations in the amount of distance covered, the exact itinerary of the journey, and the size of the barrier itself. Thus, for instance, the Vienna recension records dimensions for the barrier which appear to be mathematically impossible. Here the door panels, measured at seventy-five cubits, rise above the door frame, which is measured at only fifty cubits, such that the total length of the gate, at one hundred and fifty cubits, fails to block the width of the entire pass, at two hundred cubits.[33]

Even structurally, the two major recensions of the *Masālik* place the wall in very different locations of the text. In Bodleian MS Hunt 433, the adventure appears directly after an account of the Khazars (appendix 3), while in Vienna MS Mixt. 783, the wall is subsumed under a broader rubric on the wondrous buildings of the world (appendix 2).[34] Thus, within the manuscript tradition itself, the location of the wall travels, highlighting a shifting pattern of identification and localization fully present within the geographical projections of Gog and Magog.

While these variations may reflect distinct authorial redactions, they also suggest a process of transformation that many geographies went through in the course of their codicological reception. For instance, Muqaddasī, who had access to Sāmānid royal libraries, complains that Ibn Khurradādhbih's geography only reached him in the form of an abridgment (*mukhtaṣar*).[35] He further adds that if one were to closely examine the geography of the Sāmānid *wazīr* Jayhānī, it would be apparent that a large portion of it was based entirely upon Ibn Khurradādhbih.[36] The notable abridgment of Ibn Khurradādhbih may very well speak to a cannibalization of the geography by Jayhānī, whose text, according to Muqaddasī, was quite long.[37] Muqaddasī mentions that he saw in the royal library of the Būyid ruler ʿAḍud al-Dawla a geography in seven volumes bearing no title but ascribed to Jayhānī; it was thought, however, to have been the work of Ibn Khurradādhbih.[38] While in Nīsābūr, Muqaddasī also came across two separate abridgments ascribed to Ibn Khurradādhbih and Jayhānī respectively, which agreed in substance, though Jayhānī's was slightly longer.[39]

Of the known surviving manuscripts of Ibn Khurradādhbih's geography, the earliest dated copy is from 631/1232. The two major manuscripts appear to be abridged in some fashion and rearranged in distinct orders, indicating a process by which later redactors came to shape and even construct the work, perhaps based upon the readings of later geographies. For instance, Idrīsī, when relating Sallām's adventure to the wall, states that he draws on both Jayhānī and Ibn Khurradādhbih for his description, which diverges in notable ways from the surviving manuscripts of Ibn Khurradādhbih's geography, indicating how accretions to the text evolved through the process of dissemination (appendix 4). While it may be that Jayhānī is the source for this divergence, it is also possible that Idrīsī drew on the writing (*kitāb*) of one of his Turkish informants who might have shaped the account of the story, so as to explicitly position Gog and Magog beyond the Adhkish Turks.[40]

The polysemous manuscript transmission, with all its variants, speaks to the problems of the factual and the authentic. Yāqūt, in his geography, plays with this tension as he frames Sallām's narrative in dialogue with a host of accounts, which all authoritatively promote their own truth-claims as to where the land of Gog and Magog truly lies. Yāqūt simply concludes that, because of the divergences of the authorities, he is not convinced of the veracity of all that he has laid forth. It is God alone who knows the entire truth of the matter. However, as the wall is affirmed in the Qurʾān, Yāqūt has no doubt concerning the actual existence of these monstrous races bottled up behind a barrier.[41]

Descriptive geographies were often supplemented with a broader body of cartographical material. Like many geographers before him, Muqaddasī integrates a series of detailed maps into his work. In the opening to his geography, he describes how he color-coded his maps so that the geographical descriptions would be more readily perceptible, "In the maps, we have colored the well-known roads red, the golden sands yellow, the salt seas green, the well-known rivers blue, and the principal mountains in dust color."[42] Sallām's journey is grafted into this cartographic system of representation. Against these spatial projections, where maps themselves function as mimetic acts of possession, Sallām's course is translated from word into image, placed in physical space through an ocular vision that occurs as much in the mind's eye as in the cartographical illusion.

Masʿūdī states that he consulted a map of the earth (*ṣūrat al-arḍ*), on which were representations of large buildings and lofty palaces, including depictions of the length of Dhū 'l-Qarnayn's wall, an image reiterated in Islamic maps of the world.[43] In the *mappa mundi* integral to Idrīsī's world geography, we can trace the trajectory of the journey across the margins of the east (plates 6a and 6b). Highlighting the very toponyms described in Sallām's adventure, Idrīsī leads us to the farthest northeastern corner of his map, where the land of Gog and Magog is located. Sallām's presence is most noticeable in the case of the putrid land (*al-muntina*), which becomes a standard topographical feature in a range of cartographical projections, placed before a visual representation of the towering gate (plate 7).[44] Sallām's ekphrastic description translates into a cartographic world of representations, where maps project the variegated forms of being. Positioned on the frontier of the inhabited world, the land of Gog and Magog and the wall that bottles them up serve as sites of repeated interest in the visual representations of world maps (plate 8).

The broad range of historiographic discourse that draws on this story speaks to a larger phenomenon of incorporating an encyclopedic array of anecdotal material in an effort to record all of written history. Al-Wāthiq's embassy to discover the wall became part of the historiographic record, localized as a concrete event in time. Ibn Taghrībirdī (d. 874/1470), for instance, turns to the expedition as a historical detail in the life of al-Wāthiq; Dhahabī sees Sallām's adventure as an occasion to complete information concerning the wall; for Ibn al-Jawzī the anecdote plays a part in the larger hagiographic narrative of Alexander the Great.

Most of these authors turn to al-Wāthiq's mission as a real event and as an accurate description of the rampart. However, the debate concerning the authenticity of this story continues, despite the fact that many historians and geographers take Sallām's account to be authoritative. This anxiety over veracity resounds in a range of material. Suspicion coalesces around two interrelated problems: 1) did Sallām al-Tarjumān truly journey to the wall; and 2) was what he saw indeed the barrier mentioned in the Qurʾān. Questions plague the account from its first reception in ʿAbbāsid geography. Ibn Rusta, in his geography *Kitāb al-aʿlāq al-nafīsa* [Book of rare ornaments], is one of the earliest voices to call into question the truth of the tale. He explains that he recorded this account exactly as it appeared in the original so that we may see the confusion (*takhlīṭ*) and exaggeration (*tazyīd*) contained therein, the authenticity of which cannot be accepted.[55]

Likewise, while Thaʿālibī relies heavily on Ibn Khurradādhbih as a source for pre-Islamic material on the Persian kings, he, too, disputes Sallām's claims concerning the wall, arguing that the barrier can only be as God the Almighty has mentioned in the Qurʾān:

> That which Sallām al-Tarjumān relates when speaking of the wall, in regard to the gate and the door post, and in the description of the lock and the key and the teeth (*dandānjāt*) in the shape of pillars (*usṭuwānāt*) is not to be relied upon, for it does not agree with what the Qurʾān mentions as the description of the rampart.[56]

A similar critique is echoed in a marginal note in Hunt 433, the Bodleian manuscript of the *Masālik*, which lambastes Ibn Khurradādhbih's account of the wall as contradicting the Qurʾān.[57]

This criticism builds upon an earlier inquiry into the actual dimensions of the wall. In addition to curiosity concerning the wall's location, early Muslim scholars took an interest in the physical appearance of Alexander's barrier. A debate evidently contemporary to Ibn Khurradādhbih took place concerning the physical size of the rampart. According to Masʿūdī, the well-known caliphal astronomer Muḥammad b. Kathīr al-Farghānī (fl. 247/861) is said to have rejected claims that the wall stretched one hundred and fifty *farsakhs*.[58] While Farghānī may have sought to prove the absurdity of such tales, in his astronomical treatise, *Jawāmiʿ ʿilm al-nujūm* [Compendium on astronomy], he does not question the actual existence of Gog and Magog, whom he locates geographically in the sixth and seventh climes.[59] It is easy to imagine how such early disputes concerning the physical dimensions and location of the wall might serve as an impetus for Sallām's mission, which could then put such debates to an end.

Disagreement nonetheless continued. With serious misgivings, the polymath Bīrūnī questioned the various descriptions of the wall, singling out the anecdotes of Shahrbarāz and Sallām al-Tarjumān. He found both accounts unreliable. Focusing his attention on the story of al-Wāthiq's embassy, he argued that the veracity of the account is drawn into question when Sallām describes a Muslim community located at the edge of the earth and isolated from all other Muslims:

> The reliability [diminishes] in the description of the residents of those regions that have begun to profess Islam and speak in Arabic despite their separation from the civilized world, and [their] location right in the middle of a putrid, black land that stretches a distance of many days [in either direction] between it and them. [A people who] do not know anything about the caliph or about the caliphate, nor who he is, nor his state. We do not know of a single Muslim community cut off from the lands of Islam, save the Bulghārs and the Sawār, and they are close to the outlying regions of the civilized world, in the extreme of the seventh clime. Furthermore, they have not mentioned anything to do with this wall, and they are not ignorant of the caliphate and the caliphs, rather they are in communication with them; nor do they speak Arabic, rather a language that is a mixture of Turkish and the language of the Khazar. Since the description of this account takes on such a shape, it is not expected that this information would lead to the disclosure of the truth. This is what I wanted to relate concerning the issue of Dhū 'l-Qarnayn. God knows best about this.[60]

Bīrūnī's response underscores the fact that despite the many details woven into Sallām's narrative, the precise location of the wall he visited remained for his readers shrouded in mystery. For much of the historiographical discourse, interested merely in the fact of the journey and not the exact location of the wall, such a lacuna could be overlooked.

Needless to say, this early criticism never doubted the existence of the wall itself, but rather drew into question the authenticity of Sallām's description. For instance, Ibn Khaldūn (d. 808/1406), like Thaʿālibī before him, when describing the caliphal adventure, which he refers to as a long tale (*ḥikāya ṭawīla*), states that the true affair concerning the description of the wall is to be found in the Qurʾān.[61] Despite the tension over whether or not Sallām's account genuinely depicts the wall, the belief in the wall's physical existence plays a significant role in the popularization of the narrative.

The doubts concerning the story's veracity continue simultaneously with a broad acceptance of Sallām al-Tarjumān's role as a chief authority on the barrier. The overwhelming majority of writers present the ʿAbbāsid adventure as a historical expedition that succeeded in reaching its goal. The authority of the account forms part of a larger discursive structuring of the world, anchored in scriptural and empirical knowledge. Ibn Ḥazm, for example, in his doxography, uses Sallām's eyewitness testimony and the power of scriptural citations as proof of Dhū 'l-Qarnayn's barrier, in a rebuttal to Jews, who, he claims, doubted its existence.[62]

Sallām enters directly into the formal exegetical commentaries of the Qurʾān, aided in part by the immensely popular body of narratives dedicated to recounting the lives of the prophets (*qiṣaṣ al-anbiyāʾ*). Ibn Khurradādhbih's geographical engagements with *Sūrat al-Kahf* share in a larger practice of narrating and imagining the accounts of the People of the Cave and the wall of Dhū 'l-Qarnayn. The visual traditions representing the lives of prophets draw on these two Qurʾānic scenes as standard subjects in the broad repertoire of miniature painting.[63] Writing from Nīsābūr, Aḥmad b. Muḥammad al-Thaʿlabī (d. 427/1036), in his *ʿArāʾis al-majālis fī qiṣaṣ al-anbiyāʾ* [Ornaments of assemblies on the tales of the prophets], showcases Sallām in order to give a description of the wall and further develop the life of Dhū 'l-Qarnayn.[64] Sallām's account appears in Abū 'l-Faraj Ibn al-Jawzī's *Salwat al-aḥzān* [Comfort in times of sorrow],[65] a homiletic work that details notable pious figures in history. Likewise, in the general history ascribed to Jalāl al-Dīn al-Suyūṭī (d. 911/1505), which begins with biographical entries on the prophets, Sallām serves as the primary source for the story of the wall, described under the rubric of curious or strange tales (*al-ḥikāyāt al-gharība*).[66] Similarly, the Delhi Sultanate historian Minhāj al-Dīn Jūzjānī (fl. 658/1260) includes Sallām's adventure in his universal history, which he drew upon from a collection of stories (*qiṣaṣ*) on the adventures of Dhū 'l-Qarnayn.[67] The anecdote became such a fixture in hagiographic writings that the tale made its way into Khwārazm Turkish, translated into the *Qiṣaṣ al-anbiyāʾ* of Nāṣir al-Dīn al-Rabghūzī (d. after 710/1310), as an authoritative testament to the barrier against the monstrous races.[68]

In the field of Qurʾānic hermeneutics, the Ashʿarī theologian Fakhr al-Dīn al-Rāzī, in his major commentary of the Qurʾān, situates the wall in the farthest region of the north (*aqṣā 'l-shamāl*), at the end of the inhabited earth, as established in books of history (*kutub al-tawārīkh*). Referencing the account of Shahrbarāz's envoy to the wall beyond the Khazar, related by Ṭabarī, Rāzī describes al-Wāthiq's mission, and quotes Ibn Khurradādhbih's geography as further evidence for the northern location of the barrier. This is juxtaposed with the opinion of Bīrūnī, who, according to Rāzī, situated the wall in the northwestern quarter of the earth.[69] Niẓām al-Dīn al-Nīsābūrī (d. 730/1330) in his commentary, quotes Rāzī's account of the mission and Bīrūnī's opinion,[70] in a broader demonstration of how the life of Alexander was itself a paradigm for exploration and learning. For

Nīsābūrī, Alexander's relationship with Aristotle offers a divine confirmation of the legitimacy of philosophical inquiry.[71]

The Damascene scholar Ibn Kathīr (d. 774/1373), who details al-Wāthiq's mission in his world history, also draws upon it in his Qurʾānic commentary.[72] As a genre, Qurʾānic exegesis has tended toward conservatism in terms of privileging accounts based upon the sayings of the Prophet, early Companions, and established juridical and philological authorities. However, by the time the scholar Burhān al-Dīn al-Biqāʿī (d. 885/1480), renowned for his use of the Hebrew Bible and the Gospels to interpret the Qurʾān, referred to the authority of al-Wāthiq's mission, the account itself had long been marshaled forth into the formalized body of exegetical writing as a historical testament to the existence of the wall.[73]

Given Sallām's ability to travel through such diverse fields of scholarship, it comes as little surprise that he also makes his way into scientific cosmographical writings on the wonders of creation (*ʿajāʾib al-makhlūqāt*). As a genre, this encyclopedic body of literature focuses on natural history, in its broadest sense, as unified under the rubric of wonder and curiosity. The practice of tying exotic narratives together with the authority of scientific investigation has a long history.[74]

Arabic and Persian writings on the marvels of the world emerge as part of a broader cosmological field of inquiry that perceives, in all of creation, from the beehive to the orbit of the planets, the greater design of God's grandeur. Muḥammad b. Maḥmūd al-Ṭūsī (fl. 555/1160), author of one of the first Persian cosmographies of marvels, writes that the aim of human life is to contemplate the marvels of creation and thus come to know God; a motif that had already been fully articulated in the early formulations of Islamic theodicy on divine design and order.[75] The wonder of the tale itself is enhanced by the ocular proof that is the basis of Sallām's description. The anonymous Persian collection of historical anecdotes, the *Mujmal al-tawārīkh wa 'l-qiṣaṣ*, includes Sallām's account as part of the wonders of the world, and concludes that there is no other description of the rampart as detailed as this one, for Sallām actually sees the wall.[76]

Since writings on the wonders of creation, like descriptive geography, often recycle a set corpus of material, the question of organization and arrangement was often one of the primary means of setting a work apart from its predecessors. Thus within this field we find the adventure to the wall continually re-situated and re-contextualized. Abū Ḥāmid al-Gharnāṭī (d. 565/1169–70) draws on the anecdote for his description of marvelous buildings in his *Tuḥfat al-albāb* [Gift to the intellects].[77] Ṭūsī, in his *ʿAjāʾib-nāma*, incorporates Sallām's journey to the wall of Dhū 'l-Qarnyan and orders it into an alphabetized list of wonders that span the regions of the earth.[78] Also prominent is the tradition of quoting Sallām's anecdote as part of topographical lists of wonders lurking in the various geographical climes of the world, as is the case with Ibn al-Wardī (d. 861/1457) in his *Kharīdat al-ʿajāʾib* [The pearl of marvels].[79] Through each telling, the story is transformed, often abridged, reduced to its bare elements; indeed Sallām may be given a different name or disappear entirely.[80]

Yet beyond such truncations, there are also traditions that develop and expand Sallām's journey. Through the material that survives we are able to catch a glimpse of how, somewhere in the dissemination of the tale, other wondrous accounts were appended to the name of Sallām, the ʿAbbāsid interpreter. It is in Qazwīnī's book of wonders that Sallām's evolution as the standard-bearer of the marvelous is most prominent.

In a section treating the strange islands and marvelous creatures of the oceans, Qazwīnī tells how al-Wāthiq's ambassador visited the Caspian Sea.[81] Here Sallām describes an island inhabited with only herds of sheep. Their number was so great that there was no place on the island to escape from them. When ships arrived, the crews would catch as many fat ewes and rams as they wished. Sallām goes on to relate, "Except for these sheep, I did not see any other animals on this island. The island has springs and grass and numerous trees. Praise be to Him whose blessings are innumerable!"[82] The account of the Island of Sheep can be found in earlier Arabic geographies, with antecedents in classical antiquity.[83] This tale, nowhere to be found in the account of al-Wāthiq's mission as known in Ibn Khurradādhbih, was presumably associated with Sallām because of his status as a well-known traveler in the region.

In the same section, Qazwīnī mentions another account ascribed to our intrepid adventurer. After referencing the standard introduction to Sallām's adventure to the wall, Qazwīnī immediately digresses to a further account of marvelous phenomena. In contrast to Ibn Khurradādhbih's description, in which Sallām remained with the king of Khazar for only a day and a night,[84] Qazwīnī relates that Sallām stayed for a period of five days:

> While with [the king] I saw an amazing thing (*amr ʿajīb*): [the Khazar] had caught a fish of great size, they pierced its ear and wove cords through it and then they pulled the cords tight such that the ear of the fish split open. From inside the fish emerged a maidservant of reddish-white complexion, long hair, and a beautiful form. They took her and brought her to the land. She would hit her face, pull out her hair, and scream. God had created over her midriff a white film,

> like thick clothing that ran from her navel to her knees, as though it were a tightly woven loincloth. They held on to her until she died among them.[85]

In the illuminated manuscript tradition this account of the maidservant emerging from the body of a fish appears as a site of recurrent interest (plate 9).

Fusing the beautiful and the bestial, the image of an attractive woman taken from the belly of a giant fish borders on the grotesque. The description of how she tears her hair and screams, along with her death in the hands of her captors, adds a distinctly graphic element to the story, as does the initial splitting open of the fish to pull forth the maidservant. This account bears the hallmark of a first-person testimony, and is presented as an authoritative description of a strange occurrence that takes place at the margins of the world, in the remote land of the Khazar.

Although by the time Qazwīnī recorded this anecdote the Khazar dynasty had long disappeared, they surface in the later sources, frozen in time. Qazwīnī relates that he read this tale (*ḥikāya*) in a number of books, and mentions, in particular, the *Kitāb al-ʿajāʾib* [Book of wonders] of the Andalusian traveler, Abū Ḥāmid al-Gharnāṭī. This anecdote, which has a long pedigree, does appear in Gharnāṭī's *Tuḥfat al-albāb*, though, perhaps due to a variant manuscript recension, the ascription to Sallām is entirely missing; rather Gharnāṭī merely describes how some merchants related this tale to him.[86] Somewhere in the transmission from Gharnāṭī to Qazwīnī, the story became attached to Sallām.

The ascription of this wondrous account to al-Wāthiq's interpreter points to broader discursive strategies of the marvelous. Above all, the identification of Sallām strengthens the tale's veracity, moving it from an unspecified group of merchants to a localized, historical first-person eyewitness description, based on the authority of a known, and, presumably, respected narrator. This gesture moves us away from Gharnāṭī's account, which is set in an unspecified place, some time in the distant past (*sana min al-sinīn*), to the specific setting of Sallām's journey to the king of the Khazar.[87]

Due in large measure to the popularity of Qazwīnī's work, the anecdote of the fish and the handmaid ascribed to Sallām enjoyed a wide reception and was repeated in works such as Ibn al-Wardī's book of wonders, *Kharīdat al-ʿajāʾib*,[88] Ibn Iyās's (d. ca 930/1524) geographical compendium, *Nashq al-azhār fī ʿajāʾib al-aqṭār* [Smelling flowers through the wonders of the regions],[89] and Aḥmad b. Yūsuf al-Qaramānī's (d. 1019/1611) history, *Akhbār al-duwal wa 'l-āthār al-awwal* [Accounts of the nations and the monuments of the first civilizations].[90]

These stories of Dhū 'l-Qarnayn's wall, the Island of Sheep, and the maidservant pulled from the giant fish share part in a widely diffused discourse of the marvelous. Islamic books on the marvels of creation build upon a body of learned and popular traditions that passed through Indian, Greek, Persian, and Arabic materials. When Qazwīnī discusses islands inhabited by dog-headed men, he does not consciously evoke the Greek tradition of the Cynocephali (κυνοκέφαλοι), but rather draws on the wealth of geographical material that had entered into his sphere of knowledge.[91] The race of people known in the Indian epic the *Mahābhārata* as the *karṇaprāvaraṇa*, who can cover themselves with their long ears, perhaps lingers somewhere in the background of the various characterizations of Gog and Magog possessing ears so long that they can wrap themselves up in them when they go to sleep.[92] Ibn Ḥazm's identification of the pygmies of Greek lore with Gog and Magog also speaks to the broad circulation and appropriation of material focused on the margins of the world. The transmission of Sallām the translator, who himself is translated into the discursive field of marvels (plate 10), follows in tandem with his journey across geographies, histories, encyclopedias, prophetic tales, and Qurʾānic learning, indicating a broader paradigm of the circulation and transmission of knowledge.

The Routinization of Alterity

As a geographical authority, we can trace Sallām's presence through the thirteenth/nineteenth century with *al-Tarjumāna al-kubrā* [The great interpreter], by the Moroccan historian, statesman, and traveler, Abū 'l-Qāsim al-Zayyānī (d. 1249/1833).[93] In this work, Zayyānī mixes his own travel experiences, inspired by the autobiographical genre of the travelog (*riḥla*), with geographical information and marvelous anecdotes taken from classical Arabic sources. In connection to the wonders of the Caspian Sea, Zayyānī relates the account of Sallām's discovery of the maidservant in the belly of a giant fish.[94] For Zayyānī, there is no question about the physical existence of the wall against Gog and Magog, which he believes to be located in the northern regions of China, and which he locates on his own cartographical projection of the world (plate 11). The story of Sallām's expedition piques Zayyānī's interest, as he mentions it several times.[95] The veracity of the tale is never a problem for the Moroccan statesman, who views Sallām's report to al-Wāthiq as an authentic account of the barrier.

Just as the adventure is threaded into nineteenth-century Morocco, so, too, does it inflect the intellectual history of South Asia, and, in this way, is emblematic of the routinization of learning and the charismatic power of transmitting knowledge across various centuries and societies. The encyclopedic compendium by Amīn Aḥmad al-Rāzī (fl. 1002/1594), the *Haft iqlīm* [Seven climes], represents an intersection of geography, history, and belletristic writing, all tied together with an interest in marvelous tales. Writing in the Persian context of the Indian subcontinent, Rāzī relates the history of various Islamic dynasties and recounts biographies of important people from each region, all structured around the Ptolemaic division of the world into climes. At the very end of his compendium lies the wall of Gog and Magog, which he describes by drawing on Sallām's adventure.[96] In a similarly structured work, Ḥakīm Mahārat Khān al-Iṣfahānī, physician of the Mughal emperor Shāh ʿĀlam Bahādūr Shāh I (d. 1124/1712), relates the journey in his Persian geographical compendium, *Bahjat al-ʿālam* [Splendor of the world], which explicitly draws from earlier authorities, such as Ibn al-Wardī's *Kharīdat al-ʿajāʾib*, and is based on the Ptolemaic division of the world into seven climes.[97]

Likewise, Murtaḍā Ḥusayn Bilgrāmī (d. ca 1210/1795), who served in the Mughal administration, draws on the same anecdote at the end of his geographical and historical compendium, the *Ḥadīqat al-aqālīm* [The garden of the climes]. He uses this account in order to detail Alexander's wall and the monstrous peoples of Gog and Magog, after which he describes both Europe and America.[98] The figure of Bilgrāmī is particularly interesting, as he represents the intersection between two epistemological systems. On the one hand, he is fully immersed in Arabic–Persian fields of learning, while on the other, he is in direct contact with the colonial production of knowledge through his interaction with European scholarship. This is most clear in Bilgrāmī's association with Captain Jonathan Scott (d. 1829), who commissioned Bilgrāmī to compose the aforementioned historical geography.[99] Scott himself was a founding member of the Bengal Asiatic Society and Persian secretary to Warren Hastings (d. 1818), the first governor-general of British-ruled India.

The widespread belief that the rampart of Dhū 'l-Qarnayn described in the Qurʾān corresponds to some geographical site, and that Gog and Magog are bottled up behind this barrier, predetermines the continued interest in Sallām's journey. Almost every major geographical treatise written in Arabic and Persian discusses the lands of Gog and Magog as located in physical space, as part of the wider conception of the world (plate 12).

For instance, the Īlkhānid geographer and historian Ḥamd Allāh al-Mustawfī, in his Persian *Nuzhat al-qulūb*, prefaces the account of Sallām's journey by situating the wall at a latitude of 73°0′ and a longitude of 109°30′, deep in the seventh clime, which would be in the heart of Siberia, at the northern edge of the earth.[100] Though the various projections differ, there is an overwhelming agreement that Gog and Magog correspond to real nations located somewhere on the earth's margins.

Based on the authority of Prophetic sayings, Gog and Magog were, from an early period, associated with the Turkic tribes of Central Asia.[101] The field of descriptive geography often identified these monstrous races as directly related to the Turks.[102] The scholar and lexicographer Maḥmūd al-Kāshgharī (fl. 476/1094) affirms in his Turkish grammar and dictionary, *Dīwān lughāt al-Turk* [Compendium of the Turkic dialects], the widely held belief that the Turks all trace their ancestry back to Turk, son of Yāfith, son of Noah—the same genealogy delineated for Gog and Magog.[103]

The exegetical tradition often locates the wall of Gog and Magog in the land of the setting sun, where the Turks dwell.[104] Kāshgharī, supported by his personal experience living among the Turkic tribes of Central Asia, lists the language spoken by Gog and Magog as one of the Turkish dialects (*alsun al-turk*), though he admits that nothing is known of it because of the barrier and the interposition of the mountains that separate Gog and Magog from the rest of the world.[105] The Īlkhānid historian and statesman Rashīd al-Dīn (d. 718/1318), in his historical compendium, *Jāmiᶜ al-tawārīkh*, details a Mongolian origin myth that describes how their primogenitors had emerged from an iron mountain enclosure. The account appears to echo the barrier built against Gog and Magog and points to the appropriation and reinscription of the story among Central Asian Turks.[106]

Despite the geographical isolation suggested by the enclosure, there are reports of travelers and merchants who were able to make contact and even trade with these monstrous races. On his caliphal mission to the Bulghār, Ibn Faḍlān claims to have seen, with his own eyes, a giant carcass from the people of Gog and Magog, suggesting that contact beyond the barrier was believed to be possible. According to reports he received from the Bulghār, these monsters were said to live beyond the land of the Finnish Veps (Wīsū).[107] A similar suggestion is made by Ibn Ḥawqal, who maps Gog and Magog in the northernmost regions of the earth.[108] After describing the Khazar, the Kīmāk, the Bulghār, and the Ṣaqāliba, Ibn Ḥawqal turns to the lands of Gog and Magog, the true extent of which, he admits, only God knows. Yet he is able to provide further detail through a report that he received directly from the Sāmānid chamberlain (*ḥājib*), Abū Isḥāq Ibrāhīm b. Alptakīn (d. 356/967).[109]

According to Ibn Alptakīn, merchants from Khwārazm were able to reach these remote tribes and trade with them by climbing a series of lofty mountains that lead to the region. However, the merchants, who would acquire silk and furs, had to carry their goods on their backs, as pack animals were unable to ascend the towering peaks.[110] Ibn Ḥawqal relates that the people of Gog and Magog were hairless, and that they would only trade with merchants after plucking out all the hair from the merchants' beards.[111] Such a detail resonates with Ibn Faḍlān's astonishment at the beardless Turks he encountered on his journey who plucked all the hair off their faces,[112] and suggests that the merchant tales of Gog and Magog that reached Ibn Ḥawqal were based on the identification of these savages with Turkish nomads. Such a process of transposition seems to be the basis of the account by the Persian scholar Shahmardān b. Abī 'l-Khayr (fl. 476/1083), who describes how merchants (*bāzargānān*) were able to make contact with the monstrous races. Though unlike Ibn Ḥawqal or Ibn Faḍlān, Shahmardān situates these tribes near China.[113]

All these descriptions point to a process by which the ominous sign of the monstrous was grafted onto actual peoples and places. This multivalent act of transposing monstrosity with the foreign is reflected in the rather fluid boundaries enclosing the apocalyptic races. Thus, for instance, Muqaddasī comments that many people believed Gog and Magog dwell beyond the lands of Iberia, while he himself was of the view that they lived a two-month journey past the Khazar.[114] This northern location is one of the prevailing opinions, drawn, in large part, on the details of Sallām's journey beyond Khazaria. However, as with Shahmardān's assessment, the association with the northeast is also well documented. For instance, Qudāma, basing himself in part on material from the Pseudo-Callisthenes cycle, relates how the ruler of China beseeched Alexander the Great to build a wall against the savage tribes, who are explicitly identified as Turks.[115] Thus the rampart was at times situated between the Tughuzghuz Turks and the Chinese.[116] The Ghaznavid historian Abū Saʿīd Gardīzī (fl. 440/1049) identifies Gog and Magog as a Turkish tribe near the northern border with China, drawing apparently from the lost geography of Balkhī.[117] Gardīzī goes on to describe how Alexander erected the barrier at the bequest of the people of Turkistān, who were plagued by these savage tribes.[118]

The fluidity of shifting borders forms part of the logic of circumscribing the mark of the savage, which, as a category, was transposed and made relevant for ever-changing geopolitical realities. Writing in 625/1228, the Persian collector of anecdotes, Sadīd al-Dīn al-ʿAwfī, describes in his *Jawāmiʿ al-ḥikāyāt* [Collections of tales], the destruction of Transoxiana, Khurāsān, Iraq, and Azerbaijan by the Mongol hordes, whom he identifies, evidently not in a metaphorical sense, as the front guard of Gog and Magog, an association that was quite long lasting.[119] As each age confronted a new set of enemies and aggressors, the marginal figures of Gog and Magog linger in the background, ready to be associated with any new menace. Thus the historian, Ibn Iyās, writes in his history of Mamlūk Egypt, *Badāʾiʿ al-zuhūr fī waqāʾiʿ al-duhūr* [The wonders of blossoms and the vicissitudes of the ages], that during the year 912/1506 the Europeans (*Franj*) made their way into the Persian Gulf (Baḥr al-Ḥijāz) and started to upset the Ottoman trade monopoly in the region.[120] We are told that after years in the attempt, they finally succeeded, through their cunning, to tunnel their way under the wall built by Alexander the Great, which Ibn Iyās locates on a mountain range separating the Mediterranean (Baḥr al-Rūm) from the Indian Ocean (Baḥr al-Ṣīn).

By way of the Indian Ocean, Gog and Magog, in the guise of Europeans, are able to enter the Persian Gulf. Though evidently not aware of the full details, Ibn Iyās describes the entry of Portuguese traders into the Indian Ocean by way of the navigation route that Vasco da Gama opened during his three circumnavigations of Africa around the Cape of Good Hope (1497–9, 1502–3, 1524). For Ibn Iyās the bursting of Alexander's wall explains how European merchant boats could make their way from the Mediterranean into the Indian Ocean.

It is through these European forays into uncharted territory in the heyday of discovery that Sallām journeys from manuscript to printed page, appearing suddenly in Rome in 1592, with the first printed Arabic geography, Idrīsī's *Nuzhat al-mushtāq*.[121] The way in which Idrīsī's work traveled from the court of the Norman monarch of Sicily, Roger II (d. 1154), where it was first commissioned, across the Arabic-speaking world, to end, over four centuries later, in the Medici printing house, bespeaks the entangled lines of transmission that such material enjoyed. This Arabic printed edition of Idrīsī's geography gained an even wider circulation with the publication, in Paris, in 1619, of a Latin translation undertaken by two Arab Christian language instructors, Gabriel Sionita and Joannes Hesronita.[122] Because of a textual error in a passage that appeared to identify the author of the geography as a native of Sudan,[123] this work became known in Latin as the *Geographia Nubiensis* [The geography of the Nubian]. Though Idrīsī's identity was obfuscated for some time to come and the maps that originally accompanied his work remained largely unknown, the significance of his descriptive geography did not go unnoticed; indeed, its influence was felt in the fields of European geography and cartography.[124] For our purposes, it is through this printed translation that the story of Salam Altargiaman (*interprete*) and the adventure to the rampart (*agger*) of Dhū 'l-Qarnayn (*Bicornis*) first became widely available to an early modern European readership, who would find in the mission another kind of wonder altogether.[125]

7

BEYOND THE WALLS OF THE ORIENT

Of Encyclopedias and Fiction

Following the traces of Sallām's tale takes us to the birth of modern Orientalism. Here, the dialectic between fact and fancy plays out even more fervently on the stage of an entirely new array of cultural assumptions and epistemic paradigms. Sallām's adventure appears in the *Bibliothèque orientale, ou Dictionaire universel* (Paris, 1697) of Barthélemy d'Herbelot (d. 1695), an encyclopedia whose title page promises to contain, "everything regarding the knowledge of the peoples of the Orient, their histories and traditions, true or fabulous. . . "[1] D'Herbelot's work was posthumously edited and published by the French Orientalist Antoine Galland (d. 1715), translator/author of *Les milles et une nuits* (Paris, 1704–17),[2] the sprawling expansion of the popular Arabic collection of stories, *Alf layla wa layla* (*The Thousand and One Nights*), whose European incarnation played a central role in constituting the image of the exotic Orient in the colonial discourses of the eighteenth and nineteenth centuries.[3] In Voltaire's (d. 1778) estimation, d'Herbelot's *Bibliothèque orientale* too was a collection of "Arabic and Tartar stories,"[4] and, as such, it also formed part of an epistemological framework that attempted to possess and orientalize the Orient.[5] As a mine of information of oriental mores and customs, d'Herbelot's encyclopedia inspired the Gothic romance by William Beckford (d. 1844), originally entitled *An Arabian Tale from an Unpublished Manuscript* (London, 1786), and subsequently known simply as *Vathek*,[6] a fictional novel that detailed the fantastic adventures of the ʿAbbāsid caliph al-Wāthiq as a libidinous tyrant on a magical quest filled with debauchery and murder, all to gain supernatural powers.

In the entry on Gog and Magog (*Iagiouge et Magiouge*), d'Herbelot outlines al-Wāthiq's embassy to the rampart, drawing from the Persian account of Mustawfī's *Nuzhat al-qulūb*, which he knows to be based upon a certain *Ketab al messalek val memalek.*[7] D'Herbelot goes on to relate the anecdote of Sallām and the maidservant in the belly of a fish, quoting from Qazwīnī's *ʿAjāʾib al-makhlūqāt*, which he believes is drawn from accounts of Sirens.[8] The allure of such fabulous stories forms part of a broader view concerning the essential oriental inclination toward the fanciful and superstitious.

The English literary critic, Thomas Warton (d. 1790), in the introduction to his influential study, *The History of English Poetry* (1774–81), entitled "Of the Origin of Romantic Fiction in Europe," advances the view that the impetus of the medieval romance, as a mode of relating marvelous adventures, can be traced back to the fables of the Oriental imagination. For Warton, the story of Sallām's encounter with the wall of Gog and Magog, as culled from d'Herbelot's *Bibliothèque orientale*, is merely a footnote to his larger argument, exemplified in the case of the giant Goëmagot (i.e., Gogmagog), inhabiting Cornwall in the *Historia regum Britanniae* by the bishop Geoffrey of Monmouth (d. ca 1155). Beliefs in giants and other such superstitions, as suggested by Warton's formulation, were not natural to Europeans, but were entirely "Arabian inventions," a theory, which, while debated,[9] was repeated throughout the nineteenth century.[10] Sallām's journey, as with other fanciful oriental accounts, such as *Sindbad the Sailor*, were grouped together by the common wisdom that saw the ultimate Eastern origin behind wonder tales and childish superstitions, "half fiction, half fact, which are so universally diffused among the legendary literature of every country as to appear indigenous to each of them."[11]

While Sallām's story was repeated in the popular reception of the exotic and benighted Oriental, the first detailed study of the account was produced by the German Orientalist Theophilus (Gottlieb) Siegfried Bayer (d. 1738), in an article on the history of the fortifications of the Caucasus, according to Greek, Latin, Arabic, Persian, and Turkish sources, entitled, "De Muro Caucaseo." Best known for his work on Chinese, Bayer had an encyclopedic devotion to oriental languages, as evidenced by his work with Arabic, Persian, Syriac, Mongolian, Tibetan, and Manchu.[12] Bayer wrote this particular article in 1726, during the first year of his tenure in St. Petersburg, as the chair of Greek and Roman antiquities at the Academia Scientiarum Imperialis Petropolitanae.[13] The fledgling academy, founded by the Russian czar, Peter the Great (d. 1725), had all the outward appearance of an imperial center of learning. This setting foregrounds Bayer's treatment of the material; as Bayer himself mentions, his article on the military defenses of the Caucasus was inspired by the recent Russian conquests of the western and southern shores of the Caspian, in 1723, from the Ṣafavids of Iran. It is in this context of the Caucasus, revisited under the tutelage of Russian imperial forces, that we are reintroduced to "Alsalemus altargjeman (seu Interprete)."

Bayer's own frame of reference was inflected in great measure by his background as a German Protestant, and by the larger discourse of scientific discovery with which his philological examinations were in concert. His ironic disdain for the *fabula*, which is Sallām's story, can, in part, be explained by a trend in European epistemology, which sought to demystify the marvelous through science and reason; the discursive power of the Enlightenment attacked superstition on all fronts as 'vulgar credulity.'[14]

As shown by this one essay, the philological study of language, out of which modern Orientalism developed, for Bayer serves as a tool for parsing history from legend. One of the central thrusts of Bayer's article is an exposé of childish Muslim myths, which crescendos in an attack on the Prophet Muḥammad, who is caricatured as a coarse and foolish storyteller (*fabulatorem inficetum et ridiculum*).[15] For Bayer, the story of the wall against Gog and Magog told (sic) by 'Mahomete' in the Qur'ān is the perfect representation of such condemnable *superstitionis*.[16] Peppering his prose with allusions to classical Greek and Latin sources, Bayer quotes Horace when he cautions us to assay the true value of these fables from the oriental nations (*orientalium populorum*), so that we may distinguish the real from the false coins embedded in such dubious material, "quid distent aera lupinis."[17]

Not surprisingly, Bayer views Sallām's adventure as no different than one of the many ridiculous (*multa ridicula*) tales told by Orientals. Basing himself on what he acknowledges as the truncated Latin edition of Idrīsī, many details of Sallām's journey escape him, such as the name of the caliph who dispatches Sallām; as Bayer states, this piece of information is not present in the version of the account before him.[18] However, out of the material that is available to him, Bayer shows great zeal in relating all the particular elements that punctuate this tale, from Isaacium Eben Ismael, ruler of Armenia, to the key that locks the gate of the ominous wall. Here the pleasure of relating Sallām's account arises from taking delight in mocking the incredulous Orientals. To underscore this point, Bayer again turns to Horace—*spectatum admissi, risum teneatis, amici?*—in a passing reference to the opening of the *Ars Poetica* (1–5):

Humano capiti ceruicem pictor equinam
iungere si uelit et uarias inducere plumas
undique collatis membris, ut turpiter atrum
desinat in piscem mulier formosa superne,
spectatum admissi, risum teneatis, amici?

Were a painter to unite a horse's neck to a human head,
and spread a variety of plumage over limbs taken from every part,
so that what is the torso of a beautiful woman
terminates unsightly in an ugly fish below;
could you, my friends, refrain from laughter?

Bayer merely has to quote the last line of this opening passage of the *Ars Poetica* to set in motion a chain of associations that evoke artifice and dissimilitude. The uncanny resemblance of Horace's image of the mermaid with the account of the maidservant emerging from the body of a fish ascribed to Sallām was evidently lost on Bayer, who makes no reference to the story, though it is already detailed in d'Herbelot's *Bibliothèque orientale*.[19] Even without the maidservant and the fish, Bayer's disdain for Sallām's marvelous tale resounds through his entire presentation. It is an account that Bayer deigns to narrate with the sole aim of revealing its absurdity (*ut fabula desinat in risum*); a fable that begins with the dream of a caliph and ends with the dream of Sallām (*Ita ex somniis chaliphae exorsa fabula, in somniis Alsalemi desinit*).[20]

This negative reception in St. Petersburg, however, did little to impede Sallām's travels across the imagined geographies of Orientalists. While Bayer sets forth his own position candidly, later writers would learn to veil and obscure such contempt. With Bayer it is clear that the *multa ridicula* of oriental nations serve to disprove the validity of their faith. The *fabula* of Dhū 'l-Qarnayn's wall as represented in the Qurʾān bears testimony to this, as does the ridiculous tale of *Alsalemus,* which, according to the epistemology of Orientalism, goes part and parcel with the misguided beliefs of Orientals.

A Romantic Turn

The Swedish diplomat and Orientalist of Armenian descent, Constantin Mouradgea d'Ohsson (d. 1851), approached Sallām's adventure from a completely different perspective. As the son of Ignatius Mouradgea d'Ohsson (d.

1807), who was himself a scholar, former dragoman, and *charge d'affaires* for the Swedish mission in Istanbul, Constantin came to his field of study unlike most of his fellow Orientalists. Best known for his *Histoire des Mongols*, in 1828 Constantin d'Ohsson published a curious book entitled *Des peuples du Caucase et des pays au nord de la mer Noire et de la mer Caspienne, dans le dixième siècle*. The subtitle, *ou Voyage d'Abou-el-Cassim*, begins to explain the unique nature of this study. Basing himself on over twenty Arabic, Persian, and Turkish manuscripts scattered across Paris, Leiden, Uppsala, and Stockholm, d'Ohsson weaves together his very own travel narrative based on a fictitious adventurer, whom he invents and names Abou-el-Cassim. As d'Ohsson explains in his preface, he imagines Abou-el-Cassim as a caliphal envoy sent to the king of the Bulghārs on the Volga in the year 336/948.[21] He uses such primary sources as Masʿūdī's *Murūj al-dhahab*, Yāqūt's *Muʿjam al-buldān*, and Ṭabarī's *Taʾrīkh* to fill in the details of Abou-el-Cassim's imaginary journey through the region. D'Ohsson, along the way, glosses this work, a virtual storehouse of information, with detailed explanatory footnotes. He then concludes Abou-el-Cassim's adventure with an appendix, as long as the body of the text, wherein he supplements the information of the narrative with full explanations.

With nearly each statement accounted for by some primary source, d'Ohsson's encyclopedic display results in a recondite blend of fact and fancy. Against this backdrop we see Sallām's journey cast as a well-known authority on the wall. D'Ohsson's work is devoid of any editorial display of disdain. Rather, he lets the sources speak for themselves. Through the figure of Abou-el-Cassim, he imagines being a Muslim traveler in the tenth century. Abou-el-Cassim relates that the wall of Gog and Magog is mentioned in the Qurʾān, where God says to the Prophet, "They (that is to say the infidels) will ask you about Dhū 'l-Qarnayn" (Q. 18:83).[22] D'Ohsson showcases Abou-el-Cassim's beliefs throughout the travelog, as when he informs us, "It is certain that at the end of the world Gog and Magog will spread across the earth, according to our sacred book."[23] This serves as an occasion for a digression concerning al-Wāthiq's expedition.

With characteristic attention to detail, d'Ohsson offers an editorial footnote at the end of Sallām's account citing various Arabic, Turkish, and Persian sources that all include the adventure.[24] Here d'Ohsson makes no comment on the question of authenticity, rather he quotes from the history, *Rawḍat al-ṣafāʾ* [Garden of purity], of the Tīmūrid historian Muḥammad b. Khāwandshāh Mīr Khwānd (d. 903/1498), who, upon describing the barrier, mentions:

> Although the astronomer Muḥammad Farghānī and other recent scholars have tried to demonstrate that all these details [concerning the wall] are false, nonetheless, as it has been transmitted to us by the ancient historical works, I am not permitted to reject them, rather I have recorded all they have said faithfully.[25]

This is the only commentary accompanying the anecdote. D'Ohsson is content to let the texts speak for themselves, which, after all, is central to the larger aim of this project, namely, to present a coherent narrative of a fictional journey from the perspective of a Muslim traveler in the tenth century.

Only in a passing reference made in the prologue does D'Ohsson draw direct attention to the question of the veracity of the many fabulous accounts contained in these sources. He mentions that the same reproach made by the Greek geographer Strabo could also be applied to the authors of these manuscripts:

> Observing that those who were professedly writers of myths (*μυθογράφους*) were esteemed and honored, they supposed that they also should make their writings pleasing, if they told, in the appearance of history (*ἐν ἱστορίας σχήματι*) what they had never seen, nor even heard, at least not from eye-witnesses, with no other object in view than to tell what afforded their audience pleasure and amazement (*θαυμαστήν*).[26]

This is a fitting quote for an author of an imaginary account envisioned through the eyes of a fictional medieval Muslim traveler. We, as readers, nonetheless still feel a sweet wonder and curiosity when reading d'Ohsson's translation of such material as the legendary exploits of Anūshirwān or Sallām's marvel of the maidservant emerging from the body of a fish.[27] By projecting these diverse anecdotes through the lens of the imaginary Abou-el-Cassim, d'Ohsson masterfully escapes any responsibility for the authenticity of the material, a narrative technique fully exploited in the various traditions of marvel-writing, where the frequent citation of sources adds a veneer of authority, distancing both the author and the reader from the charge of assessing the problem of veracity.[28]

D'Ohsson demonstrates a certain romantic passion for these sources, imagining himself in the role of a caliphal envoy to the king of the Bulghārs, traveling across the hostile and savage lands of the wondrously foreign. Though he addresses the latent question of veracity obliquely, the effect of Abou-el-Cassim's narrative leaves us with the impression that one would not have to actually travel anywhere to write such a travelog. All of this material is drawn together with Mandevillean flare from the accounts of other writers and composed into the cohesive semblance of a journey. This flirtation with the fictional, though supplemented by the marginal notes and the erudite appendix, offers us the pleasure of enjoying the adventure, imagining ourselves, in exotic transference, traveling through a strange land in the distant past.

In a series of passing observations made in the nineteenth century, we can capture further glimpses of Sallām's reception by European scholars. The reaction is overwhelmingly negative, and Sallām's story is generally dismissed as a fabrication. The French Orientalist Joseph Toussaint Reinaud (d. 1867), in the introduction to his edition and translation of the *Taqwīm al-buldān* [Survey of countries] by Abū 'l-Fidā' (1848), briefly references Sallām's account.[29] By this time Sallām had become well known in the scholarship on Arabic and Persian geography, aided in large measure by the wide circulation of the French translation of Idrīsī's geography and the immense popularity of d'Herbelot's *Bibliothèque orientale*.[30] Reinaud outlines the story of al-Wāthiq's mission to the wall; he plots Sallām's course through Armenia and Georgia, across the Caucasus, his visit to the Khazar, and his travels around the Caspian and up into the Urals and the Altai mountains. He mentions that the account of Sallām was preserved by Idrīsī and others, and concludes that "unfortunately, it is overloaded with fabulous stories and from the very beginning it aroused the suspicions of Muslims themselves."[31] Even more dismissive is the remark of the Austrian Orientalist, Aloys Sprenger (d. 1893), in his monograph *Die Post- und Reiserouten des Orients* (1864), in which he claims that the journey is an intentional deception, "eine unverschämte Mystifikation des Sallām."[32]

The pendulum swings back as the French scholar Charles Barbier de Meynard (d. 1908) rejects Sprenger's claim outright. Barbier de Meynard, the first to publish an Arabic edition and translation of Ibn Khurradādhbih's *Masālik* (1865), sets forth his own hypothesis concerning "la trop fameuse relation du Sallām l'interprète."[33] He sees al-Wāthiq's mission to the People of the Cave, along with the journey to the wall of Gog and Magog, as part of a concerted theological effort on the part of the caliph to combat the ridiculous tales circulated by *ḥadīth* scholars concerning the location and identification of such Qur'ānic references. In his view, Sallām's journey had, at least, a real beginning, and he sees "les fantaisies" that conclude the adventure as a concession to the taste for the marvelous, which the scientific conquests of al-Ma'mūn were unable to weaken.[34] For this reason de Meynard refused to hold Sallām's account as merely an impudent mystification. Such a formulation is informed by a desire to see ʿAbbāsid rationalism—embodied in Muʿtazilī thought—as something which it was not, namely a precursor of Enlightenment ideals. Yet, regardless of the strength or weakness of his hypothesis, de Meynard's intention was clear; he argues that to understand this account we must historicize it. He finds in the narrative a historical journey, which, though colored by fantastical elements, bears upon the social reality of the period.

Michael Jan de Goeje

The movement to historicize Sallām's adventure continued to develop throughout the century. The Dutch Orientalist Michael Jan de Goeje (d. 1909) had a tremendous impact on the modern reception and study of Arabic descriptive geography, by editing and publishing a corpus of major Arabic geographies in his *Bibliotheca geographorum Arabicorum* (1870–94). Preceding his own edition and French translation of Ibn Khurradādhbih's *Masālik* (1889), de Goeje published, in Dutch, a short study dedicated to the question of the wall, entitled, "De Muur van Gog en Magog" (1888).[35]

Here de Goeje traces the figure of Alexander's wall in some of its various incarnations, leading us through the Pseudo-Callisthenes cycle to Shahrbarāz's envoy, and finally ending with the account of Sallām's adventure. He takes up al-Wāthiq's embassy as an occasion to plot the actual location of the wall against Gog and Magog. Situating this narrative in a physical topography of place names, de Goeje seeks to prove that not only did Sallām's journey occur, but that we can trace exactly where he traveled and uncover the very rampart described in such detail. He does this by mixing together the distinct accounts of Sallām's entry into Transoxiana as preserved in the Vienna manuscript and in Idrīsī's redaction.[36] De Goeje argues that this composite text engages with a concrete series of references, fully corresponding to a geographical and historical reality that can be traced, described, and substantiated. Filling in the lacunae of Sallām's narrative with conjecture and glossing over the many inconsistencies, de Goeje concludes that not only did Sallām al-Tarjumān reach the Jade Gate to the Great Wall of China, but that the legend of Alexander's wall in the Pseudo-Callisthenes cycle, itself the inspiration for the Qurʾānic account, finds its origin with the fortifications of the Great Wall.[37]

Ultimately, de Goeje erects the edifice of his argument on the reading of one toponym in the adventure, which he vocalizes as *Igu* and believes to correspond to a city which was known as 伊吾 (Yiwu) and 伊吾盧 (Yiwulu) during the during the Han (206 B.C.E.–220 C.E.) and Tang (618–907 C.E.) dynasties.[38] Yizhou (伊州), as it came to be known, represented for the

Tang one in a series of forward occupied positions on its western frontier, which were continually challenged by Tibetan and Uyghur competition in the region.[39] After 840, when a massive force of Qirghiz Turks destroyed the Uyghur Khanate on the Orkhon Valley of Mongolia, the political situation of the Turfan region, in general, and of Yizhou, in particular, went through a period of violent upheaval.[40] Over the course of the seventh and eighth centuries there had been a continued Uyghur presence in the Tarim Basin, and the Yizhou prefecture was no exception.[41]

Toward the end of the eighth century, the Tibetan empire succeeded in gaining control over the prefecture of Yizhou.[42] Between 842 and 851, the region witnessed a bloody civil war over a question of succession among the ruling factions of the then fragmenting Tibetan Empire.[43] While by the spring of 851 the Tang dynasty had captured Yizhou from the Tibetans, in the years that follow, fragments of the Uyghur Khanate from the Orkhon, who had fled to the region, succeeded in gaining control over both Yizhou and Gaochang (高昌).[44] The Uyghurs referred to Gaochang as Qocho, which became their capital in 856. Yizhou, they called Qomul, which through Mongolian became Khamil, whence the modern Chinese name for the city, 哈密 (Hami), in the Xinjiang province.

De Goeje admits that his reading of this toponym as *Igu* to correspond with Hami / Yizhou is conjectural, for the surviving manuscript on which he bases this reading leaves this word unvocalized.[45] Looking to support his thesis, de Goeje argues that Sallām traveled to Yizhou by way of Lake Balkhash, located in southeastern Kazakhstan. Here the putrid smell of the black land through which Sallām's expedition traveled can be explained by an alliaceous odor produced by asafœtida, an umbelliferous plant common in the region.[46]

From Yizhou, de Goeje argues that Sallām was led to the Jade Gate, known as the Yumenguan Pass (玉門關) of the Silk Road in the northwest of China.[47] This fortified pass formed part of a lengthy series of defensive walls built during the Han dynasty.[48] Looking for further support for this argument, de Goeje turns to the two rulers Sallām says he met during the return journey from the wall. This passage only occurs in the Vienna manuscript and is not picked up by the later Arabic and Persian reception of the account. The manuscript states that the expedition traveled to a place whose king was called اللب, which de Goeje vocalizes as al-Lub. It then describes, in a section that is partly illegible, that the group traveled to a place whose king appears to be طابوىن, which de Goeje reads as طبانوين, and vocalizes as Tabānūyan.[49] Turning north above the Tarim Basin, de Goeje claims that the king, al-Lub, ruled over Lake Lop-nor,[50] while he holds that Tabānūyan ruled over a region identified by Ibn Khurradādhbih as the Upper Nūshajān, on the western border of China (*ḥadd al-ṣīn*), which de Goeje believes corresponds to the city of Khotan.[51] These conjectures are all made in order to substantiate the central claim that Sallām traveled around and through the region of the Tarim Basin and that he proceeded to the Wall of China *via* the city of Yizhou.

The force of de Goeje's argument lies in his identification of this one toponym—whose vocalization and consonantal form is not substantiated by any other Arabic or Persian source—with the ancient Chinese city, Yizhou. As this is located some 220 miles (350 kilometers) from the Jade Gate, de Goeje must also overlook the way the Vienna manuscript details a three-day journey from Igu, or Īkka, to the wall of Dhū 'l-Qarnayn. Only a relay system of post horses could cover this distance in such a short time.[52]

De Goeje is also forced to explain *a fortiori* why Sallām would travel through this region during the height of instability, in the midst of a Tibetan civil war of succession (842–51). Additionally, he must account for how Sallām could travel from the Khazar capital to the Jade Gate in a period of what appears to be roughly two months, an extraordinary pace for the period considering the distance separating the two regions.[53] Likewise, he must demonstrate why a city, populated by a mix of Uyghurs and Tibetans, would be known to Sallām by a Chinese toponym. Furthermore, de Goeje must argue for the existence of an Arabic- and Persian-speaking population of Muslims living in Yizhou who have memorized the Qurʾān, built mosques and Qurʾānic schools, have never heard of the caliph, and—by the look of Sallām's account—are the rulers of the city.

The linguistic evidence for this line of argumentation is anything but conclusive. During the Tang dynasty, the term *zhou* (州) served as an administrative designation for a frontier prefecture.[54] There is documentary evidence, in both Tibetan and Khotanese, that the Tibetan empire adopted this Chinese administrative term for the names of cities that they had wrested from China, such as seems to be the case with 伊州 (Yizhou).[55] However, at a very early date this city was also known by some variant of the local Uyghur toponym Qomul, which, as noted above, transformed into the modern name Hami. It has been claimed that a variant of Qomul appears in a Sogdian document of the early fourth century C.E.[56] Though the reading of this Sogdian toponym has been disputed, there is, in an Uyghur document from the Tang period, what appears to be the early use of Qomul by the local Uyghur population.[57] Furthermore, it is by the name Qomul, and not Yizhou, that Arabic and Persian geographical sources came to know this city.[58] Lastly, in early Persian geographical texts, the Chinese designation 州 (*zhou*) for a prefecture is transliterated consistently into the Arabic script as both جو (*jū*) and چو (*chū*), while there is no indication that either كه (*kuh*) or گه (*guh*) were employed to render the Chinese.[59] Thus, even if Sallām were to have traveled to this city in the Xinjiang region during this period of violent upheaval, it is not clear that it would have been referred to as Yizhou or that he would have written the word as Īkku.

The Tibetans, Uyghurs, and Sogdians of Yizhou / Qomul were not, at that moment, Muslims, but rather Buddhists and Manicheans.[60] However, it is not beyond the pale of reason to envision a Muslim population living in the prefecture during Sallām's visit.[61] With regard to the black putrid lands, asafœtida, often identified in Greek as *silphion* (*σίλφιον*), in Arabic as *ḥiltīt*, and in Persian as *angudān* and *hing*, is a common plant found throughout Central Asia, Iran, and India, and has been used for medicinal purposes for centuries, referenced, for instance, in Ḥunayn b. Isḥāq's translation of Dioscorides' *Materia medica*.[62] It is plausible to suppose that Sallām came across fields of this plant when he traveled nearly a month through a black, putrid region. Furthermore, we could easily imagine that these fields of rancid asafœtida, a plant used as a spice for cooking even in Sallām's day,[63] could have been encountered in Lake Balkhash on the way to Yizhou.[64]

There are a variety of potential vocalizations for the names of the rulers mentioned by Sallām. These two names appear only in the Vienna manuscript and are left unvocalized and partly illegible. Since they are not substantiated in any other source, why should they not bend under the weight of de Goeje's reading? Furthermore, this thesis does not address the fact that the concept of the "Great Wall" of China, as a continuous series of unified fortifications, did not yet exist during Sallām's day.

It is this last point, namely the anachronistic configuration of the Great Wall of China as an ancient barrier stretching for thousands of miles, which is, perhaps, most problematic. The Great Wall of China, as it is known today, did not exist before the middle of the Ming dynasty (1368–1644). Prior to the Ming fortifications, a series of walls and ramparts were erected under different dynasties for ever-changing purposes, but these fortifications did not represent a continuous line of demarcation, with a unified history or purpose. The Jade Gate, which lies at the western stretch of China, was abandoned after the fall of the Han dynasty and was never connected to the much later Ming fortifications of the north that served as a buffer against Mongolian nomads.[65] Furthermore, it appears that the Tang of Sallām's day actually looked down upon the practice of wall building.[66] Various Chinese dynasties built walls and barriers, often from packed earth strengthened with wood; but these frequently disintegrated with the fall of a given dynasty.

The myth of the Great Wall of China as an ancient continuous barrier is, in large part, the product of eighteenth- and nineteenth-century European constructions of the Orient, where the Wall stood as an emblem of Chinese isolationism and oriental despotism.[67]

As European geographical knowledge transformed during the course of the Enlightenment, the exact location of Alexander's fabled barrier came under scrutiny. De Goeje's thesis that the rampart against Gog and Magog was really the Great Wall, is, itself, in dialogue with a running debate that stretches back to the seventeenth century. This debate is shaped, in large part, by pre-existing notions concerning the nature and history of the Great Wall. For instance, the editorial notes to the English (1730) translation of Abū 'l-Ghāzī Bahādur Khān's (d. 1074/1663) Chaghatay history, *Shajarat al-atrāk* [The genealogy of the Turks], itself based on an earlier French translation (1726), promoted the idea that the wall of Gog and Magog found throughout the oriental sources corresponded to the Great Wall of China and that, furthermore, al-Wāthiq's mission to Alexander's rampart most likely reached this Chinese barrier.[68] A similar conclusion is drawn by Edward Gibbon (d. 1794), in his influential history on the Roman empire; he reads Bayer's description of Sallām's adventure and concludes that the "imaginary rampart of Gog and Magog" is derived from "the gates of Mount Caucasus, and a vague report of the wall of China."[69] However, Bayer himself had rejected the notion that Alexander's barrier was to be found in the Wall of China, a theory that had been promoted earlier by the English Orientalist Thomas Hyde (d. 1703).[70]

By the time the English geographer, historian, and surveyor for the East India Company, James Rennell (d. 1830), objected to the identification of Alexander's wall against Gog and Magog with the Great Wall of China, the theory had taken on the power of common wisdom,[71] a link substantiated in the mimetic power of early modern European cartography.[72] Rennell's claim that the two walls were indeed different was met with skepticism, as reflected in an anonymous review, published in the *Asiatic Annual Register* (1801), of his study, *The Geographical System of Herodotus, Examined, and Explained* (1800):

> . . . the land of Gog and Magog is placed by Oriental geographers north-east of China and we think it rather probable that the Wall of China is the one designed by them, though the inaccuracy of their accounts and particularly those of the envoy of the caliph Wathec, have rendered its situation obscure and perplexing. . . but as for the

> existence of any other rampart than the Wall of China [this] rests upon very doubtful authority.[73]

So powerful was the Great Wall in the European imagination that it stood as a means of assessing the quality and authenticity of accounts of medieval travelers to China. Marco Polo was famously excoriated by nineteenth-century scholars for not describing the Great Wall. After all, how was it possible for him to travel to China and not mention the single most important symbol of Chinese civilization?[74] Such cognitive dissonance was itself the product of an epistemological system that reduced the Orient into an ahistorical caricature, essentialized and reified. Marco Polo does not mention the Wall of China because the Wall of China as a single unified entity did not yet exist.[75] What he did look for was the people of Gog and Magog, whom he identified as the Tatar tribes of Ong and Mongol. As for Ong, who correspond to the Turkic Önggüd tribe, many of whom had converted to a form of Nestorian Christianity,[76] Polo connected them to the descendants of Prester John, the legendary Christian patriarch of the far east who animated the imagination of medieval European Christians for centuries.[77] Despite this effort to mold the Orient into a confirmation of the pre-existing paradigms of what the Orient was, Polo did not find the wall of Gog and Magog in any massive Chinese barrier.

Just as Marco Polo's narrative was shaped by preconceived notions of what the world should be, so, too, later European constructions of the Orient were often predicated on grossly unexamined preconceptions. The observations of Sir Henry Yule (d. 1889) on Ibn Baṭṭūṭa's (d. ca 779/1377) account of the wall of Gog and Magog are particularly illustrative. According to the Arabic redaction of Ibn Baṭṭūṭa's travels, while in the Chinese city of Canton (Kalān), Ibn Baṭṭūṭa asked the Muslim population settled there about the location of the wall of Gog and Magog. He learned that the barrier was a sixty-day journey beyond the city, and that along the way were nomadic cannibals who devoured whomever they captured. For this reason, Ibn Baṭṭūṭa comments that he never encountered anyone who had seen the wall or what was beyond it.[78] Nowhere does Ibn Baṭṭūṭa claim that this barrier was the Great Wall of China. However, Yule sees the matter in an entirely different fashion:

> This is an instance of Ibn Batuta's loose notions of geography. He inquires for the Wall of China from his coreligionists at the wrong extremity of the empire... Had he inquired at Khanbalik (if he really was there) he might have received more information. The Rampart

> of Gog and Magog was believed to have been erected by Alexander the Great to shut up the fierce nations of the north and bar their irruptions into civilized southern lands. It is generally referred to Darband on the Caspian, but naturally came to be confounded with the Wall of China. Edris gives an account of the mission sent by the Khalif Wathek Billah to explore the Rampart of Gog and Magog.[79]

Contrary to Yule's reading, Ibn Baṭṭūṭa does not ask for the Wall of China, but for an apocalyptic barrier built by Alexander the Great against savage nations at the end of the earth. None of the medieval geographers confuse a Chinese barrier for Alexander's rampart, as the concept of a singular, unified Great Wall of China, an anachronism for the period, would have been entirely foreign to them.

Not only did the Great Wall of China give Europeans a mechanism to historicize and demystify medieval accounts of the barrier against Gog and Magog, but it also served as a means of stripping away the legendary material surrounding the figure of Alexander the Great. As James Dunbar (d. 1798) argued in *Essays on the History of Mankind in Rude and Cultivated Ages* (1780), as far as the wall of Gog and Magog was concerned, "the lofty spirit of Alexander would hardly have stooped to such dastardly policy,"[80] suggesting that it is rather a characteristic of oriental despotism to pen people behind walls.

In a similar vein, Richard Burton (d. 1890) comments in his annotation of the account of Dhū 'l-Qarnayn included in his sprawling translation of *The Thousand and One Nights* (1885–6), that the Great Wall of China "dates from B.C. 320 and as the Arabs knew [the Chinese city of] Canton well before Mohammed's day, they may have built their romance upon it." He claims that the myth of the barrier against Gog and Magog not only had its origins in the Great Wall, but that the Arabs themselves invented the entire account.[81] De Goeje's thesis is thus neither meant to be original nor provocative, but is rather set to marshal the authority of philology as a means of proving what was already a widespread belief, namely that the legend of Alexander's rampart found its origins in the Great Wall of China. Such a pairing not only helped to separate the Alexander of myth from the Alexander of history, but it also served to highlight the oriental character of this entire mythology and thereby assign the fiction to an oriental imagination, which, in turn, unduly shaped medieval European accounts of marvels and monsters.

The notion that the mythical origins of the wall of Gog and Magog were rooted in the Great Wall of China has been so enduring that the Sinologist

Joseph Needham, when treating the Chinese practices of wall building in his encyclopedic study *Science and Civilisation in China* (1971), argues "both Franks and Saracens knew of a Great wall, vague though their knowledge might be, and throughout the middle ages they ascribed its origins to the Macedonian world-conqueror."[82] Following de Goeje, Needham claims Sallām's adventure represents a perfect example of this very confusion. Ironically, the confusion is not with medieval travelers who mistake Chinese fortifications for Alexander's rampart, but with modern scholars who were quick to read into the sources a timeless and mythical Chinese barrier that simply was not there.

To imagine Sallām at the Jade Gate we must overlook the most obvious fact that by no means does Sallām's description match the physical form of the gate itself. Nor, for that matter, does the account evoke any section of the Great Wall of China as it came to be later constructed. We know that this wall is not made out of brass and copper, nor does it dam up a single mountain pass, nor is it carved with a Qurʾānic inscription. Sallām's account certainly does not lack detail when it comes to the description of the rampart. The image he casts before us draws on the long and polysemous traditions surrounding Alexander's barrier.

To accept de Goeje's theory in the hope of physically locating the 'real' wall of Sallām's journey, we must dissect the entire account into pieces of fact and fiction, if we are to think that what Sallām believed to be the wall of Gog and Magog was all along simply the Wall of China. As far as the Jade Gate of the Han dynasty is concerned, this would have represented a series of largely abandoned mud fortifications. In his desire to locate the origins of Alexander's barrier against Gog and Magog in the Great Wall of China, de Goeje is forced to overlook many factors which draw his reading into doubt. The question of why Sallām must have visited these particular ruins and not any of the other countless fortifications scattered across Central Asia is never addressed.[83]

Yet, to do justice to de Goeje's theory we should appreciate that he is the first major Orientalist to fully explore the narrative claims and implications of the adventure in terms of the physical world, in an attempt to give philological credence to what was already a well established trope in European letters. Restoring faith in Sallām's account, moving out of the field of marvelous fiction into the domain of historical fact, de Goeje demands that the anecdote be taken as a serious example of geographical exploration and travel.

Whither the Wall of China?

De Goeje's quest for a geographical location for Sallām's adventure parallels his argument that the Wāqwāq islands—a recurrent toponym in Arabic and Persian descriptive geography, where women grow off trees—really correspond to Japan.[84] Both arguments are built on a desire to demystify the enchanted world represented in Islamic cosmography. And both of these theories were met with controversy.[85]

The Wall of China thesis caused a stir, as scholars set off to counter, modify, or support de Goeje's argument. Immediately following its publication, Wilhelm Tomaschek, in the *Vienna Oriental Journal* (1889), wrote a short review summarizing de Goeje's main points. Despite minor differences of opinion concerning Sallām's return journey, mainly with regard to Idrīsī's recension, Tomaschek follows the outline of de Goeje's argument, elevating Sallām's narrative out of the 'realm of fable' into the world of historical reality, where, in the Wall of China the account gains factual authenticity, "dass Sallām's Bericht auf Wahrheit beruhe."[86]

In his study on the Alexander cycle, "Beiträge zur Geschichte des Alexanderromans" (1890), Theodore Nöldeke (d. 1930) upholds the view that Sallām reached the Wall of China, "wie de Goeje gezeigt hat." Nonetheless, Nöldeke also claims that Sallām's description of the wall was heavily influenced by the anonymous *Neṣḥānā d'Aleksandrōs*, which he postulates that Sallām did not actually read, but heard via some Christian acquaintance.[87] Such a move suggests again that while some of the material contained in the anecdote may well be fictitious, the underlying itinerary reflects a historical journey.

Tracing the footsteps of Abū Dulaf, another controversial medieval traveler,[88] Josef Marquart (d. 1930), in his study of geographical journeys through Asia, *Osteuropäische und ostasiatische Streifzüge* (1903), continues the tradition of attempting to fix geographical specificity to elusive texts. Marquart situates Sallām's journey to the Wall of China as a precursor to Abū Dulaf's "criss-crossing rambles" through Tibet and the Chinese frontier.[89] The explicit assumption underpinning these investigations holds that in such marvelous journeys there are kernels of truth waiting to be uncovered; this is built on the belief that the material contains authentic information, albeit in an arrangement that is not entirely genuine.[90]

As the thesis on the Wall of China came from one of the most eminent Orientalists of the day, it challenged other scholars to view Sallām's account as a historical event that occurred in time and space. Richard Henning picks up this sentiment in his multi-volume compilation of travel narratives of discovery, *Terrae incognitae* (1936), when he turns to de Goeje's reading in order to affirm that Sallām made his way to Hami in the Xinjiang province and then ultimately to the Wall of China. Admittedly, Henning finds a discrepancy between the three days it takes Sallām to reach de Goeje's Jade Gate after leaving the city of Hami and the hundreds of miles that actually separate these two locations.[91] However, this minor inconsistency does not challenge the larger frame of the narrative, which marks it as authentic; for Henning, the stinking country, the devastated localities, the city of Hami, and the Muslim municipalities in proximity to the wall all affirm the historical truth of the actual journey.[92]

Even before such scholars drew on the Wall of China thesis as historical fact, there had already been serious doubts concerning de Goeje's argument. The first significant challenge came from Étienne Zichy, in his article "Le voyage de Sallām, l'interprète, à la muraille de Gog et de Magog" (1922).[93] Zichy takes up the question of the wall, attacking de Goeje's thesis in order to re-plot what he believes to be the actual course of Sallām's adventure. To do this, he bases his argument primarily on the version of the journey to the wall as recorded in Idrīsī's geography. For the transmission of this anecdote, Idrīsī draws on both Ibn Khurradādhbih and the lost work of the statesman and geographer Jayhānī.[94] Idrīsī leaves Igu, or Īkka, out of his account altogether. Instead of mentioning Sallām's departure from the Khazars, he describes the itinerary as setting out from the Bashjirt, a Turkish tribe of the southern Ural mountains. In Idrīsī's account, the Adhkish live a short distance from the wall. Ibn Khurradādhbih's geography lists the Adhkish as a Turkic tribe. However, he makes no mention of them during Sallām's journey.[95] From here Sallām journeys to a city whose king is the ruler of the Adhkish Turks. Zichy argues that the Adhkish must be located in the Urals, near the Bulghārs along the Volga.[96] Positing new readings for each of de Goeje's conjectures, Zichy claims that Sallām actually traveled not to the Wall of China, but merely north of the Caucasus, and that it was here that the contemporaries of Sallām searched for the wall.[97]

This article was followed the next year (1923) with another rebuttal to de Goeje's hypothesis; this was made by C. E. Wilson in an essay entitled "The Wall of Alexander against Gog and Magog; and the Expedition sent out to find it by the Khalif Wāthiq."[98] Wilson also rejects de Goeje's hypothesis. He chooses instead to base himself, like Zichy before him, primarily on Idrīsī's account of Sallām's journey. However, Wilson follows the itinerary of Sallām's journey up past the northern Mongolian steppe into the region of Lake Baikal, which stretches across southeastern Siberia, where he believes "Idrīsī imagined the rampart to be."[99] For Wilson, this would position the wall at the extreme north of the Yablonoi mountain range of northern Mongolia.[100] Wilson traces the expedition from the Bashjirt, through what he terms the fetid land of the Qirghiz steppe of Mongolia, where he claims Sallām's expedition concluded. After painstakingly mapping out a new itinerary for Sallām's journey, he argues that Alexander's wall is nothing but a "legend which could not bear close investigation."[101] This, however, does not lead Wilson to doubt the broader truth claims of al-Wāthiq's intention to find the wall, and of Sallām's expedition across uncharted territory. Wilson's hypothesis ultimately points not to intentional mystification but incredulous misunderstanding, wherein Sallām, guided by a popular legend, was led to some fortification thousands of miles away in the far northeast, and when told that this was Alexander's rampart, accepted it as fact.[102]

The cartographer Konrad Miller (d. 1933) soon after published a study (1928) on Idrīsī's world map, in which he also turned to the question of Sallām's journey to the wall.[103] Miller superimposes a fallacy of psychological intention onto the account, claiming that when Sallām was unable to find the wall in the traditional location of the Caucasus, he chose instead to invent the entire affair, daring not to return to the caliph empty-handed. Here Miller claims that Sallām's fanciful imagination was mistaken by Idrīsī as truth.[104] Turning from the anecdote to Idrīsī, Miller argues that we should by no means think that the rampart described represents the Wall of China, "of which Idrīsī knows nothing at all." Rather Miller argues that Alexander's wall was always supposed to be located somewhere in the north or northeast, and that as geographical knowledge of the world increased, so, too, did geographers push the wall farther to the margins of the world. Basing himself both on Idrīsī's account of the expedition and the projection of the accompanying world map, Miller concludes that Idrīsī must have thought that the wall was located in the Altai mountain range at the headwaters of the Irtysh River.[105]

The argument over Sallām's journey continued with Andrew Anderson's monograph, *Alexander's Gate, Gog and Magog and the Enclosed Nations* (1932). Anderson prefaces his remarks by stating that the anecdote of Sallām al-Tarjumān has had "an altogether undeserved influence." In turn, Anderson goes on to reject de Goeje's Great Wall thesis, and like Zichy, Wilson, and Miller, he follows Idrīsī's account to map Sallām's itinerary. Yet Anderson concludes that the mountain chain containing Alexander's rampart, as represented by Idrīsī, does not correspond to the Altai range as Miller argues, but suggests that the name given by Idrīsī as Qūfāyā is a corruption Qaf, Qabk, or Qabkh, i.e., the various Arabic forms for the Caucasus, an argument which is nontheless not entirely convincing.[106]

After these articles, mention of the adventure often takes on the form of passing references rather than fully developed arguments. Minorsky, in his commentary on the anonymous fourth/tenth-century Persian geography, the *Ḥudūd al-ʿālam* (1938), dismisses the entire affair with a brief aside, calling Sallām's account to the wall of Gog and Magog, "a wonder tale interspersed with three or four geographical names."[107] Yet despite this flat-handed rejection, Minorsky finds in Sallām's account sufficient geographical information to refute Zichy's thesis that Sallām traveled north past the Caucasus into the Urals.[108]

On the other hand, the desire to glimpse the truth in this account echoes tangentially in A. A. Vasiliev's study, *Byzance et les Arabes* (1935), in which he is not so quick to discredit the entire affair. Rather, like al-Wāthiq's mission to the People of the Cave, Vasiliev is ready to accept the historicity of Sallām's expedition. In a brief footnote, he challenges Sprenger's claim that the entire account was purely a mystification, suggesting instead that the description of the wall probably reflects a mixture of popular legends held by the people encountered, and Sallām's own preconceived notions.[109]

Zeki Validi Togan, in his edition, translation, and commentary of Ibn Faḍlān's journey to the king of the Bulghārs (1939), also chooses to take the journey to the wall seriously.[110] In a note, Togan argues against de Goeje's hypothesis and offers instead a series of possible readings for the unidentified toponyms in Sallām's itinerary. Foremost, Togan sees in Igu, or Īkka, not the Chinese city Yizhou, but a reference to a toponym named by the Turkish lexicographer Kāshgharī as Iki-Ögüz (اكي اكز), which he identifies with a frontier town (*biʿl-thaghr*), on the Ili River, a tributary of Lake Balkhash in Kazakhstan.[111] Togan argues that since Gog and Magog were commonly held to be Turks, we should then look among the eastern Turks in order to plot Sallām's itinerary. For Togan, the adventure ends before the Iron Gate, that is the Tiemenguan (鐵門關) to the Taklamakan Desert, at the eastern stretch of the Tian Shan mountain range.[112]

Each of these scholars approaches the story from a distinct angle, adding their own voices to the fray, emphasizing certain elements and ignoring others, often to suit their own tastes and dispositions. For instance, D. M. Dunlop, in his monograph, *The History of the Jewish Khazars* (1954), speculates more about Sallām's ethnicity than the itinerary of his journey. After mentioning that Sallām stayed with the king of the Khazar, Dunlop concludes, without any textual evidence, that Sallām was probably a Khazar Jew.[113] Salo Wittmayer Baron, in his *Social and Religious History of the Jews* (1952), hypothesizes, also without evidence, that Sallām was most likely a Jew from al-Andalus.[114]

Building upon the itinerary as mapped out by de Goeje, the historian and engineer László Bendefy published an entire monograph in Hungarian (1941) on the topic. Bendefy's initial interest in the adventure appears to be based on Idrīsī's account of how Sallām visited the Bashjirt—proto-Hungarian tribes who were neighbors of the Khazar.[115] From here Bendefy follows de Goeje, tracing the caliphal mission to the Great Wall of China. Yet the location of the Jade Gate in a desert plain and the archeological description of the edifice published by the Hungarian explorer and archeologist Sir Aurel Stein (d. 1943) hardly corresponds to Sallām's description of a mountain barrier.[116] Bendefy reasons that, had Sallām traveled to the Wall of China, he would have soon realized that this barrier was not built by Alexander the Great.[117] This leads Bendefy to look to other fortifications associated with the Greek hero in order to identify the itinerary of the caliphal delegation.

Bendefy plots Sallām's adventure through Central Asia over the Hindū Kush mountain range into the Swāt Valley, in the northwest of modern-day Pakistan. Here, Bendefy reasons, Sallām must have discovered the mountain fortification of Bīr-kōṭ, which, based on the survey of Sir Aurel Stein, corresponds to Bazira (Βάζιρα). According to the Greek historian, Arrian of Nicomedia (d. ca 160 C.E.), Bazira was the location of a military campaign carried out by Alexander the Great in the Swāt Valley during the spring of 327 B.C.E.[118] In Bendefy's estimation, it was in this region that Sallām saw what he took to be Alexander's barrier against Gog and Magog. Bendefy identifies this with Aornos (*Ἄορνος*), described by Arrian as a natural rock (*πέτρα*) stronghold, which Alexander the Great had captured and which Aurel Stein sought to locate on the precipitous massif of Ūṇa-sar rising above the Indus River.[119] To support this entire hypothesis, Bendefy suggests that Idrīsī's reference to the Adhkish is a textual corruption which should be read as Badakhshān, a region in northeastern Afghanistan.[120] This leads him to argue that the toponym interpreted by de Goeje as Igu is a distortion of the fortification of Girā, or rather Rāja Girā, the local Paṭhān name for Uḍegrām, the location of another of Alexander's battles in the Swāt Valley, identified by Aurel Stein as Arrian's Ora (*Ὦρα*).[121] This entire theory, needless to say, is philologically, geographically, and historically dubious.[122]

Bendefy argues that the details of Sallām's narrative that run counter to this thesis, such as the actual description of the barrier, are themselves errors introduced into the account by Ibn Khurradādhbih, who had a penchant for fabulous tales.[123] While Sallām's account of the wall and its mountainous regions certainly does not match that of the Jade Gate, it also lacks any concrete mention of travel through the Swāt Valley and fails to match Aural Stein's descriptions in any significant way.[124] How these mountainous ruins, which have come to be associated with Alexander's Indian campaign largely through Aurel Stein's identifications,[125] could have been known to Sallām, is also not addressed. Following de Goeje's effort to concretely locate the wall, Bendefy adds the use of archeological material to the analysis of the adventure in an attempt to wed Sallām's itinerary to the historical campaigns of Alexander the Great.

Most recently three articles in the *Encyclopaedia of Islam*, all written by E. J. van Donzel, followed by a monograph (2010), co-written with Andrea Schmidt and Claudia Ott, have sought to revitalize the theory developed by de Goeje more than a hundred years ago. The first two encyclopedia articles appear side by side, under the headings, "Qočo" and "Qomul." Van Donzel uses this pair of articles to defend the argument that Sallām traveled by way of Yizhou, known by the Uyghurs as Qomul, to the Great Wall of China. Treating the journey as historical fact, van Donzel glosses over the tumult that arose to challenge de Goeje's Great Wall hypothesis.

In these two articles, van Donzel bypasses the question of authenticity altogether, using Sallām's description of Igu, or Īkka, as a way to describe what the city of Qomul once really looked like, telling us that Sallām's description of city walls stretching for a parameter of sixty kilometers corresponds to the Chinese *kuan* (*guan*), which he argues was equivalent to a fortified city.[126] Van Donzel's claim that Sallām's description of Igu, or Īkka, with its sixty-kilometer parameter, corresponds to a Chinese *guan* seems specious, as a *guan* (關), historically, was a mountain pass, barrier, or customs house.[127] The idea that there were Chinese urban centers of such a size on the frontiers is also questionable.[128] As for Yizhou, according to Tang administrative records from the ninth century, it was a relatively modest outpost with fewer than two thousand households.[129] Yet from de Goeje's thesis, van Donzel builds a historical narrative of conclusions, based on what he takes to be the first narrative of a Muslim traveler to the region. He claims Sallām's reference to the Muslims inhabiting the city Igu, or Īkka, is proof for the early presence of Islam in the Xinjiang region.

Van Donzel's last encyclopedia article takes a slightly different approach to the adventure. The subject for this article is reserved entirely for Sallām al-Tarjumān. Though van Donzel still calls Sallām an early traveler to China and supports de Goeje, he offers a more nuanced position, drawing into question the veracity of the narrative and calling the journey an alleged expedition, "Sallām *may* have traveled the Ili River upstream. The ruined towns which he then reached are *perhaps* the ruins of Peiting. . . the city of the ancient capital of the region. He *may* then have passed modern Urumchi, Guchen and Barku."[130] Van Donzel argues that though the details of Sallām's journey after having left the Caucasus might be vague, there is no good reason to doubt that Sallām made his way to the Jade Gate. He bases this conclusion on one single observation that he takes as historical fact, "Sallām did reach Hami, since his Īkku is identical with this Chinese town."[131] Here van Donzel directs us to his own entry on Qomul in the *Encyclopaedia of Islam* as proof for this claim. In this article on the Uyghur city, his identification of this unvocalized toponym with Yizhou is based on de Goeje's hypothesis, which here is presented as a historical reality. This is despite the fact that de Goeje's largely speculative argument has been a flash point for heated debate. Van Donzel does reference some of those who challenged de Goeje's claim,[132] yet, in the final analysis, he concludes that Sallām "did indeed travel to the eastern part of the Tarim basin [where] he saw the western extension of the Great Wall of China."[133]

As we have noted, the textual evidence for the claim that Sallām made his way to China is tenuous at best. Though the Vienna manuscript that de Goeje uses for his edition of Ibn Khurradādhbih's descriptive geography is far more complete than the Bodleian copy used by de Meynard, it is, as de Goeje himself acknowledges, a later abridgment.[134] The manuscript in question, Vienna Mixt. 783 (Loewenstein 2403), purchased by the Swedish Orientalist Count Carlo de Landberg (d. 1924) in Alexandria and gifted to the Imperial Library of Vienna in 1886,[135] is undated, though one of the ownership notes goes back to 756/1355.[136] The condition of the manuscript is poor and worm-eaten, with large portions having been taped over and recopied by a later hand.[137] This is the case with the section containing the unvocalized toponym that de Goeje reads for Yizhou (plate 13).

The scribe who recopied this passage does not make our job any easier, as not only is the toponym in question left without diacritical marks, but its consonantal form is ambiguous and can be read in multiple ways:

إلى مدينة يقال لها <ابله [ابكه] تربيعه عشرة فراسخ ولها> أبواب حديد

ilā madīnatin yuqālu lahā ..l.h/..k.h tarbīʿuhu ʿasharatu farāsikha wa lahā abwābu ḥadīdin

It is of note that the passage copied over does not agree grammatically with the rest of the text, suggesting that what lies beneath the medieval restoration could very well contain something else altogether.[138] The codicological record is all the more problematic. De Meynard recognized that his edition, based on the Oxford manuscript (MS Hunt 433), and the much later manuscript housed in Paris (Supplément arabe 895), represented a significant abridgment of the text, and, as such, was an imperfect reflection of the original geography. With the discovery of a new and considerably expanded manuscript (Vienna Mixt. 783), de Goeje was able to significantly improve de Meynard's text, basing his edition on three manuscripts, namely Vienna Mixt. 783, Bodleian Hunt 433, and a third manuscript in Oxford, which he did not identify, but only mentioned as containing a fragment of the geography.[139]

On close inspection, it is evident that this third manuscript is Bodleian MS Hunt 538, which contains an excerpt embedded within the larger geography of Ibn Ḥawqal, mainly treating marvelous phenomena, including the wall of Gog and Magog. This particular manuscript served as a basis for both de Goeje's edition of Ibn Ḥawqal and Johannes Kramers' subsequent re-edited improvement. Neither of these editors included this section in their editions, or found it particularly noteworthy that Ibn Khurradādhbih was quoted at length in a manuscript of Ibn Ḥawqal's geography. Indeed de Goeje seems to intentionally obfuscate the matter by not mentioning the provenance of this material.[140]

A comparison with the other manuscripts of Ibn Ḥawqal makes it readily apparent that this section is a later addition to Ibn Ḥawqal's text. Nonetheless, it is included within MS Hunt 538 as original to the manuscript, as it is written out in the same scribal hand. This speaks to how fluid and multivalent the textual reception of medieval manuscripts could be, particularly when the original form and intention of the author was often eclipsed by the tastes and desires of those responsible for a text's transmission. Ibn Ḥawqal, along with Iṣṭakhrī, and evidently Balkhī, two authors on whom he bases his own geography, are exceptional among early geographers in not mentioning al-Wāthiq's mission to the wall; the insertion of this account remedies what might have appeared to his readers as a glaring lacuna.

Illustrative of this process of adaptation and transformation is a geographical compendium made in 725/1325 in the famous crusader castle of Jordan, the fortress of Karak. This particular manuscript consists of a partial abridgment from Ibn al-Faqīh, and selections from Idrīsī, including Sallām's adventure to the wall, which is highlighted on the title page by the proclamation, "contained herein is the account (*ḥadīth*) of Gog and Magog."[141] As with the insertion in the Ibn Ḥawqal manuscript of MS Hunt 538, this tag underscores how the account to the wall came to be viewed as the *sine qua non* of Islamic descriptive geography. Perhaps even more important is how common such acts of mixing and matching geographical material were in medieval codicological practices.

Medieval manuscripts were transmitted in an evolutionary process, which often ignored authorial design or intention, wherein the practices of dissemination could give birth to multiple recensions, even within the lifetime of an author. To make sense of the significant differences between the Bodleian (B) and the Vienna (V) manuscripts, de Goeje posited a two-stage process of recension, one (B) which began during or slightly after the reign of al-Wāthiq, around 232/847, and another (V) which Ibn Khurradādhbih did not finish until after 272/885. De Goeje based this theory upon internal references to historical events dated after the reign of al-Wāthiq, which appear only in the Vienna manuscript. Such is the case with the description of the adventure in the pyramids of Giza undertaken in the service of Ibn Ṭūlūn; this is recorded only in the Vienna manuscript and historically must postdate al-Wāthiq's reign. While the Bodleian manuscript does not contain this section, it is also missing several other segments that appear to be integral to the geography.

It should be noted that much of the material datable to the latter half of the third/ninth century appears in the form of poetic citations that are almost entirely absent from the Bodleian recension. The use of verse, however, functions as an essential component to the geography, in terms of form and structure, as several of the toponyms mentioned are relatively rare, as far as geographical discourse is concerned, and are explicitly framed as catchwords to explain and geographically situate particular lines of verse that highlight or reference geographical locations. This helps to confirm that the Bodleian copy is an abridgment of a text, which like the Vienna manuscript, once contained a full range of poetic citations.[142]

It is thus not impossible to imagine that the historical references lacking from the Bodleian copy, which is missing an undetermined number of folios,[143] are not a reflection of an earlier recension, but represent a later abridgment. The radically different proemiums opening the two recensions, which have recently been studied by James Montgomery,[144] could easily be understood not as different authorial redactions, but as reflections of an even later process of abridgment. In terms of the Bodleian proemium, it was copied by a different hand from the main body of the text.[145] As for the Vienna copy, its proemium, which is wedded to the political context of the period, is also, evidently, by a later hand.[146] However, based upon the reception history, the introductory dedication in the Vienna manuscript is most likely original to the geography.[147]

This messy work of codicological analysis is not mere pedantry, for broader claims about the nature and purpose of the geography are based upon what appears to be a deceptively clean text when edited. While de Goeje's modern edition neatly smoothes out the rough edges of manuscript variation through, what is, at times, an obscure critical apparatus, just like the medieval recensions, it, too, reflects an editorial process of shaping and defining the text according to a set of particular interests. The epistemic framework informing de Goeje's notions of a critical edition would be largely foreign to the medieval copyists, who were often quite comfortable expanding, cutting, and rearranging where they saw fit. For instance, the end of Ibn Khurradādhbih's geography, as presented in the Vienna manuscript, is interrupted with what appears to be a later addendum to the text,[148] which includes, among other amazing anecdotes, an account related by an anonymous narrator (*ḥaddathanī muḥaddithun*) of a lute-playing shepherd from the region of Samarqand, who was lured into a verdant spring and disappeared, seduced by beautiful water nymphs.[149] While this could very well correspond to an authorial version, as de Goeje himself admits, there is no way of knowing, as this section does not appear in the other manuscripts. What we have of Ibn Khurradādhbih's geography is not a camera copy of an original redaction, or even two distinct authorial recensions, but a codicological record that reflects the text's medieval reception history. While what survives appears, for all intents and purposes, to correspond to material produced at some point in the third/ninth century, it is also evident that this material has been redacted, edited, and shaped in the process of transmission.

With regard to the historical record, Ibn Khurradādhbih is known to have been a companion of al-Muʿtamid, for whom he apparently wrote his work on musical history.[150] From the bibliographical accounts about Ibn Khurradādhbih, it is not at all apparent that he was affiliated with the court of al-Wāthiq, a generation earlier. Furthermore, there are many references in the geography that predate al-Wāthiq, such as the account of al-Maʾmūn receiving from ʿAbd Allāh b. Ṭāhir two thousand Ghuzz Turks as captives from Kabul in 211–2/826–7,[151] and the narrative based on Tamīm b. Baḥr's journey to the Uyghur Turks on the Orkhon, which, according to Minorsky, appears to have occurred around 206/821.[152] It is reasonable to assume that a good portion of the historical and geographical information that Ibn Khurradādhbih gathered is based on previous existing data collected by and for the secretariat, in circulation well before he actually began to compile his work.[153] The modern notion of authorship and authorial design is entirely anachronistic to the period and to this particular text. This is highlighted in the Bodleian manuscript in which Ibn Khurradādhbih is explicitly mentioned as an authority within the narrative (*wa qāla Abū 'l-Qāsim. . .*),[154] suggesting a form of authorship that is as much a process of emendation, arrangement, and authorial certification as actual composition.

While it is clear that there were at least two recensions of Ibn Khurradādhbih's geography, the assumption that the manuscript divergence that we have today reflects two different stages of authorial design is based, more than anything, on a desire to see the manuscripts for something which they are clearly not, i.e., authorial redactions. However, by recognizing the surviving codicological record for what it is, namely stages in the reception history of third/ninth century geography, we risk losing authorial, and thus epistemological control over the text. While the Bodleian manuscript, which at points reads very much like an abridgment when compared to the Vienna recension, is missing apparent references to later historical events and contains several notable variants in order and content, these differences appear, above all, to reflect a historical process of reception and abridgment. De Goeje's claim that there were two original redactions gives both levels of variants, which are quite significant as far as al-Wāthiq's mission goes, a veneer of authorial intention. This, after all, forms the basis of textual source criticism, which seeks to reconstitute an ideal 'original' text out of the morass of manuscript recensions. Yet such a framework, which privileges an original authorial design, overlooks how, in the course of publication, either in manuscript or print form, texts and their meanings become collaborative events which are, necessarily, part of a process of veiling the author, however construed, within an ever collapsing horizon of intention.[155]

As for the reception history of Sallām's adventure, the surviving record is quite telling. The ʿAbbāsid geographer Ibn Rusta was one of the first to copy out the adventure, which he does as a means of demonstrating Ibn Khurradādhbih's own exaggeration (*tazyīd*), very much in keeping with Iṣfahānī's assessment of Ibn Khurradādhbih as seldom discriminate in what he relates and in the books he writes.[156] Raising doubt about the veracity of the journey, Ibn Rusta's version does not mention a city near the mountain pass. This is also the case with Ibn al-Faqīh, who composed his geography during the reign of al-Muʿtaḍid (r. 279–89/892–902).[157] While Ibn al-Faqīh transmits the account as authentic, he makes no reference to the enormous city located on the road to the barrier. Ibn Rusta and Ibn al-Faqīh, who testify to the earliest surviving reception of Ibn Khurradādhbih, both plot Sallām's journey through the lands beyond the Khazar, without mentioning specific toponyms that could concretely locate the wall. In his edition of these two geographies, de Goeje chooses not to copy out these transmissions of Sallām's journey, evidently because he saw no need to replicate an account already contained in Ibn Khurradādhbih's work.[158]

The result of passing over this reception history as redundant is to efface the early record of the adventure. The succeeding generation of geographical writing, as represented by Ibn al-Qāṣṣ, Ibn al-Munādī, Muqaddasī, and Abū ʿUbayd al-Bakrī, is also unanimous on this issue. None of these authors makes reference to a named toponym before the wall. Even Idrīsī's apparent redaction of Jayhānī, which de Goeje believes is closer to the Vienna recension, offers us no insight into the name of this city.[159]

This reception history is further supported by the codicological evidence from the surviving manuscripts of Ibn Khurradādhbih's geography, for only Vienna Mixt. 783 identifies a toponym before the wall. Even here there is doubt, for what appears to be the name of this city survives only after the restoration of damage to the manuscript, by means of a later scribal hand, which has pasted a sheet of paper over the effaced section in question. Whether what is written on this restoration corresponds to the original manuscript remains to be seen, as we are effectively left only with a palimpsest. Perhaps more importantly, neither the Bodleian nor Paris manuscripts, nor the excerpt in Ibn Ḥawqal, make reference to a city before the wall. This is completely in line with the early reception of the account, which maps the adventure in the ambiguous space of *terra incognita,* beyond the lands of the Khazar.

Through the positivism necessary to construct the illusion of a definitive and stable *urtext,* de Goeje, in the process of his edition and translation, pushes the messy history of textual reception into the margins of a critical apparatus. The hypothesis of two authorial redactions neatly explains the discrepancies in the two major manuscript groupings. That these stemmata represent the only recensions, authorial or otherwise, however, remains to be seen. The transmission of learning within Islamic intellectual history followed both oral and written lines of dissemination, often extending from the lifetime of the author and beyond. This is evidently the case for Ibn al-Munādī and Ibn al-Qāṣṣ, whose respective receptions of the adventure are based upon the formalized structure of *isnād* transmission, which suggests that Ibn Khurradādhbih himself could have circulated the account at various points in time. Whatever might have constituted the published text(s), it is clear from its early reception that the section treating a named city before the wall is missing.

While the sources converge in the absence of any concrete toponym next to the barrier, the reception history itself points to multiplicity and heterogeneity in the process of transmission. Thus, when tracking the distance covered between the Khazar and the fortifications before the wall, through the putrid land and destroyed cities to the series of fortifications, the two recensions of the geography offer distinctly different calculations: the Vienna manuscript gives a total of fifty-six days, while the Bodleian manuscript claims it took sixty-six. Ibn Rusta, Muqaddasī, and Yāqūt state that it took sixty-three days to reach the fortifications. Ibn al-Faqīh skips over this section entirely, claiming earlier in his geography that a journey of two months separates the Khazar and the wall of Gog and Magog.[160] Ibn al-Qāṣṣ states authoritatively that the wall of Gog and Magog is located seventy-two days north of the Khazar, while his actual description of the adventure adds up to a total of seventy-four. Idrīsī's account describes the journey as seventy-three days, though from the borders of the Bashjirt. While this polysemous divergence reflects the multiple lines of transmission and transformation in the history of reception, all of the writers are clear about one thing, namely that the wall of Gog and Magog is located somewhere beyond the land of the Khazar. Not one of them directly references China or a Chinese fortification.

The Bodleian recension presents a shorter account of the anecdote, which does not contain many of the same details found in the Vienna manuscript. These include the description of an enormous named city before the barrier, the small crack discovered in the wall, the Qurʾānic inscription written in the first language, and certain details of the return journey, such as the frontier regions visited and the numerous casualties suffered. Yet, these added elements are missing in the later accounts of al-Wāthiq's mission, starting immediately with the likes of Ibn al-Faqīh, Ibn Rusta, Ibn al-Qāṣṣ, and Ibn al-Munādī, and continuing after Idrīsī. While this could indicate an early abridgment of the account within the body of ʿAbbāsid descriptive geography, it could also point to a later expansion and improvement of the adventure as preserved within the Vienna recension. It is the Bodleian version, or more likely an earlier redaction quite similar to it and not the extended account in the Vienna recension, which serves as the general basis for the reception history of Sallām's adventure.

As we have noted, the recension that passes through Jayhānī and is picked up by Idrīsī and those who follow him, such as Ibn al-Athīr,[161] only mentions a city ruled by the Khāqān of the Adhkish Turks. This continues the long tradition that associates Gog and Magog with Turkic tribes. In the process of reception, several significant details, which do not appear in the manuscripts of Ibn Khurradādhbih's geography, creep into the account of the mission. For example, in Ibn al-Qāṣṣ's account, Sallām learns that the horrible smell in the black putrid land was caused by the rotting carcasses of the people destroyed by Gog and Magog. Likewise in Idrīsī, the anecdote of a camel-riding missionary who converted the Turks before the wall and taught them the Qurʾān does not have an analog in the surviving manuscripts of the *Masālik*. While these variations could, indeed, find their genesis in the original authorial composition of Sallām al-Tarjumān, it is just as likely that such additions are themselves later exegetical expansions of the account.

So what of the mysterious toponym in the Vienna manuscript? As the name of the city is left unvocalized there are numerous possible readings, and thus the original intent must remain open to speculation. Barring evidence from any future manuscript discovery, there is nothing to ground the text to one authoritative interpretation. While this toponym could be original to the authorial design of the text, given that it is entirely absent from the reception history, it is also plausible that it represents a later accretion or 'improvement' to the story. While de Goeje has argued for Igu, there are other possible readings of note.

One possibility is that the word is merely a garbled form of Adhkish, an interpretation which perhaps has textual support in Idrīsī's recension.[162] It is noteworthy that what de Goeje transcribes here as the letter *kāf*, he renders elsewhere as *lām*; thus, based on the same principle, the toponym could be read as some variant of Īla, Abla, or Unla.[163] The ambiguity of the unmarked and unvocalized grapheme, which as a cypher both produces and annihilates meaning within each new context of reception, has led Sallām through Central Asia, from the Urals, to the high steppes of Mongolia, across the Taklamakan Desert on the northern stretch of the Silk Road, and beyond the Hindū Kush into the Swāt Valley.

The palimpsest invites such interpretive engagement. One hitherto unexplored solution could come from the Mongols. The Īlkhānid historian and statesman Rashīd al-Dīn, in his historical compendium, *Jāmiʿ al-tawārīkh*, describes the Önggüt, from the so-called White Tatars,[164] as a Turkish tribe of some four thousand families, who were one of the first groups to affiliate with the Mongols. According to Rashīd al-Dīn, the Önggüt originally received a stipend from the Golden Emperor (*Āltān khān*) of the Chin dynasty for protecting a walled fortification that stretched from the Yellow River (*qarā-mūrān*) to the Bohai Gulf of the Yellow Ocean (*daryā-i jūrchih*).[165] This barrier, Rashīd al-Dīn likens, in terms of its size, to the wall of Alexander the Great (*mānand-i sadd-i Iskandar*), which evidently he believed to have been another structure altogether.[166] Rashīd al-Dīn explains how the Önggüt, who were originally descendants of the Shato Turks, received their name from the Mongols, based upon their status as guardians over these fortifications, for, according to him, the word *öngü* means, in Mongolian, wall or barrier.[167]

Although de Goeje imagined that the Vienna manuscript is extremely old, he admits that the scribal emendations and corrections occurred much later.[168] While the production of the manuscript would have to precede the ownership note of 756/1355, it is not clear if the emendations, which appear to be responsible for the section in question, were made at an earlier or later date. Given the absence of this toponym in the reception of the account, it is as reasonable to assume that it represents a scribal addition, as it is to posit an authorial origin behind the word. It could very well be the case that this mysterious toponym was introduced after the Mongol invasions of Central Asia, as the word may be a corruption of *öngü* (انگو), and would thus be based upon a known folk etymology for the word wall.

Not only is this vocalization more philologically plausible than that offered by Yizhou, but it also has the added benefit of semantically echoing the location that it purports to represent. Furthermore, Rashīd al-Dīn explicitly identifies *öngü* as a Mongolian word for a walled fortification which he likens to Alexander's rampart (*sadd*), suggesting a reasonable means for reckoning how this word could have been grafted onto a description of the wall against Gog and Magog.[169] While it is unlikely that Sallām al-Tarjumān would have come across such a word, the idea that he encountered the Önggüt, who guarded fortifications for the Chin dynasty (1115–1234) along the borders of Mongolia, would be entirely anachronistic. The word itself appears to belong to a different historical sphere of linguistic exchange; one that developed well after the third/ninth-century ʿAbbāsid encounters along the march-lands of Central Asia. Such a hypothesis would thus be predicated on the multivalent reception that Ibn Khurradādhbih's geography enjoyed, or suffered, depending on one's perspective.

Yet this, too, is unsatisfying, if not also unconvincing, as such a reduction limits and closes off the conceptual fluidity of the frontier. Focusing on the problem solely from the question of where Sallām actually ended up, or whether his journey was a historical fact, risks overlooking the complex narrative structures that have animated this anecdote for centuries. For though de Goeje's Wall of China thesis does a great service by taking the material seriously, the positivism of trying to give historical and geographical specificity to Sallām's journey forces us to ignore all the deliberate ambiguity and indeterminacy that weds this narrative to the fluid space of the marvelous.

CONCLUSION

The Limits of Knowledge

The anecdote as a vehicle for historical knowledge is limited by its own narrative form and generic expectations. The ʿAbbāsid adventure to discover the land of Gog and Magog does not lead us to a physical wall, but to epistemic multiplicity. The narrative resists bringing us closer to ʿAbbāsid relations with Khazaria, the reconfiguration of the Uyghur Khanate, or Sogdian trade routes through Central Asia—though all these are parts of frontier history which loom large during the period. Such historical configurations, rather, form the imagined and largely unspoken landscape of the adventure, whose underlying concern is not in the world of ontology. While outwardly a physical barrier appears to be the focus of Sallām's mission, like descriptive geography, such semiotic emplotment serves to fashion existence within a discrete, manageable narrative, which, in this particular case, means grafting ʿAbbāsid dominion within the arc of salvation.

The dissemination, translation, and reception of such anecdotes reflects the broader transmission and circulation of knowledge and its expansion through the accretions of new iterations. Following the intricate turns of the thread, as the adventure weaves back and forth through the fabric of its interpreters, we may behold a discernible pattern of storytelling recurrent in both the sources and the scholarship that traces them. From the beginning, the tension between the authentic and spurious forms a well-defined motif.

Sallām's narrative anticipates the generations of readers who will try to fathom and transmit the real with exacting certainty. All the names assigned to it—*khabar, qiṣṣa, ḥikāya, fabula, mystifikation, legende, récit, relation, report, narrative, story, tale, text*—attempt to account for the words and their effect, and yet none of the categories, with their own valences and predispositions, bring us any closer to apprehending the historical reality of the event itself. This ambiguity, found throughout the marvelous, between what André Miquel calls the verisimilar and the legendary, is at the heart of the problem.[1]

There is an inherent challenge in using such categories as the legendary, fabulous, or marvelous to interpret and explain the impressive dissemination of Sallām's journey. Even those, such as Ibn Rusta, Thaʿālibī, and Bīrūnī, who objected to the evident contradictions and ambiguities in the account, held the belief that the wall of Gog and Magog exists; this premise foregrounds the medieval reception of the adventure. As Ibn al-Wardī states in his cosmographical book of wonders, Gog and Magog must be located on the map, for there is Qurʾānic proof (*naṣṣ al-kitāb*) of their physical existence.[2] For us, the problem of the category of the marvelous is that it is inflected with an implicit sense of the fictitious; and though some medieval Muslims voice suspicion concerning the authenticity of Sallām's journey, their broader worldview embraces a universe populated with marvels and monsters. This is a world affirmed in the Qurʾān itself,[3] where the talking *hudhud* (hoopoe), the *jinn* and angels, Moses and the fish, the People of the Cave, the wall holding back Gog and Magog are all generally taken as literal accounts of reality.

To begin to appreciate the narrative of al-Wāthiq's embassy, we have had to explore the cultural assumptions and social logic surrounding its production and reception. By mapping out the various contingencies that inflect Ibn Khurradādhbih's descriptive geography, we have seen why this particular anecdote is emblematic of how other such tales are in commerce with discourses of the marvelous. This structure is enacted through a mimetic illusion that manages the vertiginous world of diversity through the power of text and image. All of this is predicated on the belief that the marvelous is part of a reality that can be verified through empirical observation. Needless to say, this particular framework of ocular authority runs counter to Enlightenment epistemologies.

Confronted with a world stripped of such medieval enchantment, modern analysis has centered on three basic propositions: 1) the expedition itself never occurred; 2) the expedition occurred, yet Sallām, not finding the wall, made up the entire affair so as not to anger the caliph; 3) the expedition occurred, yet Sallām reached a fortification which he incorrectly thought to be the rampart of Dhū 'l-Qarnayn. All three of these responses ultimately doubt the central claim of the account, that Sallām reached Alexander's wall, built to protect humankind against a race of monsters destined to overrun the world at the end of time. While these conclusions may be bolstered by the fact that we lack the material evidence for the existence of a wall built by Alexander against Gog and Magog, they also run the risk of ignoring the broader significance of the tale itself.

Those who sought to give more credence to Sallām's itinerary as a historical event, have invariably turned to Idrīsī's version of the account to supplement their analysis. More often than not, this supplementation has occurred without consideration of how the variations in Idrīsī's text do not necessarily reflect a more accurate or truly original version of events and may well be indicative of how later readers altered or changed Sallām's account in the course of its reception. This is a process that is also likely at play in the codicological recensions as preserved in the two major manuscript groupings of Ibn Khurradādhbih's geography.

Models of Imperial Dominion

In dialogue with Syriac, Persian, and Arabic narratives of the rampart, Sallām sets his course in line with a tradition of following the tracks of Alexander the Great. The implicit logic operating within the text affirms the truth of Sallām's experience and the unquestionable existence of the wall itself. As with the gem offered to Shahrbarāz and the shovel presented to Muʿāwiya, the chip of iron that Sallām scratches off with his knife serves as a testament to the physical existence of the ominous boundary.

Despite the many divergences, ultimately, the various recensions position Sallām's wall in a remote and largely untraceable land at the margins of existence. The topographical specificity that frames the entire affair, tantalizingly fans out precisely at the moment the wall is unveiled, revealing and simultaneously concealing, to keep ever present and ever distant the object desired. The putrid-smelling land, the ruined cities, and the unvocalized toponym all take us out of the discourse of exactitude and into the world of indeterminacy.

From its initial reception, the adventure has been framed by a discourse of the marvelous. Within Islamic configurations, marvel-writing has developed a concern with the apocalypse and the destruction of the earth. The wall itself is a visual testament to the broad design of salvation history, which will level the threatening diversity of existence in apocalyptic fury.[4] A discourse of wonder permeates the Qurʾān, which refers to itself (Q. 72:1) as a marvel (*ʿajab*). Muslim exegetes took the primary meaning of the word for a Qurʾānic verse (*āya*) to be equivalent to a marvel (*ʿajab*), demonstrating a deeper symbolic relationship between the Qurʾān as a linguistic phenomenon and the human reaction of astonishment at the reception of divine revelation.[5] The marvelous is part of the very Qurʾānic narrative that foregrounds the People of the Cave and Dhū 'l-Qarnayn's campaign against Gog and Magog, as the word marvel frames the entire *sūra* (Q. 18:9; cf. 18:63).

Ibn Khurradādhbih's account of the missions sent by al-Wāthiq to discover the locations of these two stories suggests not only the incorporation of Qurʾānic material within the field of descriptive geography, but also a vision of caliphal power as interconnected with religious knowledge and imperial surveillance. As such, these missions form part of an articulation of ʿAbbāsid dominion, where the relics of Byzantium are disproved, while the wall of Gog and Magog is not only located but controlled, under the rule of Muslims, in what appears to be a divinely orchestrated progression of history.

As for this imperial projection of power, given the state of the codicological evidence, we can only speculate as to the original contexts for the reception of Ibn Khurradādhbih's geography. In the cases of Sallām's journey to the wall and Muḥammad b. Mūsā's encounter with the false Byzantine relics, Ibn Khurradādhbih claims to have heard both accounts directly from the adventurers themselves, perhaps at some point not too long after the events occurred. How much time might have separated Ibn Khurradādhbih's reception of this material and the composition of his geography, nonetheless, remains to be seen. The adventures were most likely disseminated within a courtly context during Ibn Khurradādhbih's own lifetime, as Sarakhsī, the ill-fated tutor and *nadīm* of al-Muʿtaḍid, appears to have related both stories in his no longer extant geography.[6]

We know from the biographic record that Ibn Khurradādhbih, the companion of al-Muʿtamid, was a denizen of the court. Among his works, considered lost, are the *Kitāb al-ṭabīkh* [Book on the culinary arts], the *Kitāb al-sharāb* [Book on drinking], and the *Kitāb al-nudamāʾ wa 'l-julasāʾ* [Book on boon companions and table companions], all of which speak to a belletristic intersection with court culture. This proximity to centers of power suggests not only a caliphal audience, but also larger networks connecting the ruling elite, the bureaucratic interests of the secretariat, and the social circles of littérateurs. Ibn Khurradādhbih's audiences with al-Muʿtamid, as well as his association with the Christian aristocrat ʿAbdūn b. Makhlad (d. 310/922–3), brother of Ṣāʿid b. Makhlad (d. 276/889), the *wazīr* to both al-Muʿtamid and the prince regent al-Muwaffaq, highlight points of interconnectivity along which the marvelous stories and the poetical citations of his geography could well have circulated. His friendship with the court poets Ibn al-Rūmī (d. 283/896) and Buḥturī further adumbrate a backdrop of literary salons (*majālis*) that were the occasion for poetry and wondrous tales.[7]

In a description of Transcaucasia and the kingdom of the Khazar, Ibn Khurradādhbih cites a verse from Buḥturī's elegiac poem dedicated to Isḥāq b. Kundajīq, a military commander and governor of Mawṣil and Jazīra, of Khazar descent:

شَــرَفٌ تَزَيَّدَ بِٱلْعِــرَاقِ إِلَى ٱلَّذِي   عَــهَدُوهُ فِي خَمْلِيجَ أَوْ بِبَلَنْجَــرا

He has gained honor in Iraq in addition
to that which he has been pledged in Khamlīj or Balanjar.[8]

Like most of the poetic citations in the Vienna recension, this line of verse is missing from the Bodleian manuscript. As for its placement within the *Masālik*, this verse with its reference to Khazar cities situates the land beyond the frontiers within the orbit of ʿAbbāsid influence. Buḥturī composed this particular elegy in 269/883 for the ceremonial investiture in which Isḥāq b. Kundajīq was crowned and given two swords, and conferred the title Dhū 'l-Sayfayn ('Possessor of two swords').[9] A similar honorific is found in Dhū 'l-Wazīratayn ('Possessor of the two vizierates'), the title granted in the same year to Ṣāʿid b. Makhlad, in a sardonic reference to his service to both al-Muwaffaq, de facto ruler of the empire, and his imprisoned brother, the caliph al-Muʿtamid. Ṭabarī relates that during this same year Isḥāq b. Kundajīq was instructed by Ṣāʿid, acting on the orders of al-Muwaffaq, to capture the caliph al-Muʿtamid, who sought refuge from his brother with the general Ibn Ṭūlūn. Isḥāq b. Kundajīq, after having detained al-Muʿtamid, returned him disgraced in chains back to Sāmarrāʾ, in Shaʿbān 269 / February 883.[10] The citation of this verse within the *Masālik* has led James Montgomery to argue that the unnamed patron mentioned in the opening dedication of the Vienna recension could not have been the caliph al-Muʿtamid, as it would be unlikely for Ibn Khurradādhbih to reference an elegy in honor of a figure who participated so prominently in the caliph's humiliation. This line of analysis would point rather to al-Muʿtamid's rival, the prince regent al-Muwaffaq, as the addressee elliptically referenced in the Vienna exordium, or to someone within al-Muwaffaq's entourage, such as his son, the future caliph al-Muʿtaḍid.[11]

Ibn Khurradādhih's acquaintance with Ṣāʿid's brother perhaps suggests an affiliation with the partisans of al-Muwaffaq, a point which strengthens the claim that the geography, at least as preserved in the Vienna manuscript, would not have been dedicated to al-Muʿtamid. Similarly, the reference in the adventure through the Giza pyramids to the general Luʾluʾ, who abandoned his former master Ibn Ṭūlūn to join forces with al-Muwaffaq, may also offer a further indication of an alignment in the Vienna recension with the partisans of al-Muwaffaq. This is admittedly more problematic, as the discoveries in the pyramids appear to lionize Ibn Ṭūlūn, ally of the imprisoned al-Muʿtamid, for his ability to have the pharaonic treasures unearthed. It may suggest that the anecdote of the pyramid, as well as the allusion to Isḥāq b. Kundajīq, were deployed within a political context in which such material had already been neutralized and was therefore no longer politically charged or relevant.

The appendix at the end of the Vienna manuscript, with its account of seductive water nymphs, the adventure in the pyramids, many details of the mission to the wall, and the majority of the verse citations, are entirely missing from the Bodleian recension. Significant portions of the poetry, however, are preserved within the reception history of the *Masālik*.[12] Nonetheless, the appendix, the Giza foray, and the various particularities of Sallām's adventure found only in the Vienna manuscript are also absent in the geographers that follow Ibn Khurradādhbih, pointing to the limited circulation of this particular manuscript. While the Vienna copy preserves details that suggest a greater proximity to the court, it also contains evident accretions that have been introduced into the text at some point in the course of its transmission. The limited dissemination of the prototype for the Vienna manuscript points to multivalency in the production of the geography, both in the recensions and in the diachronic reception. There may well have been multiple copies produced within the lifetime of the author and disseminated in a host of individual occasions, in piecemeal, or as a set body of anecdotes, or in a formalized redaction deposited within the treasury. The present codicological evidence nonetheless limits a full clarification of the original courtly contexts of production and reception.

As for the broader audience, Ibn Khurradādhbih's social universe suggests a cosmopolitan urban literary culture. Among Ibn Khurradādhbih's associates was Ibn al-Marzubān (d. 309/920), a philologist, historian, and Qurʾānic exegete of Persian descent, who, according to Yāqūt, translated over fifty works from Persian into Arabic.[13] Ibn al-Marzubān was a student of the Baghdadi historian and man of letters Ibn Abī Ṭāhir (d. 280/893), who, likewise, was of Persian stock, and, according to Ibn al-Nadīm, had a penchant for collecting fables (*khurāfāt*) and evening tales (*asmār*).[14] In his treatment of literati and the denizens of the court, Ibn al-Nadīm situates Ibn Khurradādhbih between these men, underscoring an associative proximity in the literary universe of ʿAbbāsid writerly culture during the latter half of the third/ninth century.[15] As for the intersection between storytelling and imperial administration, there is also the case of Ibn Khurradādhbih's contemporary, the Persian courtier, Abū 'l-ʿAnbas al-Ṣaymarī (d. 275/888), *nadīm* to both al-Mutawakkil and al-Muʿtamid. Like Ibn Khurradādhbih, Ṣaymarī appears in Ibn al-Nadīm's chapter on boon companions, table companions, men of letters, singers, buffoons, clowns, and comedians.[16] Ṣaymarī, who was a judge and jurist, wrote on a wide array of subjects, including astrology and oneiromancy.[17] He is, however, also remembered for his obscene humor and his role as a court humorist. His treatise, *Faḍl al-surm ʿalā 'l-fam* [Superiority of the anus to the mouth], gives a taste of this largely court-sanctioned vulgarity. Ṣaymarī had his own run-in with Buḥturī, and like Ibn Khurradādhbih, had an interest in marvelous tales, as is evident in his no longer extant collection *ʿAjāʾib al-baḥr* [Wonders of the sea] which, based on Ibn al-Nadīm's classification, would be in the realm of fables of dubious authenticity.[18] Ibn al-Nadīm also points out that the ʿAbbāsid caliphs were particularly fond of listening to evening tales and fables.[19] It is through this larger social network of belletristic writing, with its attendant interest in poetry and storytelling, that Ibn Khurradādhbih's geography, and with it Sallām's adventure, is shaped and disseminated.

And it is in this light that we should re-evaluate Iṣfahānī's strong condemnation that Ibn Khurradādhbih was unreliable. One of the explicit reasons given by Iṣfahānī is Ibn Khurradādhbih's claim that the caliphs, beginning with ʿUmar b. al-Khaṭṭāb and continuing through the Umayyads and the ʿAbbāsids, were all skilled singers. Accordingly, Ibn Khurradādhbih argued that singing was something the caliphs inherited as part of the caliphate, as one of the pillars of their rule (*rukn min arkān al-imāma*)—a notion that Iṣfahānī rejects outright. According to him, Ibn Khurradādhbih's examples of the material sung and composed by these caliphs are all pitiful and not worth mentioning.[20]

It is of note, however, that Iṣfahānī's *Kitāb al-aghānī* depicts al-Wāthiq as a connoisseur of music and poetry who played the lute and sung his own compositions. Al-Wāthiq studied closely with the renowned musician Isḥāq al-Mawṣilī (d. 235/850); the latter helped al-Wāthiq improve his skills.[21] The caliph famously sought to establish a canon of the best musical compositions under Isḥāq's supervision. According to Isḥāq, of all the caliphs, al-Wāthiq was the most skilled singer.[22] While the *Kitāb al-aghānī* indicates that later ʿAbbāsid caliphs did not attain the same skill in music or poetry, the tradition of caliphal compositions and performances continued after al-Wāthiq, until al-Muʿtaḍid, who, according to Iṣfahānī, was the last accomplished musician among the caliphs.[23] Thus it stands to reason that when Ibn Khurradādhbih traced the practice of singing and composing poetry to the earliest caliphs, he was appealing to a particular conception of the caliphate and court culture.

The surviving sections of Ibn Khurradādhbih's *Kitāb al-lahw wa 'l-malāhī*, which was evidently composed for al-Muʿtamid,[24] himself an ardent aficionado of music, offer a full-throated defense of singing and musical performance as grounded in the tradition of the Prophet, the theories of ancient philosophers, and the patronage of emperors.[25] The discipline of music (*mūsīqā*), according to Ibn Khurradādhbih, represents a philosophical system that leads to all other sciences (*sāʾir al-ʿulūm*), combining perfectly rational principles (*ʿuqūl*) with physical perceptions (*ḥawāss*).[26] To this end, Alexander the Great paid great respect to musicians, as did Khusraw Parwīz, who would sing with his beloved Shīrīn.[27] Such a configuration serves not only to legitimate musical performance, but also positions it as part of the cosmopolitan character of the caliphate.

As with his book on music, Ibn Khurradādhbih's administrative geography promotes a very specific image of the caliph and caliphal dominion. While his geography deals with the reality of competing powers, both within and beyond the political territories of Islam, represented, for instance, by the Rustamids, the Idrīsids, the Umayyads of al-Andalus, and the Byzantines, it locates the focus of attention on the centers of ʿAbbāsid rule. To evoke, as Ibn Khurradādhbih does, the Sāsānian usage, it is the 'heart of Iran' (*dil-i Īrānshahr*) that serves as the central node through which the routes of the world pass. From the sacred landscape of Mecca and Medina, to the wastelands before the wall of Gog and Magog, Ibn Khurradādhbih positions the caliphate as the *axis mundi* around which revolves an expansive, divine cosmography. This process of imperial self-fashioning frames the geography and its placement of ever-marvelous anecdotes along the frontiers. The *Masālik* opens up the itineraries of Rūs traders, the expansive network of polyglot Jewish merchants, and Sallām's adventure beyond the Khazars. The extent to which these descriptions reflect historical reality, has, nonetheless, received a considerable amount of debate. The geography's relationship to the larger constellation of ʿAbbāsid writerly culture and its adherence to the expectations of belletristic pleasure point to a process of not only describing the world, but also shaping it through a set of literary conventions.

The Task of the Translator

There are many parallels between Sallām's adventure to the wall and Ibn Faḍlān's narrative concerning his travels to the king of the Bulghārs nearly a century later. Both are caliphal envoys sent to the far reaches of the world.

Both encounter wondrous phenomena at the margins of existence. Yet Ibn Faḍlān's narrative is a much longer account, more developed and substantial, and offers a fuller array of historical and geographical contingencies.

Ibn Faḍlān also describes his own encounter with Gog and Magog. He relates that the Bulghār king found a giant man from these monstrous races.[28] Eventually, the king had the man killed and hung from a tree. Curious, Ibn Faḍlān requested to be taken to see the carcass, still hanging from the tree. He describes for us the immensity of this giant from the people of Gog and Magog, who, he is told, live a three-month journey beyond the Finnish Veps (Wīsū), a group themselves three months away from the Bulghārs (plate 14).

A giant from a far-off land, a wall at the end of the earth; both of these intrepid adventurers cast their eyes onto the wondrous material reality of being. Led by guides, who point the way and help interpret and translate the margins of the world, our adventurers, in turn, guide us to behold the marvelous. The interpretative lenses that frame their comprehension of existence lead them to see a world that largely corresponds to their preconceptions. Ibn Faḍlān, when confronted with this giant figure, draws upon a particular vocabulary to fathom the phenomenon. As with Ibn Faḍlān's act of beholding, the ocular proof of the witness confronted with alterity stands at the heart of Sallām's translation project. Central to both adventures is the allure of storytelling through the exotic tales of travelers to remote lands. There is ample evidence to suggest that the very centrality of the marvelous in Islamic intellectual history, so much a part of scientific constructions of the natural world, reflects a desire to indulge in the narrative pleasures of the strange and uncanny.[29]

The backdrop of the ʿAbbāsid translation movement, the transmission of knowledge through various linguistic fields, the rise of administrative geography matched with imperial anxieties over the frontier, the value of verse, the role of dream interpretation, the development of marvel-writing, the eschatological projections of time all play in concert with the social contingencies that frame the production of Ibn Khurradādhbih's geography and the ʿAbbāsid reception of Sallām's adventure. Without this broader social matrix we have only a narrative utterly inconsistent with our own assumptions of the world. As the debate that follows Sallām demonstrates, the open field of the anecdote allows, and even encourages, such slippage in comprehension. The geographical rendering of the margins through the power of anecdotes hides the complex work inherent in the task of the translator, concealing the incongruous moments with diegetic continuity, emplotting narrative unity across the heterogeneity of existence.

POSTSCRIPT

ROYAL GRAFFITI

Well before becoming one of the most powerful rulers of the Islamic East, and before acquiring a vast library which would include a copy of the Ibn Khurradādhbih's *Masālik*, the Būyid prince ʿAḍud al-Dawla, at the fresh age of nineteen, visited the ruins of Persepolis, once the center of the Sāsānian empire. He took an interest in the ancient inscriptions lining the walls of the ruined city, which centuries before had been sacked by Alexander the Great *en route* to the wonders of the east. We know this because ʿAḍud al-Dawla had his own inscription made on the doorway between the portico and the main hall of Darius' palace in commemoration of his visit:

> حَضَرَهُ ٱلْأَمِيرُ أَبوُ شُجاع عَضُدُ ٱلدَّولة أَيَّدَهَ ٱللّٰهُ في صَفرٍ سَنَة
> أَرْبَعَ وَأَرْبَعِينَ وَثَلاثْمائةٍ وَقُرِئً مَا فِي هٰذه ٱلآثارِ مِن ٱلْكِتابَةِ قَرأَهُ
> عَلي بنُ ٱلسَّري ٱلْكَاتِب ٱلْكَرَجي وَمارَسفَنْد ٱلمَوْبَد ٱلْكَازَرُوني

> The amīr Abū Shujāʿ ʿAḍud al-Dawla, may God aid him, appeared here in Ṣafar of the year 344 [June 955]. The inscriptions on the ruins were read to him. The scribe ʿAlī b. al-Sarī ʽl-Karajī and the Zoroastrian priest Mārasfand al-Kāzarūnī read them to him.[1]

Through this act of translation, the mute ruins speak their secrets, uniting the Persian prince with the magnificent Sāsānian past. The symbolic significance of the *amīr* carving his name on the ruins comes into relief with another inscription from the same year. Here ʿAḍud al-Dawla appears as Fannā Khusraw b. al-Ḥasan, affirming through his name (the refuge of Khusraw) a royal Persian ancestry, and through his genealogy (the son of al-Ḥasan) his rightful claim as heir to the Būyid dynasty.[2]

This particular act of translation, in the form of inscription, cuts across temporal divides, recovering the mark of the past in the present, which is, in turn, recorded for future eyes to uncover and decode. The inscriptions on the ruins, which are really nothing more than royal graffiti, form the basic structure of all anecdotes, themselves accounts of events, whether real or imagined—deceptively simple. Yet the anecdote, as opposed to the past or the present, or whatever ontological category of being we may choose, is a way of ordering the world with meaning, and is never neutral. ʿAḍud al-Dawla has the royal inscriptions translated for him and on the palimpsest of history he signs his own name. In a not entirely unrelated way, al-Wāthiq's adventure, or at least Ibn Khurradādhbih's vision of it, is another example of royal graffiti, a discursive suturing of the caliphal name to the memory of someone else's architectural grandeur. These accretions of meaning, of readers and writers, are common to the anecdote, which is in a continual process of transformation, through the inscription of new readers, each marking their place in a continuing narrative.

The illusion of the anecdote lies in its minimalist reduction of ontology—of what occurred, whether real or imagined—into the basic expression of events, in the story of what happened where and when, to whom, and for what reasons. In contrast to its simplicity of form, the processes of decoding the broader logic of the tale, the assumptions and networks through which it travels and on which it relies, require another illusion, namely encyclopedic totality. To understand each of the constituent elements of such narratives, we must also understand the larger assumptions and values in play. Ultimately, it is an interpretive process of mapping meaning. For to decode ʿAḍud al-Dawla's inscriptions on the ruins of Persepolis, or al-Wāthiq's caliphal reach before the wall, we must turn to notions of dynastic authority, and the power of language and memory, not in isolation, but through a larger semiotics of statecraft, which, from our vantage, survives only in such fragmentary inscriptions.

We may remember al-Wāthiq for yet another act of royal graffiti, which also fits into a paradigm of caliphs and kings confronting the impermanence of power. An account preserved in the *Adab al-ghurabāʾ* [The etiquette of strangers] ascribed to Isfāhānī, relates that al-Wāthiq held a drinking party with his boon companions and singers in al-Mukhtār, one of the palaces of Sāmarrāʾ, decorated with beautiful paintings (*ṣuwar ʿajība*). Once drunk, al-Wāthiq took in the beauty of the murals and the splendor of the evening, and with a pocketknife, he inscribed (*kataba*) on the wall a set of verses, which concluded:

مَجْلِسٌ حُفَّ بِٱلسُّرُورِ وَٱلنَّرْجِسِ وَٱلْآسِ وَٱلْغِنا وَٱلْبَهـارِ
لَيْسَ فيهِ عَيْبٌ سَوى أَنَّ مَا فيهِ سَيُفْنيهِ نَازِلُ ٱلْمِقْدارِ

A gathering overtaken by cheer, narcissus,
myrtle, singing, and fragrance.
It suffers no fault, save that
it will be effaced by the reverses of fate.[3]

The poetry is not only a gloss on the ephemeral evening, but also on the transience of the mimetic illusion that the paintings of the palace represent. Not surprisingly, nostalgia serves as a prominent trope in the reconstituted textual memory of such poetic graffiti. Unlike the inscriptions of ʿAḍud al-Dawla, what survives of this caliphal encounter with the fragility of existence is the narrative performance of the graffiti, which simultaneously fulfills and contradicts the prediction of its own effacement.

As critical observers, our entry into the past occurs through these fragments, through the textual and semiotic, etched in the monuments erected, the words inscribed, the bones entombed. All of these are traces of the past that we try to recuperate into a meaningful order. To uncover such meaning we must seek out additional pieces to set together, so as to reconstruct a conceptual mosaic, which, in the realm of being, can only be a pale simulacrum of the past, achieved by a swift *léger de main*. Our own endeavors of recuperation are likewise historical acts to be contextualized and decoded, circumscribed by our own assumptions and values.

The motif of melancholy before the ruins—the *aṭlāl* and *āthār*—resounds in the very origin of Arabic poetry, in the generic form of the opening verses (*naṣīb*) of the classical ode (*qaṣīda*). This modality of longing (*ḥanīn*) in dislocation marks an established conceit in ʿAbbāsid descriptive geography,[4] and suggests already, in the beginning, a loss, a nostalgic estrangement.

Our strategy for understanding the paradigmatic patterns enveloping the intersection of salvation history and geography has been to draw on the power of the anecdote as a point of entry into the larger discursive assumptions and values surrounding the anxieties of translation. The ʿAbbāsid expedition sent to discover Dhū ʿl-Qarnayn's wall that holds back the tribes of Gog and Magog serves as an emblem for the coalescence of eschatology and geography, drawn together in the metaphor of translation. To understand the larger workings of such anecdotes, we must diagram the core individual elements against which historical material is cast and disseminated. Yet, as we have acknowledged, from such encyclopedic grandeur the sum of the parts can never truly make the whole.

The case of Sallām al-Tarjumān's journey to the wall at the edge of the world first appears along the frontiers of the ʿAbbāsid empire, as part of a body of geographical writing that details the administrative concerns of the state with belletristic attention to poetry and marvelous anecdotes. When seen within the larger pattern of looking for geographical confirmation of Qurʾānic material, Sallām's adventure evokes a tradition of mapping scripture across the contours of the globe. The strong parallels between the caliphal mission and earlier Syriac, Sāsānian, and Umayyad accounts further suggests the lasting effect of translation in the formation of Arabic and Persian descriptive geography. Furthermore, the prominent role of translators and acts of translation in geography, and the concomitant tradition on the wonders of creation, indicates the important conceptual role that translation has played in conceiving and imagining frontier spaces. Standing between the savage and the civilized is the figure of the interpreter, who domesticates alterity into the sublimated form of the anecdote. The fact that many readers, over time, have come to question such anecdotes highlights the lasting tensions surrounding the widely disseminated accounts of *ʿajāʾib* literature. This is further accentuated by the fact that a similar anxiety envelops the potentially distorting effects of translation, a semantic resonance that inflects the very category of the *tarjumān*.

While the marvels of existence become a fixture in a wide range of fields, the concern for fidelity is matched with an aesthetic that flirts with what modern readers might anachronistically wish to call fiction. In the apprehension of marvelous phenomenon mediated between layers of transmitters, the translator's integrity is continually under scrutiny. While a deep strain of positivism inflects much of the material, in the reconstruction of events through the stable transmission over time, there is a counter voice of doubt and speculation, autochthonous in the primary sources, which questions the reliability of such transmission.

An entire range of metaphors and anecdotes accounting for translation evolve as central tropes in the *imaginaire*, concerned in the most basic sense with understanding the diversity of existence. The conceptual borders mapped out in a geography of salvation serve as imagined conceits, and thus are not to be found in being, but in language. These discourses enveloping the construction and dissolution of such borders are circumscribed by an imperial logic of dominion; yet they also point to the subversive power of translation in the slippage of communication, as a veil (*ḥijāb*) that conceals as much as it reveals. Ultimately, such frontiers are epistemic in nature. They are used in the production of meaning, in distinguishing alterity through deictic acts of communication, through gesture (*īmāʾ*) and pointing (*ishāra*) with the finger of astonishment (*angusht-i taʿajjub*). This leads us both here and there, from apprehending the unfettered marvel, to moving off the page, attempting to internalize the sublime design of difference itself.

APPENDIX 1

THE DISSEMINATION OF THE ADVENTURE

Manuscripts of Ibn Khurradādhbih, *al-Masālik wa 'l-mamālik*

Bodleian Library, Oxford University
B = MS Hunt 433, *al-Masālik wa 'l-mamālik fī ṣifat al-arḍ* [Uri, *Bibliothecae Bodleianae*, §993], 82 fols. An abridgment, dated 631/1232. Opening folio in a different hand. Lacuna between fol. 81b–82a.
H = MS Hunt 538, excerpt of Ibn Khurradādhbih in Ibn Ḥawqal, *al-Masālik wa 'l-mamālik* [Uri, *Bibliothecae Bodleianae*, §963], fols. 139b–145b.

Bibliothèque national de France, Paris
P = Supplément arabe 895, *Kitāb fīhi ṣifat al-arḍ. . . wa 'l-masālik wa 'l-mamālik* [de Slane, *Catalogue des manuscrits arabes*, §2213], 54 fols. A nineteenth-century copy based on Bodleian, MS Hunt 433.

Österreichische Nationalbibliothek, Vienna
V = MS Mixt. 783, *Kitāb masālik wa 'l-mamālik ʿan Ibn Khurradādhbih* [Loebenstein, *Katalog*, §2403], 77 fols. Undated, provenance note dated 756/1355. Worm-eaten, damaged by moisture, several portions have been taped over and recopied, three different hands, last section appears to be a later addition, fols. 75a–77a.

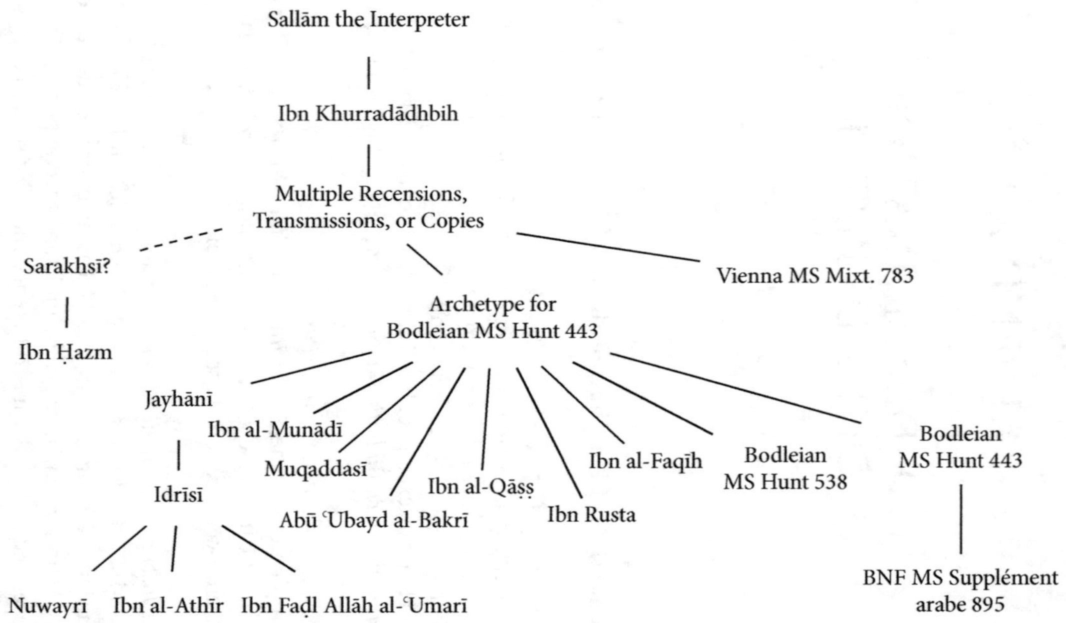

Figure 3: Recensions of Sallām's Adventure

APPENDIX 2

THE VIENNA RECENSION

The following is a translation of Sallām's adventure as it appears in the copy of *al-Masālik wa 'l-mamālik*, housed in Vienna MS Mixt. 783 [MS V, fols. 68b–72a]. Double brackets mark sections that have been copied or glued over in the manuscript and recopied; bracketed parentheses indicate marginal notes, while single brackets indicate my own clarifications. The paragraph numbers are collated with appendices 3 and 4; the asterisks mark notable divergences, and paragraph numbers marked with asterisks indicate sections not present in the Bodleian and Paris recensions.

Description of the Barrier of Gog and Magog

[§1] Sallām the Interpreter informed me that when al-Wāthiq bi'llāh dreamt in his sleep that the barrier which Dhū 'l-Qarnayn had built between us and Gog and Magog had opened, he asked for a man to set out to its location and seek information about its condition.

[§2*] So Ashinās said, "There is no one more appropriate than Sallām the Interpreter." [For] he could speak thirty languages.

[§3] [Sallām] said: So al-Wāthiq summoned me and said, "I want you to set out for the wall in order to inspect it and return to me with an account (*khabar*) of it."

[§4*] He outfitted me with fifty strong young men and gave me five thousand dinars and a personal indemnity of ten thousand dirhams and he ordered that each man be given a thousand dirhams and daily sustenance to last a year.

[§5*] He ordered that there be prepared for the men felt coats wrapped in leather, and that there be made ready for them fur saddlecloths and wooden stirrups. [§6] He gave me two hundred mules for carrying supplies and water.

[§7] So we set out [V 69a] from Sāmarrāʾ with a dispatch from al-Wāthiq biʿllāh to Isḥāq b. Ismāʿīl, the ruler of Armenia. He was in Tiflīs on our arrival. Isḥāq dispatched us to the ruler of al-Sarīr and the ruler of al-Sarīr dispatched us to the king of the Alāns and the king of the Alāns dispatched us to the Fīlān Shāh and the Fīlān Shāh dispatched us to the Ṭarkhān, king of the Khazar. We remained with the king of the Khazar for a day and a night, until he sent us off with five guides. We traveled away from [the king of the Khazar] for twenty-six days.

[§8] Then we came upon a putrid black land. Before entering this land, we had prepared for ourselves vinegar to smell in lieu of the vile odor. For ten days we traveled in this land. Then we reached ruined cities and we traveled through them for twenty days.* We inquired about these cities and were informed that Gog and Magog had breached them and then destroyed them. Then we traveled through fortifications near the mountain range on a branch [of which] is located the barrier [cf. *Masālik*, 163, note i].

[§9] A tribe who speak Arabic and Persian populate these fortifications. They are Muslims and they recite the Qurʾān; they have Qurʾānic schools and mosques. They asked about us and where we were from. We informed them that we were messengers of the Commander of the Faithful.

> They grew astonished and exclaimed, "The Commander of the Faithful!?"
>
> We replied, "Yes."
>
> They asked, "Is he old or young?"
>
> We replied, "He is young."
>
> They were equally astonished and inquired, "Where is he?"
>
> We responded, "In Iraq, in a city called Sāmarrāʾ."
>
> They replied, "We have never heard of this before."

[§10*] The distance between one fortification to the next ranges from one to two *farasakhs*.

[§11*] Then we traveled [69b] [[to a city called Unkuh [?]. Its perimeter is ten *farsakhs* and it has iron gates which are lowered from above]]. In the city are cultivated fields and mills. This is the city in which Dhū 'l-Qarnayn resided with his army. A distance of three days' journey separates the city from the rampart. Fortifications and towns line the way until the rampart is reached on the third day. The barrier is [located in] a mountain enclosure.

[§12*] They say that Gog and Magog live in [this enclosure] and that they are of two kinds. They mention that [those of] Gog are taller than [those of] Magog and that one of them is an arm's length or an arm's length and a half tall [[more or less]].

[§13*] Then [[we reached a high mountain on which is a fortification and the barrier]] that Dhū 'l-Qarnayn had built. This is the pass, [(which is a valley)], between the two mountain sides, the width of which is two hundred cubits. This is the path from which [Gog and Magog] will set off to scatter across the earth.

[§14*] So [Dhū 'l-Qarnayn] dug the foundation of the rampart thirty cubits into the ground and he built it up with iron and copper until the foundation reached the surface of the earth. Then he erected two doorposts, which are next to the mountain on both sides of the pass.

[§15] The width of each doorpost is twenty-five cubits, and they are fifty cubits high. [(At their base each of these posts protrudes ten cubits from the gate.)] All of this is constructed with bricks of iron set into copper.

[§16] Each brick measures a cubit and a half squared by four fingers thick.

[§17] A lintel (*darwand*) of iron, five cubits thick, stretches across the two doorposts, the length of which is one hundred and twenty-five cubits, mounted over the doorposts extending on each side for a distance of ten cubits.

[§18] Over the lintel [V 70a] is a wall of iron bricks set in copper that extends to the top of the mountain. It rises as far as the eye can see, stretching above the lintel for about sixty cubits.*

[§19] Above this are iron merlons; on top of each merlon are two angled points (*qurnatān*) that face each other.

[§20*] Each merlon is five cubits tall by four cubits wide, and there are a total of thirty-seven merlons [lining the wall].

[§21] As for the iron gate, it has two door panels which are sealed shut, each panel is fifty cubits long, seventy-five cubits high, and five cubits thick.* The two panels hinge on thick vertical pivot bars set into the lintel.

[§22*] No wind enters either through the gate or the mountain pass, as though it were made of one single mass.

[§23] On the gate is a bolt, which is seven cubits long and the thickness of an arm-span in circumference.

[§24*] Two men alone would be unable to fasten the bolt.

[§25] The bolt is twenty-five cubits above the ground. Five cubits above the bolt is the lock, which is longer than the bolt. It is secured by two hasps, which are each two cubits long. On the lock is attached a key, which is a cubit and a half long; it has twelve teeth, each tooth is in the form of a pestle used in mortars. The key's circumference is four handspans; it is connected to a chain welded to the gate,* which is eight cubits long and four fingers thick in circumference. Each ring on the chain is like the ring of a ballista.

[§26] The lower threshold (*ʿataba*) of the gate is ten cubits wide and one hundred cubits long, not including what is under the base of the two doorposts, and rises up five cubits. [V 70b] All of this is measured [[in the black cubit.

[§27] Along the gate are two fortifications]], a fresh spring is located [[at the gates of each of these two fortifications]] and before [[each one are two trees. Located in one of the fortifications]] are the construction tools with which the barrier was built, including iron cauldrons and iron mixing rods. On each trivet are four cauldrons, similar to cauldrons for making soap. Here the remaining iron bricks have all clumped together with rust.

[§28] The guardian of these fortifications rides in every Monday and Thursday.* They inherit [watch over] the gate just as the caliphs inherit the caliphate.* He rides in with three men who bear around their necks an iron mallet.

[§29*] At the gate are stairs which he climbs to the highest step, whereupon he strikes the bolt, once in the early morning, in order to listen to [Gog and Magog], who clamor up like a nest of hornets, and only after a while do they quiet down. In the afternoon he will strike it once more, and he will lean in with his ear against the gate. They clamor the second time more fiercely than the first, and after a bit they quiet down. Come evening he will strike it a third time and again they will make tremendous noise. He will then wait until sunset.

[§31] Then once again he will strike the bolt so that those behind [the gate] can hear and understand that there are guards there. And the guards inspect to see that those on the other side have not damaged the gate in any way.

[§32] Near this spot is a large fortification ten *farsakhs* by ten *farsakhs*, with an area of one hundred *farsakhs*.

[§33*] Sallām said: I asked those who were present from the people of the fortifications [V 71a], "Has there ever been any kind of damage to the gate?"

> They said, "Nothing has ever occurred except for this crack." The crack was the width of a thin thread.
>
> I then replied, "Are you nervous at all about [this crack]?"
>
> They responded, "No. For this gate is five cubits wide using the Alexandrian cubit." This cubit measures a cubit and a half according to the black cubit. Each cubit was the length of Alexander's forearm.
>
> Sallām stated: I drew close and I took out from my leggings a knife and I scraped the spot of the crack, and there broke off a piece the size of half a dirham. So I packed it securely into a cloth in order to show it to al-Wāthiq bi'llāh.

High above the right doorpost there was an inscription in iron, written in the first language: *When the promise of my Lord comes to pass, He will flatten [the rampart], the promise of my Lord is true* [Q. 18:98].

[§34*] We examined the structure and the majority of it is lined with rows of yellow bricks made from copper and rows of black bricks made from iron.

[§35*] There was a place dug out on the mountain in which the gates were cast, along with the location where the cauldrons were used to mix the copper, and where the lead and copper were poured out. The cauldrons looked to be of brass. On each one were handles on which hung chains with prongs which were used to carry the copper to the top of the wall.

[§36] We asked those present, "Have any one of you seen Gog and Magog?" They mentioned that they had seen them several times atop the wall, whereupon a dark wind would descend and push them back onto their side. Measuring by eyesight, the male stands one and a half handspans tall.

[§37] The mountain on the outer side has no slope nor craggy base, no plants grow, nor grass, nor trees, nor anything else. It is a flat mountain (*musaṭṭaḥ*), rising up with a sheer white face.* [V 72b]

[§38] When we set off we took with [[us guides to the region of Khurāsān.]]

[§39*] And the king was called al-L.b. [[We traveled from that spot and reached an area]] whose king is called Ṭ.ā.ū.n, and he was a director of taxation. We stayed with them for several days.

[§40*] We traveled from that place until we arrived at Samarqand, this took eight months. We reached Isbīshāb and we crossed the river at Balkh. Then we traveled to Sharūsana and then on to Bukhārā and then to Tirmidh. Then we reached Nīsābūr.

[§41*] Of the men that were with us twenty-two died of illness on our way to the wall. Those that died we buried in their clothes. [[And those that got sick we had to leave in villages along the way.]] On the return fourteen men died. So when we arrived at [[Nīsābūr we were only fourteen men.

[§42] The people]] of the fortifications had outfitted us with everything we needed.

[§43] Then we reached ʿAbd Allāh b. Ṭāhir. He granted me eight thousand dirhams and gave each of my companions five hundred dirhams, and granted to each horseman five dirhams and to the footmen three dirhams for each day of travel until reaching Rayy.

[§44*] Of the mules only twenty-three survived.

[§45] We arrived at Sāmarrāʾ.

[§46*] I went to al-Wāthiq and informed him of the account and I showed him the iron which I had scratched off from the gate. He praised God. He ordered that alms be given out and he gave each man one thousand dinars.

[§47] It took us sixteen months to reach the rampart and twelve months [f. 72b] [[and some days]] to return.*

[§48] Sallām the Interpreter related to me this report in its entirety, then he dictated it to me from his own draft which he had drawn up for al-Wāthiq biʿllāh.

APPENDIX 3

THE BODLEIAN RECENSION

The following is a translation of Sallām's adventure as related in the copies of *al-Masālik wa 'l-mamālik* of Bodleian MS Hunt 433 [MS B, fols. 61a–64a] and Bibliothèque national de France, Arabic Supplément 895 [MS P, fols. 40b–42b]. Asterisks mark notable divergences with the Vienna recension.

After Samandar is the Rampart of Gog and Magog*

[§1] Abū 'l-Qāsim related:* Sallām the Interpreter informed me that when al-Wāthiq dreamt in his sleep that the barrier which Dhū 'l-Qarnayn had built between us and Gog and Magog was open, [§3] he summoned me and said, "Examine [the barrier] and bring me back information concerning its condition."

[§4] He outfitted me with fifty men and gave me five thousand dinars and a personal indemnity of ten thousand dirhams and he ordered that each man be given a thousand dirhams and daily sustenance to last a year.

[§6] He gave me two hundred mules for carrying supplies and water.

[§7] So we set out from Sāmarrāʾ with a dispatch from al-Wāthiq to Isḥāq b. Ismāʿīl, the ruler [B 61b] of Armenia. He was in Tiflīs on our arrival. Isḥāq dispatched us to the ruler of al-Sarīr and the ruler of al-Sarīr dispatched us to the king of the Alāns and the king of the Alāns dispatched us to the Fīlān Shāh and the Fīlān Shāh dispatched us to the Ṭarkhān, king of the Khazar. We remained with the king of the Khazar for a day and a night, until he sent us off with five [P 41a] guides. We traveled away from [the king of the Khazar] for twenty-nine days.

[§8] Then we reached a putrid black land. Before entering this land, we had prepared for ourselves vinegar to smell in lieu of the loathsome odor. For ten days we traveled in this land. Then we reached ruined cities and we traveled through them for twenty-seven days.* We inquired about these cities and were informed that Gog and Magog had breached them. Then we traveled through fortifications near the mountain range on a branch of which is located the barrier.

[§9] A tribe who speak Arabic and Persian populate these fortifications. They are Muslims and they recite [B 62a] the Qurʾān; they have Qurʾānic schools and mosques. They asked about us and where we were from. We informed them that we were messengers of the Commander of the Faithful.

> They grew astonished and exclaimed, "The Commander of the Faithful!?"
>
> We replied, "Yes."
>
> They asked, "Is he old or young?"
>
> We replied, "He is young."
>
> They were equally astonished and inquired, "Where is he?"
>
> We responded, "In Iraq, in a city called Sāmarrāʾ."
>
> They replied, "We have never heard of this before."

[§37] Then we traveled to a sheer mountain face with no vegetation.*

[§13] A valley, the width of which is one hundred and fifty cubits,* cuts through the mountain.

[§15] There are two doorposts constructed on each side of the mountain through which the valley runs. The width of each doorpost is twenty-five cubits, and they extend ten cubits from the gate. All of this is constructed with bricks of iron set into copper. [The doorposts] rise up fifty cubits.

[§17] There is a lintel of iron which stretches across the two doorposts, the length of which is one hundred and twenty cubits. The lintel, mounted over the two doorposts [P 41b], extending for a width of ten cubits along each doorpost [B 62b], is five cubits thick.

[§18] Over the lintel rises a wall of iron bricks set in copper that extends to the top of the mountain. It rises as far as the eye can see.

[§19] Above this are iron merlons; on each merlon are two angled tips of equal size.

[§21] As for the iron gate, it has two door panels which are sealed shut, each panel is fifty cubits long and five cubits thick.* The two panels hinge on thick vertical pivot bars set into the lintel.

[§23] On the gate is a bolt, which [[is seven cubits wide]] and the thickness of an arm-span in circumference.

[§25] The bolt is twenty-five cubits above the ground. Five cubits above the bolt is the lock, which is longer than the bolt. It is secured by two hasps which are each two cubits long. On the lock is attached a key, which is a cubit and a half long and has twelve teeth, and it is as if each one is larger than the pestle used in mortars [cf. MS H, fol. 142a]. Connected to the key is a chain [B 63a] eight cubits long and four fingers thick. Each ring on the chain is like the ring of a ballista.

[§26] The lower threshold of the gate is ten cubits wide and is a hundred cubits long, not including what is under the base of the two doorposts, and rises up five cubits. All of this is measured in the black cubit.

[§28] The guardian of these fortifications rides in every Friday with ten knights, each knight bears an iron mallet, each one weighing fifty *mann*s.*

[§31*] The guardian pounds the bolt with these mallets three times so that those behind [the gate] can hear and understand that there are guards there. And the guards inspect to see [P 42a] that those on the other side have not damaged the gate in any way. When our companions struck the gate they placed their ears on it and heard from within a roar.

[§32] Near this spot is a large fortification ten *farsakh*s by ten *farsakh*s.

[§27] Along the gate are two fortifications [B 63b], each two hundred cubits squared. At each of the gates of these two fortifications are two trees, and between these two fortifications is a fresh water spring. Located in one of the fortifications are the tools with which the barrier was built, including iron cauldrons and iron mixing rods. On each trivet are four cauldrons similar, but larger, than soap cauldrons. Here the remaining iron bricks have all clumped together with rust.

[§16*] The bricks measure a cubit and a half squared by four fingers thick.

[§36] We asked those present, “Have any one of you seen Gog and Magog?” They mentioned that they had seen them several times atop the wall, whereupon a dark wind would descend and push them back onto their side. By the looks of it, the male measures only one and a half handspans.

[§38] When we set off we took with us guides [who led us] to the region of Khurāsān. We traveled through it until reaching the back side of Samarqand.

[§42] The guardian [B 64a] of the fortifications had outfitted us with everything we needed.

[§43] Then we reached Abū 'l-ʿAbbās ʿAbd Allāh b. Ṭāhir. Sallām the Interpreter said: He granted me one hundred thousand dirhams* and gave each of my companions five hundred dirhams, and granted to [P 42b] each horseman five dirhams and to the footmen three dirhams for each day of travel until reaching Rayy.

[§47] I returned to Sāmarrāʾ twenty-eight months after having departed.*

[§48] Sallām informed me the entirety of this account and he dictated it to me from his own draft which he had drawn up for al-Wāthiq.

APPENDIX 4

THE IDRĪSĪ RECENSION

The following are excerpts of Sallām's adventure related by Idrīsī, *Nuzhat al-mushtāq* [2:934–8]. Asterisks mark notable variations, asterisks followed by roman numerals mark significant divergences with the Vienna, Bodleian, and Paris recensions.

[*I] As for the rampart of Gog and Magog, books reference it and accounts circulate about it, among them is what Sallām the Interpreter related. ʿUbayd Allāh b. Khurradādhbih reported from [Sallām] in his book; likewise Abū Naṣr al-Jayhānī reported this account. They both relate that:

[§1] When al-Wāthiq saw while sleeping that the barrier which Dhū 'l-Qarnayn had built between us and Gog and Magog was open, he summoned Sallām the Interpreter and said to him, "Go and inspect this barrier and bring me back information about it and its condition and what is going on with it."

[§6] He then ordered a group of fifty men to accompany [Sallām] and he gave to [Sallām] five thousand dinars and an indemnity of ten thousand dirhams and he commanded that each man be given five thousand dirhams and daily sustenance to last a year. He ordered that they be supplied with two hundred mules for carrying supplies and water.

[§7] Sallām the Interpreter related: So we set out from Sāmarrāʾ with a dispatch from al-Wāthiq bi'llāh to Isḥāq b. [p. 935] Ismāʿīl, the ruler of Armenia, with the aim that he send on our delegation from there.* So we set out to Tiflīs and when we met with him he drew up a dispatch for us to the ruler of al-Sarīr and we set out toward him and when we reached him he directed us to the king of the Alāns.

[*II] And he sent along with us an exchange of letters. When we reached [the king of the Alāns] he dispatched us to the ruler of Fīlān Shāh and when we reached him we stayed with him for some days and he chose for us five guides who would lead us along our journey.

[*IV] So we traveled away from him for twenty-seven days on the borders of the Bashjirt until we reached a long, expansive black land with a horrible smell.

[§8] We traversed this land for ten days, having prepared ourselves with items which we would smell in order to block out [the stench], fearful of being harmed by the loathsome odor.* We finally passed through it and traveled for a period of a month through a destroyed land, whose buildings had been decimated and only ruins remained which indicated what was once there.* We asked those traveling with us about these cities and they informed us that they were cities that Gog and Magog had raided and destroyed. Then we reached fortifications near the mountain range on a branch of which is located the barrier. And that was in six days.*

[§9] A tribe who speak Arabic and Persian populate these fortifications.

[*VI] Here is a city whose king is called the Khāqān of the Adhkish.

[§9] The people are Muslims who have mosques and Qurʾānic schools. . . .

[*VII] We asked them about their conversion to Islam, when did it come about and who taught them the Qurʾān. They replied [p. 936], "Many years back a man reached us riding a four-legged beast with a long neck with a hump on its back." We realized that they were describing a camel. They went on, "He stayed with us and communicated with us in a language we could understand and he taught us the precepts (*sharāʾiʿ*) of Islam and how to follow them, so we accepted them and also he taught us the Qurʾān and its meanings and we learned and memorized it from him." Sallām reported: Then we went from there to the barrier to inspect it.

[§10] We traveled from the city for a distance of two *farsakh*s and then we reached the barrier.

[§13] There is a mountain. A valley, the width of which is one hundred and fifty cubits, cuts through it. In the middle of this location is a gate of iron, fifty cubits long, flanked on each side by two doorposts.

[§15] The width of each doorpost is twenty-five cubits. . .

[§17] The *darwand* is the upper lintel (*al-ʿataba al-ʿulyā*) which had been mounted over each doorpost,* extending for a width of ten cubits.

[§18] Above the lintel is a solid structure of iron bricks set into copper, reaching up to the top of the mountain. It rises up as high as can be seen.

[§19] Above this are iron merlons; on the edges of each [merlon] are two horns (*qarnān*) of equal size.*

• • •

[§28 / p. 937] The guardian of these fortifications rides in every Friday with ten knights bearing iron mallets,* each weighing fifty *mann*s.

[§31] He pounds the bolt with these mallets each day three times so that those behind [the gate] can hear and understand that there are guards there. And the guards inspect to see that Gog and Magog have not damaged the gate in any way. When those bearing the mallets strike the gate they place their ears on it, listening to what is on the other side; they could hear a roar from within the gate pointing to creatures on the other side.*

• • •

[*VIII / p. 938] Sallām the Interpreter related: I wrote down all of these descriptions and I took them with me.

[§38] Then we set off with guides from the people of the fortifications. And they led us up to the region of Khurāsān.

[*IX] We traveled from these fortifications to the city of Lakmān, to the city of Gharyān, then to the city of Barsākhān, then to Ṭarāz and finally to Samarqand.

[§43] Then we reached ʿAbd Allāh b. Ṭāhir and stayed with him for several days. He granted me one hundred thousand dirhams and gave each of my companions five thousand dirhams, and granted to each horseman five dirhams and to the footmen three dirhams for each day of travel until reaching Rayy.

[§47] Then we reached Sāmarrāʾ after having set out and traveled for twenty-eight months.

[*X] This is all that Sallām the Interpreter reported concerning the descriptions of the barrier and the regions through which he traveled and the nations which he met along the way and the dialogue which he had with those he met.

LIST OF ABBREVIATIONS

Journals and Reference Works

AEMA	*Archivum Eurasiae Medii Aevi*
AOASH	*Acta Orientalia Academiae Scientiarum Hungaricae*
BSOAS	*Bulletin of the School of Oriental and African Studies*
BSOS	*Bulletin of the School of Oriental Studies*
EAL	*Encyclopedia of Arabic Literature*. London: Routledge, 1998.
EI^2	*The Encyclopaedia of Islam*. 2nd ed. Leiden: Brill, 1954–2005.
EI^3	*The Encyclopaedia of Islam*. 3rd ed. Leiden: Brill, 2007–.
EIr	*The Encyclopaedia Iranica*. London: Routledge, 1982–.
EQ	*The Encyclopaedia of the Qurʾān*. Leiden: Brill, 2001–6.
GAL	Brockelmann, Carl. *Geschichte der arabischen Litteratur*. 2nd ed. Leiden: Brill, 1943–9.
GALS	Brockelmann, Carl. *Geschichte der arabischen Litteratur Supplement*. Leiden: Brill, 1937–42.
GAS	Sezgin, Fuat. *Geschichte des arabischen Schrifttums*. Leiden: Brill, 1967–2010.
IJMES	*International Journal of Middle East Studies*
JAOS	*Journal of the American Oriental Society*
JRAS	*Journal of the Royal Asiatic Society of Great Britain and Ireland*
JWCI	*Journal of the Warburg and Courtauld Institutes*
MEL	*Middle Eastern Literatures*
ZGAIW	*Zeitschrift für Geschichte der Arabisch-Islamischen Wissenschaften*

Primary Sources

Aghānī	Abū ʿl-Faraj al-Iṣfahānī. *Kitāb al-aghānī*. Edited by ʿAbd al-Sattār Aḥmad Farrāj. Beirut: Dār al-Thaqāfa, 1957–64.
ʿAjāʾib	Zakariyyāʾ b. Muḥammad al-Qazwīnī. *ʿAjāʾib al-makhlūqāt wa gharāʾib al-mawjūdāt*. Edited by F. Wüstenfeld. Göttingen: Verlag de Dieterichschen Buchhandlung, 1849.

Azraqī	Abū 'l-Walīd al-Azraqī. *Akhbār Makka*. Edited by ʿAbd al-Malik b. ʿAbd Allāh b. Duhaysh. Mecca: Maktabat al-Asadī, 2003.
Bakrī	Abū ʿUbayd al-Bakrī. *al-Masālik wa 'l-mamālik*. Edited by André Ferré and Adrian van Leeuwen. Carthage: al-Dār al-ʿArabiyya li'l-Kitāb, 1992.
Bayān	al-Jāḥiẓ. *al-Bayān wa 'l-tabyīn*. Edited by ʿAbd al-Salām Muḥammad Hārūn. Cairo: Maṭbaʿat Lajnat al-Taʾlīf wa 'l-Tarjuma wa 'l-Nashr, 1948.
BGA	*Bibliotheca geographorum Arabicorum*. Edited by M. J. de Goeje. Leiden: Brill 1870–94.
Bilād	Zakariyyāʾ b. Muḥammad al-Qazwīnī. *Āthār al-bilād wa akhbār al-ʿibād*. Beirut: Dār Ṣādir, 1960.
Buldān	Ibn al-Faqīh. *Kitāb al-buldān*. Edited by Yūsuf al-Hādī. Beirut: ʿĀlam al-Kutub, 1996.
CSCO	*Corpus Scriptorum Christianorum Orientalium*
Dodge	Ibn al-Nadīm. *The Fihrist of al-Nadīm: A Tenth-Century Survey of Muslim Culture*. Translated by Bayard Dodge. New York: Columbia University Press, 1970.
Fākihī	Muḥammad b. Isḥāq al-Fākihī. *Akhbār Makka*. Edited by ʿAbd al-Malik b. ʿAbd Allāh b. Duhaysh. Beirut: Dār Khiḍr, 1994.
Fihrist	Ibn al-Nadīm. *al-Fihrist*. Edited by Ayman Fuʾād Sayyid. London: Al-Furqan Islamic Heritage Foundation, 2009.
Futūḥ	Aḥmad b. Yaḥyā 'l-Balādhurī. *Kitāb futūḥ al-buldān = Liber expugnationis regionum*. Edited by M. J. de Goeje. Leiden: Brill, 1866.
Ghurar	ʿAbd al-Malik al-Thaʿālibī. *Ghurar akhbār mulūk al-furs wa siyarihim*. Edited by Zotenberg Hermann. Paris: Imprimerie Nationale, 1900.
Ḥayawān	al-Jāḥiẓ. *Kitāb al-ḥayawān*. Edited by ʿAbd al-Salām Muḥammad Hārūn. Cairo: Maktabat Muṣṭafā 'l-Bābī 'l-Ḥalabī, 1938–45.
Hitti	Aḥmad b. Yaḥyā 'l-Balādhurī. *The Origins of the Islamic State*. Translated by Philip Khuri Hitti. New York: Columbia University, 1916.
Ḥudūd	*Ḥudūd al-ʿālam*. Edited by Maryam Mīr Aḥmadī and Ghulām Riḍā Warahrām. Tehran: Dānishgāh al-Zahrāʾ, 2003.
IFG	Ibn al-Faqīh. *Kitāb al-buldān*. *BGA*, vol. 5, 1885.
IḤG	Ibn Ḥawqal. *Ṣūrat al-arḍ*. *BGA*, vol. 2, 1873.
Iṣṭakhrī	Ibrāhīm b. Muḥammad al-Iṣṭakhrī. *al-Masālik wa 'l-mamālik*. Edited by Jābir ʿAbd al-ʿĀl al-Ḥīnī. Cairo: Dār al-Qalam, 1961.
Jāmiʿ	Muḥammad b. Jarīr al-Ṭabarī. *Jāmiʿ al-bayān ʿan taʾwīl al-Qurʾān*. Cairo: Muṣṭafā 'l-Bābī 'l-Ḥalabī, 1954.
Jazīrat	al-Ḥasan b. Aḥmad al-Hamdānī. *Ṣifat jazīrat al-ʿArab*. Edited by David Heinrich Müller. Leiden: Brill, 1891.
Kashf	Muṣṭafā b. ʿAbd Allāh Ḥājjī Khalīfa. *Kashf al-ẓunūn ʿan asāmī 'l-kutub wa 'l-funūn*. Edited by Muḥammad Sharaf al-Dīn Yāltaqāyā and Rifʿat Bīlka al-Kilīsī. Istanbul: Wikālat al-Maʿārif al-Jalīla, 1941.

Kharāj	Qudāma b. Jaʿfar. *Kitāb al-kharāj wa ṣināʿat al-kitāba*. Edited by Muḥammad Ḥusayn al-Zubaydī. Baghdad: Dār al-Rashīd, 1981.
Lahw	Ibn Khurradādhbih. *Mukhtār min kitāb al-lahw wa 'l-malāhī*. Edited by Ighnāṭiyūs ʿAbduh Khalīfa. Beirut: al-Maṭbaʿa al-Kāthūlīkiyya, 1961.
Masālik	Ibn Khurradādhbih. *al-Masālik wa 'l-mamālik*. *BGA*, vol. 6, 1889.
Meynard	Ibn Khurradādhbih. "Livre des routes et des provinces." Edited by Charles Barbier de Meynard. *Journal Asiatique* 5 (1865): 5–127, 227–96, 446–527.
MḤudūd	*Ḥudūd al-ʿālam = The Regions of the World: A Persian Geography, 372 A.H. (982 A.D.)*. Translated by Vladimir Minorsky. Cambridge: E. J. W. Gibb Memorial, 1982.
Miʿṭār	Muḥammad b. ʿAbd Allāh al-Ḥimyārī. *Kitāb al-rawḍ al-miʿṭār*. Edited by Iḥsān ʿAbbās. Beirut: Maktabat Lubnān, 1975.
Muʿjam	Yāqūt al-Rūmī. *Muʿjam al-buldān*. Beirut: Dār Ṣādir, 1955–7.
Murūj	al-Masʿūdī. *Murūj al-dhahab*. Edited by Charles Pellat. Beirut: al-Jāmiʿa al-Lubnāniyya, 1966–79.
Nafīsa	Ibn Rusta. *al-Aʿlāq al-nafīsa*. *BGA*, vol. 7, 1882.
Nuzhat	Abū ʿAbd Allāh al-Idrīsī. *Opus geographicum = Nuzhat al-mushtāq fī ikhtirāq al-āfāq*. Edited by E. Cerulli, et al. Naples: Brill, 1970–8.
RIF	Aḥmad b. Faḍlān. "Ibn Fadlan's Reisebericht." In *Abhandlungen für die Kunde des Morgenlandes*, edited by Ahmed Zeki Velidi Togan. Vol. 24. Leipzig: F. A. Brockhaus, 1939.
Ṣūrat	Ibn Ḥawqal. *Kitāb ṣūrat al-arḍ*. Edited by J. H. Kramers. Leiden: Brill, 1938–9.
Tanbīh	al-Masʿūdī. *al-Tanbīh wa 'l-ishrāf*. *BGA*, vol. 8, 1894.
Taqāsīm	Muḥammad b. Aḥmad al-Muqaddasī. *Aḥsan al-taqāsīm fī maʿrifat al-aqālīm*. *BGA*, vol. 3, 1877.
Tījān	ʿAbd al-Malik b. Hishām. *Kitab al-tījān fī mulūk Ḥimyar wa 'l-Yaman*. Edited by F. Krenkow. Hyderabad: Maṭbaʿat Majlis Dāʾirat al-Maʿārif al-ʿUthmāniyya, 1928.
TRM	al-Ṭabarī. *Taʾrīkh al-rusul wa 'l-mulūk = Annales quos scripsit Abu Djafar Mohammed ibn Djarir at-Tabari*. Edited by M. J. de Goeje, et al. Leiden: Brill, 1879–1901.
Udabāʾ	Yāqūt al-Rūmī. *Muʿjam al-udabāʾ*. Edited by Iḥsān ʿAbbās. Beirut: Dār al-Gharb al-Islāmī, 1993.
Yaʿqūbī	Aḥmad b. Abī Yaʿqūb al-Yaʿqūbī. *Taʾrīkh al-Yaʿqūbī*. Beirut: Dār Ṣādir, 1960.
YBN	Aḥmad b. Abī Yaʿqūb al-Yaʿqūbī. *Kitāb al-buldān*. *BGA*, vol. 7, 1892.

NOTES

Introduction

1 Clifford Geertz, "Thick Description," in *The Interpretation of Culture* (New York: Basic Books, 1973), 5–30.

2 On the broader epistemological implications of translation, see George Steiner, *After Babel* (New York: Oxford University Press, 1975), 47.

3 See Roy Mottahedeh, "ʿ*Ajāʾib* in *The Thousand and One Nights*," in *The Thousand and One Nights in Arabic Literature and Society* (Cambridge: Cambridge University Press, 1997), 29–39.

4 For a fuller description of Qazwīnī and his work, see my article, "The Wiles of Creation: Philosophy, Fiction, and the ʿ*Ajāʾib* Tradition," *MEL* 13 (2010): 21–48.

5 On medieval European intellectual contexts for the marvelous, see Caroline Walker Bynum, "Wonder," *American Historical Review* 102 (1997): 1–26. See also, Lorraine Daston and Katharine Park, *Wonders and the Order of Nature, 1150–1750* (New York: Zone Books, 1998); also, John Friedman, *The Monstrous Races in Medieval Art and Thought* (Cambridge: Harvard University Press, 1981); Paul Freedman, "The Medieval Other: The Middle Ages as Other," in *Marvels, Monsters, and Miracles* (Kalamazoo, MI: Medieval Institute Publications, 2002), 1–24.

6 Cf. Q. 16:68–9; see the work ascribed to Jāḥiẓ, *al-ʿIbar wa ʾl-iʿtibār* (Cairo: Maṭbaʿat al-Nīl, n.d.), 75; Ikhwān al-Ṣafāʾ, *Rasāʾil* (Beirut: Dār Ṣādir, 1957), 2:301–2; Abū Ḥāmid al-Ghazālī, *al-Ḥikma fī makhlūqāt Allāh* (Beirut: Tawzīʿ Dār Iḥyāʾ al-ʿUlūm, 1978), 90–1; Abū Ḥāmid al-Gharnāṭī, *Tuḥfat al-albāb*, ed. Gabriel Ferrand in *Journal Asiatique* 207 (1925), 33; ʿ*Ajāʾib*, 5.

7 *Ḥayawān*, 1:208–9; cf. Abū Ḥāmid al-Ghazālī, "Ḥaqīqat al-tawḥīd," in *Iḥyāʾ ʿulūm al-dīn* (Egypt: al-Maktaba al-Tijāriyya al-Kubrā, n.d.), 4:258; cited in Eric Ormsby, *Theodicy in Islamic Thought* (Princeton: Princeton University Press, 1984), 45.

8 *Ḥayawān*, 2:109–10.

9 Michel Foucault, *The Order of Things* (New York: Vintage Books, 1994), 34–5.

10 *Ḥayawān*, 1:204.
11 *Galeni compendium Timaei Platonis*, in *Plato Arabus* (London: Warburg Institute, 1943–51), 5, §c; cited in Ormsby, *Theodicy*, 83.
12 Ghazālī, "al-Imlāʾ ʿan ishkālāt al-Iḥyāʾ," appendix to the *Iḥyāʾ*, 5:35; for this formulation and its broader impact, see Ormsby, *Theodicy*, 32–91.
13 See G. E. von Grunebaum, "Observations on the Muslim Concept of Evil," *Studia Islamica* 31 (1970): 117–34.
14 See chapter 7, 155ff.
15 Rashīd Riḍā, *Fatāwā* (Beirut: Dār al-Kitāb al-Jadīd, 1970), from the journal, *al-Manār*, 2:650–3.
16 See Remke Kruk, "Gog and Magog in Modern Garb," in *Gog and Magog* (Amsterdam: Rozenberg Publications, 2007), 53–68.
17 See chapter 7, 149.
18 Bynum, "Wonder," 24.
19 See Raymond Prier, *Thauma idesthai* (Tallahassee: Florida State University Press, 1989).
20 For the emphasis on ʿ*iyān* as ontological proof within descriptive geography, see André Miquel, *La Géographie humaine du monde musulman* (Paris: Mouton, 1967–87), 1:277–8; Paul Wheatley, *The Places Where Men Pray Together* (Chicago: Chicago University Press, 2001), 64–6.
21 Ibn Jinnī, *al-Khaṣāʾiṣ* (Beirut: Dār al-Kutub al-ʿIlmiyya, 2001), 1:97.
22 Seeger Bonebakker, "*Nihil Obstat* in Storytelling?" in *The Thousand and One Nights in Arabic Literature and Society*, 56–77; Rina Drory, "Legitimizing Fiction in Classical Arabic Literature," in *Models and Contacts* (Leiden: Brill, 2000), 37–47, and "Medieval Fiction," *EAL*. Also see the collected volume of essays edited by Stefan Leder, *Story-telling in the Framework of non-Fictional Arabic Literature* (Wiesbaden: Harrassowitz, 1998); and Philip Kennedy, ed., *On Fiction and Adab in Medieval Arabic Literature* (Wiesbaden: Harrassowitz, 2005).
23 See Syrinx von Hees, "The Astonishing: A Critique and Re-reading of ʿ*Aǧāʾib* Literature," *MEL* 8 (2005): 101–20.
24 *Kharāj*, 132; cf. Isḥāq b. al-Ḥasan al-Zayyāt (fl. fifth/eleventh century), *Dhikr al-aqālīm* (Barcelona: CSIC, 1989), 85; see the opening anecdote to Idrīsī's (d. 560/1165) geography, *Nuzhat*, 6–7.
25 *Tanbīh*, 30.
26 See Charles Pellat, "Akhbār al-Ṣīn wa 'l-Hind," *EI*².
27 *Fihrist*, 2:321–2, 332; cf. 1:305, 468, 471.
28 *Kitāb al-tabaṣṣur* (Cairo: al-Maṭbaʿa al-Raḥmāniyya, 1935), 25–9; on the question of attribution, see Charles Pellat, "Ǧāḥiziana i. Le *Kitāb al-tabaṣṣur bi 'l-tijāra* attribué à Ǧāḥiẓ," *Arabica* 1 (1954): 153–65.
29 ʿAbd al-Malik al-Thaʿālibī, *Laṭāʾif al-maʿārif* (Cairo: Dār Iḥyāʾ al-Kutub al-ʿArabiyya, 1960), 233–9.
30 *Ṣūrat*, 329.
31 *Taqāsīm*, 43.

32 Jāḥiẓ, *Majmūʿ rasāʾil al-Jāḥiẓ* (Cairo: Lajnat al-Taʾlīf wa ʿl-Tarjuma wa ʿl-Nashr, 1943), 24–5.

33 See Stephen Greenblatt's treatment of mimetic capital in *Marvelous Possessions* (Chicago: University of Chicago Press, 1991), 6–8.

34 James Montgomery, "Serendipity, Resistance, and Multivalency: Ibn Khurradādhbih and his *Kitāb al-masālik wa-l-Mamālik*," in *On Fiction and Adab in Medieval Arabic Literature*, 177–232.

Chapter 1: Routes and Realms

1 According to the title page of Bodleian MS Hunt 433 (= MS B), the full title is *Kitāb al-masālik wa ʿl-mamālik fī ṣifat al-arḍ*.

2 See *Kashf*, 1:278; M. Hadj-Sadok, "Ibn Khurradādhbih," *EI*²; C. Bosworth, "Ebn Ḵordāḏbeh," *EIr*; also Ignatii Krachkovskii, *Istoriia arabskoi geograficheskoi literatury* (Moscow: n.p., 1957), trans. Ṣalāḥ al-Dīn ʿUthmān Hāshim as *Taʾrīkh al-adab al-jughrāfī ʿl-ʿarabī* (Cairo: Lajnat al-Taʾlīf wa ʿl-Tarjuma wa ʿl-Nashr, 1963–5), 147–51; *GAL*, 1:225–6; see also Tadeusz Lewicki, *Źródła arabskie do dziejów słowiańszczyzny* (Warsaw: Zakład imienia Ossolińskich, 1956–88), 1:43–50. *Kh.r.dā.dh.b.h.*, it can be read as Khurdādhbih, after the Zoroastrian deity Khurdād, meaning 'Khurdād is best' (Middle Persian, Xordād-weh). Khurradādhbih is admittedly the *lectio difficilior*; see Philippe Gignoux, *Noms propres sassanides* (Vienna: Österreichische Akademie der Wissenschaften, 1986), vol. 2, fasc. ii, 187, §1035; cf. Krachkovskii, 147. There is some confusion over the dates of his birth and death, which are variously given as 205/820 and 211/826, for the former, and 300/912, for the latter. Regarding the date of composition of the *Masālik*, de Goeje argues for a two-stage process: the first, during the reign of al-Wāthiq, in the year 232/846, and the second, which was not completed until after 272/885, *Masālik*, xx. See chapters 6 and 7 for the manuscript recensions of Ibn Khurradādhbih's geography, p. 133–4, 169–71.

3 See Meynard, 8.

4 *TRM*, ser. 3, 2:1014–5.

5 See Ibn Najjār (d. 643/1245), *Dhayl Taʾrīkh Baghdād* (Hyderabad: Dāʾirat al-Maʿārif al-ʿUthmāniyya, 1978–86), 2:11–3, §269.

6 Dodge, 326. See Lucien Bouvat, *Les Barmécides d'après les historiens arabes et persans* (Paris: Ernest Leroux, 1912); Dominique Sourdel, *Le vizirat ʿabbāside* (Damascus: Institut français, 1959–60), 1:127–81; Dimitri Gutas, *Greek Thought, Arabic Culture* (New York: Routledge, 1998), 53, 72, 128–9.

7 Sayyid Maqbul Ahmad, *A History of Arab-Islamic Geography* (Amman: al-Bayt University, 1995), 58–9.

8 According to Ibn al-Nadīm, Abū ʿl-ʿAbbās Jaʿfar Aḥmad al-Marwazī was the first to compose a work entitled *al-Masālik wa ʿl-mamālik*, though he did not finish it. Ibn al-Nadīm relates that, after his death, the books of Marwazī were taken from al-Awāz to Baghdad and sold there, in the year 274/887–8, *Fihrist*, 1:463, Dodge, 329; *Udabāʾ*, 2:776–7. As for other contemporaries of

Ibn Khurradādhbih who wrote on the subject of "Routes and Realms," Ibn al-Nadīm mentions the Baghdadi historian Aḥmad b. al-Ḥārith al-Kharrāz (d. ca 258/872), along with Aḥmad b. al-Ṭayyib al-Sarakhsī (d. 285/899), Dodge, 227–8; *Udabāʾ*, 1:23, 292; Sarakhsī was a pupil of the philosopher Kindī (d. ca 260/874), and an intimate of the caliph al-Muʿtaḍid (r. 279–89/892–902), who ultimately executed him, Dodge, 326, 626–8; see Franz Rosenthal, *Aḥmad b. aṭ-Ṭayyib as-Saraḫsī* (New Haven: American Oriental Society, 1943), 13–39, 58–80.

9 See de Goeje's introduction, *Masālik*, xvff.; also see Barthold and Krachkovskii concerning the issue of the original size of this work.

10 See, in particular, the audit (*taqdīr*) of revenue and agricultural capacity for the Sawād, *Masālik*, 8–15.

11 De Goeje puts forth the hypothesis that, after working as the postmaster for the Jabal during his youth, Ibn Khurradādhbih was promoted to the position of minister responsible for overseeing the central bureau of communication at either Sāmarrāʾ or Baghdad, and that it was there that he gathered the material for his descriptive geography, *Masālik*, ix; cf. *GAL*, 1:225. De Goeje's statement is later turned from supposition to fact, with M. Hadj-Sadok, who claims that Ibn Khurradādhbih was "promoted to the office of director-general of the same department in Baghdād and later in Sāmarrāʾ." The sources only mention Ibn Khurradādhbih's position as *ṣāḥib al-barīd wa ʾl-khabar* for the Jabal, see Dodge, 326. More broadly, Muqaddasī attests that Ibn Khurradādhbih held a bureaucratic position at the court as a *wazīr*, which itself might be an error; he does not specify that he was the postmaster general of either Sāmarrāʾ or Baghdad.

12 Ibn al-Nadīm, "*nādama ʾl-Muʿtamida wa khuṣṣa bihi*," *Fihrist*, 1:458; Dodge, 326; cf. *Murūj*, §§3213–27.

13 See *Murūj*, §578.

14 Muqaddasī, "*kāna wazīra ʾl-khalīfati wa aqdara ʿalā waḍāʾiʿi ʿulūm khizānati amīri ʾl-muʾminīn*," *Taqāsīm*, 362; see de Goeje, *Masālik*, ix.

15 See Ibn Najjār, *Dhayl Taʾrīkh Baghdād*, 2:11, §269.

16 See Shawkat Toorawa, *Ibn Abī Ṭāhir Ṭayfur and Arabic Writerly Culture* (London: Routledge Curzon, 2005), 102–8.

17 See *Murūj*, §§3213–27; Ibn Khurradādhbih joined Buḥturī in 269/882–3 in the *dayr* of Sāmarrāʾ associated with the Christian notable, ʿAbdūn b. Makhlad (d. 310/922–3), brother of Ṣāʿid b. Makhlad (d. 276/889), who was a vizier to al-Muʿtamid and al-Muwaffaq, see Ibn Faḍl Allāh al-ʿUmarī (d. 749/1349), *Masālik al-abṣār*, 1:311; cf. Buḥturī, *Dīwān* (Cairo: Dār al-Maʿārif, 1963–4), 1:456, 554, §§184, 232; 4:2300, §864; on Ṣāʿid and his brother, see Robert McKinney, *The Case of Rhyme Versus Reason* (Leiden: Brill, 2004), 96–7.

18 Buḥturī, "*ibnu mulūkin sādatin nujub*," *Dīwān*, 1:253–4, §84, line 11; we may speculate as to the political implications of the *faraj baʿd al-shidda* motif in the poem itself, which was composed, according to Ṣayrafī, in 269/882–3, i.e.,

during the beginning of the imprisonment in Sāmarrā᾽ of Ibn Khurradādhbih's patron, al-Muᶜtamid, by his brother al-Muwaffaq.

19 Yāqūt, *"wa in yakun kādhiban fa-ᶜalayhi kadhibuhu," Udabā᾽*, 4:1573; this is quoted from Abū 'l-ᶜAlā᾽ al-Maᶜarrī (d. 449/1058), *Risālat al-ghufrān* (Beirut: Dār al-Kitāb al-ᶜArabī, 2001), 350; cf. Khalīl b. Aybak al-Ṣafadī, *al-Wāfī* (Beirut: Dār Iḥyā᾽ al-Turāth al-ᶜArabī, 2000), 9:239.

20 *Tanbīh*, 75; *Murūj*, §9.

21 *Ṣūrat*, 329; see Ch. Pellat, "al-Djayhānī," *EI*[2]; see also Hansgerd Göckenjan and István Zimonyi, *Orientalische Berichte über die Völker Osteuropas und Zentralasiens im Mittelalter* (Wiesbaden: Harrassowitz in Kommission, 2001), 1–28.

22 *Murūj*, §503; *Ṣūrat*, 3, 5.

23 On the administrative role of the *kātib*, see M. Carter, "The *Kātib* in Fact and Fiction," *Abr Nahrain* 11 (1971): 42–55; for the development of various governmental agencies under the heading of *dīwān*, see Reuben Levy, *The Social Structure of Islam* (Cambridge: Cambridge University Press, 1957), 325ff.; Saiyid Abdul Qadir Husaini, *Arab Administration* (Madras: M. Abdur Rahman, 1949), 76ff., 149ff.

24 James Montgomery has treated the issue of the two distinct proemiums in the surviving manuscript tradition, "Serendipity," 202–9.

25 *Masālik*, 4. See P. Crone, "Mawlā," *EI*[2].

26 See references to the genre in *Fihrist*, 1:324, 428, 458–9, 463.

27 See Paul Heck, *The Construction of Knowledge in Islamic Civilization* (Leiden: Brill, 2002).

28 *Kharāj*, 102.

29 Adam Silverstein, *Postal Systems in the pre-Modern Islamic World* (Cambridge: Cambridge University Press, 2007), 90–140.

30 *Kharāj*, 78.

31 Ibid., 77.

32 Gutas, *Greek Thought*, 20–7; Mohsen Zakeri, "Translation from Middle Persian (Pahlavi) into Arabic to the Early Abbasid Period," in *Übersetzung* (Berlin: Walter de Gruyter, 2007), 2:1199–1205.

33 See Parvaneh Pourshariati, *Decline and Fall of the Sasanian Empire* (London: I.B.Tauris, 2008).

34 See Richard Bulliet, *Conversion to Islam in the Medieval Period* (Cambridge: Harvard University Press, 1979), 1–6, 128–38.

35 For the heterogeneous form that state administration initially took on under the Umayyads, see E. Ashtor, *A Social and Economic History of the Near East in the Middle Ages* (London: Collins, 1976), passim, and specifically, 39.

36 Gerald R. Hawting, *The First Dynasty of Islam* (London: Croom Helm, 1986), 8–9, 79; cf. Daniel Clement Dennett, *Conversion and the Poll Tax in Early Islam* (Cambridge: Harvard University Press, 1950).

37 See Gutas, *Greek Thought*, 29.

38 For the respective positions in the debate over the origins of the *wazīr*, see M. Sprengling, "From Persian to Arabic," *American Journal of Semitic Languages and Literatures* 57 (1940), 331–6; Sourdel likewise outlines a Persian precedent, *Le vizirat ʿabbāside*, 41–61; cf. S. D. Goitein, "The Origin of the Vizierate and its True Character," followed by his Appendix, *Studies in Islamic History and Institutions* (Leiden: Brill, 1966), 168–96; also see Richard Kimber who traces this debate and the respective positions therein back to the Muslim sources themselves, "The Early Abbasid Vizierate," *Journal of Semitic Studies* 37 (1992): 65–85; cf. Michael Morony, *Iraq after the Muslim Conquest* (Princeton: Princeton University Press, 1984), 71.

39 See Abū ʿAbd Allāh al-Jahshiyārī (d. 331/942), *Kitāb al-wuzarāʾ wa ʿl-kuttāb* (Cairo: Muṣṭafā ʿl-Bābī ʿl-Ḥalabī, 1938), 2–9.

40 See the history of Persian kings by Ḥamza b. al-Ḥasan al-Iṣfahānī, *Taʾrīkh sinī mulūk al-arḍ* (Beirut: Dār Maktabat al-Ḥayāh, 1961), 32–3; *TRM*, ser. 1, 2:692. See D. Sourdel, "Barīd," *EI²*; C. E. Bosworth, "Barīd," *EIr;* cf. Silverstein, *Postal Systems*, 9–10, 28–30, 40–2, 49–51. For the etymology of *barīd* in relation to the propaganda that linked the ʿAbbāsids with the great Iranian empires of the past, see Roy Mottahedeh, "The ʿAbbāsid Caliphate in Iran," in *The Cambridge History of Iran* (Cambridge: Cambridge University Press, 1975), 4:85.

41 See *Buldān*, 314; al-Khaṭīb al-Baghdādī, *Taʾrīkh Baghdād* (Beirut: Dār al-Gharb al-Islāmī, 2001), 1:386–7.

42 For the position that Iraq is the center of the world, see *YBN*, 233; *Kharāj*, 139; *Murūj*, §978. This is an idea continued with Baghdādī, *Taʾrīkh Baghdād*, 1:319–20. By the time Muqaddasī writes, however, the splendor of Baghdad had diminished, 36. The view that the title 'navel of the world' is reserved for Mecca appears throughout the sources, see *Muʿjam*, 4:463.

43 For a survey of the translation movement in its entirety, see Gutas, *Greek Thought*.

44 See A. I. Sabra, "The Appropriation and Subsequent Naturalization of Greek Science in Medieval Islam," *History of Science* 25 (1987): 223–43; S. D. Goitein, "A Turning Point in the History of the Muslim State," in *Studies in Islamic History*, 160.

45 *Masālik*, 3; cf. Montgomery, "Serendipity," 204–9.

46 *Masālik*, 5; Masʿūdī gives a number of both 4,200 and 4,500 cities, which he claims is based on Ptolemy, *Murūj*, §191, note 4, cf. §1327.

47 *MḤudūd*, 14.

48 De Goeje catches Ibn Khurradādhbih's mistake in a footnote to his French translation, *Masālik*, 121, Arabic, 159; cf. *Tanbīh*, 129. Masʿūdī rejects the identification of Ptolemy the scientist with one of the Hellenistic kings of Egypt as fallacious.

49 See chapter 4, 90–4.

50 *Kharāj*, 139; cf. *Tanbīh*, 31; *Buldān*, 404–5; see the *Muqaddima* of Abū Manṣūr Maʿmarī's *Shāh-nāma*, written in 346/957, "Muqaddima-i qadīm-i *Shāh-nāma*,"

in *Hazāra-i Firdawsī* (Tehran: Dunyā-i Kitāb, 1983–4), 166; translated by Vladimir Minorsky, "The Older Preface to the *Shāh-nāma*," *Studi Orientalistici in onore di Giorgio Levi Della Vida* (1956), 2:171; and Johannes Kramers, "L'influence de la tradition iranienne dans la géographie arabe," *Analecta Orientalia* (Leiden: Brill, 1954–6), 1:150.

51 *Masālik*, 155.

52 See Christopher Brunner, "Geographical and Administrative Divisions: Settlements and Economy," in *The Cambridge History of Iran*, 3:747–77.

53 See C. A. Nallino, "al-Khuwārizmī e il suo rifacimento della Geografia di Tolomeo," *Raccolta di scritti editi e inediti* 5 (1944): 458–532. Sezgin, however, raises doubts as to whether the work edited by Mžik is indeed to be ascribed to Khwārazmī. Yet, Sezgin does believe that this work represents geographical coordinates recorded for the no longer extant world map commissioned by al-Maʾmūn, see *GAS*, 12:4, and Sezgin, *The Contribution of the Arabic-Islamic Geographers to the Formation of the World Map* (Frankfurt: Johann Wolfgang Goethe-Universität, 1987), 14–5.

54 See Maqbul Ahmad, "Kharīṭa," *EI²*. Masʿūdī relates that he saw a series of maps dated to the period of al-Maʾmūn that represented "the universe with spheres, the stars, land and the seas, inhabited and barren regions of the world, settlements of peoples, cities, and these were more exquisite than the maps that Ptolemy laid out in his *Geography*, or those in the *Geography* of Marinos, or those of others," *Tanbīh*, 33. Based on the surviving coordinates, this geography would have featured the lands of Gog and Magog in the far northeast, see *GAS*, 12:2–4, §§1a–b.

55 *Tanbīh*, 25, 51.

56 See R. Rashed and R. Morelon, "Thābit b. Ḳurra," *EI²*. On the translations and adaptations made of Ptolemy's *Geography* in the third/ninth century, see *MḤudūd*, 7–15; see also Ahmet Karamustafa, "Introduction to Islamic Maps," in *Cartography in the Traditional Islamic and South Asian Societies* (Chicago: University of Chicago Press, 1992), 10–1.

57 *Masālik*, 5–6.

58 Morony, *Iraq after the Muslim Conquest*, 128–9.

59 See *Kharāj*, 159–62.

60 See *A Catalogue of the Provincial Capitals of Ērānshahr*, ed. Giuseppe Messina with commentary by Josef Marquart (Rome: Pontificio Istituto Biblico, 1931); Touraj Daryaee, ed. and trans., *Šahrestānīhā-ī Ērānšahr* (Costa Mesa, CA: Mazda, 2002), 1–12; Carlo Cereti, "Middle Persian Geographical Literature," *Contributions à l'histoire et la géographie historique* (Leuven: Peeters, 2004), 11–36.

61 *Masālik*, 5.

62 Ibid.

63 Maʿmarī, *Muqaddima*, 168; English, Minorsky, "The Older Preface to the *Shāh-nāma*," 172.

64 *Masālik*, 18–72.
65 Ibid., 72–118.
66 Ibid., 118–25; MS B, fols. 60b–61a, Meynard, 99–102.
67 *Masālik*, 125–53; cf. *Akhbār al-Ṣīn wa 'l-Hind* (Paris: Les Belles Lettres, 1948), §4.
68 *Masālik*, 64; on the belief in the gigantic status of the first humans, see Brannon Wheeler, *Mecca and Eden, Ritual, Relics, and Territory in Islam* (Chicago: University of Chicago, 2006), 99–122.
69 *Masālik*, 133.
70 Ibid., 129–30.
71 Ibid., 79, 123, 126.
72 Ibid., 144.
73 Ibid., 123–4, 174–5.
74 See Sarah Savant's penetrating study on early narrative strategies of assimilation within the process of conversion, "Finding Our Place in the Past: Genealogy and Ethnicity in Islam" (Ph.D. diss., Harvard University, 2006).
75 *Masālik*, 5–6; cf. *Nafīsa*, 107. These divisions and terminology were not uniform throughout either Sāsānian or ʿAbbāsid administration; see Michael Morony, "Continuity and Change in the Administrative Geography of Late Sasanian and Early Islamic al-ʿIrāq," *Iran* 20 (1982): 1–49; for pre-Islamic Persian administrative categories, see Geo Widengren, "Recherches sur le féodalisme iranien," *Orientalia Suecana* (1956), 5:122–48.
76 *Masālik*, 6; *"kawwara 'l-kūr wa 'l-ṭasāsīj,"* *TAY*, 1:164–5, a process of administrative division and taxation continued by Anūshirwān. See Morony, "Continuity and Change," 4, 6, and *Iraq after the Muslim Conquest*, 126, 129; Løkkegaard, *Islamic Taxation in the Classic Period* (Copenhagen: Branner and Korch, 1950), 164; for the Middle Persian etymology of *ṭassūj*, see Widengren, "Recherches sur le féodalisme iranien," 122n4.
77 *Masālik*, 47. In MS B, Dārābjird and Fasā apparently constitute a single district, fol. 26; cf. Iṣṭakhrī, 66.
78 Richard Frye, *The History of Ancient Iran* (München: Beck, 1984), 333–4; cf. *A Catalogue of the Provincial Capitals*, 8–23; *Šahrestānīhā-ī Ērānšahr*, 10–1. Though Arabic and Persian sources often treat *kūra* as a loanword from Persian, it is of Greek origin, from *χώρα*, see Morony, *Iraq after the Muslim Conquest*, 126; D. Sourdel "Kūra," *EI*^{2}.
79 Steingass glosses *kurr* as a "Babylonian dry measure of six ass-loads."
80 See Morony, *Iraq after the Muslim Conquest*, 125–64.
81 *Masālik*, 14; cf. *Nafīsa*, 104–5.
82 Jahshiyārī, *Kitāb al-wuzarāʾ*, 4–5.
83 *Masālik*, 15–6.
84 See Aḥmad Tafażżole, "Ferēdūn," *EIr*.
85 Firdawsī, *Shāh-nāma* (New York: Bibliotheca Persica, 1988–2008), 1:107–11, lines 286–338.
86 Masʿūdī quotes these same verses, stating that Persian poets in the period of

Islam recall such boastful poetry in pride of their ancestry, which ostensibly links these lines of verse with the broader *shuʿūbiyya* movement, *Tanbīh*, 37.

87 *Murūj*, §9, cf. §503.

88 On the issue of Abū Manṣūr Thaʿālibī's authorship of *Ghurar*, see Franz Rosenthal, "From Arabic Books and Manuscripts III: The Author of the *Ġurar as-siyar*" *JAOS* 70 (1950): 181–2; cf. C. E. Bosworth, "al-Thaʿālibī, Abū Manṣūr," *EI*².

89 *Ghurar*, 130.

90 Ibid., 257, 415, 444, 604, see also, 257, 262, 378, 458, 486, 556–7.

91 Cf. *Taqāsīm*, 335.

92 See Gilbert Lazard, "Darī," *EIr* and "The Rise of the New Persian Language," in *The Cambridge History of Iran*, 4:595–632; cf. Bo Utas, "Semitic in Iranian: Written, Read and Spoken Language" in *Linguistic Convergence and Areal Diffusion* (London: Routledge, 2005), 65–78.

93 *Masālik*, 118; cf. A. J. Arberry, *Classical Persian Literature* (London: G. Allen and Unwin, 1958), 30–1. On the oral transmission of Sāsānian verse, see Lazard, "The Rise of the New Persian Language," 604.

94 *Ghurar*, 557. On this particular verse, see M. R. Shafīʿī Kadkanī, "Kuhantarīn namūna-i shiʿr-i fārsī," *Ārash* 6 (1963), 21–2. Admittedly the transmission of this Persian citation, as with others from the period, is slightly jumbled. See also Dhabīḥ Allāh Ṣafā, *Tārīkh-i adabiyyāt dar Īrān* (Tehran: Ibn Sīnā, 1956–7), 1:177–6. This version alludes to Bahrām Gūr's hunting prowess; see W. L. Hanaway, "Bahrām Gūr," *EIr*; Cl. Huart, "Bahrām," *EI*².

95 During the ʿAbbāsid period the figure of Bahrām Gūr was closely linked to the heroic feats of the pre-Islamic Persian kings in a discourse that often highlighted the grandeur of the Persians in comparison to that of the Arabs, cf. *Faḍl al-ʿArab wa 'l-tanbīh ʿalā ʿulūmihā* (Abu Dhabi: al-Mujammaʿ al-Thaqāfī, 1998), ascribed to Ibn Qutayba (d. 276/889), 86–7.

96 *Masālik*, 26. De Goeje misreads the *kunyā* of the poet. Both verses appear to be garbled in the manuscript transmission, see Vienna MS Mixt. 783 (= MS V), fol. 13b. My translation is based on Marquart's reading in *A Catalogue of the Provincial Capitals*, 33; however, for a different interpretation which presents Samarqand in a positive light, see ʿAlī Akbar Dihkhudā, *Lughat-nāma*, s.v. "Shāsh," and Dhabīḥ Allāh Ṣafā, *Tārīkh-i adabiyyāt*, 1:149. According to Ibn Khurradādhbih, al-ʿAbbās b. Ṭarkhān was a shameless buffoon; see his encounter with al-Maʾmūn in Muʿāfā b. Zakariyyāʾ al-Nahrawānī (d. 390/1000), *al-Jalīs al-ṣāliḥ al-kāfī* (Beirut: ʿĀlam al-Kutub, 1981–93), 4:162–3; on his *kunyā* as an allusion to his imprisonment by al-Wāthiq for satirizing al-Faḍl b. Marwān, see Ibn al-Muʿtazz, *Ṭabaqāt al-shuʿarāʾ* (Egypt: Dār al-Maʿārif, 1956), 130–2; cf. Ṣafadī, *al-Wāfī*, 16:378–9.

97 *Aghānī*, 1:357.

98 Ibid., 5:265–6.

99 Ibid., 5:307; see C. E. Bosworth, "The Persian Impact on Arabic Literature,"

in *The Cambridge History of Arabic Literature*, 1:493–4; Aḥmad Mahdawī Dāmghānī, "Fāresīyāt," *EIr*.

100 *Murūj*, §§3213–27; *Aghānī*, 8:276; 10:119; 15:24; 16:133; on Iṣfahānī's negative assessment of Ibn Khurradādhbih as an unreliable source, see conclusion, 185–6.

101 *Lahw*, 16; see Shafīʿī Kadkanī, "Kuhantarīn," 25–8; Philippe Gignoux and Aḥmad Tafażżole, "Some Middle-Persian Quotations in Classical Arabic and Persian Texts," in *Mémorial Jean de Menasce* (Leuven: Imprimerie Orientaliste, 1974), 338. On the minstrel poet, see Aḥmad Tafażżole, "Bārbad," *EIr*.

102 As Shafīʿī Kadkanī notes, the transmission of these verses, both the Arabic and the Persian, seems to be garbled, ibid.

103 When considering the quantity of Arabic poetic material showcased, it seems perhaps incongruous to classify his work as part of the *shuʿūbiyya* movement of Persian writers, mainly of verse, who lambasted the putative primacy of the Arabs, as scholars such as Krachkovskii have suspected, 167–71.

104 *Masālik*, 59, 162. On Khawarnaq, see *TRM*, ser. 1, 2:850–1.

105 *Masālik*, 136. On Nāʿiṭ, see Abū ʿUbayd al-Bakrī, *Muʿjam mā istaʿjam* (Beirut: Dār al-Kutub al-ʿIlmiyya, 1998), 1:314, 4:137; cf. *Muʿjam*, 5:253; cf. Murtaḍā ʾl-Zabīdī, *Tāj al-ʿarūs* (Beirut: Dār al-Fikr, 1994), 10:432.

106 *Masālik*, 152.

107 Ibid., 101; cf. Abū Tammām (d. 231/845), who evokes the power of Iskandar and Khusraw in a famous victory ode on al-Muʿtaṣim's conquest of ʿAmmūriya, analyzed in Suzanne Stetkevych, *The Poetics of Islamic Legitimacy* (Bloomington: Indiana University Press, 2002), 152–79.

108 In the over eighty verse citations, there are several references to battle days (*ayyām*) and to lands obtained through conquest (*futūḥāt*). See, for example, *Masālik*, 7, 18–9, 22, 25, 100–1, 119, 146, 152. However, of all the citations, there are only a handful of references to lands beyond Muslim territory, which are themselves connected to military expansion or the projection of ʿAbbāsid power, e.g., 124; cf. Buḥturī, *Dīwān*, 2:974–9, §386, line 36.

Chapter 2: Models of Translation

1 See James S. Romm, *The Edges of the Earth in Ancient Thought* (Princeton: Princeton University Press, 1992), 82–120.

2 See, for instance, *TRM*, ser. 3, 2:1301, 3:1413, 1424; cf. how the Sāmānid *wazīr* Jayhānī gathered information for his descriptive geography, *Taqāsīm*, 4–5; Adam Mez, "Die Verwaltung," *Die Renaissance des Islâms* (Heidelberg: C. Winter, 1922), 70–1; Silverstein, *Postal Systems*, 20–3, 65–7.

3 See *Tanbīh*, 190–1; *Masālik*, 105–6; an account in both MS B, fol. 53a–b, and in MS V, fol. 44a–b. While Jarmī's writings may have circulated among the secretariat during the reign of al-Wāthiq, or shortly thereafter, there is nothing to indicate, from the line of transmission recorded in the *Masālik*, that Ibn Khurradādhbih's geography is contemporary to Jarmī's account, contra Lewicki, *Źródła arabskie*, 1:59–60.

4 On the speculation concerning the identity and nature of this network of itinerant Jewish merchants, and whether or not such an international network even existed, see Ch. Pellat "Rādhāniyya," *EI*[2].

5 *Masālik*, 105–6; cf. *Buldān*, 540.

6 See Lewicki, *Źródła arabskie*, 1:126–52; Omeljan Pritsak, "An Arabic Text on the Trade Route of the Corporation of Ar-Rūs in the Second Half of the Ninth Century," *Folia Orientalia* 12 (1970): 241–59; and Thomas Noonan, "When did Rūs/Rus' merchants first visit Khazaria and Baghdad?" *AEMA* 7 (1987–91): 213–9. On the identity of the Rūs, see Omeljan Pritsak, *The Origin of Rus'* (Cambridge: Harvard University Press, 1981); Peter Golden, "The Question of the Rus' Qağanate," *AEMA* 2 (1982): 77–97.

7 *Masālik*, 154; cf. *Buldān*, 540–1; *Murūj*, §§458–61.

8 This was an interpretation offered by James Montgomery in a roundtable discussion at the tenth conference of the School of ʿAbbāsid Studies, Leuven (2010).

9 R. Paret, "Aṣḥāb al-kahf," *EI*[2].

10 Muḥammad b. Mūsā b. Shākir appears to have been from the Banū Mūsā, who had close ties to the ʿAbbāsid court, cf. *GAS*, 13:243–4; on the Banū Mūsā, see *GAS*, 5:245–52; 6:147–8; D. R. Hill, "Mūsā, Banū," *EI*[2]. In the sources and in the secondary scholarship there is some debate concerning whether the famous polymath Muḥammad b. Mūsā 'l-Khwārazmī and Muḥammad b. Mūsā b. Shākir were the same person. See D. M. Dunlop, "Muḥammad b. Mūsā al-Khwārizmī," *JRAS* (1943): 248–50. Dunlop's thesis is not entirely conclusive, as the surviving material on the life of Muḥammad b. Mūsā 'l-Khwārazmī is such that it is difficult to conclude with certainty whether or not these two figures are indeed one and the same. Following Dunlop, Sezgin lists them separately, *GAS*, 13:238, 244. Cf. *Taqāsīm*, 362.

11 *Masālik*, 106–7.

12 Cf. *Tanbīh*, 134; *Murūj*, §730–1, Masʿūdī relates here that Sarakhsī, who was the author of a descriptive geography entitled *al-Masālik wa 'l-mamālik*, recounted a similar tale, directly on the authority of Muḥammad b. Mūsā b. Shākir. Sarakhsī also wrote *Risāla fī aṣḥāb al-kahf wa 'l-raqīm*, *GAS*, 12:245; cf. *Muʿjam*, 3:60–2 and *Miʿṭār*, 49. Abū 'l-Rayḥān al-Bīrūnī (d. ca 442/1050) describes Muḥammad b. Mūsā's embassy and concludes what the other sources seem to overlook, namely, that the embassy did not succeed in locating the People of the Cave, see *al-Āthār al-bāqiya* (Tehran: Mīrāth-i Maktūb, 2001), 360; trans. Edward Sachau, *The Chronology of Ancient Nations* (London: W. H. Allen, 1879), 286–7.

13 Muḥammad b. Najīb Bakrān, *Jahān-nāma* (Tehran: Ibn Sīnā, 1963), 108

14 *Buldān*, 634–5; *Muʿjam*, 2:24. Josef Marquart, "Skizzen zur geschichtlichen Völkerkunde von Mittelasien und Sibirien," in *Festschrift für Friedrich Hirth* (Berlin: Oesterheld and Co., 1920), 289–93.

15 Ibn Saʿd, *al-Ṭabaqāt al-kubrā* (Beirut: Dār Ṣādir, 1960), 1:258.

16 *RIF*, §1.
17 For Takīn, or *tegīn*, signifying a prince, but in this context applied to a *ghulām* (servant, slave), and for various interpretations concerning the significance of the name Bāris, see Togan's commentary in *RIF*, 4; Lewicki, *Źródła arabskie*, 3:123, §§27–8; and James McKeithen, *The Risalah of Ibn Fadlan* (Ph.D. diss., Indiana University, 1979), 28.
18 *RIF*, §17. The statement 'there is no deity but God' (*lā ilāha illā 'llāh*) is the first part of the profession of faith (*shahāda*).
19 *RIF*, §22 & passim.
20 For the body tattoos, see *RIF*, §81. For a description of one of the more graphic scenes in *RIF*, §§89–92, see Albert S. Cook, "Ibn Fadlān's Account of Scandinavian Merchants on the Volga in 922," *Journal of English and Germanic Philology* 22 (1923): 54–63.
21 *Masālik*, 65; cf. *Akhbār al-Ṣīn wa 'l-Hind*, 5, §8.
22 *Masālik*, 66.
23 Ibid; cf. R. A. Donkin, *Dragon's Brain Perfume: An Historical Geography of Camphor* (Leiden: Brill, 1999), 105–42.
24 *Ṭabāʾiʿ al-ḥayawān*, ed. and trans. Vladimir Minorsky as *Sharaf al-Zamān Ṭāhir Marvazī on China, the Turks, and India* (London: Royal Asiatic Society, 1942), Arabic, ch. 9, §8, 45, trans., 34 (hereafter *Ṭabāʾiʿ al-ḥayawān*). Minorsky draws from only a selection of Marwazī's *Ṭabāʾiʿ al-ḥayawān*, while the complete work remains in manuscript form. Minorsky doubts that this tribe described by Marwazī truly refers to the Kīmāk, 107–8; cf. *MḤudūd*, 304ff., along with C. E. Bosworth, "Kimäk," *EI²*. Cf. *Masālik*, 28.
25 Marwazī, *Ṭabāʾiʿ al-ḥayawān*, Arabic, 45.
26 Ibid., 44–5. The Yūra depicted appear to be identical with the Siberian Yugra, see Minorsky's commentary, 113; cf. Peter Golden, "The Peoples of the Russian Forest Belt," in *The Cambridge History of Early Inner Asia* (Cambridge: Cambridge University Press, 1990), 1:229–55. In regard to *mughāyaba*, Marwazī thrice uses this specific word to describe silent trade, Arabic, ch. 15, §§3, 12, 16, cf. ch. 9, §8. The Arabic term denotes mutual absence; the trilateral root *ghayn/yāʾ/bāʾ* etymologically signifies absence. MS Delhi Arabic 1949 of the British Library presents no ambiguity concerning the word in question, cf. fols. 14a, 42b, 44b, which is consistently given as *mughāyaba*. Minorsky, in his critical apparatus, offers *muʿāyana* as a possible reading, Arabic, 45. However, *mughāyaba* is justified, as it agrees with the codicological record, as well as other sources; cf. Abū 'l-Fidāʾ (d. 732/1331), *Taqwīm al-buldān* (Paris: Imprimerie nationale, 1840), 201–2; Aḥmad b. ʿAlī 'l-Qalqashandī (d. 821/1418), *Ṣubḥ al-aʿshā* (Cairo: al-Muʾassasa al-Miṣriyya, n.d), 4:466; 5:422.
27 Cf. Minorsky's commentary, *Ṭabāʾiʿ al-ḥayawān*, 113.
28 Marwazī, *Ṭabāʾiʿ al-ḥayawān*, Arabic, ch. 15, §§12, 48; English, 58.
29 Ibid., ch. 15, §§16, 49; English, 58–9; Minorsky's commentary, 159. Cf. *Buldān*, 69; Bīrūnī, *Taḥqīq mā li'l-Hind* (Beirut: ʿĀlam al-Kitāb, 1983), 236; *Alberuni's*

India, trans. Sachau (London: K. Paul, Trench, Trübner & Co., 1910), 299–300; Marwazī, ch. 15, §12; *Bilād*, 81–2; *Miʿṭār*, 90; Masʿūdī [pseud.], *Akhbār al-zamān* (Beirut: Dār al-Andalus, 1966), 46. None of these authors use the word *mughāyaba*, rather they paraphrase. See also Herodotus, *The Histories of Herodotus* (New York: G. P. Putnam's Sons, 1921–4), vol. 4, §196. Cf. E. W. Bovill, "The Silent Trade of Wangara," *Journal of the Royal African Society* 29 (1929): 27–38; Philip Grierson, *The Silent Trade* (Edinburgh: W. Green, 1903); on Chinese accounts of a similar practice, see Paul Pelliot, *Notes on Marco Polo* (Paris: Imprimerie nationale, 1959–63), 2:622–4.

30 Ptolemy, *Geographia* (Leipzig: Sumptibus et typis Caroli Tauchnitii, 1843), 3; trans. J. Lennart Berggren and Alexander Jones as *Ptolemy's Geography* (Princeton: Princeton University Press, 2000), 57.

31 Regarding the Arabic vocalization for Gog and Magog, there are two accepted Qurʾānic readings, Yājūj and Mājūj without the *hamza*, which was preferred in the Ḥijāz and Iraq, versus Yaʾjūj and Maʾjūj with the *hamza*. See Ṭabarī, who considers the former to be the correct reading (*al-qirāʾa al-ṣaḥīḥa*), *Jāmiʿ*, 16:16.

32 For an overview of Islamic eschatological traditions see, David Cook, *Studies in Muslim Apocalyptic* (Princeton: Darwin Press, 2002).

33 Flavius Josephus, *Antiquitatum iudaicorum*, bk. 1, §123, in *Opera* (Cambridge: Harvard University Press, 1926–65); idem, *De bello iudaico*, bk. 7, §§244–5; Andrew R. Anderson, *Alexander's Gate, Gog and Magog and the Enclosed Nations* (Cambridge: Mediaeval Academy of America, 1932), 8; Matthias Henze, ed., *The Syriac Apocalypse of Daniel* (Tübingen: Mohr Siebeck, 2001), 12; see Károly Czeglédy, "The Syriac Legend Concerning Alexander the Great," *AOASH* 7 (1957): 231–49.

34 See Gerrit J. Reinink, "Alexander the Great in Seventh-Century Syriac 'Apocalyptic' Texts," in *Syriac Christianity under Late Sasanian and Early Islamic Rule* (Aldershot: Ashgate, 2005), art. 6, 150–78.

35 Ephraem [pseud.], Sermo V, *Des heiligen Ephraem des Syrers Sermones III*, (Leuven: Secrétariat du CSCO, 1972), 320:63–4; Methodius [pseud.], *Die syrische Apokalypse*, ed. and trans. Reinink (Leuven: Peeters, 1993), 540:14–6, §§3–10; Reinink, "Pseudo-Ephraem's 'Rede über Das Ende,'" *Syriac Christianity*, art. 4, 437–63; idem, "Ps.-Methodius: A Concept of History in Response to the Rise of Islam," *Syriac Christianity*, art. 9, 166–7.

36 On the Islamic exegetical tradition of the epithet Dhū 'l-Qarnayn, see Israel Friedländer, *Die Chadhirlegende und der Alexanderroman* (Leipzig: Teubner, 1913), 276ff; cf. Andrew Anderson, "Alexander's Horns," *Transactions and Proceedings of the American Philological Association* 58 (1927): 100–22.

37 *Neṣḥānā d'Aleksandrōs* [The triumph of Alexander], edited and translated in Ernest Budge, *The History of Alexander the Great, Being the Syriac Version of the Pseudo-Callisthenes* (Cambridge: Cambridge University Press, 1889), Syriac, 257, English, 146.

38 On the question of the prophethood of Dhū 'l-Qarnayn, see Ibn Hishām, *al-Sīra al-nabawiyya* (Beirut: Dār al-Maʿrifa, 2006), 289; he is often considered merely a pious servant of God (*ʿabd ṣāliḥ*), see ʿAbd al-Razzāq, *Tafsīr* (Beirut: Dār al-Kutub al-ʿIlmiyya, 1999), 3:234–5; *Jāmiʿ*, 16:9. There are various interpretations as to whether or not this figure corresponded to Alexander the Great, in addition to the speculations concerning the origin and signification of the epithet 'Dhū 'l-Qarnayn,' see *Murūj*, §§124, 671; *Buldān*, 125–6; *Jāmiʿ*, 16:9; Fakhr al-Dīn al-Rāzī, *al-Tafsīr al-kabīr* (Beirut: Dār al-Fikr, 1981–3), 21:164–6.

39 See Brannon Wheeler, "Moses or Alexander? Early Islamic Exegesis of Qur'an 18:60–65," *Journal of Near Eastern Studies* 57 (1998): 191–215.

40 Anderson, *Alexander's Gate*, 12–4.

41 MS B, fol. 61a; cf. *Masālik*, 163.

42 *Masālik*, 4.

43 Abū Maʿshar's description, as quoted in Thaʿālibī, contains more detail than Ibn Khurradādhbih's passage, which suggests that Ibn Khurradādhbih is not the source for Abū Maʿshar, Thaʿālibī, *Laṭāʾif*, 164–5; see *Murūj*, §1419; Dodge, 656–8; David Pingree, *The Thousands of Abū Maʿshar* (London: Warburg Institute, 1968), 15n6.

44 Pingree, *Thousands*, 14–6. More broadly on the Hermetic association with the pyramids, see A. Fodor, "The Origins of the Arabic legends of the Pyramids," *AOASH* 23 (1970): 335–63, and Michael Cook, "Pharaonic History in Medieval Egypt," *Studia Islamica* 57 (1983): 67–103.

45 *Buldān*, 123; cf. *Masālik*, 159; *Nafīsa*, 80. The talismans appear in Ibn al-Faqīh's account, and in MS B, fol. 77b, Meynard, 126, and in Abū Maʿshar's account, in Thaʿālibī, *Laṭāʾif*, 165; but are not referenced in MS V; on *musnad* as an ancient script, see *Murūj*, §827; in the transmission of Ibn al-Kalbī's (d. 206/821) book of genealogy, the philologist Abū Saʿīd al-Sukkarī (d. 275/888) cites Ibn Khurradādhbih's writing (*kitāb*), which preserves an example of the *musnad* script, *Jamharat al-nasab* (Beirut: ʿĀlam al-Kutub, 1986), 614, cf. 11. Cf. Edward Lane, *An Arabic-English Lexicon* (London and Edinburgh: Williams and Norgate, 1863–93), s.v. "Musnad." As for the motif of attempting to destroy the pyramids, *Murūj*, §814; cf. Taqī 'l-Dīn al-Maqrīzī (d. 845/1442), *al-Mawāʿiẓ wa 'l-iʿtibār* (Cairo: al-Maktabat Madbūlī, 1998), 1:328.

46 Similar accounts concerning Ibn Ṭūlūn and the pyramids are detailed in several later sources, all of which appear not to be aware of the episode as recorded in MS V, a possible indication of the limited circulation of the Vienna recension; the adventure is also absent from the later geographies, see Abū Muḥammad al-Balawī (fl. 330/941), *Sīrat Ibn Ṭūlūn* (Damascus: al-Maktaba al-ʿArabiyya, 1939), 194–6; Abū Jaʿfar al-Idrīsī (d. 649/1251), *Kitāb anwār ʿulwiyy al-ajrām fī 'l-kashf ʿan asrār al-ahrām* (Beirut: Franz Steiner, 1991), 35–6, 132; Maqrīzī, *al-Mawāʿiẓ*, 1:128, cf. 339.

47 Alexandre Popović, *Revolt of African Slaves in Iraq in the Third/Ninth Century* (Princeton: Markus Wiener Publishers, 1999), 119ff.

48 *TRM*, ser. 3, 4:2028–9, 2080–2.

49 In 273/887 Luʾluʾ was imprisoned by Abū Aḥmad al-Muwaffaq for nearly ten years, *TRM*, ser. 3, 4:2112, 2146. Only MS V contains the adventure related by Muhallabī; on the question of the dating of these two recensions, see chapter 7, 171.

50 *Masālik*, 160.

51 See Patrick Geary, *Furta Sacra: Thefts of Relics in the Central Middle Ages* (Princeton: Princeton University Press, 1978).

52 See Idrīsī, *al-Anwār*, 33–5, 106–7; Maqrīzī, *al-Mawāʿiẓ*, 1:324–6, 330. I would like to thank Michael Cooperson for sharing with me a pre-publication version of his article, "Al-Maʾmūn, the Pyramids, and the Hieroglyphs," in *ʿAbbāsid Studies II* (Leuven: Peeters, forthcoming), which argues for the historicity of al-Maʾmūn's excavation of the pyramids; see also J. M. F. van Reeth, "Caliph al-Maʾmūn and the Treasure of the Pyramids," *Orientalia Lovaniensia Periodica* 25 (1994): 221–36; and more broadly, Ulrich Haarmann, "Muslim Medieval Perceptions of Pharaonic Egypt," in *Ancient Egyptian Literature* (Leiden: Brill, 1996), 605–28, along with Mark Pettigrew, "The Wonders of the Ancients" (Ph.D. diss., University of California at Berkeley, 2004), 146–92.

53 *Masālik*, 156–7. See Ibn ʿAbd al-Ḥakam, *Futūḥ Miṣr wa ʾl-Maghrib* (New Haven: Yale University Press, 1922), 206; Rodrigo Ximénez de Rada (d. 1247), *Historia de rebus hispanie* (Turnhout, Belgium: Brepols, 1987), 99–100; Alfonso X (d. 1284), *La Primera crónica general de España* (Madrid: Gredos, 1955), 1:307, §553.

54 *Masālik*, 156–7; *Nafīsa*, 79. Cf. Garth Fowden, *Quṣayr ʿAmra, Art and the Umayyad Elite in Late Antique Syria* (Berkeley: University of California Press, 2004), 197–226.

55 See Masʿūdī's account of the geographical description of the world allegedly presented to ʿUmar b. al-Khaṭṭāb after the early Muslim conquests, *Murūj*, §§973–85.

56 *Masālik*, 157; *Nafīsa*, 80. On the Arab conquest of Paykand, see Étienne de la Vaissière, *Sogdian Traders* (Leiden: Brill, 2005), 268–73.

57 *Masālik*, 115–6; *Nafīsa*, 78–9.

58 Iṣfahānī, *Kitāb adab al-ghurabāʾ* (Beirut: Dār al-Kitāb al-Jadīd, 1972), 30–1, §8; on the question of authorship, see Sebastian Günther, "Abū l-Faraj al-Iṣfahānī," *EI*[3].

59 *Murūj*, §491.

Chapter 3: Al-Wāthiq and the Translators

1 Matthew Gordon, *A Breaking of a Thousand Swords, A History of the Turkish Military of Samarra* (Albany: State University of New York Press, 2001), 47–74.

2 *YBN*, 255.

3 Ibid., 264–5.

4 Alastair Northedge, *The Historical Topography of Samarra* (London: British School of Archaeology in Iraq, 2005), 166–93.

5 *Masālik*, 31.

6 On ethnic demarcations see, *YBN*, 258–9; on religious practice see Gordon, *Thousand Swords*, 4–5, 147–9; on the Sogdian military institution of the *chākar* (i.e., *shākiriyya*), see Étienne de la Vaissière, *Samarcande et Samarra* (Paris: Association pour l'avancement des études iraniennes, 2007), 68–77, 187–9; Patricia Crone, *Slaves on Horses* (Cambridge: Cambridge University Press, 1980), 78–9.

7 For general sources on al-Wāthiq's life, see Yaʿqūbī, 2:479–84; *YBN*, 264–5; *TRM*, ser. 3, 2:1330–64; *Aghānī*, 9:267–93; Baghdādī, *Taʾrīkh Baghdād*, 16:22–8; Ṣafadī, *al-Wāfī*, 27:201–4; Suyūṭī, *Taʾrīkh al-khulafāʾ* (Beirut: Dār al-Turāth, 1969), 315–20. As for al-Wāthiq's death of "insufferable thirst," Max Meyerhof has speculated that this was caused by diabetes, see his article, "ʿAlī aṭ-Ṭabarī's 'Paradise of Wisdom,' One of the Oldest Arabic Compendiums of Medicine," *Isis* 16 (1931), 9.

8 *Aghānī*, 9:267–8; "*kāna 'l-Wāthiqu aʿlama 'l-khulafāʾi bi'l-ghināʾ*," 285.

9 *Aghānī*, 1:18–9, 4:117, 5:60, 9:285; cf. *Fihrist*, 1:437, Dodge, 309; Hilary Kilpatrick, *Making the Great Book of Songs* (London: Routledge, 2003), 28, 40.

10 On al-Wāthiq's fondness for eggplant, see Ibn ʿAbd Rabbih (d. 328/939), *al-ʿIqd al-farīd* (Beirut: Dār al-Kutub al-ʿIlmiyya, 1987), 6:300; Ibn Sayyār al-Warrāq (fl. 338/950), *Kitāb al-ṭabīkh = Annals of the Caliph's Kitchens* (Leiden: Brill, 2007), passim. For an astrological reading of al-Wāthiq's death, see Abū Maʿshar, *Kitāb al-milal wa 'l-duwal = On Historical Astrology: The Book of Religions and Dynasties* (Leiden: Brill, 2000), 110.

11 *Aghānī*, 4:118; on Farīda, 4:116–22, cf. 9:274.

12 *Nafīsa*, 149; cf. Bakrī, 1:455; *Miʿṭār*, 310.

13 Ibn Abī Uṣaybiʿa (d. 668/1270), *ʿUyūn al-anbāʾ* (Beirut: Dār Maktabat al-Ḥayāh, 1965), 258; see Ibn al-Qifṭī (d. 646/1248), *Taʾrīkh al-ḥukamāʾ* (Leipzig: Dieterich'sche Verlagsbuchhandlung, 1903), 174.

14 Artemidorus, *Taʿbīr al-ruʾyā = Le livre des songes par Artémidore d'Éphèse* (Damascus: Institut français, 1964); on the debate concerning the authenticity of this translation, see below, 229n69. For a reference to Ḥunayn's translation of the *Septuagint* into Arabic, see *Tanbīh*, 112.

15 The physician named here is Bukhtīshūʿ b. Jibrīl, ultimately exiled by al-Wāthiq to Jundaysābūr, see Ibn al-Qifṭī, *Taʾrīkh al-ḥukamāʾ*, 102; D. Sourdel, "Bukhtīshūʿ," *EI²*; Ibn Māsawayh was a physician from the time of Hārūn al-Rashīd until the reign al-Mutawakkil, see Ibn Abī Uṣaybiʿa, *ʿUyūn al-anbāʾ*, 175; J. C. Vadet, "Ibn Māsawayh," *EI²*.

16 *Murūj*, §2857.

17 On his treatment of teeth, see Ḥunayn b. Isḥāq, *Fī ḥifẓ al-asnān* (Aleppo: Dār al-Qalam al-ʿArabī, 1996).

18 *Murūj*, §2863; cf. Sezgin, *GAS*, "Sharḥ masāʾil Ḥunayn b. Isḥāq fī 'l-umūr al-ṭabīʿiyya," 2:251, excerpt A.

19 See A. K. S. Lambton, "Khalīfa," *EI²*; more specifically for the authority of the caliphate, see Patricia Crone and Martin Hinds, *God's Caliph* (Cambridge:

Cambridge University Press, 1986).

20 See, Hayrettın Yücesoy, "Translation as Self-Consciousness," *Journal of World History* 20 (2009): 523–57.

21 *Ḥayawān*, 1:74–9.

22 Ibid., 1:74–5.

23 Ibid., 1:75–9.

24 Ibid., 1:76.

25 Muḥammad b. Idrīs al-Shāfiʿī, *al-Risāla* (Baltimore: Johns Hopkins Press, 1961), 32, §134.

26 See Q. 14:4; 16:105; 39:29; 41:44; 43:1–2; 92:5.

27 See A. L. Tibawi, "Is the Qurʾān Translatable?" *Moslem World* 52 (1962): 4–16.

28 See Sherman Jackson, "Al-Jahiz on Translation," *Alif: Journal of Comparative Poetics* 4 (1984): 99–107; also Myriam Salama-Carr, "Translation as seen by al-Jahiz and by Hunayn Ibn Ishaq—Observer versus Practitioner," in *International Medieval Research I* (Turnhout, Belgium: Brepols, 1997), 386–93.

29 Ḥunayn b. Isḥāq, *Risālat Ḥunayn b. Isḥāq* (Tehran: Muʾassasa-i Muṭālaʿāt-i Islāmī, 2001), passim.

30 See Ibn al-Qifṭī, *Taʾrīkh al-ḥukumāʾ*, 415–6.

31 Ibid.

32 See Gutas, *Greek Thought*, 136–41.

33 Abū Ḥayyān al-Tawḥīdī, *Kitāb al-imtāʿ wa ʾl-muʾānasa* (Beirut: al-Maktaba al-ʿAṣriyya, 1953), 1:107ff. See D. S. Margoliouth's translation of this debate, "The Discussion between Abū Bishr Mattā and Abū Saʿīd al-Sīrāfī on the Merits of Logic and Grammar," *JRAS* (1905): 79–129; cf. Muhsin Mahdi, "Language and Logic in Classical Islam," in *Logic in Classical Islamic Culture* (Wiesbaden: Harrassowitz, 1970), 51–83. See also C. Versteegh, "Logique et grammaire au dixième siècle," *Histoire, épistémologie, langage* 2 (1980): 39–52.

34 Tawḥīdī, *al-Imtāʿ*, 1:108.

35 Cf. Heck, *Construction of Knowledge*, 24.

36 Tawḥīdī, *al-Imtāʿ*, 1:111.

37 An edition of Abū Bishr Mattā's translation appears in ʿAbd al-Raḥmān Badawī's study of the Arabic reception of the *Poetics* of Aristotle, *Fann al-shiʿr* (Cairo: Maktabat al-Nahḍa al-Miṣriyya, 1953), 85–145. Cf. Margoliouth "The Discussion," 86; Badawī's notes, 85ff. See also Shukrī Muḥammad ʿAyyād, *Kitāb Arisṭūṭālīs fī ʾl-shiʿr* (Cairo: Dār al-Kātib al-ʿArabī, 1967), 180–90.

38 Aristotle, *Fann al-shiʿr*, ed. Badawī, 85.

39 Ibid.

40 Fārābī, *Risāla fī qawānīn ṣināʿat al-shuʿarāʾ*, included in Aristotle, *Fann al-shiʿr*, ed. Badawī, 149–58.

41 See Fārābī's treatment of tragedy and comedy, for instance, ibid., 153.

42 In a surviving fragment of his *Kitāb al-nuqaṭ*, Ḥunayn b. Isḥāq discusses the limitations of Arabic for the expression of foreign terms. The fragment, which may well be spurious, is quoted in the *Kitāb al-majālis*, written in 417/1026–7

by the Nestorian bishop of Nisibis (Naṣībīn), Īliyā b. Shīnā (d. 439/1047–8), ed. L. Cheikho, *al-Mashriq* 20 (1922), 373.

43 See *tarjamahu* in Lane's *Arabic Lexicon*. Cf. Q. 18:22.

44 See Frederic Delitzsch, *The Hebrew Language Viewed in the Light of Assyrian Research* (London: Williams and Norgate, 1883), 50; cf. William Muss-Arnolt, *Assyrisch-English-Deutsches Handwörterbuch* (Berlin: Reuther und Reichard, 1905), 2:953–4.

45 Jāḥiẓ, "Tafḍīl al-nuṭq ʿalā 'l-ṣamt," *Rasāʾil al-Jāḥiẓ* (Egypt: Maktabat al-Khānjī, 1964–79), 4:235.

46 Ghazālī, "*al-lisānu tarjumānun yaṣduqu marratan yakdhibu ukhrā*," *Iḥyāʾ*, 1:34.

47 One version of this *ḥadīth* states that "There is not one among you who the Lord will not speak to [directly], there is neither an interpreter between [the Lord] and him, nor a veil that will veil him" (*mā minkum min aḥadin illā sayukallimuhu rabbuhu, laysa baynahu wa baynahu tarjumānun wa lā ḥijābun yaḥjubuhu*). See Bukhārī, "Kitāb al-zakāt," 1:266–7, §1434; idem, "Kitāb al-manāqib," 3:707, §3637; cf. Muslim b. al-Ḥajjāj (d. 261/875), *Ṣaḥīḥ*, "Kitāb al-zakāt," 1:400–1, §2399; Ibn Māja (d. 273/887), *Sunan*, "al-Muqaddima," 31, §190; idem, "Kitāb al-zakāt," 268, §1916; Abū ʿĪsā 'l-Tirmidhī (d. 279/892), *Sunan*, "Kitāb ṣifat al-qiyāma," 2:617, §2599; all *ḥadīth* citations from the canonical six books are listed by the individual volumes of each respective collection in *Mawsūʿat al-ḥadīth al-sharīf* (Vaduz: Jamʿiyyat al-Maknaz al-Islāmī, 2000–1).

48 Ibn al-ʿArabī develops the gnostic role of the interpreter in the communication of revelation in *al-Futūḥāt al-Makkiyya* (Cairo: al-Hayʾa al-Miṣriyya al-ʿĀmma liʾl-Kitāb, 1972–92), see particularly, 8:188–9; 9:461–2; 10:176. Following the same figurative line, he uses the metaphor of translation and interpretation as a title for a collection of his mystical and erotic verse, *Tarjumān al-ashwāq* [The interpreter of desires].

49 See A. Dietrich, "Ibn Djuldjul," *EI*[2].

50 Ibn Abī Uṣaybiʿa's biography of Ibn Juljul from *ʿUyūn al-anbāʾ*, 493–5, cf. R. Arnaldez, "Iṣṭifan b. Basīl," *EI*[2]. Though here Ḥunayn is referred to as a *mutarjim*, in other instances the title *tarjumān* is used, Ibn al-Qifṭī, *Taʾrīkh al-ḥukamāʾ*, 25. Cf. Ibn Abī Uṣaybiʿa, *ʿUyūn al-anbāʾ*, 257, who also records the term *nāqil* to describe Ḥunayn, though the context suggests that this appellation is used as a slight by his slanderers, 265. In other contexts, Ḥunayn is described as a *nāqil*, 259, 279. *Tarjumān* is clearly used as a professional title, as is the case of Mūsā b. Khālid al-Tarjumān, 262, who nonetheless does not reach the same rank as Ḥunayn, 281; the same is true for Fathyūn al-Tarjumān, whose translations are said to be filled with errors, 280. Muqaddasī calls Sallām a *mutarjim*, reflecting a certain interchangeability of the terms, 362–5.

51 Ḥunayn b. Isḥāq, *Risāla*, 2.

52 Ibn Abī Uṣaybiʿa, *ʿUyūn al-anbāʾ*, 265; for the treatment of this piece as an autobiographical account, see Dwight Reynolds, ed., *Interpreting the Self, Autobiography in the Arabic Literary Tradition* (Berkeley: University of

California Press, 2001), 107–19.

53 S.v. "nāqil," *Lisān al-ʿArab*.

54 Ḥunayn b. Isḥāq, *Risāla*, 29; see also *Fihrist*, 2:278; Dodge, 684.

55 See Hayrettın Yücesoy, *Messianic Beliefs and Imperial Politics in Medieval Islam* (Columbia: University of South Carolina Press, 2009), 24–8, 40–58.

56 See Leah Kinberg's introduction to her translation of Ibn Abī 'l-Dunyā (d. 281/894), *Kitāb al-manām*, entitled *Morality in the Guise of Dreams* (Leiden: Brill, 1994), 22–3.

57 See Gutas, *Greek Thought*, 96–104.

58 *Murūj*, §1233ff. See Ibn Khaldūn, *Kitāb al-ʿibar* (Beirut: Dār al-Kitāb al-Lubnānī, 1961), 1:882, 886; trans. Franz Rosenthal as *The Muqaddimah* (Princeton: Princeton University Press, 1967), 367–71, cf. 80–3; see also Toufic Fahd, *La divination arabe* (Leiden: Brill, 1966), 91–130.

59 See Q. 12:4–6, and the story of Yūsuf and his vision and his divinely instructed ability to interpret dreams and portents (Q. 12:6, 12, 101, *taʾwīl al-aḥādīth*). See John Lamoreaux, *The Early Muslim Tradition of Dream Interpretation* (Albany: State University of New York Press, 2002), 107–34.

60 Ibn Khaldūn, *Kitāb al-ʿibar*, 1:882.

61 Ibn Qutayba, *Kitāb taʿbīr al-ruʾyā* (Damascus: Dār al-Bashāʾir, 2001), 95; *Fihrist*, 2:351, Dodge, 742; see Lamoreaux, *Early Muslim Tradition*, 19–25.

62 Ibn Qutayba, *Kitāb taʿbīr al-ruʾyā*, 103.

63 Ibid., 100, 134, 166.

64 See Gutas, *Greek Thought*, 45–52, 108–10.

65 See Toufic Fahd, "The Dream in Medieval Islamic Society," in *The Dream and Human Societies* (Berkeley: University of California Press, 1966), 351–63.

66 See, for instance, al-Maʾmūn's dream as precipitating the translation movement, *Fihrist*, 2:141–2; Dodge, 583–4; Ibn al-Qifṭī, *Taʾrīkh al-ḥukamāʾ*, 29; Ibn Abī Uṣaybiʿa, *ʿUyūn al-anbāʾ*, 259; cf. Ṣafadī, *al-Wāfī*, 216–7. See Gutas, *Greek Thought*, 95–104.

67 See Lamoreaux, *Early Muslim Tradition*, 76–7; see also Maria Mavroudi, *A Byzantine Book on Dream Interpretation* (Leiden: Brill, 2002), 168–236.

68 Abū Saʿīd Naṣr b. Yaʿqūb al-Dīnawarī (fl. 397/1006), *Kitāb al-taʿbīr fī 'l-ruʾyā* (Beirut: ʿĀlam al-Kutub, 1997), 114–6.

69 *Fihrist*, 2:181, Dodge, 614. On the question of the authenticity of the attribution to Ḥunayn, see Mavroudi, *A Byzantine Book*, 135–42. Whether or not the translation at hand is that of Ḥunayn himself or one of his disciples, all internal indications of the text point to a translation of the third/ninth century or possibly the fourth/tenth century. The only translation that we know from the period is the one ascribed to Ḥunayn.

70 See, for example, Bukhārī, *Ṣaḥīḥ*, "Kitāb al-fitan," 2:1428, §7146; Muslim, *Ṣaḥīḥ*, "Kitāb al-fitan," 2:1211, §7416.

71 Bukhārī, "Kitāb aḥādīth al-anbiyāʾ," 2:654, §3380; Muqātil b. Sulaymān, *Tafsīr* (Beirut: Dār al-Kutub al-ʿIlmiyya, 2003), 2:301; *Jāmiʿ*, 16:23.

72 See *Kashf*, 1:316–8.
73 See Dīnawarī, *Kitāb al-taʿbīr*, 2:390; 1:610–1.
74 See Muṭahhar b. Ṭāhir al-Maqdisī (fl. 355/966), *Kitāb al-badʾ wa ʾl-taʾrīkh* (Paris: Leroux, 1899–1919), 2:204–9.
75 Artemidorus, *Taʿbīr al-ruʾyā*, 335n4, cf. xxii–xxiii.
76 See Mavroudi, *A Byzantine Book*, 256–352.
77 See the section inserted into the Arabic translation of Artemidorus, 335, along with Ibn Qutabya, *Kitāb al-taʿbīr*, 103; Dīnawarī, *Kitāb al-taʿbīr*, 551–2; Ibn Sīrīn [pseud.], *Tafsīr al-aḥlām al-kabīr* (Tripoli, Lebanon: Dār al-Īmān, 1998), 97–9. Each give similar interpretations for dreams concerning the apocalypse. See also Khargūshī (d. 407/1016) on dreaming of Gog and Magog, in Lamoreaux, *Early Muslim Tradition*, 97.
78 See Abū ʿUbayd Allāh al-Marzubānī (d. 384/994), *Nūr al-qabas* (Wiesbaden: Franz Steiner, 1964), 211ff.

Chapter 4: A Geography of Neighbors

1 Yaʿqūbī, 2:481; cf. *YBN*, 256.
2 See *Futūḥ*, 297, Hitti, 460; Ibn al-ʿAdīm (d. 660/1262), *Zubdat al-ḥalab* (Damascus: Institut français, 1951–68), 1:69–70; also see Charles Pellat's gloss on Ashinās in his edition of *Murūj*, 6:158.
3 See *Murūj*, §2817.
4 Yaʿqūbī, 2:585. On this ceremony, see *TRM*, ser. 3, 2:1330. See also Ṭabarī, *The History of al-Ṭabarī*, trans. Joel Kraemer as *The Incipient Decline* (Albany: State University of New York Press, 1989), especially his note to this section, 34:4; Gordon, *Thousand Swords*, 78–9; de la Vaissière, *Samarcande et Samarra*, 194–202.
5 This section appears only in the Vienna recension, MS V, fol. 68b; on this reading of *kushtubān*, see de Goeje's glossary, *Masālik*, 6.
6 See C. E. Bosworth, "Ḳabq," *EI*[2].
7 *Masālik*, 123–4; cf. M. Streck, "Ḳāf," *EI*[2].
8 *Buldān*, 584.
9 On the authority of ʿAṭāʾ al-Khurāsānī, Ṭabarī quotes Ibn ʿAbbās as having interpreted Q. 18:93, "*bayna ʾl-saddayni*" as two mountains, across which is the rampart (*radm*) of Dhū ʾl-Qarnayn, holding back the peoples of Gog and Magog, thought to correspond to Armenia and Azerbaijan, *Jāmiʿ*, 16:16. Cf. *Tījān*, 103; Anderson, *Alexander's Gate*, vii–viii.
10 See E. Kettenhofen, "Darband," *EIr*. Cf. *Darband-nāma* (St. Petersburg: Academy of Sciences, 1851), appendix 7, 194–204.
11 'Armenia' was used as a blanket term to include a variety of regions including what is today Georgia. Following a Sāsānian tradition, Ibn Khurradādhbih divides Armenia into four sections, of which Tiflīs is located in the first, *Masālik*, 122; cf. *Futūḥ*, 194; C. E. Bosworth, "al-Kurj" *EI*[2].
12 *Murūj*, §498; *TRM*, ser. 3, 2:1414–6.

13 *Murūj*, §498.
14 Yaʿqūbī, 2:481–2.
15 Fragments of the anonymous *Taʾrīkh Bāb al-Abwāb* survive through quotations recorded by the seventeenth-century Turkish historian Aḥmad b. Luṭf Allāh in his history *Jāmiʿ al-duwal*. Vladimir Minorsky prepared the Arabic text, with a translation and commentary, *A History of Sharvān and Darband in the 10th-11th Centuries* (Cambridge: W. Heffer and Sons, 1958).
16 Minorsky, *History of Sharvān*, §4.
17 Ibid., §5.
18 Ibid.; cf. Dhahabī, *Taʾrīkh al-Islām*, 17:26.
19 "*Yukhḍabu biʾl-wasma*," *TRM*, ser. 3, 3:1415–6. On the identification of the *ṣāḥib al-sarīr* with this region, see Minorsky, *History of Sharvān*, 167.
20 *Masālik*, 124.
21 Ibid., 123–4.
22 *Futūḥ*, 193–7, Hitti, 305–9; see *Murūj*, §444; also *Kharāj*, 193–4. For the title of Wahrārzān and the possible variants, see Minorsky, *History of Sharvān*, 97–9; cf. *MḤudūd*, 447–50.
23 Gaston Wiet identifies the People of the Throne with the Avars in Dāghistān, see Ibn Rusta, *Les atours précieux: par Ibn Rusteh* (Cairo: Publications de la Société de géographie d'Égypte, 1955), 165; Minorsky, *History of Sharvān*, 97–9.
24 Iṣṭakhrī, 130.
25 *Murūj*, §478.
26 *Nafīsa*, 147–8.
27 See Agustí Alemany, *Sources on the Alans* (Leiden: Brill, 2000), 244–75, with attention to 246–7.
28 *Murūj*, §479.
29 *Nafīsa*, 148.
30 Cf. Ehsan Yarshater, "Esfandīār," *EIr*.
31 Masʿūdī, §480; cf. F. Gabrieli, "Ibn al-Muḳaffaʿ," *EI*[2] and John D. Latham, "Ebn al-Moqaffaʿ," *EIr*.
32 *Futūḥ*, 198, Hitti, 308–9.
33 Ḥamza al-Iṣfahānī, *Taʾrīkh sinī*, 45.
34 On the fortification of Fīlān Shāh, see *Muʿjam*, 1:304. Cf. Minorsky, *History of Sharvān*, 100–1.
35 The Arabic reads, "*ṭarkhān malik al-khazar*." De Goeje understands *ṭarkhān* as a sobriquet for the king of the Khazar, *Masālik*, French, 125. Ibn Khurradādhbih uses this term to refer to the prince of Samarqand and as a title for lesser Turkish rulers, *Masālik*, 40–1. See Minorsky, *History of Sharvān*, 101. The *ṭarkhān*, signifying a lesser official, may allude to the phenomenon of the double kingship of the Khazar state, in which there existed a figurehead potentate who ruled merely in name, referred to as the *Khāqān*, while the real power resided in the hands of another king. See *Ḥudūd*, §50.1: "The Khazar king (*pādshāh*) is called the Ṭarkhān of the Khāqān (*ū-rā ṭārkhān-i khāqān*

khwāndan)," Minorsky suggests that the anonymous author of the *Ḥudūd* drew here from Sallām's account. On the issue of the double kingship, see *Murūj*, §453; *Nafisa*, 139; Iṣṭakhrī, 131; *RIF*, 169–70. J. G. Frazer, using these sources as his guide, presents an interesting reading of double kingship and regicide among the Khazar, "The Killing of the Khazar Kings" *Folklore* 28 (1917): 382–407.

36 *Taqāsīm*, 362. This is picked up by Ḥājjī Khalīfa in his *Kitāb-i jahān-numā*, who situates Khwārazmī in al-Wāthiq's expedition to find the wall. This appears to be based on a confused reading of Muqaddasī's transmission of the adventure, *Kitāb-i jahān-numā* (Istanbul: Ibrāhīm Mutafariqqa, 1732), 379. Cf. Jean-Louis Bacqué-Grammont, François de Polignac, and Georges Bohas, "Monstres et murailles," *Revue des mondes musulmans et de la Méditerranée*, 89–90 (2000), 118, 121.

37 Masʿūdī gives the reign of the ʿAbbāsid caliph Hārūn al-Rashīd (r. 140–93/786–809) as the period for the Khazar conversion, *Murūj*, §448. See Peter Golden, "The Conversion of the Khazars to Judaism," in *The World of the Khazar* (Leiden: Brill, 2007), 123–62.

38 See Peter Golden, "The Khazar Sacral Kingship" in *Pre-modern Russia and its World* (Wiesbaden: Harrassowitz, 2006), 79–102.

39 See Richard Mason, "The Religious Beliefs of the Khazars," *Ukrainian Quarterly* 51 (1995): 383–415.

40 *Murūj*, §447; Iṣṭakhrī, 129.

41 *Murūj*, §§447, 450–2; see Thomas Noonan, "Some Observations on the Economy of the Khazar Khaganate," in *The World of the Khazar*, 207–44.

42 de la Vaissière, *Sogdian Traders*, 292–3; see Thomas Noonan, "Why Dirhams First Reached Russia," *AEMA* 4 (1984): 151–282; idem, "Fluctuations in Islamic Trade with Eastern Europe during the Viking Age," *Harvard Ukrainian Studies* 16, nos. 3–4 (1992): 237–59.

43 Minorsky, *History of Sharvān*, 101.

44 *Murūj*, §446.

45 Ḥasan b. Aḥmad al-Muhallabī (d. 380/990), *al-Masālik wa 'l-mamālik* (Damascus: al-Takwīn liʾl-Ṭibāʿa, 2006), 60; Ibn Saʿīd al-Maghribī (d. 685/1286), *Kitāb al-jughrāfiyā* (Beirut: Manshūrāt al-Maktab al-Tijārī, 1970), 196.

46 *Ṣūrat*, 347–9.

47 Ibid.

48 *Buldān*, 591; *Muʿjam*, 4:306; 5:11.

49 *Muʿjam*, 1:303.

50 *Murūj*, §505.

51 Ibid., §504.

52 *Buldān*, 588.

53 *ʿAjāʾib*, 129. The same account appears in *Buldān*, 584–5.

54 The dream of the creature from the water echoes an account in the romance cycle of Alexander's dream of founding the city of Alexandria on the Nile

Delta. Masʿūdī records Alexander's dream and then his subsequent submarine adventure in the diving bell, *Murūj*, §§831–2; see Callisthenes [pseud.], trans. Minoo Southgate, *Iskandarnamah* (New York: Columbia University Press, 1978), 194–5.

55 *Ghurar*, 636.

56 This verse only appears in MS V, fol. 68a; see *Masālik*, 162; Buḥturī, *Dīwān*, 2:1152–62, §470, line 43; on the date of composition, see Ṣayrafī's note, 1152; cf. J. S. Meisami, "Buḥturī," *EAL*; see also Akiko Motoyoshi Sumi, *Description in Classical Arabic Poetry* (Leiden: Brill, 2004), 92–121.

57 Muḥammad b. Maḥmūd al-Ṭūsī, *ʿAjāʾib-nāma* (Tehran: Nashr-i Kitāb, 1966), 383.

58 Andrew Anderson, "Alexander at the Caspian Gates," *Transactions and Proceedings of the American Philological Association* 59 (1928): 130–63.

59 *Mujmal al-tawārīkh wa 'l-qiṣaṣ* (Tehran: Muʾassasa-i Khāwar, 1939), 76.

60 *TRM*, ser. 1, 5:2669–71; Ṭabarī, *The History of al-Ṭabarī*, trans. Gerald Smith as *The Conquest of Iran* (Albany: State University of New York Press, 1994), 14:40–2.

61 Ṭabarī relates that ʿAbd al-Raḥmān had wanted to push his conquests to the wall (*sadd*), *TRM*, ser. 1, 5:2667–8; Balʿamī explicitly reads this rampart as that of Gog and Magog, Balʿamī, *Tārīkh-nāma-i Ṭabarī* (Tehran: Surūsh, 1995–9), 3:532–4.

62 St. Epiphanius, "De XII gemmis," *Opera* (Leipzig: Weigel, 1862), 4:190–1; Julius Ruska, *Das Steinbuch des Aristoteles* (Heidelberg: C. Winter, 1912), 14–5; Berthold Laufer, *The Diamond: A Study in Chinese and Hellenistic Folk-lore* (Chicago: Field Museum of Natural History, 1915), 9.

63 Laufer, *Diamond*, 6–20.

64 See Ruska, *Steinbuch des Aristoteles*, §9, 105–6.

65 See Ibn Mākūlā (d. ca 475/1082), *al-Ikmāl* (Cairo: Dār al-Kitāb al-Islāmī, 1962–7), 1:351–2.

66 See Ch. Pellat, "ʿAmr b. Maʿdīkarib," *EI*[2].

67 Balʿamī, *Tārīkh-nāma*, 3:533–4.

68 Rāzī, *al-Tafsīr al-kabīr*, 21:171; Dhahabī, *Taʾrīkh al-Islām*, 2:244–8; *Miʿṭār*, 310–1.

69 See *GAS*, 1:361; M. Makkī, "Egipto y los orígenes de la historiografía arábigo-española," *Revista del Instituto de Estudios Islámicos en Madrid* 5 (1957): 185–8; *Buldān*, 123; *Muʿjam*, 1:184; 3:344; 5:401.

70 Bakrī, 1:455; *Miʿṭār*, 310.

71 See W. Barthold, "Khazar," *EI*[2].

72 Compare this with the case of Maslama b. ʿAbd al-Malik (d. 122/740), the Umayyad governor of Mesopotamia and Azerbaijan, who, according to Muqaddasī, sought the cave of darkness (*kahf al-ẓulamāt*) that Dhū 'l-Qarnayn had entered, near a fortification (*ribāṭ*) built by the legendary hero, *Taqāsīm*, 146; cf. Nabia Abbott, *Studies in Arabic Literary Papyri* (Chicago: University of Chicago Press, 1957–72), 1:55. Maslama's rebuilding of the defensive walls at Bāb al-Abwāb is also positioned as paralleling Alexander's barrier against Gog and Magog, a topic explored by Antoine Borrut, who kindly shared with

me a pre-publication version of his book, *Entre mémoire et pouvoir: l'espace syrien sous les derniers Omeyyades et les premiers Abbassides (v. 72–193/692–809)* (Leiden: Brill, forthcoming), chapter 5, section B.2.

73 *Buldān*, 110–1.

74 Ibid., 110; *Muʿjam*, 1:8; according to Iṣfahānī, this verse, however, was composed originally by Ibn Jāmiʿ in honor of a victory of Hārūn al-Rashīd in Byzantium, *Aghānī*, 18:174.

75 *Buldān*, 109.

76 MS B, fols. 60b–61a.

77 Maqdisī, *Kitāb al-badʾ*, 4:91–2.

78 Ibn al-Qāṣṣ, British Library, MS Or. 13315, fols. 25b–26a; *GALS*, 1:306–7; *GAS*, 1:496–7; Tāj al-Dīn al-Subkī (d. 771/1370), *Ṭabaqāt al-shāfiʿiyya al-kubrā* (Cairo: ʿĪsā 'l-Bābī 'l-Ḥalabī, 1964–76), 3:59–63.

79 The *kishwar* system is outlined in the Pahlavi *Zand-Ākāsīh, Iranian or Greater Bundahish* (Bombay: Rahnumae Mazdayasnan Sabha, 1956), ch. 8. See Abū Manṣūr Maʿmarī, "Muqaddima-i qadīm-i *Shāh-nāma*," 166–8; English, 171–2.

80 See Michael Witzel, "The Home of the Aryans," *Anusantatyai* (Dettelbach: J. H. Röll, 2000), 299–301.

81 Bīrūnī, *Taḥdīd nihāyāt al-amākin* (Ankara: Dogus, 1962), 106–7; trans. Jamil Ali as *The Determination of the Coordinates* (Beirut: American University of Beirut, 1967), 101–2.

82 Bīrūnī, *Taḥdīd*, 107–8, and English, 102–3.

83 See, *Murūj*, §369.

84 See, for example, Iṣṭakhrī, 15–9.

85 Ibn Ṣāʿid, *Ṭabaqāt al-umam* (Cairo: Dār al-Maʿārif, 1998), 16–7.

86 *Ḥudūd*, §8.1.

87 *Jazīrat*, 26ff.

88 See Ralph Brauer, "Boundaries and Frontiers in Medieval Muslim Geography," *Transactions of the American Philosophical Society* 85, no. 6 (1995), 11ff.

89 Such is the case, for instance, when Iṣṭakhrī uses the phrase "in Islam" (*fī 'l-islām*) as a geographical demarcation in opposition to the *dār al-kufr*, Iṣṭakhrī, 153.

90 See, for instance, ʿAbd al-Razzāq, *al-Muṣannaf*, "Bāb al-Muḥāriba," ed. Ḥabīb al-Raḥmān al-Aʿẓamī (Beirut: al-Maktab al-Islāmī, 1970–2), 10:110, §18547.

91 See Muḥammad b. al-Ḥasan al-Shaybānī, *Kitāb al-siyar*, ed. Majid Khadduri (Beirut: Dār al-Muttaḥida li'l-Nashr, 1975), 129–96. Cf. Majid Khadduri's translation, *The Islamic Law of Nations* (Baltimore: Johns Hopkins Press, 1966), 130–94, particularly 130n1.

92 See Gutas, *Greek Thought*, 178.

93 *YBN*, 233.

94 See *YBN* for references to the *arḍ al-islām* in opposition to the *ghayr arḍ al-islām*, 234, and also *bilād al-islām*, 334.

95 For example, Iṣṭakhrī makes a clear geographical projection of Islam as a kingdom (*mamlakat al-islām*) like the kingdoms of China and India, which,

given the title of the genre, fits into a larger conception of the world divided into the temporal rule of kingdoms, Iṣṭakhrī, 16. Thus are referenced the lands (*bilād*), kingdoms (*mamālik*), the end (*ilā ākhir*), the frontiers (*ḥudūd*), and the abode (*dār*) of Islam, Iṣṭakhrī, 15, 17–8, 157. This variety in naming is clearly connected to its opposite, namely *kufr*, cf. Iṣṭakhrī, 33, 35, 110. Though there is a fluidity in the categorical terms, the division between *kufr* and *islām* is certainly present in the early geographical projection of space, and speaks to the formation of collectives in negative dialectic. The same follows with Ibn Ḥawqal, who draws directly on Iṣṭakhrī's model, *Ṣūrat*, 1, 5, 8–10, 13.

96 See *Murūj*, §3202; here evidently the context is not geographical but political, set against Byzantium.

97 *Taqāsīm*, 9. As for Islam as a geographical category, Muqaddasī relates, "I have traveled across Islam, far and wide," and uses "farthest reaches of Islam (*aqāṣī 'l-islām*)," *Taqāsīm*, 116, 241.

98 *Kharāj*, *mamlakat al-islām*, 130, 159, 181; *ḥadd al-islām*, 172; *thughūr al-islām*, 130–1, 185; *buldān al-islām*, 186; *bilād al-islām*, 196; *bilād al-ʿaduww*, 186.

99 It is important to note that even the demarcations of *dār al-islām* and *dār al-kufr* are also constructed around projected notions of Islamic orthodoxy; see Abū Manṣūr al-Baghdādī (d. 429/1037), *Kitāb uṣūl al-dīn* (Istanbul: Maṭbaʿat al-Dawla, 1928), 270.

100 Cf. A. Miquel, "Iḳlīm," *EI*^{2}.

101 For an outline of the Persian terminology of the *kishwar* system, see Shahmardān b. Abī 'l-Khayr (fl. 476/1083), *Nuzhat-nāma-i ʿalāʾī* (Tehran: Muʾassasa-i Muṭālaʿāt wa Taḥqīqāt-i Farhangī, 1983–4), 307–8.

102 *YBN*, 233; *Masālik*, 5; Ibn al-Qāṣṣ gives also the appellation *dil-i zamīn / qalb al-arḍ*, British Library, MS Or. 13315, fol. 26a; as part of a larger articulation of ʿAbbāsid ideology, Qudāma refers to *dil-i Īrānshahr* as the capital of the empire of Islam (*qaṣabat mamlakat al-islām*), *Kharāj*, 159; a similar categorization is given in Iṣṭakhrī, 15; *Ṣūrat*, 9; Kramers, "L'influence de la tradition iranienne," 151–2.

103 *Muʿjam*, 1:34, cf. 24.

104 On the notion of the encircling ocean as linked to ancient Greek geographical writings, s.v. 'Atlanticum Mare,' *Dictionary of Greek and Roman Geography*, William Smith (London: Walton and Maberly, 1854).

105 The *Ṣūrat al-arḍ* ascribed to Muḥammad b. Mūsā 'l-Khwārazmī describes the encircling ocean as forming the shape of a *ṭaylasān* around the lands of the earth, *Kitāb ṣūrat al-arḍ* (Leipzig: Harrassowitz, 1926), 82; cf. *Taqāsīm*, 10–1; Masʿūdī describes a similar map ascribed to Ptolemy, §193; see, however, Kramers, "L'influence de la tradition iranienne," 148–9.

106 *Buldān*, 59; *Taqāsīm*, 10.

107 *Masālik*, 155.

108 *Buldān*, 62.

109 *Jazīrat*, 31–44.

110 Ptolemy, *Geographia*, bk. 7.5, 2:176; see trans. Berggren and Jones, 22, 108.
111 *Ḥudūd*, §8.2–4; cf. *Tanbīh*, 31.
112 Yāqūt quotes Bīrūnī, *Muʿjam*, 1:54; see a similar division, *Kharāj*, 140.
113 See Ptolemy, *Kitāb al-arbaʿa*, Bodleian MS Marsh 206, fols. 53a–63a.
114 By the third/ninth century, the *Tetrabiblos* had already become well-known in Arabic, with two translations completed before Ḥunayn b. Isḥāq's corrections, see *GAS*, 7:41–5.
115 Ptolemy, *Kitāb al-arbaʿa*, Bodleian MS Marsh 206, fol. 54b.
116 *Masālik*, 157–8.
117 MS B, fol. 77a.
118 *Masālik*, 157.
119 *Nafisa*, 23–4, cf. 99–103; cf. *Tanbīh*, 29.
120 Marwazī, British Library, MS Delhi Arabic 1949, fol. 10b.
121 Ibid., fols. 39a–b.
122 *YBN*, 257; *Buldān*, 367.
123 A. Rippin, "Sām," "Yāfith"; G. Vajda, "Hām," *EI*^{2}.
124 See, for instance, *Jazīrat*, 35–6.
125 Cf. Ibn Khaldūn, *Kitāb al-ʿibar*, 1:141–50.
126 See s.v. 'Scythia,' Smith, *Dictionary*.
127 Herodotus, *Histories*, vol. 2, bk. 4, lines 64–5.
128 Ibid., bk. 4, lines 71–3; cf. Ibn Faḍlān's description of the funeral rites of a high Rūs chief, §§88–92.
129 Ptolemy and the commentary of Abū 'l-Ḥasan ʿAlī b. Riḍwān al-Miṣrī (d. 453/1061), *Kitāb al-arbaʿa*, Bodleian MS Marsh 206, fols. 59b–60a; cf. *GAS*, 1:484; *GAL*, 7:44, §g.
130 *Jazīrat*, 32, 37.
131 Anderson, *Alexander's Gate*, 3ff.
132 Ibn Ḥazm, *al-Faṣl fi 'l-milal* (Beirut: Dār al-Kutub al-ʿIlmiyya, 1999), 1:143–4.
133 Aristotle, *Historia animalium, Books VII–X* (Cambridge: Harvard University Press, 1991), bk. vii (viii) 597a, 3–9. The story of the pygmies and the cranes is a well established tradition in the world of Greek wonders, appearing in the *Iliad* (iii, 6), along with Herodotus (iii, 116; iv, 13), see Rudolf Wittkower, "Marvels of the East," *JWCI* 5 (1942): 159–97; 160n2.
134 See Romm, *Edges of the Earth*, 92ff.
135 Ibn al-Baṭrīq's translation does, however, gloss the Greek term Scythia as the region of Khurāsān, an addition either by the translator himself, or a later copyist, Aristotle, *Historia animalium* = *Ṭibāʿ al-ḥayawān* (Kuwait: Wikālat al-Maṭbūʿāt, 1977), 330n2. On the small stature of Gog and Magog, see *Jāmiʿ*, 16:19.
136 See Ṭūsī, *ʿAjāʾib-nāma*, 535; *Nuzhat*, 964; cf. Muḥammad b. Mūsā 'l-Damīrī (d. 808/1405), *Ḥayāt al-ḥayawān al-kubrā* (Cairo: Muṣṭafā 'l-Bābī 'l-Ḥalabī, 1956), 2:103; this identification makes its way into European geographical traditions, see the Genoese map of 1457, "Isti sunt ex Gog generacione qui. . .

continue a grubius infestantur," *Genoese World Map, 1457* (New York: DeVinne Press, 1912), 39–40.

137 Ibn Ḥazm, *Faṣl fī 'l-milal*, 143–4.

138 Khwārazmī locates the city of Magog in the seventh clime, and the interior city of Gog, which lies beyond the seven clime, in the far northeast, above the arctic circle, *Ṣūrat al-arḍ*, 32, 34, 37.

139 After describing the visit with the Khazar king, Idrīsī, basing himself on Ibn Khurradādhbih and on Jayhānī's no longer extant geography, states that Sallām passes through the borders (*tukhūm*) of the Bashjirt, *Nuzhat*, 934–5. These are Turkish tribes living in what is Bashkurdistan in the southern Ural mountains, see Z. V. Togan, "Bashdjirt," EI^2; *MḤudūd*, 318–9.

140 Ibn Khurradādhbih refers to the Dead Sea beyond Jerusalem as the 'fetid sea' using the same term (*al-buḥayra al-muntina*), 79; cf. *IḤG*, 111, with *mayyita* in *Ṣūrat*, 170.

141 *Nuzhat*, 929. This fetid odor may be contrasted to the amazingly pleasant smell (*rāʾiḥa ṭayyiba ʿajība*), which, according to Ibn Khurradādhbih, is to be found in Medina, suggesting a broader cosmographic pattern of natural dispositions, *Masālik*, 171.

142 See Q. 30:9; 35:44; 40:21; cf. Q. 3:137; 6:11; 12:109; 16:36; 28:69; 30:42 on calamities and the destruction around the earth (*kharābāt al-bilād*) in divine confirmation of the Qurʾān (i.e., 18:58), as projected geographically, see Ibn al-Qāṣṣ, British Library, MS Or. 13315, fols. 55a–b.

Chapter 5: A Wondrous Barrier

1 See the recent attempts by Faustina Doufikar-Aerts to reconstruct the stemma of the Arabic Alexander cycle and its relationship to the Syriac and Ethiopian traditions, "Alexander the Flexible Friend," *Journal of Eastern Christian Studies* 55 (2002): 195–210; idem, "*Sīrat al-Iskandar*: An Arabic Popular Romance of Alexander," *Oriente Moderno* 22 (2003): 505–20; see also idem, "Alexander Magnus Arabicus" (Ph.D. diss., Leiden University, 2003), 9–81; an English revision is forthcoming (Leuven: Peeters). On the Ethiopian translation, see Andrew Anderson, "The Arabic History of Dulcarnain and the Ethiopian History of Alexander," *Speculum* 6 (1931): 434–45. See also an Arabic version, edited and translated by Emilio García Gómez, *Ḥadīth Dhī 'l- Qarnayn = Un Texto árabe occidental de la leyenda de Alejandro* (Madrid: Instituto de Valencia de D. Juan, 1929), hereafter referred to as *Ḥadīth Dhī 'l-Qarnayn*. Developing out of the Arabic tradition is the Spanish *aljamiado* translation, *Historia de Dulcarnain*, ed. F. Guillén Robles, in *Leyendas de José hijo de Jacob y de Alejandro Magno* (Zaragoza: Impresa del Hospicio provincial, 1888). As for the Persian recension, Theodore Nöldeke argued for a Pahlavi version made sometime during the late sixth century C.E., Nöldeke, "Beiträge zur Geschichte des Alexanderromans," *Denkschriften der Kaiserlichen Akademie der Wissenschaften* 38 (1890), 30–2. However, see Richard Frye, "Two Iranian

Notes," *Papers in Honour of Professor Mary Boyce* (Leiden: Brill, 1985), 185–8; and Claudia Ciancaglini, "The Syriac Version of the Alexander *Romance*," *Le Muséon* 114 (2001): 120–40.

2 See *Qiṣṣat al-Iskandar*, ascribed to Abū Zayd ʿUmāra b. Zayd (d. ca 200/815), presumed compiler, British Library, MS Add. 5928, fol. 3b; cf. Abbott, *Studies in Arabic Literary Papyri*, 1:51–6; Wilferd Madelung, *Der Imam al-Qāsim ibn Ibrāhīm* (Berlin: de Gruyter, 1965), 69–71; Doufikar-Aerts, *Alexander Magnus Arabicus*, 29–39; opening sections of this work are edited by Israel Friedländer, *Die Chadhirlegende*, 308–16.

3 *Tījān*, 110; Nashwān b. Saʿīd al-Ḥimyarī (d. 573/1178), *Mulūk Ḥimyar* (Cairo: Quṣayy Muḥibb al-Dīn al-Khaṭīb, 1975), 107–8.

4 *Tījān*, 115; Ḥimyarī, *Mulūk Ḥimyar*, 111–2.

5 Ḥimyarī, *Mulūk Ḥimyar*, 98–101; Ḥassān b. Thābit, *Dīwān* (Beirut: Dār Ṣādir, 1974), 1:471–3; see Hamdānī, *Kitāb al-iklīl* (Sanaa: Maktabat al-Irshād, 2008), 1:123; cf. 2:171, 241.

6 Ḥassān b. Thābit, *Dīwān*, 1:472, lines 19, 21; for further references to the ropes of heaven motif, see Kevin van Bladel, "Heavenly Cords and Prophetic Authority in the Qurʾān and its Late Antique Context," *BSOAS* 70 (2007): 223–46.

7 Ḥassān b. Thābit, *Dīwān*, 1:473, line 37; see W. ʿArafāt, "Ḥassān b. Thābit," *EI*^{2}.

8 See *TRM*, ser. 2, 3:1303–4; cf. Ibn ʿIdhārī (fl. 712/1312), *Kitāb al-bayān* (Leiden: Brill, 1948–51), 1:27.

9 Ḥimyarī, *Mulūk Ḥimyar*, 98–113, 104; on the question of the authorship of the *Sharḥ*, see vii; cf. Ilse Lichtenstädter, "Nashwān b. Saʿīd," *EI*^{2}. For an Ottoman perspective on the Greek origins of Dhū ʾl-Qarnayn, see Ḥājjī Khalīfa, *Kitāb-i jahān-numā*, 377.

10 See Reinink, "Die Entstehung der syrischen Alexanderlegende als politisch-religiöse Propagandaschrift für Herakleios' Kirchenpolitik," in *Syriac Christianity*, art. 3, 263–81.

11 Ibn ʿAbd al-Ḥakam, *Futūḥ Miṣr*, 38–9.

12 Ibid., 38.

13 *Jāmiʿ*, 16:8; see ʿUmāra b. Zayd, British Library, MS Add. 5928, fol. 5a.

14 Ibn Hishām, *al-Sīra al-nabawiyya*, 288; ʿUmāra b. Zayd, British Library, MS Add. 5928, fol. 5a.

15 Muqātil b. Sulaymān, *Tafsīr*, 2:299.

16 Ibn Qutayba, *Kitāb al-maʿārif* (Cairo: Dār al-Kutub, 1960), 54; Dīnawarī, *Akhbār al-ṭiwāl* (Beirut: Dār al-Arqām, 1995), 31–9.

17 *Tanbīh*, 116; cf. *Murūj*, §§669–98. See also Zachary Zuwiyya, *Islamic Legends Concerning Alexander the Great* (New York: Global Publications, 2001), 42–5.

18 See ʿUmāra b. Zayd, British Library, MS Add. 5928, fol. 17a.

19 Ṭabarī, *Jāmiʿ*, 16:19.

20 See *Murūj*, §§447, 450–2; *RIF*, §§47–8, 70; cf. István Zimonyi, *The Origins of the Volga Bulghars* (Szeged, Hungary: Universitas Szegediensis de Attila József Nominata, 1990), 102, 137–8.

21 See *Nuzhat*, 935–6.

22 See *Masālik*, 31. Cf. *Buldān*, 637–9. Minorsky posits the date of 206/821 for Tamīm's journey among the Uyghurs on the Orkhon, "Tamīm ibn Baḥr's Journey," *BSOAS* 12 (1948): 275–305.

23 *Masālik*, 70; see *Fihrist*, 2:401–2, Dodge, 802; H. A. R. Gibb, "Chinese Records of the Arabs in Central Asia," *BSOS* 2 (1923): 613–22; Marwazī, *Ṭabāʾiʿ al-ḥayawān*, §16. See also Abū Dulaf, *Majmūʿ fī ʾl-jughrāfiyā*, facs. ed. Fuat Sezgin (Frankfurt am Main: J. W. Goethe University, 1987), 350; recorded in *Muʿjam*, 3:442; Josef Marquart, *Osteuropäische und ostasiatische Streifzüge* (Leipzig: Dieterich'sche Verlagsbuchhandlung, 1903), 7.

24 ʿAbd al-Razzāq, *Muṣannaf*, "Kitāb al-jāmiʿ," 11:376–8, §20890; Bukhārī, *Ṣaḥīḥ*, "Kitāb al-tawḥīd," 3:1532, §7657; Abū Dāwūd al-Sijistānī (d. 275/889), *Sunna*, "Kitāb al-sunna," 2:803–4, §4770, in *Mawsūʿat al-ḥadīth al-sharīf*; Abū Yaʿlā ʾl-Mawṣilī (d. 307/919–20), *Musnad* (Damascus: Dār al-Maʾmūn liʾl-Turāth, 1984), 2:408–9, §219. Similarly, Ibn al-Faqīh describes how he read from the Gospel (*al-Injīl*) that one of the signs of the end of time was the advent of a nation (*qawm*) from the east; this is a reference to the apocalyptic vision in the Book of Revelation (12:12–6), which describes how demonic eastern kings emerge in preparation for the battle of Armageddon, *Buldān*, 609.

25 MS V, fol. 69, see chapter 7, 155ff., 169.

26 Walther Hinz, *Islamische Masse und Gewichte* (Leiden: Brill, 1955), 62–3.

27 Compare this, for instance, with the circumference of the city of Iṣfahān, which, according to Ibn Rusta, was one *faraskh* with walls defended by one hundred towers and four gates, *Nafīsa*, 160–1.

28 See Peter Clayton and Martin Price, eds., *The Seven Wonders of the Ancient World* (London: Routledge, 1989).

29 *Masālik*, 159–62.

30 Cf. Murray Krieger, *Ekphrasis: The Illusion of the Natural Sign* (Baltimore: Johns Hopkins University Press, 1992), 6. As for the modern genealogy of this term, see Ruth Webb, "Ekphrasis Ancient and Modern," *Word and Image* 15 (1999): 7–18.

31 The notion of *ʿiyān* within geographical discourse as akin to the concept of *autopsia* is developed by James Montgomery, "Travelling Autopsies: Ibn Faḍlān and the Bulghār," *MEL* 7 (2004): 3–32.

32 *Nuzhāt*, 938.

33 The reading *qurnatān* is confirmed in all three manuscripts: MS B, fol. 62b, Paris Supplément arabe 895 (= MS P), fol. 41b, and MS V, fol. 70a. However, horns (*qarnān*), is also attested, see *Nuzhat*, 936; cf. de Goeje's translation, *Masālik*, 127; see also the emendation to Jean Gagnier's (d. 1740) transcription of MS B, MS Bodleian Or. 306, fol. 71b.

34 *Masālik*, 166, as for the term *dastaj al-hawāwīn*, a bundle of mortars, see Steingass, *Persian-English Dictionary*, s.v. *hāwan-dasta*, mortar and pestle.

35 This is the title given by *Murūj*, §1419; Ḥājjī Khalīfa draws from Masʿūdī in

his description of this work, 2:1397; cf. Julius Lippert, "Abū Maʿshar's *Kitāb al-Ulūf*," *Wiener Zeitschrift für die Kunde des Morgenlandes* 9 (1895): 351–8; Pingree, *Thousands*, 1–21.

36 Masʿūdī relates that people dispute the actual dimensions and location of the wall, *Murūj*, §1419.

37 Abū Hilāl al-ʿAskarī, *Kitāb al-ṣināʿatayn* (Cairo: ʿĪsā 'l-Bābī 'l-Ḥalabī, 1971), 134. See also Sumi, *Description in Classical Arabic Poetry*, 1–17.

38 Fārābī, "Risāla fī qawānīn ṣināʿat al-shiʿr," Aristotle, *Fann al-shiʿr*, ed. Badawī, 157–8.

39 Aristotle, *Kitāb Arisṭūṭālīs*, ed. ʿAyyād, 87.

40 *Bayān*, 1:76

41 Ibid.

42 Ibid., 77.

43 For visual reconstructions of Sallām's account, see Miquel, *La Géographie humaine*, 2:505, fig. 33; and László Bendefy, *Szallam tolmács küldetése Nagy Sándor falához* (Budapest: Szentföldi Ferencrendi Zárda, 1941), 74–5, 77. For the various discrepancies in the arithmetic of Sallām's barrier, see chapter 6, 133.

44 See Reinink's introduction to his edition of Pseudo-Jacob of Sarug, *Das syrische Alexanderlied*, *CSCO* (Leuven: Peeters, 1983), 455:1–15; idem, "Alexander the Great in Seventh-Century Syriac 'Apocalptic' Texts," *Syriac Christianity*, sec. 4, 165–8.

45 Jacob of Sarug [pseud.], *Das syrische Alexanderlied*, 454:76, rez. 2, lines 406–8, 411–4; cf. Carl Hunnius, "Das syrische Alexanderlied," *Zeitschrift der Deutschen Morgenländischen Gesellschaft*, 60 (1906): 564–7, lines 402, 404, 408–11; trans. Budge, *History of Alexander*, 183–4.

46 Jacob of Sarug [pseud.], *Das syrische Alexanderlied*, 454:30, rez. 2, line 73; Hunnius, 178, line 73, trans. Budge, *The History of Alexander*, 167; compare with the *Neṣḥānā d'Aleksandrōs*, edited and translated by Budge, in *The History of Alexander*, Syriac 256ff. Budge designates this work as, 'The Christian Legend,' to distinguish it from the *Tashʿītā d'Aleksandrōs*, the Syriac translation of the Pseudo-Callisthenes cycle. I refer to the work by its Syriac title, *Neṣḥānā d'Aleksandrōs*, 256, signifying a victory, triumph, or trophy, such as with the heroic acts of martyrs or Christian heroes.

47 Reinink, "Die Entstehung der syrischen Alexanderlegende," *Syriac Christianity*, sec. 3, 263–81.

48 *Neṣḥānā*, Syriac, 263; English, 150.

49 Methodius [pseud.], *Die syrische Apokalypse*, 520:15, §6.

50 *Neṣḥānā*, Syriac, 271; English, 155.

51 *Neṣḥānā*, Syriac, 268; English, 153. In the description of the key, Budge's translation disregards the Syriac *shnānāṯā*, which can mean both grooves, rocks, and mountains, etymologically connected to the word for teeth, *shennē*. Instead, Budge offers cubits (*ammīn*), 268n5, cf. 267n9, and xviii. However, the various MSS (ABCDE) attest to this word. For the meaning of this word

as teeth or points, see Carl Brockelmann, *Lexicon Syriacum* (Berlin: Reuther & Reichard, 1895), 380–1; Smith, *Dictionary*, 587; also see Nöldeke, "Beiträge," 29n3. Justin Perkins, in a translation of MS B of Budge's edition, published as "Notice of the Life of Alexander the Great," *JOAS* 4 (1854): 359–440, reads "he fastened iron spikes in the cliff, and nailed the iron key which had twelve notches. And he encompassed it with brazen chains." The interpretation of the twelve notches agrees with the Arabic Alexander cycle as it is expressed in Berlin MS Or. 2195, fol. 39a, and in Callisthenes [pseud.], *Ḥadīth Dhī 'l-Qarnayn*, 53; likewise in the Ethiopic translation of the Arabic prepared by Budge himself, *The Life and Exploits of Alexander the Great* (London: C. J. Clay, 1896), 238.

52 See Nöldeke, who believes this Syriac work to be the inspiration of the Qurʾānic account of Dhū 'l-Qarnayn's wall against Gog and Magog, "Beiträge," 26ff. Though this thesis has had a lasting effect on modern readings of the sources for the Qurʾān, it has not gone entirely without criticism, see Wheeler, "Moses or Alexander?" 191–215.

53 There are striking parallels between the Qurʾānic passage and both the Syriac *mēmrā* and the *Neṣḥānā*, viz. the eschatological significance of the wall, the prophetic role of Alexander in foreseeing its destruction, along with the details of the wall itself being constructed of iron and copper. However, assuming that these two Syriac accounts are genuinely from the beginning of the seventh century, they do not speak *a fortiori* to a direct line of causality for the formation of the Qurʾānic tradition. Take, for instance, the use of the words for copper and iron to describe the wall in the *Neṣḥānā* and in the accounts ascribed to Jacob of Sarug and Methodius; both of these terms are incorporated into the Qurʾānic account. Yet, the Arabic word used for iron, *ḥadīd* (18:96), is not etymologically linked to the Syriac *parzlā*, found in the Syriac accounts, while the Arabic cognate *firzil* is, though this is not used in the Qurʾānic description. As for the term for copper, the Syriac *nḥāshā* is etymologically linked to the Arabic *nuḥās*. Rather than this shared cognate, the Qurʾān uses *qiṭra* (Q. 18:96); cf. the use of *nuḥāṣ* (Q. 55:35). Many structural elements of the Qurʾānic tale, in a very general sense, parallel the Syriac tradition, which appears to predate the Qurʾān, see Nöldeke, "Beiträge," and Kevin van Bladel, "The Alexander Legend in the Qurʾan 18:83–102," in *The Qurʾan in its Historical Context* (London: Routledge, 2008), 175–203. At a linguistic level, however, the significant instances of divergence point to an oblique course of transmission and appropriation, both orally and textually, that emerges in dialogue with the eschatological discourse on the life of Alexander, widely diffused throughout the seventh century. The epithet of Dhū 'l-Qarnayn is itself an indication of this, for while the Syriac cycle references the horns of Alexander, it consistently refers to the hero by his Greek name, and not by a variant epithet, cf. *Neṣḥānā*, Syriac, 257, English, 146.

54 See Sourdel, *Le vizirat ʿabbāside*, 1:295, 312–3, 316, 328, 378; on Ibn Khurradādhbih's relationship with the Christian aristocrat, ʿAdūn b. Makhlad, see ʿUmarī,

Masālik al-abṣār, 1:311.

55 Cf. Callisthenes [pseud.], *Ḥadīth Dhī 'l-Qarnayn*, 53; the date of this work is based on what appears to be a seventh/thirteenth-century Maghribī manuscript; to what degree this manuscript draws on an earlier tradition of Arabic translations of the Syriac versions of the Pseudo-Callisthenes cycle remains to be seen, see Zuwiyya, *Islamic Legends,* 41–2.

56 See Berlin MS Or. 2195, fol. 39a; Callisthenes [pseud.], *Ḥadīth Dhī 'l-Qarnayn*, 53; *Sharḥ sīrat Iskandar Dhū 'l-Qarnayn*, dated 1104/1693, BNF MS Arabe, ancien fonds, 1494a, fol. 76b; cf. Doufikar-Aerts, *Alexander Magnus Arabicus*, 141–2, 144.

57 *Masālik*, 168. The two trees here may be an oblique reference to the speaking trees of the Sun and the Moon found in the Alexander cycle, while the spring may echo Alexander's quest for the fountain of life.

58 See M. L. Chaumont, "Callisthenes" *EIr*; Nöldeke argued, rather speculatively, that the Syriac *Tashʿīta d'Aleksandrōs* was based on a lost Middle Persian text, "Beiträge," 14ff. Ciancaglini has sought to discredit this theory; though her argumentation, particularly regarding the stages of translation from Pahlavi into Syriac, awaits further evaluation, "The Syriac Version." Nonetheless, even her theory does not exclude the circulation of the Alexander Romance within a pre-Islamic Persian milieu, 135–7.

59 *Fihrist*, 1:99, Dodge, 84; cf. Baghdādī, *Taʾrīkh Baghdād*, 5:110–2, §1959. See Ibn al-Munādī, *al-Malāḥim*, ed. ʿAbd al-Karīm al-ʿUqaylī (Qom: Dār al-Sīra, 1998), 38–48.

60 Ibn al-Jawzī, *al-Muntaẓam* (Beirut: Dār al-Kutub al-ʿIlmiyya, 1992–3), 1:294–7; Ibn al-Jawzī repeats Ibn al-Munādī's transmission of Sallām's adventure in *Tanwīr al-ghabash* (Riyadh: Dār al-Sharīf, 1998), 88–93.

61 Ibn al-Jawzī, *al-Muntaẓam*, 1:294–7.

62 See the account of Abū Sahl al-Faḍl b. Nawbakht (d. ca 193/809), *Fihrist*, 2:133; Dodge, 574–5; *Ghurar*, 485; Ḥamza al-Iṣfahānī, *Taʾrīkh sinī*, 37; cf. Gutas, *Greek Thought*, 39–40.

63 Dīnawarī, *Akhbār*, 31–2; *TRM*, ser. 1, 2:696–7, 700–1; cf. Firdawsī, *Shāh-nāma*, 5:523–6, lines 95–136; *Iskandar-nāma*, ed. Īraj Afshār (Tehran: Bungāh-i Tarjuma wa Nashr-i Kitāb, 1964), 3–4; William Hanaway, "Eskandar-nāma," *EIr.*

64 *Masālik*, 168.

65 Ibid., 166; see W. Hinz, who calculates this at 0.5405 meters, *Islamische Masse und Gewichte*, 54–64; however, Alastair Northedge, based upon the archeological measurements of bricks in Sāmarrāʾ, puts the black cubit at 0.526 meters, "The Racecourses at Sāmarrāʾ," *BSOAS* 53 (1990), 54.

66 *Masālik*, 168.

67 MS B, fol. 63a; cf. MS V, fol. 70b.

68 See C. C. Berg, "Ṣawm," *EI*[2]; Georges Vajda, "Fasting in Islam and Judaism," in *The Development of Islamic Ritual* (Aldershot: Ashgate, 2006), 144–7.

69 See *YBN*, 261; cf. Dominique Sourdel, "Questions de cérémonial ʿabbaside,"

Revue des études islamiques 28 (1960), 126.

70 See Azraqī (fl. 250/865), 619–20, 642, 644, 650; Fākihī (fl. 272/885), 2:63–5, 5:182.

71 Azraqī, 548–58; Fākihī, 2:11–22; *Nafīsa*, 40–2; cf. Wheeler, *Mecca and Eden*, 19–29.

72 *Masālik*, 90.

73 Azraqī, 599–627; Fākihī, 2:162–75; *Nafīsa*, 43.

74 Azraqī, 401, 637, 644–5, cf. 575–82; Fākihī, 2:79, 83–5, 3:62. On the consumption of *nabīdh*, a fermented beverage, at the *siqāya*, see Azraqī, 570–2; Fākihī, 2:59–62; cf. Maurice Gaudefroy-Demombynes, *Le pèlerinage à la Mekke* (Paris: P. Geuthner, 1923), 89–101; Gerald Hawting, "The 'Sacred Offices' of Mecca," *Jerusalem Studies in Arabic and Islam* 13 (1990): 62–84.

75 Azraqī, 322–7.

76 Azraqī, 325; Fākihī, 5:236.

77 See Janine Sourdel-Thomine, "Clefs et serrures de la Kaᶜba," *Revue des études islamiques* 39 (1971): 29–86.

78 See Wheeler, *Mecca and Eden*, 28, and 155–6.

79 See *Masālik*, 132–3; YBN, 314–6; *Buldān*, 74–8; *Nafīsa*, 24–58; *Taqāsīm*, 71–5.

80 Azraqī, 737; Fākihī, 4:37–45.

81 On the prophesied destruction of the Kaᶜba by the Ethiopian Dhū 'l-Suwayqatayn ('The one with two thin legs'), see Ibn al-Munādī, *al-Malāḥim*, 168–9; cf. Wilferd Madelung, "Apocalyptic Prophecies in Ḥimṣ in the Umayyad Age," *Journal of Semitic Studies* 31 (1986), 177–8; Cook, *Studies in Muslim Apocalyptic*, 78–9.

82 Dīnawarī, *Akhbār*, 35; Fākihī, 1:394, 2:9, 3:221; cf. Firdawsī, *Shāh-nāma*, 5:48–9, lines 627–36; cf. *Iskandar-nāma*, 101–6.

83 *Neṣḥānā*, Syriac, 268–71, English, 154–6; Jacob of Sarug [pseud.], *Das syrische Alexanderlied*, 454:84ff., rez. 2, lines 432ff.; Methodius [pseud.], *Die syrische Apokalypse*, 520:15–6, §9; and Ephraem [pseud.], *Des Syrers Sermones*, 320:63–4, lines 169–225.

84 Berlin MS Or. 2195, fols. 38b–39a; Callisthenes [pseud.], *Ḥadīth Dhī 'l-Qarnayn*, 53.

85 See *Jāmiᶜ*, 16:27.

86 James L. Kugel, *Traditions of the Bible* (Cambridge: Harvard University Press, 1998), 227–42.

87 Ibn Qutayba, *Kitāb al-maᶜārif*, 28; cf. *Jāmiᶜ*, 14:97; *Tanbīh*, 197.

88 *Jāmiᶜ*, 14:97; Ibn Qutayba, *Faḍl al-ᶜArab*, 53; Dīnawarī, *Akhbār*, 8–9.

89 *Tanbīh*, 197; cf. J. Pedersen, "Ādam," *EI*².

90 See, *TRM*, ser. 3, 2:1343–9.

91 For an overview of the ᶜAbbāsid *miḥna*, see W. M. Patton, *Aḥmed ibn Ḥanbal and the Miḥna* (Leiden: Brill, 1897).

92 *TRM*, ser. 3, 2:1113.

93 *Neṣḥānā*, Syriac, 263; English, 150; cf. Ephraem [pseud.], *Des Syrers Sermones*, 320:64, lines 199–202.

94 Ṭabarī offers the reading of the Kufans as "*yufqihūna qawlan*," from *afqaha*, to make understood, suggesting that they could barely make themselves intelligible, *Jāmiᶜ*, 16:16.

95 See, for instance, Thaʿlabī (d. 427/1036), *al-Kashf wa 'l-bayān* (Beirut: Dār Iḥyāʾ al-Turāth al-ʿArabī, 2002), 4:151; al-Ḥusayn b. Masʿūd al-Baghawī (d. ca 516/1122), *Maʿālim al-tanzīl* (Riyadh: Dār al-Ṭība, 2002), 5:201–2; Ibrāhīm b. ʿUmar al-Biqāʿī (d. 885/1480), *Naẓm al-durar* (Hyderabad: Maṭbaʿat Majlis Dāʾirat al-Maʿārif al-ʿUthmāniyya, 1976–8), 12:134.

96 *Tījān*, 101; cf. Aḥmad b. Muḥammad al-Thaʿlabī, *ʿArāʾis al-majālis* (Cairo: al-Maktaba al-ʿĀlāmiyya, 1929), 240.

97 *Jāmiʿ*, 16:18.

98 Ibid.

99 *Tījān*, 103.

100 Callisthenes [pseud.], *Tashʿītā d'Aleksandrōs*, ed. Budge, *History of Alexander the Great*, Syriac, 164; English, 92.

101 Cf. Mark Lidzbarski, "Zu den arabischen Alexandergeschichten," *Zeitschrift für Assyriologie* 8 (1893), 305.

102 See A. R. Nykl, *Compendium of Aljamiado Literature* (Paris: Protat, 1929), 113–2, fol. 74a–b; cf. Zuwiyya, *Islamic Legends*, 18n59.

103 MS B, fols. 63b–64a; Meynard, 102.

104 See, for instance, Ibn Rusta, British Library, MS Add. 23378, fol. 98b; Ibn al-Munādī's account as preserved in Ibn al-Jawzī, *al-Muntaẓam*, 1:297; Ibn al-Qāṣṣ, British Library, MS Or. 13315, fol. 48b; *Taqāsīm*, 365; Bakrī, 1:458; *Muʿjam*, 3:200. On Idrīsī's description, see chapter 5, 123–4.

105 MS V, fol. 71b.

106 *Masālik*, 169, note c; cf. de Goeje, "De Muur," 108.

107 De Goeje suggests that the original reading was the river of Ilakh, i.e., the Jaxartes, which he believes was corrupted into the river of Balkh, i.e., the Oxus, *Masālik*, 169, note d. In his French translation he changes the order of the itinerary to make it more plausible, to "Samarkand, Isbyschāb, Oschrousana, Bokhāra, Tirmidh, le fluve de Balkh (l'Oxus)," *Masālik*, 131. This reading still does not explain why Sallām would leave Samarqand for Isbījāb and then head back to Bukhārā.

108 See Dīnawarī, *Akhbār*, 31–2.

109 *Nuzhat*, 935.

110 Ibid., 938; *Masālik*, 169, note b.

111 See V. V. Barthold, "History of Semirechyé," in *Four Studies on the History of Central Asia* (Leiden: Brill, 1956), 1:86–92. On Barskhān as the correct reading for Idrīsī's Barsākhān, see *Taqāsīm*, 263; Minorsky, "Tamīm ibn Baḥr," 277, 290; cf. *MḤudūd*, 292–3; on Nūshjān, see *Masālik*, 28.

112 *Nuzhat*, 932–3, Khūrīn Barkhān Mand al-Turkī, the name is evidently garbled in the manuscript recensions, note line 4; this might be a distorted form of the name of the Kīmāk informant mentioned at the beginning of the geography, *Nuzhat*, 5.

113 Idrīsī locates the Adhkish Turks north of the Kīmāk who are themselves east of the Qarluq, *Nuzhat*, 712, 843–4; cf. Konrad Miller, *Charta Rogeriana:*

Weltkarte des Idrisi (Stuttgart: Konrad Miller, 1928).

114 Cf. *Masālik*, 169, note b.

115 See Peter Golden, "The Migrations of the *Oğuz*," *Archivum Ottomanicum* 4 (1972), 59–61.

116 See P. Golden, "Toghuzghuz," *EI²*.

117 *YBN*, 255; Gordon, *Thousand Swords*, 33; de la Vaissière, *Samarcande et Samarra*, 148, 168–81.

118 de la Vaissière, *Samarcande et Samarra*, 167ff.

119 de la Vaissière, *Sogdian Traders*, 279–84; 299–319.

120 See E. Kohlberg, "Shahīd," *EI²*.

121 See *TRM*, ser. 3, 2:1338; cf. *Masālik*, 34, 39; E. Marin, "ʿAbd Allāh b. Ṭāhir," *EI²*.

122 The description of the report as a *qiṣṣa* and the distribution of alms appears only in MS V, fol. 71b.

Chapter 6: To Live to Tell

1 See Stefan Leder, "Prose, non-Fiction, Medieval," *EAL*.

2 *Nuzhat*, 938.

3 See Michael Cooperson, "Probability, Plausibility, and 'Spiritual Communication,'" in *On Fiction and Adab*, 69–71.

4 See Stefan Leder, "The Use of Composite Form," in *On Fiction and Adab*, 125–9.

5 See Lane's entry for *qaṣṣahu*; Ch. Pellat "Ḳiṣṣa," *EI²*.

6 See *qiṣṣa* in the index of Charles Pellat's edition of Jāḥiẓ's *Kitāb al-tarbīʿ wa 'l-tadwīr* (Damascus: Institut français, 1955), 182.

7 Ibn al-Nadīm mentions that Sarakhsī wrote a geography, *al-Masālik wa 'l-mamālik*, *Fihrist*, 1:459, Dodge, 628; *GAS*, 11:244–5. Ibn Ḥazm states that Sarakhsī, presumably in this geography, recorded the story of Sallām al-Tarjumān; Ibn Ḥazm also lists Qudāma b. Jaʿfar as relating the adventure, while the surviving geographical material from the ʿAbbāsid administrator does not include the account, Ibn Ḥazm, *al-Faṣl fī 'l-milal*, 1:144.

8 British Library, MS Add. 7496, fol. 83b; I.O. Islamic 617, fol. 99a–b; de Goeje omits the full account, *IFG*, 301, note h. Yūsuf al-Hādī, who bases his revision of de Goeje's edition on Mashhad MS 5229, which omits this section, copies Ibn Khurradādhbih's text as edited by de Goeje, *Buldān*, 600n1; cf. facsimile edition of the Mashhad MS, *Majmūʿ fī 'l-jughrāfiyā*, 292–3.

9 British Library, MS Add. 23378, fols. 169b–173a; British Library, MS Or. 4895, fols. 97a–98b; de Goeje also omitted this account in his edition of *Nafīsa*, 149, note c.

10 Cf. Göckenjan and Zimonyi, *Orientalische Berichte*, 25–6.

11 British Library, MS Or. 13315, fols. 48a–b.

12 *Taqāsīm*, 362–5.

13 Bakrī, 1:454–8.

14 *Nuzhat*, 934–8.

15 *Muʿjam*, 3:199–200.

16 *Bilād*, 597–9.
17 *Miʿṭār*, 310–1.
18 Bakrān, *Jahān-nāma*, 109–14. Cf. C. A. Storey, *Persian Literature* (London: Luzac and Co., 1970), 2:120. Bakrān dedicated this work to Sulṭān Muḥammad, ruler of Khwārazm (r. 596–617/1200–20); cf. Krachkovskii, *Istoria arabskoi*, 325–6; Ahmad, *History of Arab-Islamic Geography*, 167; Storey, 2:123.
19 Ḥamd Allāh al-Mustawfī, *Nuzhat al-qulūb* (Leiden: Brill 1915–9), 1:243–5; English, 2:235–6.
20 On the Turkish translation of Ibn Khurradādhbih's geography, see *Kashf*, 2:1665; cf. Maḥmūd Efendī 'l-Khaṭīb's (fl. 970/1563) translation of Ibn al-Wardī's *Kharīdat al-ʿajāʾib*, Bodleian MS Turk d. 39, fols. 66a–67b; also Muṣṭafā b. Aḥmad ʿAlī (d. 1008/1600), *Kunh al-akhbār* (Istanbul: n.p. 1861–9), 2:133–5, cf. 1:160; see also Surūrī's (d. 969/1561–2) Turkish translation of Qazwīnī's *ʿAjāʾib al-makhlūqāt*, Bodleian MS Turk d. 2, fol. 139b. See Ḥājjī Khalīfa, *Kitāb-i jahān-numā*, 379; cf. Bacqué-Grammont, et al., "Monstres et murailles," 118, 121. On the translation of Arabic material into Persian and Turkish, see Anja Pistor-Hatam, "Übersetzungen innerhalb des islamischen Kulturraums," in *Übersetzung*, 2:1220–30.
21 *Ṣūrat*, 14.
22 *Taqāsīm*, 3, 6.
23 Ibid., 362.
24 Ibid. According to this statement, Muqaddasī probably read the geographies of Ibn Khurradādhbih and Jayhānī in the royal library of Nīsābūr, a testament to their reception histories, *Taqāsīm*, 4.
25 See Etan Kohlberg, *A Medieval Muslim Scholar at Work* (Leiden: Brill, 1992), 142, §103.
26 Ibn al-Qāṣṣ, British Library, MS Or. 13315, fols. 30a, 57a.
27 Ibid., fol. 4a.
28 Samʿānī, *Kitāb al-ansāb* (Beirut: Dar al-Kutub al-ʿIlmiyya, 1998), 4:410–1.
29 This reading is based on Cairo, Egyptian National Library, MS Aḥmad Taymūr, *Buldān*, 103, fasc. ed. Fuat Sezgin, "Kitāb dalāʾil al-qibla," *ZGAIW* 4 (1987–8), 55 (Arabic section); British Library, MS Or. 13315, reads "under Muḥammad b. ʿAbd Allāh b. Khurradādh," fol. 48a; Istanbul, MS Walī 'l-Dīn 2453 abridges the *isnād* altogether, facs. ed. Sezgin, "Kitāb dalāʾil al-qibla," in *ZGAIW* 5 (1989), 45 (Arabic section).
30 Cf. Ibn al-Jawzī's *isnād* transmission of the account, which he takes from Ibn al-Munādī, who reports to have received Sallām's adventure from Ibn Khurradādhbih, *al-Muntaẓam*, 1:294.
31 See Ibn al-Najjār, *Dhayl*, 2:11; cf. Baghdādī, *Taʾrīkh al-Baghdād*, 2:85–8, 8:647, §4132.
32 See Gregor Schoeler, "Schreiben und Veröffentlichen," *Der Islam* 69 (1992), 30.
33 MS V, fol. 69b; see de Goeje's translation, *Masālik*, 127n1, 128n1.
34 MS V, fol. 66a.

35 *Taqāsīm*, 3–4
36 Ibid., 241.
37 Ibid., 4.
38 Ibid., 4, note l.
39 Ibid.
40 In addition to the Turkish informant who discusses the area adjacent to the wall, Idrīsī lists as one of his sources the writing of a certain Khānākh (var. Jānākh), the son of the Kīmāk ruler (*khāqān*), of whom nothing is known, *Nuzhat*, 5, 933; cf. *MḤudūd*, 297.
41 *Muʿjam*, 3:200.
42 *Taqāsīm*, 9; cf. *Murūj*, §191.
43 *Murūj*, §731.
44 Bodleian MS Pococke 375, fols. 3b–4a; Bodleian MS Arab c. 90, fols. 27b–28a. On this last manuscript, see Jeremy Johns and Emilie Savage-Smith, "The Book of Curiosities: A Newly Discovered Series of Islamic Maps," *Imago Mundi* 55 (2003): 7–24.
45 *Ghurar*, 440–2.
46 Bīrūnī, *al-Āthār al-bāqiya*, 48–9.
47 Ibn al-Jawzī, *al-Muntaẓam*, 1:294–7.
48 Sibṭ Ibn al-Jawzī, grandson of Ibn al-Jawzī, *Mirʾāt al-zamān fī taʾrīkh al-aʿyān* (Beirut: Dār al-Shurūq, 1985), 1:327–8.
49 Nuwayrī, based on Idrīsī, *Nihāyat al-arab* (Cairo: Dār al-Kutub al-Miṣriyya, 1923), 1:374–8.
50 Dhahabī, *Taʾrīkh al-Islām* (Beirut: Dār al-Kitāb al-ʿArabī, 1987), 2:243–8.
51 Ibn Faḍl Allāh al-ʿUmarī bases himself on Idrīsī, see ʿUmarī, *Masālik al-abṣār*, 2:137–40.
52 Ibn Kathīr, *al-Bidāya wa 'l-nihāya* (Cairo: Dār al-Ḥadīth, 1992), 2:112–3.
53 Ibn Khaldūn, *Kitāb al-ʿibar*, 1:136–7.
54 Ibn Taghrībirdī, *al-Nujūm al-zāhira* (Cairo: al-Muʾassasa al-Miṣriyya al-ʿĀmma, 1963), 2:259.
55 *Nafīsa*, 149; cf. Miquel, *La Géographie humaine*, 2:503.
56 *Ghurar*, 440–2.
57 MS B, fol. 64a; this note appears to be in the same hand as the note on the frontispiece by the jurist ʿAbd al-Laṭīf b. al-Ghaffār who read through the work in the year 1040/1630–1.
58 *Murūj*, §731; cf. Mīr Khwānd, *Tārīkh-i rawḍat al-ṣafāʾ* (Tehran: Markazī-i Khayyām Pīrūz, 1960), 1:93; though contra Mīr Khwānd, given the dimensions of the wall debated, as described by Masʿūdī, it does not appear that Farghānī is responding directly to Sallām's account.
59 Muḥammad b. Kathīr al-Farghānī, *Kitāb jawāmiʿ ʿilm al-nujūm* (Cambridge: Harvard University Press, 1998), 39–40.
60 Bīrūnī, *al-Āthār al-bāqiya*, 48–9.
61 Ibn Khaldūn, *Kitāb al-ʿibar*, 1:137.

62 Ibn Ḥazm, *al-Faṣl fī 'l-milal*, 1:143–4.
63 Rachel Milstein, Karin Rührdanz, and Barbara Schmitz, *Stories of the Prophets* (Costa Mesa, CA: Mazda, 1999), 7–15, 32–8, 328–30.
64 Thaʿlabī, *ʿArāʾis al-majālis*, 243–4; while this account is not present in Brinner's translation, *The Lives of the Prophets* (Leiden: Brill, 2002), it is part of the early manuscript tradition, see British Library, MS Or. 1494, dated 513/1119, fols. 195b–196b.
65 See the partial manuscript of Ibn al-Jawzī's work, in CSIC, Madrid, Almonacid MS Junta 38, fols. 4a–5b; cf. L. P. Harvey, *Muslims in Spain, 1500 to 1614* (Chicago: University of Chicago Press, 2005), 153–4.
66 Ḥājjī Khalīfa credits Suyūṭī with the title *Badāʾiʿ al-zuhūr*, which he differentiates from the work with the same title by Ibn Iyās, Mamlūk historian, and occasional student of Suyūṭī, *Kashf*, 1:229. Modern popular editions of this collection of prophetic tales, however, ascribe the authorship of this work to Ibn Iyās, *Badāʾiʿ al-zuhūr* (Istanbul: Maṭbaʿat al-Dawla, 1931), 162–3.
67 Minhāj al-Dīn Jūzjānī, *Ṭabāqāt-i Nāṣirī* (Tehran: Dunyā-i Kitāb, 1983–4), 1:149–50.
68 Rabghūzī ascribes this adventure not to Sallām but to Abū Yaʿqūb Tarjumānī, on the authority of Majd al-Dīn Andījānī, who includes the account in his own Qurʾānic commentary; in this account the key has eighteen teeth, *Qiṣaṣ al-anbiyāʾ, An Eastern Turkish Version*, trans. H. E. Boeschoten, J. O'Kane, and M. Van Damme (Leiden: Brill, 1995), fols. 175v–176r9.
69 Rāzī, *al-Tafsīr al-kabīr*, 21:170–1, cf. 164.
70 Niẓām al-Dīn al-Nīsābūrī, *Tafsīr gharāʾib al-Qurʾān* (Beirut: Dār al-Kutub al-ʿIlmiyya, 1996) 3:460.
71 Nīsābūrī, *Tafsīr*, 3:457; cf. Robert Morrison, "Reasons for a Scientific Portrayal of Nature in Medieval Commentaries on the Qurʾān," *Arabica* 52 (2005): 182–203.
72 Ibn Kathīr, *Tafsīr al-Qurʾān al-ʿaẓīm* (Riyadh: Dār Ṭiba li'l-Nashr wa 'l-Tawzīʿ, 1999), 5:196.
73 Biqāʿī, *Naẓm al-durar*, 12:138–9.
74 See Romm, *Edges of the Earth*, 92ff.
75 Ṭūsī, *ʿAjāʾib-nāma*, 6; cf. Abū 'l-Shaykh al-Iṣfahānī (d. 369/979), *Kitāb al-ʿaẓama* (Beirut: Dār al-Kutub al-ʿIlmiyya, 1994), 17–38.
76 "*Az īn khabar nazdīktar bi-dīdār-i sadd-i Iskandar hīch riwāyat nīst*," *Mujmal al-tawārīkh*, 493.
77 Gharnāṭī, *Tuḥfat al-albāb*, 217–8.
78 Ṭūsī, *ʿAjāʾib-nāma*, 235–6.
79 Ibn al-Wardī, *Kharīdat al-ʿajāʾib* (Beirut: Dār al-Sharq al-ʿArabī, 1991), 102–4. Ibn al-Wardī's text on this section follows closely Ibn al-Athīr al-Jazarī, *Tuḥfat al-ʿajāʾib*, SOAS MS 372, fols. 81b & ff. Both follow the Jayhānī / Idrīsī narrative. The text ascribed to Ibn al-Wardī is a compilation of the earlier work of Aḥmad b. Ḥamdān al-Ḥarrānī (fl. 732/1332), *Jāmiʿ al-funūn*, cf. "Ibn al-Wardī," *EI*².
80 See the Persian cosmographical work, *Majmaʿ al-gharāʾib*, Bodleian MS Ouseley

47, fol. 47b. This work, compiled by Muḥammad b. Darwīsh al-Balkhī for the Afghān ruler Pīr Muḥammad Khān (r. 963–75/1556–67), relates that al-Wāthiq sent an unidentified group to the wall. See also Maḥmūd Efendī 'l-Khaṭīb, who mistakenly copies 'Sallām' as 'Sulaymān,' Bodleian MS Turk d. 39, fols. 66a–67b.

81 *ʿAjāʾib*, 128.

82 Ibid.

83 *Nuzhat*, 220; Ferrand appends this account to Gharnāṭī, *Tuḥfat al-albāb*, 233–4.

84 *Masālik*, 163.

85 *ʿAjāʾib*, 128–9.

86 Gharnāṭī, *Tuḥfat al-albāb*, 119n2. Gharnāṭī's *Tuḥfat* contains no reference to Sallām in this anecdote. A manuscript of the *Tuḥfat* copy gives certifications of oral transmission (*samāʿāt*) that date to a copy made during Gharnāṭī's lifetime in Mawṣil, 557/1162 (British Library, Add. 18535, fol. 122b). This manuscript is also missing the ascription to Sallām. Abū 'l-Fatḥ al-Ibshīhī (d. ca 850/1446) relates the same story; however, on the authority of neither Sallām nor Abū Ḥāmid, but rather a certain Shaykh Abū 'l-ʿAbbās al-Ḥijāzī, suggesting a different genealogy altogether, *al-Mustaṭraf* (Sidon, Lebanon: al-Maktaba al-ʿAṣriyya, 1996), 2:215. Also see César E. Dubler, *Abū Ḥāmid el Granadino* (Madrid: Editorial Maestre, 1953), 309–14; cf. René Basset, *Mille et un contes* (Paris: Maisonneuve Frères, 1924), 192.

87 Gharnāṭī, *Tuḥfat al-albāb*, 199.

88 Ibn al-Wārdī, *Kharīdat al-ʿajāʾib*, 152; see also the anonymous *ʿAjāʾib al-makhlūqāt*, drawn from Qazwīnī and others, British Library, MS Or. 1528/1, fol. 15a.

89 Ibn Iyās, *Nashq al-azhār*, British Library, MS Add. 7503, fol. 195a.

90 Aḥmad b. Yūsuf al-Qaramānī, *Akhbār al-duwal* (Beirut: ʿĀlam al-Kutub, 1992), 3:260.

91 The *jazīrat al-saksār* mentioned by Qazwīnī is based on the Persian, *sag* (dog) and *sar* (head), suggesting the ancient origin of such material. For the Greek tradition, see J. W. McCrindle's translation and notes, *Ancient India as Described by Ktêsias the Knidian* (London: Trübner and Co., 1882), 22. The loanword *μαρτιχόρας* (manticore), also belies the Persian *mard* (man) and *khwār* (eater), McCrindle, 11–2; cf. Wittkower, "Marvels of the East," 162; and, in general, for the Qazwīnī context, Julie Badiee, "An Islamic Cosmography" (Ph.D. diss., University of Michigan, 1978), 128–41.

92 See Wittkower, "Marvels of the East," 164; cf. *Jāmiʿ*, 16:19.

93 Zayyānī, *al-Tarjumāna al-kubrā* (Rabat: Wizārat al-Anbāʾ, 1967), 248–9; 298–9; 498.

94 Ibid., 248–9, where this entire tale is related on the authority of Gharnāṭī, however, see above, 249n86.

95 In addition to referencing the story twice in *al-Tarjumāna al-kubrā*, Zayyānī recalls his description of Sallām in his unpublished work, *al-Tarjumān al-muʿarrib* [The Arabic interpreter], 248.

96 Amīn Aḥmad al-Rāzī, *Haft iqlīm* (Tehran: Kitāb-furūshī-i Adabiyya, 1960), 3:517–8.

97 British Library, MS Or. 2409, fol. 104a, cf. fol. 2a.

98 Allāh-yār ʿUthmān al-Bilgrāmī, *Ḥadīqāt al-aqālīm*, litho. ed. (Lucknow: Newal Kishore Press, 1897), 492–3. Cf. H. Beveridge, "The Garden of Climes," *Asiatic Quarterly Review* (Jan. 1900): 145–62; Gulfishan Khan, *Indian Muslim Perceptions of the West During the Eighteenth Century* (Karachi: Oxford University Press, 1998), 78–84, 132–8.

99 Bilgrāmī, *Ḥadīqāt al-aqālīm*, 2–4.

100 Mustawfī, *Nuzhat al-qulūb*, 1:243; cf. Khwārazmī, who locates Gog and Magog further in the northeast, *Ṣurat al-arḍ*, 32, 34, 37.

101 See Rāzī, *al-Tafsīr al-kabīr*, 21:164.

102 *Buldān*, 594; *Muʿjam*, 3:197; cf. *Kharāj*, 199.

103 Kāshgharī, *Dīwān lughāt al-Turk* (Istanbul: Dār al-Khilāfa al-ʿAliyya, 1915–17), 1:27; *Compendium of the Turkic Dialects*, trans. Robert Dankoff and James Kelly (Buxbury, MA: Harvard University, 1982–5), 1:82, §21; see *GAS*, 12:35, §14.

104 See *Jāmiʿ*, 16:20.

105 Kāshgharī, *Dīwān lughāt al-Turk,* 1:29; *Compendium*, trans. Dankoff and Kelly, 1:83, §21.

106 Rashīd al-Dīn, *Jāmiʿ al-tawārīkh* (Tehran: Iqbāl, 1959), 1:113–4; John Boyle, "The Alexander Legend in Central Asia," *Folklore* 85 (1974): 217–28; idem, "Alexander and the Mongols," *JRAS* 2 (1979): 123–36.

107 *RIF*, §72; cf. Minorsky's commentary in Marwazī, *Ṭabāʾiʿ al-ḥayawān*, 113; Lewicki, *Źródła arabskie,* 3:163, §299.

108 *Ṣūrat,* 12, 14; for a map of Ibn Ḥawqal's projection of Gog and Magog in the north, see *GAS*, 12:32, §11.

109 See Abū Saʿīd al-Gardīzī (fl. 440/1049), *Zayn al-akhbār* (Tehran: Bunyād-i Farhang-i Īrān, 1968), 160–1; Muḥammad Nāẓim, *The Life and Times of Sulṭān Maḥmūd of Ghazna* (Cambridge: Cambridge University Press, 1931), 26–7.

110 *Ṣūrat*, 14.

111 Ibid., 482.

112 *RIF*, §32.

113 Shahmardān, *Nuzhat-nāma-i ʿalāʾī*, 308–9.

114 *Taqāsīm*, 46, 361–2.

115 *Kharāj*, 199.

116 Zayyāt, *Dhikr al-aqālīm*, 295–9.

117 Gardīzī, *Zayn al-akhbār*, 269, cf. 255.

118 Ibid., 282.

119 ʿAwfī, *Jawāmiʿ al-ḥikāyāt*, British Library, MS Or. 11676, fol. 132b; in Muḥammad Niẓām al-Dīn, *Introduction to the Jawāmiʿu 'l-ḥikāyāt* (London: Luzac and Co., 1929), 13; cf. Boyle, "Alexander and the Mongols."

120 Ibn Iyās, *Badāʾiʿ al-zuhūr*, 4:109.

121 Idrīsī, *Fī jughrāfiyā 'l-kulliyya = De geographia universali* (Rome: In Typographia Medicea, 1592), 315–18. Cf. Marina Tolmacheva, "The Medieval Arabic Geographers and the Beginnings of Modern Orientalism," *IJMES* 27 (1995):

141–56.
122 Tolmacheva, "Medieval Arabic Geographers," 144.
123 Idrīsī, *Geographia Nubiensis*, trans. Gabriel Sionita and Joannes Hersonita (Paris: H. Blageart, 1619).
124 Tolmacheva, "Medieval Arabic Geographers," 141–52.
125 Idrīsī, *Geographia Nubiensis*, 267–70.

Chapter 7: Beyond the Walls of the Orient

1 "Tout ce qui regarde la connoissance des Peuples de l'Orient, leurs histoires et traditions véritables ou fabuleuses," Barthélemy d'Herbelot, *Bibliothèque orientale, ou, Dictionaire universel* (Paris: Compagnie des Libraires, 1697).
2 See Nicholas Dew, "The Making of d'Herbelot's *Bibliothèque Orientale*," in *Debating World Literature* (London: Verso, 2004), 233–52.
3 On Galland's 'translation,' see Muhsin Mahdi, *The Thousand and One Nights* (Leiden: Brill, 1995), 11–50.
4 Voltaire, 11 December 1742, *Correspondence* (Geneva: Institut et Musée Voltaire, 1955), 12:174, §2523; in Dew, "The Making," 234–5.
5 See Edward Said, *Orientalism* (New York: Pantheon Books, 1978), 65.
6 Cf. d'Herbelot, *Bibliothèque orientale*, 911–2. See Muna Al-Alwan, "The Orient 'Made Oriental'" *Arab Studies Quarterly* 30 (2008): 43–52.
7 D'Herbelot, *Bibliothèque orientale*, 470.
8 Ibid., 471.
9 For a negative reception of Warton's thesis, see John Dunlop (d. 1842), *The History of Fiction* (London: Longman, 1814), 1:137–40.
10 See John Brady (d. 1814), *Varieties of Literature* (London: G. B. Whittaker, 1826), 116–8; Frederick Fairholt (d. 1866), *Gog and Magog* (London: J. C. Hotten, 1859), 21.
11 "History of Discovery Relative to Magnetism," *Annual Report of the Board of Regents of the Smithsonian Institution*, Misc. Doc. 82 (1864), 288.
12 See Knud Lundbæk, *T. S. Bayer (1694–1738), Pioneer Sinologist* (Copenhagen: Curzon Press, 1986), 3–4.
13 T. S. Bayer, "De Muro Caucaseo," *Commentarii Academiae Scientiarum Imperialis Petropolitanae* 1 (1726): 425–63, with particular focus on the section treating Sallām, 438–42.
14 On this issue, see Daston and Park, *Wonders and the Order of Nature*, particularly ch. 9, "The Enlightenment and the Anti-Marvelous," 329–63.
15 Bayer, "De Muro Caucaseo," 446.
16 Ibid., 438.
17 Ibid., 446, this quotation is from Epistula VII of Horace. Lundbæk describes how Bayer was known for his "immoderate use of quotations" from Greek and Latin, *T.S. Bayer*, 6.
18 Bayer, "De Muro Caucaseo," 439. The Medici Arabic edition, however, does

mention al-Wāthiq, while the Latin translation printed in Paris obfuscates al-Wāthiq biʿllāh by translating his name as "Fidelis Deo," *Geographia Nubiensis*, 267.

19 In addition to d'Herbelot, *Bibliothèque orientale*, this story appears later in Latin with Johann Bernhard Koehler's (d. 1802) translation of excerpts from Ibn al-Wārdī's book of marvels, *Abulfedae Tabula Syriae* (Leipzig: Litteris Schoenermarkii, 1766).

20 Bayer, "De Muro Caucaseo," 442.

21 Constantin d'Ohsson, *Des peuples du Caucase* (Paris: Firmin Didot, 1828), ii. D'Ohsson's account very much echoes the trajectory of the caliphal envoy Ibn Faḍlān to the king of the Bulghārs on the Volga in 309/921.

22 D'Ohsson, "Ils (c'est-à-dire les infidèles) t'interrogeront sur Zoul-Carnéin," *Des peuples*, 131.

23 "Il est certain qu'à la fin du monde les Yadjoudjes et Madjoudjes se répandront sur la terre, selon notre livre sacré." Ibid., 133.

24 Ibid., 139.

25 Mīr Khwānd, *Tārīkh-i rawḍat al-ṣafāʾ*, 1:93.

26 For Strabo this includes the likes of Ctesias, Herodotus, and most of those who have written on the life of Alexander, *Geographica* (Leipzig: Teubner, 1877–98), 2:713, C. 507–8.

27 D'Ohsson, *Des peuples*, 8–12; d'Ohsson sets the account of the *jeune fille* emerging from the body of a fish with the Yūra and not the Khazar, 83.

28 See Zadeh, "The Wiles of Creation."

29 *Geographie d'AboulFéda*, ed. and trans. Reinaud, *Introduction Générale a la Géographie des Orientaux* (Paris: Imprimerie nationale, 1848), 1:lv–lvi, cccxiii–cccxiv.

30 See *Géographie d'Edrisi*, trans. Jaubert, 2:416.

31 Reinaud, "Malheureusement, elle est surchargée de récits fabuleux, et, dès son origine, elle excita les défiances des musulmans eux-mêmes," *Geographie d'AboulFéda*, 1:lv–lvi.

32 Aloys Sprenger, *Die Post- und Reiserouten des Orients* (Leipzig: F. A. Brockhaus, 1864), xv.

33 "The all too notorious account of Sallām the interpreter," Meynard, 23.

34 Ibid., E. J. van Donzel makes a similar point, basing himself on the Christian apocalypse of Baḥīrā, which he argues provides a rationalized reading of the Qurʾānic stories of the People of the Cave and Dhū 'l-Qarnayn's barrier, *Gog and Magog* (Leiden: Brill, 2010), 176–7. However, such a critique is not to be found in the Syriac or Arabic versions of the legend edited by Barbara Roggema, *The Legend of Sergius Baḥīrā* (Leiden: Brill, 2009), 294–6, 368, 414, 506.

35 De Goeje, "De Muur van Gog en Magog," *Verslagen en Mededeelingen der Koninklijke Akademie van Wetenschappen*, ser. 3 (Amsterdam, 1888), 5:87–124.

36 Ibid., 5:113–4.

37 Ibid., 5:116.

38 For the evolution of this toponym from 伊吾 (Yiwu), 伊吾盧 (Yiwulu), and 伊州 (Yizhou), see British Library, MS Dunhuang S. 367, reproduced and translated by Lionel Giles as "A Chinese Geographical Text of the Ninth Century," *BSOS* 6 (1932), 834–7. See also Pelliot, *Notes on Marco Polo*, 1:159; Stein, *Serindia*, 3:1147–51.

39 See Paul Demiéville, *Le concile de Lhasa* (Paris: Imprimerie nationale, 1952), 171–3; cf. Christopher Beckwith, *The Tibetan Empire in Central Asia* (Princeton: Princeton University Press, 1987), s.v. Hami.

40 Beckwith, *Tibetan Empire*, 168–71; Michael Drompp, *Tang China and the Collapse of the Uighur Empire* (Leiden: Brill, 2005), 7–38.

41 The Uyghurs were known in Tang dynastic sources as 回鶻 (Huihu). After the fall of the Uyghur Khanate in 840 C.E., the factions that fled toward China posed a serious problem for the Tang state, see Drompp, *Tang China*, 39–69. For the presence of Sogdians in the local population of Yizhou, referred to as barbarians, 胡 (*hu*)—i.e., any foreigner in the western provinces outside of China—see Giles, "A Chinese Geographical Text," 841.

42 Giles, "A Chinese Geographical Text," 834–6; cf. Beckwith, *Tibetan Empire*, 143–72.

43 Ibid., 170–1n179.

44 On the Uyghur state that hence developed, see James Hamilton, *Les Ouïghours à l'époque des cinq dynasties* (Paris: Imprimerie national, 1955).

45 *Masālik*, 164 note g; De Goeje, "De Muur van Gog en Magog," 110.

46 De Goeje, "De Muur van Gog en Magog," 110–1; an argument also advanced by van Donzel, *Gog and Magog*, 192.

47 Cf. Demiéville, *Le concile de Lhasa*, 269–71.

48 For images and a historical overview of the pass and surrounding defensive walls, see William Lindesay, *The Great Wall Revisited* (Cambridge: Harvard University Press, 2008), 60–79.

49 De Goeje, "De Muur van Gog en Magog," 108.

50 Ibid., 111–3.

51 Ibid., 113–4; for Nūshajān al-ʿAlā, see *Masālik*, 29–30; for de Goeje's identification of the king Ṭabānūyan with this region see his French translation, *Masālik*, 131.

52 See Silverstein, *Postal Systems*, 192. C. Wessels describes a nine-day journey between Hami and the Jade Gate in *Early Jesuit Travellers in Central Asia, 1603–1721* (The Hague: Nijhoff, 1924), 37.

53 Based on van Donzel's own estimation, a journey between the edge of the Kazakh city of Atyrau (Gurjev) to the Jade Gate would stretch between 3,290 km and 3,460 km. Both the Vienna and Bodleian accounts suggest that it took roughly two months to travel from the Khazar capital, on the Volga, to the barrier. Adding the extra distance from the Volga capital of approximately 320 km to Atyrau in van Donzel's itinerary would mean that Sallām would have had to travel approximately 60 km per day. Even using the claim of Ibn al-Qāṣṣ that it took seventy-four days to reach the wall from the Khazar as

an upper limit, this would mean traveling approximately 50 km per day to reach the Jade Gate. Both of these estimates would be significantly more than the comfortable per diem average of 12 km to 17.5 km for the entire itinerary suggested by van Donzel, *Gog and Magog*, 218, 242.

54 For the designation of this city as a prefecture during the Tang dynasty in 630, see Pelliot, *Notes on Marco Polo*, "Camul," 1:153–6.

55 For the Tibetan translation during the eighth century of the Chinese *zhou* into *cu*, see F. W. Thomas, "Tibetan Documents Concerning Chinese Turkestan," *JRAS* (1927): 51–86, 807–44, particularly, 807–8; also see G. Uray, "The Old Tibetan Sources of the History of Central Asia up to 751 A.D.: A Survey," in *Prolegomena to the Sources on the History of Pre-Islamic Central Asia* (Budapest: Akadémiai Kiadó, 1979), 286–7. For the Khotanese translation of Yizhou into Ī-cū, see Sten Konow, "The Khotanese Text of the Staël-Holstein Scroll," *Acta Orientalia* 20 (1947): 131–60, specifically line 17.3 of the Khotanese text, dated 865; H. W. Bailey, "The Staël-Holstein Miscellany," *Asia Major* 2 (1951), 13.

56 On the Sogdian *km'yδ* = *kamēl* for the city Qomul, see Hans Reichelt, *Die soghdischen Handschriftenreste des Britischen museums* (Heidelberg: C. Winter's Universitätsbuchhandlung, 1928), 2:14, §2.23; see H. W. Bailey, *Indo-Scythian Studies, Being Khotanese Texts* (Cambridge: Cambridge University Press, 1985), 2:10; also Pelliot, *Notes on Marco Polo*, 1:153–6. However, see W. B. Henning, "The Date of the Sogdian Ancient Letters," *BSOAS* 12 (1948): 601–15. Henning draws into question the reading by Reichelt, of the Sogdian text itself, and believes *km'yδ* to be a misreading, 604.

57 As for the Uyghur toponym, see Tôru Haneda, "A propos d'un text fragmentaire de prière manichéenne en ouigour provenant de Turfan," *Memoirs of the Research Department of the Toyo Bunko* 6 (1932), 3, fol. a, line 1. Haneda argues for an ancient use of some variation of Qomul, as distinct from Yizhou in the early Tang period, 9–10, 17–21.

58 In Arabic and Persian geographical sources, Yizhou is known through the Uyghur as Qumūl or Qāmul and not by the Tang administrative term. Even the *Ḥudūd*, which renders all these prefectures as چو (*chū*) or جو (*jū*), accounts for Yizhou by the Uyghur name Qomul, albeit in a muddled form (خمود), see §12.9 and *MḤudūd*, 275; Gardīzī knows Hamī as Qumūl, *Zayn al-akhbār*, 268.

59 Had Sallām indeed traveled to Yizhou he probably would have transcribed it as ایجو (*ījū*) or ایچو (*īchū*) and not ایکه (*īkuh*) or ایگه (*īguh*). See, for example, the transliterations of the Chinese prefectures 甘州 (Ganzhou) = خمچو; 蘇州 (Suzhou) = سوکجو; 沙州 (Shazhou) = ساجو, in *Ḥudūd* §9.7–15, cf. *MḤudūd*, 232. See Rashīd al-Dīn, *Jāmiʿ al-tawārikh*, 1:321–2, 325, 329–30. With regard to the above cited toponyms in *Ḥudūd*, see Pelliot, *Notes on Marco Polo*, 1:150, 2:838, 822; James Hamilton, "Autour du Manuscrit Staël-Holstein," *T'oung Pao* 46 (1958), 138.

60 See Beckwith, *Tibetan Empire*, passim; on the seventh-century Sogdian temple of Hami/Yizhou, see de la Vaissière, *Sogdian Traders*, 128–9.

61 On the role of Muslims in the Tibetan Empire during the second/eighth and third/ninth centuries, see Beckwith, *Tibetan Empire*, 55–83.

62 See, Mahmoud Sadek, *The Arabic Materia Medica of Dioscorides* (Québec: Les Éditions du Sphinx, 1983), 102; Ibn Bayṭār (d. 646/1248), *Tafsīr Kitāb Dīyāsqūrīdūs* (Beirut: Dār al-Gharb al-Islāmī, 1989), bk. 3, 239–40, §76.

63 See, for instance, Ibn Sayyār al-Warrāq, *Kitāb al-ṭabīkh*, 330–1.

64 See ʿAlī b. Sahl Rabbān al-Ṭabarī (fl. third/ninth century), *Firdaws al-ḥikma* (Berlin: Sonne, 1928), 395; Meyerhof, "ʿAlī aṭ-Ṭabarī's '*Paradise of Wisdom*,'" 6–54.

65 See Aurel Stein, *Ruins of Desert Cathay* (London: Macmillan and Co., 1912), 2:117–8, 120–2.

66 Arthur N. Waldron, *The Great Wall of China* (Cambridge: Cambridge University Press, 1992), 47–8.

67 Arthur N. Waldron, "The Problem of the Great Wall of China," *Harvard Journal of Asiatic Studies* 43 (1983): 643–63; idem, *The Great Wall of China*, passim.

68 Abū 'l-Ghāzī Bahādur Khān al-Khwārazmī, *A General History of the Turks, Moguls and Tatars* (London: Knapton, 1729–30), 2:519–20; cf. trans. Bentinck, *Histoire genéalogique des Tatars* (Leiden: A. Kallewier, 1726), 117–21, 148–9.

69 Edward Gibbon, *The History of the Decline and Fall of the Roman Empire* (London: A. Strahan and T. Cadell, 1791–2), 7:141–2nn140–1.

70 Bayer, "De Muro Caucaseo," 437–8; cf. Thomas Hyde, *Epistola de mensuris et ponderibus serum seu sinensium* (Oxford: E. Theatro Sheldoniano, 1688), [unnumbered, page 29].

71 James Rennell, *The Geographical System of Herodotus, Examined, and Explained* (London: W. Bulmer, 1800), 111–2.

72 See, for instance, the map of Mongolia, "Description de la Tartarie" (1654), by the French cartographer Nicolas Sanson (d. 1667), which locates the Wall of China beneath the lands of Gog and Magog, situated in the far north of Mongolia, *Cartes générales* (Paris: P. Mariette, 1658), no. 11.

73 *The Asiatic Annual Register*, s.v. 'Account of Books for the year 1800' (1801), 2:24.

74 See Sir Henry Yule, *Cathay and the Way Thither* (London: The Hakluyt Society, 1866), 1:cxxix, note 2; cf. Igor de Rachewiltz, "Marco Polo went to China," *Zentralasiatische Studien* 27 (1997), 37.

75 de Rachewiltz, "Marco Polo went to China," 63–4.

76 See David Morgan, "Prester John and the Mongols," in *Prester John, the Mongols, and the Ten Lost Tribes* (Aldershot: Variorum, 1996), 159–70; on the Nestorian Önggüd, see Paul Pelliot, "Chrétiens d'Asie centrale et d'Extrême-Orient," *T'oung Pao* 15 (1914): 623–44.

77 Marco Polo, *Le devisement du monde* (Paris: La Découverte, 1998), 1:179–80.

78 Ibn Baṭṭūṭa, *Riḥla* (Beirut: Dār Ṣādir, 1960), 634–5.

79 Yule, *Cathay*, 2:490n1.

80 James Dunbar, *Essays on the History of Mankind in Rude and Cultivated Ages* (London: W. Strahan, 1780), 264.

81 *The Book of the Thousand Nights and a Night*, trans. Richard Burton (Benares: Kamashastra Society, 1885–6), 5:252n2.
82 Joseph Needham, et al., *Civil Engineering and Nautics* in *Science and Civilisation in China* (Cambridge: Cambridge University Press, 1971), vol. 4, part 3, 56.
83 Cf. de Rachewiltz, "Marco Polo went to China," 64–5.
84 de Goeje, "Le Japon connu des Arabes," in Buzurg b. Shahriyār, *Kitāb ʿajāʾib al-Hind = Livre des Merveilles de l'Inde* (Leiden: Brill, 1883–6), 295–307; see Shawkat Toorawa, "Wāq al-wāq: Fabulous, Fabular, Indian Ocean (?) Island(s)," *Emergences: Journal for the Study of Media and Composite Cultures* 10 (2000): 387–402.
85 See Shawkat Toorawa, "Wāḳwāḳ," EI^2.
86 Wilhelm Tomaschek, "De Muur van Gog en Magog," *Vienna Oriental Journal* 3 (1889): 103–8.
87 Nöldeke, "Beiträge," 33.
88 *Muʿjam*, 3:440–8; see V. Minorsky, "Abū Dulaf," EI^2; R. Bulliet, "Abū Dolaf," *EIr*; Clifford E. Bosworth, *The Mediaeval Islamic Underworld* (Leiden: Brill, 1976), 48–79; cf. Sezgin, who, in contrast, believes Abū Dulaf's journey to China and India to be an authentic account written by a skilled littérateur but amateur geographer, *Majmūʿ fī 'l-jughrāfiyā*, 8–10.
89 Marquart, *Osteuropäische*, 74–95; he argues that the expedition was motivated by the overthrow of the Uyghur state in 840, 90.
90 Ibid., 83–4; cf. Yule, *Cathay*, 1:clxxxvi–cxciii.
91 Richard Hennig, *Terrae incognitae* (Leiden: Brill, 1936–9), 2:173.
92 Ibid., 2:175.
93 Étienne Zichy, "Le voyage de Sallām, l'interprète, à la muraille de Gog et de Magog," *Kőrösi Csoma-Archivum*, 1, part 3 (1922): 190–204.
94 *Nuzhat*, 935; cf. Göckenjan and Zimonyi, *Orientalische Berichte*, 25–6; Zimonyi, *Origins*, 14–5.
95 *Masālik*, 31; cf. *IFG*, 329, note f; *Buldān*, 634; on the tribe of the Adhkish, see Kāshgharī, *Dīwān lughāt al-Turk*, Arabic, 1:89, *Compendium*, trans. Dankoff and Kelly, 1:129, §61.
96 Zichy, "Le voyage de Sallām," 199; cf. Zimonyi, *Origins*, 101–2.
97 Zichy, "Le voyage de Sallām," 205.
98 C. E. Wilson, "The Wall of Alexander against Gog and Magog," *Hirth Anniversary Volume* (London: Probsthain, 1923), 575–612.
99 Ibid., 606.
100 Ibid.
101 Ibid., 611.
102 Ibid.
103 Miller, *Charta Rogeriana*, 29–33.
104 Ibid., 30; this is a line of argumentation taken up by van Donzel, *Gog and Magog*, 244–5.
105 Miller, *Charta Rogeriana*, 32.

106 Anderson, *Alexander's Gate*, 96; cf. Miller, *Charta Rogeriana*, 31. Anderson, who did not have access to Idrīsī in the original Arabic, is mistaken. The text reads Qūqāyā, with a manuscript variant as Qūfāyā, and it explicitly states that this mythical mountain range is located in the far east (*aqṣā 'l-mashriq*), *Nuzhat*, 910.
107 *MḤudūd*, 225.
108 Ibid.
109 A. A. Vasiliev, *Byzance et les Arabes* (Brussels: Institut de philologie et d'histoire orientales, 1935), 1:8–9.
110 *RIF*, 196–8.
111 Ibid., see Kāshgharī, *Dīwān lughāt al-Turk*, Arabic, 1:58; *Compendium*, trans. Dankoff and Kelly, 1:103, §42; also see W. Barthold, *Zwölf Vorlesungen über die Geschichte der Türken Mittelasiens* (Berlin: Deutsche Gesellschaft für Islamkunde, 1935), 95; *MḤudūd*, 276–7.
112 *RIF*, 196; see Aurel Stein, *Serindia* (Oxford: Clarendon Press, 1921), 2:783, 3:1228.
113 Dunlop, *History of the Jewish Khazars* (Princeton: Princeton University Press, 1954), 193; idem, *Arab Civilization to A.D. 1500* (London: Longman, 1971), 313n122.
114 Salo Wittmayer Baron, *Social and Religious History of the Jews* (New York: Columbia University Press, 1952–83), 4:73.
115 Bendefy, *Szallam*, 5–8, 83; see Z. V. Togan, "Bashdjirt," *EI*².
116 Bendefy, *Szallam*, 20; Stein, *Serindia*, 2:683–97.
117 Bendefy, *Szallam*, 91.
118 Ibid., 53–64, 89–90; Aurel Stein, *On Alexander's Track to the Indus* (London: Macmillan and Co., 1929), 47; Arrian of Nicomedia, *Alexandri anabasis* (Leipzig: Teubner, 1907), 1:226–9, bk 4, §§27–8.
119 Bendefy, *Szallam*, 58–64, 92–3; Stein, *On Alexander's Track*, 152.
120 Bendefy, *Szallam*, 46–7, 89.
121 Ibid., 67–8, 86n150, 92; Stein, *On Alexander's Track*, 60.
122 As for the Adhkish Turks, see *Masālik*, 31; *Nuzhat*, 843–4. Bendefy offers no explanation as to how de Goeje's Igu could be mistakenly transcribed as Girā, that is Rāja Girā, which appears to have been an onomastic corruption that occurred after Maḥmūd of Ghazna's (d. 421/1030) invasions of the Swāt Valley; see Abdur Rehman, "Ethnicity of the Hindu Shahis," *Journal of the Pakistan Historical Society* 51, no. 3 (2003), 9. Bendefy claims that, because the toponym is unpointed, we are free to imagine what the proper transcription would have been, *Szallam*, 67.
123 Bendefy, *Szallam*, 74–7, 93.
124 Cf. Stein, *On Alexander's Track*, 53–61.
125 Ibid., 115.
126 Van Donzel, "Ḳomul," *Supplement*, *EI*²; cf. idem, *Gog and Magog*, 208. In the work cited, Luo Zhewen and Zhao Luo, *The Great Wall of China in History and Legend* (Beijing: Foreign Languages Press, 1986), there is no description here that readily parallels Sallām's layout of this enormous city, 39–41.

127 S.v. 關, R. H. Mathews, *Chinese-English Dictionary* (Cambridge: Harvard University Press, 1941), 527–8, §3571.
128 See Sen-Dou Chang, "Some Observations on the Morphology of Chinese Walled Cities," *Annals of the Association of American Geographers* 60 (1970), 70–2.
129 See Giles, "A Chinese Geographical Text," 836.
130 Van Donzel, "Sallām al-Tardjumān," *Supplement, EI²* (italics added).
131 Ibid; on the centrality of the identification of this toponym with the modern Chinese Hami for de Goeje's thesis, see van Donzel, *Gog and Magog*, 207.
132 Van Donzel, "Sallām al-Tardjumān," *Supplement, EI²*; he does not, however, engage directly with the scholarly criticism of de Geoje's thesis in his monograph, *Gog and Magog*.
133 Ibid.
134 See *Masālik*, xvff.
135 De Goeje, "De Muur van Gog en Magog," 104.
136 *Masālik*, xviii.
137 Helene Loebenstein, *Katalog der arabischen Handschriften der Österreichischen Nationalbibliothek* (Vienna: Hollinek, 1970), 1:197, 2403 (Mixt. 783); cf. *Masālik*, xviii.
138 The pronominal masculine suffix added to *tarbīᶜ* does not agree with its grammatically feminine antecedent (*madīna*). De Goeje corrects this in his edition, *Masālik*, 164, note h. However, not noted by de Goeje is how the pronominal feminine ending at the end of the taped over passage (*lahā*) appears not to agree with the partly legible masculine pronoun which starts the original text (. . . *hu 'l-abwāb*).
139 *Masālik*, xiv.
140 For a similar confusion in another critical apparatus prepared by de Goeje, see Jan Just Witkam, "Manuscripts and Manuscripts," *Manuscripts of the Middle East* 1 (1986), 111–4, cited in Montgomery, "Serendipity," 199.
141 British Library, MS I.O. Islamic 617, fol. 1a.
142 MS B contains less than ten verse citations, fols. 10a, 15a–b, 43b, 65b, 78a, 79a; cf. *Masālik*, 15–6, 82, 128–9, 162, 181. The thesis that the prototype for MS B contained more poetic material is substantiated by the excerpt in Bodleian MS Hunt 538 (= MS H), which, based on its parallels with Sallām's anecdote and its placement of the account beyond the Khazar, derives from the same archetype, see MS H, fol. 142a–b; MS B, fols. 61a–64a; cf. MS V, fol. 72a. MS H includes a verse found only in the Vienna redaction, further suggesting that the Bodleian manuscript is descended from a copy that originally had more poetry in it, see MS B, fol. 65b, MS H, 142b.
143 MS B, fols. 81b–82a, a Latin note draws attention to the lacuna in the margin, highlighting the catch word at the bottom of fol. 81b that does not match the first word at the top of fol. 82a; the same lacuna is transmitted in MS P, fol. 94a.
144 Montgomery, "Serendipity," 202–9.
145 The opening folio is written out in a heavier ink, the paper appears to have

been re-appended to replace a lost opening sheet, additionally the number of lines on the folio is thirteen, which deviates from the consistent eleven lines per folio throughout MS B.

146 *Masālik*, xviii; MS V, fol. 1a; cf. Loebenstein, *Katalog*, 1:197.

147 Ḥājjī Khalīfa outlines a very similar incipit as MS V, *Kashf*, 2:1665n3. While this does not mean it is original to the text, Montgomery's reading of the Vienna encomium suggests that it is deeply embedded within ʿAbbāsid politics, "Serendipity," 202–9; the same, however, cannot be said for the Bodleian encomium, which may well be a perfunctory addition by a later scribe.

148 A *bismillāh* marks a new section in MS V, fol. 75a; cf. *Masālik*, Arabic text 177, note h, French translation, 138n1; cf. Loebenstein, *Katalog*, 1:197.

149 *Masālik*, 181–2.

150 *Murūj*, §§3213–27.

151 *Masālik*, 37, cf. 39.

152 Minorsky, "Tamīm ibn Baḥr's Journey," 303–4.

153 A similar observation is made by P. G. Bulgakov, who argues for a single recension circa 885 and suggests that the lack of poetry in the Bodleian recension is a result of an abridgment, while the references to early historical details are anachronisms, "'*Kniga putei i gosudarstv*' Ibn Xordāḏbeha (K izucheniiu i datirovke redaktsii)," *Palestinskii Sbronik*, vol. 66 = vol. 3 (1958): 127–36. Such a thesis would restore the force of Ibn al-Nadīm's claim that the first person to write under the heading *al-Masālik wa 'l-mamālik* was Abū 'l-ʿAbbās al-Marwazī (d. 274/887–8), *Fihrist*, 1:463; cf. *MḤudūd*, 13; Marquart, *Osteuropäische*, 390.

154 MS B, fol. 54a, 78a.

155 Jerome McGann, *The Textual Condition* (Princeton: Princeton University Press, 1991), 60.

156 Iṣfahānī, "*qalīlu 'l-taṣḥīḥi li-mā yarwīhi wa yuḍamminuhu kutubahu*," *Aghānī*, 1:47; also "*qalīlu 'l-taṣḥīl*," 5:144; cf. 9:242, 267–8; 15:24, 106; 18:259; see *Masālik*, xi; Montgomery, "Serendipity," 193–4; Kilpatrick, *Making the Great Book of Songs*, 44, 112–3.

157 Ibn al-Faqīh, listing the conquests of caliphs, mentions al-Muʿtaḍid as *khalīfatunā*, *Buldān*, 111.

158 *Nafīsa*, 149, note c; *IFG*, 301, note h.

159 See *Masālik*, xx.

160 *Buldān*, 593.

161 *Mushtāq*, 2:395; Ibn al-Athīr al-Jazarī, *Tuḥfat al-ʿajāʾib*, SOAS MS 372, fol. 81b.

162 The word Adhkish is frequently spelled in the sources as Atkish, which would explain the first three letters of the Vienna *hapax legomenon*; the final letter thus would have been incorrectly transcribed. Such an interpretation is further supported by the syntactical parallelism in Idrīsī's account, which, instead of directly introducing the name of a city, describes the *khāqān* of the Adhkish with a parallel passive voice in reference to an unnamed toponym (*hunāka*

madīnatun yudʿā malikuhā khāqāna Adhkish), *Nuzhat*, 935.

163 See de Goeje's transcription of the *lām* in al-L.b, which, though not marked with as strong a cant, is similarly missing the angled marker of the *kāf*; using the same reasoning as Īkka, this could be transcribed as al-K.b, etc., MS V, fol. 71b.

164 Paul Buell, "The Role of the Sino-Mongolian Frontier Zone in the Rise of Chinggis-Qan," *Studies on Mongolia* (Bellingham: Western Washington University, 1979), 63–76; İsenbike Togan, *Flexibility and Limitation in Steppe Formations* (Leiden: Brill, 1998), 27–8, 157, 159, 162. See also Michal Biran, *The Empire of the Qara Khitai in Eurasian History* (Cambridge: Cambridge University Press, 2005), 26, 115, 133.

165 Rashīd al-Dīn, *Jāmiʿ al-tawārīkh*, 1:99, cf. 122; cf. d'Ohsson, *Histoire des Mongols* (The Hague: Les frères Van Cleef, 1834–5), 1:84–5; cf. d'Ohsson, *Histoire des Mongols*, 1:84–5. See also Henry Serruys, "Mongol Altan 'gold' = 'imperial'," *Monumenta Serica* 21 (1962): 357–78.

166 Rashīd al-Dīn, *Jāmiʿ al-tawārīkh*, 1:165; see Abū 'l-Ghāzī Bahādur Khān al-Khwārazmī, *Shajara-i Turk* (St. Petersburg: Imprimerie de l'Académie Impériale des sciences, 1871–4), 1:48.

167 This appears to be a folk etymology with no clear analogue in Mongolian, see Gerhard Doerfer, *Türkische und mongolische Elemente im Neupersischen* (Wiesbaden: F. Steiner, 1963–75), 1:152–3, "انكو (öngü?) 'Mauer.'"

168 *Masālik*, xviii.

169 Rashīd al-Dīn, "*saddī sākhta kih bi-mughūlī ān-rā ungū mī-gūyand*," *Jāmiʿ al-tawārīkh*, 165, cf. 122.

Conclusion

1 Miquel, *La geógraphie humaine*, 2:503.

2 Ibn al-Wardī, *Kharīdat al-ʿajāʾib*, 11.

3 Mohammed Arkoun, "Peut-on parler de merveilleux dans le Coran?" *L'Etrange et le merveilleux dans l'islam médiéval* (Paris: Editions J.A., 1978), 1–25; Waḥīd Saʿfī, *al-ʿAjīb wa 'l-gharīb fī kutub tafsīr al-Qurʾān* (Tunis: Tibr al-Zamān, 2001).

4 See the intersection between the discourses of wonder and eschatology in Ibn al-Wardī, *Kharīdat al-ʿajāʾib*, 289–324.

5 Muḥammad b. Bahādur al-Zarkashī, *al-Burhān fī ʿulūm al-Qurʾān* (Cairo: Dār Iḥyāʾ al-Kutub al-ʿArabiyya, 1957), 1:266; see Ṭabarī, who lists both 'sign' (*ʿalāma*) and 'account' (*qiṣṣa*) as primary meanings, *Jāmiʿ*, 1:47.

6 See above, 221n12, 245n7.

7 See Ibn al-Rūmī, *Dīwān* (Beirut: Dār al-Kutub al-ʿIlmiyya, 1994), 1:347–8; cf. Said Boustany, *Ibn ar-Rūmī* (Beirut: Publications de l'Université Libanaise, 1967), 258; Robert McKinney, *Ibn al-Rūmī*, 96–8.

8 *Masālik*, 124; cf. Buḥturī, *Dīwān*, 974–9, §386, lines 35–6.

9 *TRM*, ser. 3, 4:2037–9.

10 See *TRM*, ser. 3, 4:2083. On Isḥāq b. Kundājīq al-Khazarī, see Peter Golden, *Khazar Studies* (Budapest: Akadémiai Kiadó, 1980), 202–3; Marius Canard,

Histoire de la dynastie des H'amdanides de Jazîra et de Syrie (Paris: Presses universitaires de France, 1953), 294–8.

11 Montgomery, "Serendipity," 209–10.

12 See the verses cited in *Masālik*, 7, 16, 32–3, 162; *Buldān*, 383, 616, 420; *Tanbīh*, 37.

13 *Udabāʾ*, 4:1574; 6:2645–6, §1115; *Fihrist*, 1:461–2; Baghdādī, *Taʾrīkh Baghdād*, 3:127–30, §748.

14 *Fihrist*, 2:331; *Udabāʾ*, 1:282–6; cf. Toorawa, *Ibn Abī Ṭāhir*, 46–50.

15 *Fihrist*, 1:451–62; cf. Toorawa, *Ibn Abī Ṭāhir*, 102–8.

16 *Fihrist*, 2:435; Dodge, 307. See Shawkat Toorawa, "Proximity, Resemblance, Sidebars and Clusters: Ibn al-Nadīm's Organizational Principles in *Fihrist* 3.3," *Oriens* (forthcoming). I would like thank the author for sharing with me his article prior to its publication.

17 *Fihrist*, 1:467–9; Dodge, 332–3.

18 *Fihrist*, 2:332; Dodge, 724.

19 *Fihrist*, 2:331; Dodge, 723–4.

20 *Aghānī*, 9:242; cf. Maʿarrī, *Risālat al-ghufrān*, 350.

21 *Aghānī*, 9:277.

22 Ibid., 9:285.

23 Ibid., 9:338; Kilpatrick, *Making the Great Book of Songs*, 21–2, 263.

24 See *Murūj*, §§3213–27.

25 *Lahw*, 12–20.

26 Ibid., 14–5.

27 Ibid., 18.

28 *RIF*, §72.

29 Cf. Seeger Bonebakker, "Some Medieval Views on Fantastic Stories," *Quaderni di studi arabi* 10 (1992): 21–42.

Postscript

1 For this inscription of ʿAḍud al-Dawla, see Sheila Blair, *The Monumental Inscriptions from Early Islamic Iran and Transoxiana* (Leiden: Brill, 1992), §6, 32–3.

2 Ibid., §7, 34–5.

3 Iṣfahānī, *Kitāb adab al-ghurabāʾ*, §3, 24–5; var. "*bi-nāzili 'l-aqdār*," *Muʿjam*, 5:70–1; Northedge, *Historical Topography*, 208, 331.

4 See *Buldān*, 105–14.

BIBLIOGRAPHY

Manuscripts

Austria

Österreichische Nationalbibliothek, Vienna
MS Mixt. 783, Ibn Khurradādhbih, *Kitāb masālik wa 'l-mamālik.*

France

Bibliothèque nationale, Paris
MS Arabe, ancien fonds, 1494a (MS arabe 3687), anon., *Sharḥ sīrat Iskandar Dhū 'l-Qarnayn.*
MS Supplément arabe 895 (MS arabe 2213), Ibn Khurradạ̄dhbih, *al-Masālik wa 'l-mamālik.*

Germany

Staatsbibliothek, Berlin
MS Or. 2195, anon. *Kitāb sīrat al-Iskandar.*

Spain

Consejo Superior de Investigaciones Cientifícas, Madrid
Almonacid MS Junta 38, Ibn al-Jawzī, *Salwat al-aḥzān.*

United Kingdom

Bodleian Library, Oxford University
MS Arab c. 90, anon., *Kitāb gharāʾib al-funūn.*
MS Hunt 433, Ibn Khurradādhbih, *al-Masālik wa 'l-mamālik fī ṣifat al-arḍ.*
MS Hunt 538, Ibn Ḥawqal, *al-Masālik wa 'l-mamālik.*
MS Marsh 206, Abū 'l-Ḥasan ʿAlī b. Riḍwān al-Miṣrī, commentary on Ptolemy, *Kitāb al-arbaʿa.*

MS Or. 306, Jean Gagnier, transcription of selections from medieval Arabic geographies.
MS Ouseley 47, Muḥammad b. Darwīsh al-Balkhī, *Majmaʿ al-gharāʾib.*
MS Turk d. 2, Muṣliḥ al-Dīn Surūrī, translation of Zakariyyāʾ al-Qazwīnī, *ʿAjāʾib al-makhlūqāt.*
MS Turk d. 39, Maḥmūd Efendī 'l-Khaṭīb, translation of Ibn al-Wardī, *Kharīdat al-ʿajāʾib.*

British Library, London
MS Add. 5928, Abū Zayd ʿUmāra b. Zayd, *Qiṣṣat al-Iskandar.*
MS Add. 7503, Ibn Iyās, *Nashq al-azhār.*
MS Add. 7496, Ibn al-Faqīh, *al-Ikhtiṣār min kitāb al-buldān.*
MS Add. 23378, Ibn Rusta, *Kitāb al-aʿlāq al-nafīsa.*
MS Delhi Arabic 1949, Sharaf al-Zamān Ṭāhir al-Marwazī, *Ṭabāʾiʿ al-ḥayawān.*
MS I.O. Islamic 617, selections from Ibn al-Faqīh, *Kitāb al-buldān*, and Idrīsī, *Nuzhat al-mushtāq.*
MS Or. 1494, Aḥmad b. Muḥammad al-Thaʿlabī, *ʿArāʾis al-majālis.*
MS Or. 1528/1, anon., *ʿAjāʾib al-makhlūqāt.*
MS Or. 2409, Ḥakīm Mahārat Khān al-Iṣfahānī, *Bahjat al-ʿālam.*
MS Or. 4895, Ibn Rusta, *Kitāb al-aʿlāq al-nafīsa.*
MS Or. 11676, Sadīd al-Dīn al-ʿAwfī, *Jawāmiʿ al-ḥikāyāt.*
MS Or. 13315, Ibn al-Qāṣṣ, *ʿAjāʾib al-samāwāt wa 'l-arḍ = Dalāʾil al-qibla.*

School of Oriental and African Studies, London
MS 372, Ibn al-Athīr al-Jazarī, *Tuḥfat al-ʿajāʾib.*

Primary Sources

ʿAbd al-Razzāq. *al-Muṣannaf.* Edited by Ḥabīb al-Raḥmān al-Aʿẓamī. Beirut: al-Maktab al-Islāmī, 1970–2.
———. *Tafsīr.* Edited by Maḥmūd Muḥammad ʿAbduh. Beirut: Dār al-Kutub al-ʿIlmiyya, 1999.
Abū 'l-Fidāʾ. *Taqwīm al-buldān.* Edited by Joseph Reinaud and William de Slane. Paris: Imprimerie nationale, 1840.
———. *Taqwīm al-buldān = Geographie d'AboulFéda.* Translated by Joseph Reinaud. Paris: Imprimerie nationale, 1848.
Abū Maʿshar. *Kitāb al-milal wa 'l-duwal = On Historical Astrology: The Book of Religions and Dynasties.* Edited and translated by Keiji Yamamoto and Charles Burnett. Leiden: Brill, 2000.
Abū Yaʿlā 'l-Mawṣilī. *Musnad.* Edited by Ḥusayn Salīm Asad. Damascus: Dār al-Maʾmūn liʾl-Turāth, 1984.
Akhbār al-Ṣīn wa 'l-Hind. Edited and translated by Jean Sauvaget. Paris: Les Belles Lettres, 1948.
Alfonso X. *La Primera crónica general de España.* Edited by Ramón Menéndez Pidal. Madrid: Gredos, 1955.

ʿAlī, Muṣṭafā b. Aḥmad. *Kunh al-akhbār.* Istanbul: n.p. 1861–9.

Aristotle. *Fann al-shiʿr: maʿ al-tarjuma al-ʿarabiyya al-qadīma wa shurūḥ al-Fārābī wa Ibn Sīnā wa Ibn Rushd.* Edited by ʿAbd al-Raḥmān Badawī. Cairo: Maktabat al-Nahḍa al-Miṣriyya, 1953.

———. *Kitāb Arisṭūṭālīs fī 'l-shiʿr.* Edited by Shukrī Muḥammad ʿAyyād. Cairo: Dār al-Kātib al-ʿArabī, 1967.

———. *Historia animalium = Ṭibāʿ al-ḥayawān.* Translated by Yūḥannā b. al-Baṭrīq and edited by ʿAbd al-Raḥmān Badawī. Kuwait: Wikālat al-Maṭbūʿāt, 1977.

———. *Historia animalium (Books VII–X).* Edited and translated by D. M. Balme. Cambridge: Harvard University Press, 1991.

Arrian of Nicomedia. *Alexandri anabasis.* Edited by A. G. Roos. Leipzig: Teubner, 1907.

Artemidorus. *Taʿbīr al-ruʾyā = Le livre des songes par Artémidore d'Éphèse, Traduit du grec en arabe, par Ḥunayn b. Isḥāq.* Edited by Toufic Fahd. Damascus: Institut français, 1964.

al-ʿAskarī, Abū Hilāl. *Kitāb al-ṣināʿatayn.* Edited by ʿAlī Muḥammad al-Bajāwī and Muḥammad Abū 'l-Faḍl Ibrāhīm. Cairo: ʿĪsā 'l-Bābī 'l-Ḥalabī, 1971.

al-Baghawī, al-Ḥusayn b. Masʿūd. *Maʿālim al-tanzīl.* Riyadh: Dār al-Ṭība, 2002.

al-Baghdādī, Abū Bakr al-Khaṭīb. *Taʾrīkh Baghdād aw Madīnat al-Salām.* Bashshār ʿAwwād Maʿrūf. Beirut: Dār al-Gharb al-Islāmī, 2001.

al-Baghdādī, Abū Manṣūr. *Kitāb uṣūl al-dīn.* Istanbul: Maṭbaʿat al-Dawla, 1928.

Bakrān, Muḥammad b. Najīb. *Jahān-nāma.* Edited by Muḥammad Amīn Riyāḥī. Tehran: Ibn Sīnā, 1963.

al-Bakrī, Abū ʿUbayd. *Muʿjam mā istaʿjam min asmāʾ al-bilād wa 'l-mawāḍiʿ.* Edited by Jamāl Ṭulba. Beirut: Dār al-Kutub al-ʿIlmiyya, 1998.

al-Balʿamī, Abū ʿAlī. *Tārīkh-nāma-i Ṭabarī.* Edited by Muḥammad Rawshan. Tehran: Surūsh, 1995–9.

al-Balawī, Abū Muḥammad. *Sīrat Ibn Ṭūlūn.* Edited by Muḥammad Kurd ʿAlī. Damascus: al-Maktaba al-ʿArabiyya, 1939.

al-Bilgrāmī, Allāh-yār ʿUthmān. *Ḥadīqāt al-aqālīm.* Lithograph edition. Lucknow: Newal Kishore Press, 1897.

al-Biqāʿī, Ibrāhīm b. ʿUmar. *Naẓm al-durar.* Hyderabad: Maṭbaʿat Majlis Dāʾirat al-Maʿārif al-ʿUthmāniyya, 1976–8.

al-Bīrūnī, Abū 'l-Rayḥān. *al-Āthār al-bāqiya ʿan al-qurūn al-khāliya.* Edited by Parwīz Adhkāʾī. Tehran: Mīrāth-i Maktūb, 2001.

———. *al-Āthār al-bāqiya ʿan al-qurūn al-khāliya = The Chronology of Ancient Nations.* Translated by Edward Sachau. London: W. H. Allen, 1879.

———. *Taḥdīd nihāyāt al-amākin.* Edited by Muḥammad b. Tāwīt al-Ṭanjī. Ankara: Doğus, 1962.

———. *Taḥdīd nihāyāt al-amākin = The Determination of the Coordinates of Positions for the Correction of Distances Between Cities.* Translated by Jamil Ali. Beirut: American University of Beirut, 1967.

———. *Taḥqīq mā li'l-Hind.* Beirut: ʿĀlam al-Kitāb, 1983.

———. *Taḥqīq mā li'l-Hind = Alberuni's India*. Translated by Edward C. Sachau. London: K. Paul, Trench, Trübner and Co., 1910.

al-Buḥturī, Abū ʿUbāda. *Dīwān*. Edited by Ḥasan Kāmil al-Ṣayrafī. Cairo: Dār al-Maʿārif, 1963–4.

al-Bukhārī, Muḥammad b. Ismāʿīl. See under *Mawsūʿat al-ḥadīth*.

Buzurg b. Shahriyār. *Kitāb ʿajāʾib al-Hind = Livre des Merveilles de l'Inde*. Edited by P. A. van der Lith. Translated by L. Marcel Devic. Leiden: Brill, 1883–6.

Callisthenes [pseud.]. *Ḥadīth Dhī 'l-Qarnayn = Un Texto árabe occidental de la leyenda de Alejandro*. Edited by Emilio García Gómez. Madrid: Instituto de Valencia de Don Juan, 1929.

———. *Historia de Dulcarnain*. Edited by F. Guillén Robles. *Leyendas de José hijo de Jacob y de Alejandro Magno*. Zaragoza: Impresa del Hospicio provincial, 1888.

———. *Iskandar-nāma*. Edited by Īraj Afshār. Tehran: Bungāh-i Tarjuma wa Nashr-i Kitāb, 1964.

———. *Iskandarnamah, A Persian Medieval Alexander-Romance*. Translated by Minoo Southgate. New York: Columbia University Press, 1978.

———. *The Life and Exploits of Alexander the Great: Being a Series of Translations of the Ethiopic Histories of Alexander*. Edited by Ernest Budge. London: C. J. Clay, 1896.

———. *Neṣḥānā d'Aleksandrōs*. In *The History of Alexander the Great: Being the Syriac version of the Pseudo-Callisthenes*. Edited by Ernest Budge. Cambridge: Cambridge University Press, 1889.

al-Damīrī, Muḥammad b. Mūsā. *Ḥayāt al-ḥayawān al-kubrā*. Cairo: Muṣṭafā 'l-Bābī 'l-Ḥalabī, 1956.

Darband-nāma. Edited by Mirza A. Kazem-Beg. St. Petersburg: Imperial Academy of Sciences, 1851.

al-Dhahabī, Muḥammad b. Aḥmad. *Taʾrīkh al-Islām wa wafayāt al-mashāhīr wa 'l-aʿlām*. Edited by ʿUmar ʿAbd al-Salām Tadmurī. Beirut: Dār al-Kitāb al-ʿArabī, 1987.

al-Dīnawarī, Abū Ḥanīfa. *Akhbār al-ṭiwāl*. Edited by ʿUmar Fārūq al-Ṭabbāʿ. Beirut: Dār al-Arqām, 1995.

al-Dīnawarī, Abū Saʿīd Naṣr b. Yaʿqūb. *Kitāb al-taʿbīr fī 'l-ruʾyā*. Edited by Fahmī Saʿd. Beirut: ʿĀlam al-Kutub, 1997.

Ephraem. *Des heiligen Ephraem des Syrers Sermones III*. Edited and translated by Edmund Beck. *CSCO* 320–1. Leuven: Secrétariat du CSCO, 1972.

Epiphanius, Saint, Bishop of Constantia. "De XII gemmis," *Opera*, edited by G. Dindorf. Vol. 4, 169–224. Leipzig: Weigel, 1862.

al-Farghānī, Muḥammad b. Kathīr. *Kitāb jawāmiʿ ʿilm al-nujūm*. Edited by Yavuz Unat. Cambridge: Harvard University Press, 1998.

al-Firdawsī, Abū 'l-Qāsim. *Shāh-nāma*. Edited by Jalāl Khāliqī Muṭlaq. New York: Bibliotheca Persica, 1988–2008.

Galen. *Galeni compendium Timaei Platonis*. In *Plato Arabus*, edited by Richard Walzer, et al. London: Warburg Institute, 1943–51.

al-Gardīzī, Abū Saʿīd. *Zayn al-akhbār*. Edited by ʿAbd al-Ḥayy Ḥabībī. Tehran: Bunyād-i Farhang-i Īrān, 1968.

Genoese World Map, 1457. Edited by Edward Stevenson. New York: DeVinne Press, 1912.

al-Gharnāṭī, Abū Ḥāmid. *Tuḥfat al-albāb*. Edited by Gabriel Ferrand. *Journal Asiatique* 207 (1925): 1–148, 193–304.

al-Ghazālī, Abū Ḥāmid. *al-Ḥikma fī makhlūqāt Allāh*. Edited by Muḥammad Rashīd Qabbānī. Beirut: Tawzīʿ Dār Iḥyāʾ al-ʿUlūm, 1978.

———. *Iḥyāʾ ʿulūm al-dīn*. Egypt: al-Maktabat al-Tijāriyya al-Kubrā, n.d.

al-Hamdānī, al-Ḥasan b. Aḥmad. *Kitāb al-iklīl min akhbār al-Yaman*. Edited by Muḥammad b. ʿAlī. Sanaa: Maktabat al-Irshād, 2008.

Ḥassān b. Thābit. *Dīwān*. Edited by Walīd ʿArafāt. Beirut: Dār Ṣādir, 1974.

Herbelot, Barthélemy d'. *Bibliothèque orientale, ou, Dictionaire universel*. Paris: Compagnie des Libraires, 1697.

Herodotus. *The Histories of Herodotus*. Edited and translated by A. D. Godley. New York: P. G. Putnam's Sons, 1921–4.

al-Ḥimyarī, Nashwān b. Saʿīd. *Mulūk Ḥimyar wa aqyāl al-Yaman*. Edited by ʿAlī b. Ismāʿīl al-Muʾayyad and Ismāʿīl b. Aḥmad al-Jarāfī. Cairo: Quṣayy Muḥibb al-Dīn al-Khaṭīb, 1975.

Ḥunayn b. Isḥāq. *Fī ḥifẓ al-asnān*. Edited by Muḥammad Fuʾād al-Dhākirī. Aleppo: Dār al-Qalam al-ʿArabī, 1996.

———. *Risālat Ḥunayn b. Isḥāq ilā ʿAlī b. Yaḥyā fī dhikr mā tarjama min kutub Jālīnūs*. Edited by Mahdī Muḥaqqiq. Tehran: Muʾassasa-i Muṭālaʿāt-i Islāmī, 2001.

Hyde, Thomas. *Epistola de mensuris et ponderibus serum seu sinensium*. Oxford: E. Theatro Sheldoniano, 1688.

Ibn ʿAbd al-Ḥakam. *Futūḥ Miṣr wa 'l-Maghrib*. Edited by Charles Torrey. New Haven: Yale University Press, 1922.

Ibn ʿAbd Rabbih. *al-ʿIqd al-farīd*. Edited by Mufīd Muḥammad Qumayḥa. Beirut: Dār al-Kutub al-ʿIlmiyya, 1987.

Ibn Abī 'l-Dunyā. *Kitāb al-manām*. Edited and translated by Leah Kinberg as *Morality in the Guise of Dreams*. Leiden: Brill, 1994.

Ibn Abī Uṣaybiʿa. *ʿUyūn al-anbāʾ fī ṭabaqāt al-aṭibbāʾ*. Edited by Nizār Riḍā. Beirut: Dār Maktabat al-Ḥayāh, 1965.

Ibn al-ʿAdīm. *Zubdat al-ḥalab min taʾrīkh Ḥalab*. Edited by Sāmī 'l-Dahhān. Damascus: Institut français, 1951–68.

Ibn al-ʿArabī. *al-Futūḥāt al-Makkiyya*. Edited by ʿUthmān Yaḥyā. Cairo: al-Hayʾa al-Miṣriyya al-ʿĀmma li'l-Kitāb, 1972–92.

Ibn Baṭṭūṭa. *Riḥla*. Beirut: Dār Ṣādir, 1960.

Ibn Bayṭār. *Tafsīr Kitāb Dīyāsqūrīdūs*. Edited by Ibrāhīm b. Murād. Beirut: Dār al-Gharb al-Islāmī, 1989.

Ibn Faḍlān, Aḥmad. *The Risalah of Ibn Fadlan*. Translated by James McKeithen. Ph.D. dissertation, Indiana University, 1979.

Ibn Ḥazm. *al-Faṣl fī 'l-milal wa 'l-awhā' wa 'l-niḥal*. Edited by Aḥmad Shams al-Dīn. Beirut: Dār al-Kutub al-ʿIlmiyya, 1999.

Ibn Hishām. *al-Sīra al-nabawiyya*. Edited by Ibrāhīm al-Ibyārī, Muṣṭafā 'l-Saqqā, and ʿAbd al-Ḥafīẓ Shabalī. Beirut: Dār al-Maʿrifa, 2006.

Ibn ʿIdhārī. *Kitāb al-bayān al-mughrib fī akhbār al-Andalus wa 'l-Maghrib*. Edited by G. S. Colin and E. Lévi-Provençal. Leiden: Brill, 1948–51.

Ibn Iyās. *Badāʾiʿ al-zuhūr fī waqāʾiʿ al-duhūr*. Edited by Muḥammad Muṣṭafā, et al. Istanbul: Maṭbaʿat al-Dawla, 1931.

Ibn al-Jawzī. *al-Muntaẓam fī taʾrīkh al-mulūk wa 'l-umam*. Edited by Muḥammad ʿAbd al-Qādir ʿAṭāʾ and Muṣṭafā ʿAbd al-Qādir ʿAṭāʾ. Beirut: Dār al-Kutub al-ʿIlmiyya, 1992–3.

———. *Tanwīr al-ghabash fī faḍl al-Sūdān wa 'l-Ḥabash*. Edited by Marzūq ʿAlī Ibrāhīm. Riyadh: Dār al-Sharīf, 1998.

Ibn Jinnī. *al-Khaṣāʾiṣ*. Edited by ʿAbd al-Ḥamīd Hindāwī. Beirut: Dār al-Kutub al-ʿIlmiyya, 2001.

Ibn al-Kalbī. *Jamharat al-nasab*. Edited by Nājī Ḥasan. Beirut: ʿĀlam al-Kutub, 1986.

Ibn Kathīr. *al-Bidāya wa 'l-nihāya*. Edited by Aḥmad ʿAbd al-Wahhāb Futayḥ. Cairo: Dār al-Ḥadīth, 1992.

———. *Tafsīr al-Qurʾān al-ʿaẓīm*. Edited by Sāmī b. Muḥammad al-Salāma. Riyadh: Dār Ṭība li'l-Nashr wa 'l-Tawzīʿ, 1999.

Ibn Khaldūn. *Kitāb al-ʿibar*. Edited by Yūsuf Asʿad Dāghir. Beirut: Dār al-Kitāb al-Lubnānī, 1961.

———. *Kitāb al-ʿibar = The Muqaddimah: An Introduction to History* (abridged). Edited by N. J. Dawood. Translated by Franz Rosenthal. Princeton: Princeton University Press, 1967.

Ibn Māja. See under *Mawsūʿat al-ḥadīth*.

Ibn Mākūlā. *al-Ikmāl fī rafʿ al-irtiyāb*. Edited by ʿAbd al-Raḥmān b. Yaḥyā 'l-Muʿallimī. Cairo: Dār al-Kitāb al-Islāmī, 1962–7.

Ibn al-Munādī. *al-Malāḥim*. Edited by ʿAbd al-Karīm al-ʿUqaylī. Qom: Dār al-Sīra, 1998.

Ibn al-Muʿtazz. *Ṭabaqāt al-shuʿarāʾ*. Edited by ʿAbd al-Sattār Aḥmad Farrāj. Egypt: Dār al-Maʿārif, 1956.

Ibn Najjār. *Dhayl Taʾrīkh Baghdād*. Hyderabad: Dāʾirat al-Maʿārif al-ʿUthmāniyya, 1978–86.

Ibn al-Qāṣṣ. "Kitāb dalāʾil al-qibla." Facs. edition, Fuat Sezgin. *ZGAIW* 4 (1987–8): 7–81 (Arabic section) and *ZGAIW* 5 (1989): 1–45 (Arabic section).

Ibn al-Qifṭī, ʿAlī b. Yūsuf. *Taʾrīkh al-ḥukamāʾ*. Edited by Julius Lippert. Leipzig: Dieterich'sche Verlagsbuchhandlung, 1903.

Ibn Qutayba. *Faḍl al-ʿArab wa 'l-tanbīh ʿalā ʿulūmihā*. Edited by Walīd Maḥmūd Khāliṣ. Abu Dhabi: al-Mujammaʿ al-Thaqāfī, 1998.

———. *Kitāb al-maʿārif*. Edited by Saroite Okacha. Cairo: Dār al-Kutub, 1960.

———. *Kitāb taʿbīr al-ruʾyā*. Edited by Ibrāhīm Ṣāliḥ. Damascus: Dār al-Bashāʾir, 2001.

Ibn al-Rūmī. *Dīwān*. Edited by Aḥmad Ḥasan Basaj. Beirut: Dār al-Kutub al-ʿIlmiyya, 1994.

Ibn Rusta. *Les atours précieux: par Ibn Rusteh*. Translated by Gaston Wiet. Cairo: Publications de la Société de géographie d'Égypte, 1955.

Ibn Saʿd. *al-Ṭabaqāt al-kubrā*. Beirut: Dār Ṣādir, 1957–8.

Ibn Ṣāʿid. *Ṭabaqāt al-umam*. Edited by Ḥusayn Muʾnis. Cairo: Dār al-Maʿārif, 1998.

Ibn Sayyār al-Warrāq. *Kitāb al-ṭabīkh = Annals of the Caliph's Kitchens*. Translated by Nawal Nasrallah. Leiden: Brill, 2007.

Ibn Sīrīn [pseud.]. *Tafsīr al-aḥlām al-kabīr*. Edited by Muḥammad al-Muʿtaṣim biʾllāh al-Baghdādī. Tripoli, Lebanon: Dār al-Īmān, 1998.

Ibn Taghrībirdī. *al-Nujūm al-zāhira fī mulūk Miṣr wa ʾl-Qāhira*. Cairo: al-Muʾassasa al-Miṣriyya al-ʿĀmma, 1963.

Ibn al-Wardī. *Abulfedae Tabula Syriae*. Translated by Johann Bernhard Koehler. Leipzig: Litteris Schoenermarkii, 1766.

———. *Kharīdat al-ʿajāʾib wa farīdat al-gharāʾib*. Edited by Maḥmūd Fākhūrī. Beirut: Dār al-Sharq al-ʿArabī, 1991.

al-Ibshīhī, Muḥammad b. Aḥmad. *al-Mustaṭraf fī kull fann mustaẓraf*. Edited by Darwīsh al-Juwaydī. Sidon, Lebanon: al-Maktaba al-ʿAṣriyya, 1996.

al-Idrīsī, Abū ʿAbd Allāh. *Fī jughrāfiyā ʾl-kulliyya = De geographia universali*. Rome: In Typographia Medicea, 1592.

———. *Geographia Nubiensis*. Translated by Gabriel Sionita and Joannes Hersonita. Paris: H. Blageart, 1619.

al-Idrīsī, Abū Jaʿfar. *Kitāb anwār ʿulwiyy al-ajrām fī ʾl-kashf ʿan asrār al-ahrām*. Edited by Ulrich Haarmann. Beirut: Franz Steiner, 1991.

Ikhwān al-Ṣafāʾ. *Rasāʾil*. Beirut: Dār Ṣādir, 1957.

Īliyā b. Shīnā. *Kitāb al-majālis*. Edited by Louis Cheikho. *al-Mashriq* 20 (1922): 33–44, 112–22, 267–82, 366–77.

al-Iṣfahānī, Abū ʾl-Faraj. *Kitāb adab al-ghurabāʾ*. Edited by Ṣalāh al-Dīn al-Munajjid. Beirut: Dār al-Kitāb al-Jadīd, 1972.

al-Iṣfahānī, Abū ʾl-Shaykh. *Kitāb al-ʿaẓama*. Edited by Muḥammad Fāris. Beirut: Dār al-Kutub al-ʿIlmiyya, 1994.

al-Iṣfahānī, Ḥamza b. al-Ḥasan. *Taʾrīkh sinī mulūk al-arḍ*. Beirut: Dār Maktabat al-Ḥayāh, 1961.

Jacob of Sarug [pseud.]. "Das syrische Alexanderlied." Edited by Carl Hunnius. *Zeitschrift der Deutschen Morgenländischen Gesellschaft* 60 (1906): 169–209, 558–89.

———. *Das syrische Alexanderlied: die drei Rezensionen*. Edited and translated by G. J. Reinink. *CSCO* 454–5. Leuven: Peeters, 1983.

al-Jāḥiẓ, Abū ʿUthmān. *Kitāb al-tabaṣṣur biʾl-tijāra*. Edited by ʿAbd al-Wahhāb al-Tanūsī. Cairo: al-Maṭbaʿa al-Raḥmāniyya, 1935.

———. *Kitāb al-tarbīʿ wa ʾl-tadwīr*. Edited by Charles Pellat. Damascus: Institut français, 1955.

——. *Majmūʿ rasāʾil al-Jāḥiẓ*. Edited by Paul Kraus and Muḥammad Ṭāhā 'l-Ḥājirī. Cairo: Lajnat al-Taʾlīf wa 'l-Tarjuma wa 'l-Nashr, 1943.

——. *Rasāʾil al-Jāḥiẓ*. Edited by ʿAbd al-Salām Muḥammad Hārūn. Egypt: Maktabat al-Khānjī, 1964–79.

al-Jāḥiẓ, Abū ʿUthmān [pseud.]. *al-ʿIbar wa 'l-iʿtibār*. Edited by Ṣābir Idrīs. Cairo: Maṭbaʿat al-Nīl, n.d.

al-Jahshiyārī, Abū ʿAbd Allāh. *Kitāb al-wuzarāʾ wa 'l-kuttāb*. Edited by Ibrāhīm al-Ibyārī and Muṣṭafā 'l-Saqqā. Cairo: Muṣṭafā 'l-Bābī 'l-Ḥalabī, 1938.

Josephus, Flavius. *Opera*. Edited and translated by Henry St. John Thackeray, et al. Cambridge: Harvard University Press, 1926–65.

Jūzjānī, Minhāj al-Dīn. *Ṭabāqāt-i Nāṣirī*. Edited by ʿAbd al-Ḥayy Ḥabībī. Tehran: Dunyā-i Kitāb, 1983–4.

al-Kāshgharī, Maḥmūd. *Dīwān lughāt al-Turk*. Edited by Aḥmad Rifʿat b. ʿAbd al-Karīm. Istanbul: Dār al-Khilāfa al-ʿAliyya, 1915–7.

——. *Dīwān lughāt al-Turk = Compendium of the Turkic Dialects*. Translated by Robert Dankoff and James Kelly. Duxbury, MA: Harvard University Printing Office, 1982–5.

al-Khwārazmī, Abū 'l-Ghāzī Bahādur Khān. *A General History of the Turks, Moguls and Tatars*. London: Knapton, 1729–30.

——. *Histoire genéalogique des Tatars*. Translated by Bentinck. Leiden: A. Kallewier, 1726.

——. *Shajara-i Turk*. Edited by Jean Desmaisons. St. Petersburg: Imprimerie de l'Académie Impériale des sciences, 1871–4.

al-Khwārazmī, Muḥammad b. Mūsā. *Kitāb ṣūrat al-arḍ*. Edited by Hans von Mžik. Leipzig: Harrassowitz, 1926.

al-Maʿarrī, Abū 'l-ʿAlāʾ. *Risālat al-ghufrān*. Edited by Muḥammad al-Iskandarānī and Inʿām Fawwāl. Beirut: Dār al-Kitāb al-ʿArabī, 2001.

al-Maghribī, Ibn Saʿīd. *Kitāb al-jughrāfiyā*. Edited by Ismāʿīl al-ʿArabī. Beirut: Manshūrāt al-Maktab al-Tijārī li'l-Ṭibāʿa wa 'l-Nashr wa 'l-Tawzīʿ, 1970.

Majmūʿ fī 'l-jughrāfiyā. Facs. edition, Fuat Sezgin. Frankfurt am Main: J. W. Goethe University, 1987.

Maʿmarī, Abū Manṣūr. *Shāh-nāma*. "Muqaddima-i qadīm-i *Shāh-nāma*." Edited by M. Qazwīnī in *Hazāra-i Firdawsī*, pp. 151–76. Tehran: Dunyā-i Kitāb, 1983–4.

al-Maqdisī, Muṭahhar b. Ṭāhir. *Kitāb al-badʾ wa 'l-taʾrīkh*. Edited by Clément Huart. Paris: Leroux, 1899–1919.

al-Maqrīzī, Taqī 'l-Dīn. *al-Mawāʿiẓ wa 'l-iʿtibār bi-dhikr al-khiṭaṭ wa 'l-āthār*. Edited by Muḥammad Zaynahum and Madīḥa al-Sharqāwī. Cairo: al-Maktabat Madbūlī, 1998.

al-Marwazī, Sharaf al-Zamān Ṭāhir. *Ṭabāʾiʿ al-ḥayawān = Sharaf al-Zamān Ṭāhir Marvazī on China, the Turks, and India; Arabic text (circa A.D. 1120)*. Edited and translated by Vladimir Minorsky. London: Royal Asiatic Society, 1942.

al-Marzubānī, Abū ʿUbayd Allāh. *Nūr al-qabas al-mukhtaṣar min al-Muqtabas*. Edited by Rudolf Sellheim. Wiesbaden: Franz Steiner, 1964.

al-Masʿūdī, Abū ʻl-Ḥasan [pseud.]. *Akhbār al-zamān*. Beirut: Dār al-Andalus liʻl-Ṭibāʿa wa ʻl-Nashr, 1966.

Mawsūʿat al-ḥadīth al-sharīf: Jamʿ jawāmiʿ al-aḥādīth wa ʻl-asānīd. Vaduz: Jamʿiyyat al-Maknaz al-Islāmī, 2000–1.

Methodius [pseud.]. *Die syrische Apokalypse*. Edited and translated by G. J. Reinink. *CSCO* 540–1. Leuven: Peeters, 1993.

Mīr Ḳhwānd, Muḥammad b. Khāwandshāh. *Tārīkh-i rawḍat al-ṣafāʾ*. Tehran: Markazī-i Khayyām Pīrūz, 1960.

al-Muhallabī, Ḥasan b. Aḥmad. *al-Masālik wa ʻl-mamālik*. Edited by Taysīr Khalaf. Damascus: al-Takwīn liʻl-Ṭibāʿa, 2006.

Mujmal al-tawārīkh wa ʻl-qiṣaṣ. Edited by Bahār Muḥammad Taqī and Muḥammad Ramaḍānī. Tehran: Muʾassasa-i Khāwar, 1939.

Muqātil b. Sulaymān. *Tafsīr*. Edited by Aḥmad Farīd. Beirut: Dār al-Kutub al-ʿIlmiyya, 2003.

Muslim b. al-Ḥajjāj. See under *Mawsūʿat al-ḥadīth*.

al-Mustawfī, Ḥamd Allāh. *Nuzhat al-qulūb*. Edited and translated by Guy Le Strange. Leiden: Brill 1915–19.

al-Nahrawānī, Muʿāfā b. Zakariyyāʾ. *al-Jalīs al-ṣāliḥ al-kāfī*. Edited by Iḥsān ʿAbbās and Muḥammad Mursī Khawlī. Beirut: ʿĀlam al-Kutub, 1981–93.

al-Nīsābūrī, Niẓām al-Dīn. *Tafsīr gharāʾib al-Qurʾān*. Edited by Zakariyyāʾ ʿUmayrāt. Beirut: Dār al-Kutub al-ʿIlmiyya, 1996.

al-Nuwayrī, Aḥmad b. ʿAbd al-Wahhāb. *Nihāyat al-arab fī funūn al-adab*. Cairo: Dār al-Kutub al-Miṣriyya, 1923.

Nykl, Alois Richard. *Compendium of Aljamiado Literature*. Paris: Protat, 1929.

Polo, Marco. *Le devisement du monde*. Edited by A. C. Moule and Paul Pelliot. Paris: La Découverte, 1998.

Ptolemy. *Geographia*. Edited by Karl Friedrich August Nobbe. Leipzig: Sumptibus et typis Caroli Tauchnitii, 1843.

———. *Ptolemy's Geography: An Annotated Translation of the Theoretical Chapters*. Translated by J. Lennart Berggren and Alexander Jones. Princeton: Princeton University Press, 2000.

———. *Tetrabiblos*. Edited and translated by F. E. Robbins. Cambridge: Harvard University Press, 1940.

al-Qalqashandī, Aḥmad b. ʿAlī. *Ṣubḥ al-aʿshā fī ṣināʿat al-inshāʾ*. Cairo: al-Muʾassasa al-Miṣriyya al-ʿĀmma, n.d.

al-Qaramānī, Aḥmad b. Yūsuf. *Akhbār al-duwal*. Edited by Fahmī Saʿd and Aḥmad Ḥuṭayṭ. Beirut: ʿĀlam al-Kutub, 1992.

al-Rabghūzī, Nāṣir al-Dīn. *Qiṣaṣ al-anbiyāʾ, An Eastern Turkish Version*. Edited and translated by H. E. Boeschoten, J. O'Kane, and M. Van Damme. Leiden: Brill, 1995.

Rashīd al-Dīn, Abū ʻl-Khayr. *Jāmiʿ al-tawārīkh*. Edited by Bahman Karīmī. Tehran: Iqbāl, 1959.

al-Rāzī, Amīn Aḥmad. *Haft iqlīm*. Edited by Jawād Fāḍil. Tehran: Kitāb-furūshī-i Adabiyya, 1960.
al-Rāzī, Fakhr al-Dīn. *al-Tafsīr al-kabīr*. Beirut: Dār al-Fikr, 1981–3.
Riḍā, Muḥammad Rashīd. *Fatāwā*. Edited by Ṣalāḥ al-Dīn al-Munajjid and Yūsuf Khūrī. Beirut: Dār al-Kitāb al-Jadīd, 1970.
al-Ṣafadī, Khalīl b. Aybak. *Kitāb al-wāfī biʾl-wafayāt*. Edited by Aḥmad al-Arnāʾūṭ and Turkī Muṣṭafā. Beirut: Dār Iḥyāʾ al-Turāth al-ʿArabī, 2000.
Šahrestānīhā-ī Ērānšahr, A Middle Persian Text on Late Antique Geography, Epic, and History. Edited and translated by Touraj Daryaee. Costa Mesa, CA: Mazda, 2002.
al-Samʿānī, ʿAbd al-Karīm. *Kitāb al-ansāb*. Edited by Muḥammad ʿAbd al-Qādir ʿAṭāʾ. Beirut: Dār al-Kutub al-ʿIlmiyya, 1998.
Sanson, Nicolas. *Cartes générales de toutes les parties du monde*. Paris: P. Mariette, 1658.
al-Shāfiʿī, Muḥammad b. Idrīs. *Risāla = Islamic jurisprudence, Shāfiʿī's Risāla*. Translated by Majid Khadduri. Baltimore: Johns Hopkins Press, 1961.
Shahmardān b. Abī ʾl-Khayr. *Nuzhat-nāma-i ʿAlāʾī*. Edited by Farhang Jahānpūr. Tehran: Muʾassasa-i Muṭālaʿāt wa Taḥqīqāt-i Farhangī, 1983–4.
al-Shaybānī, Muḥammad b. al-Ḥasan. *Kitāb al-siyar*. Edited by Majid Khadduri. Beirut: Dār al-Muttaḥida liʾl-Nashr, 1975.
———. *The Islamic Law of Nations*. Translated by Majid Khadduri. Baltimore: Johns Hopkins Press, 1966.
Sibṭ Ibn al-Jawzī. *Mirʾāt al-zamān fī taʾrīkh al-aʿyān*. Beirut: Dār al-Shurūq, 1985.
al-Sijistānī, Abū Dāwūd. See under *Mawsūʿat al-ḥadīth*.
Strabo. *Geographica*. Edited by Augustus Meineke. Leipzig: Teubner, 1877–98.
al-Subkī, Taqī ʾl-Dīn. *Ṭabaqāt al-shāfiʿiyya al-kubrā*. Edited by ʿAbd al-Fattāḥ Muḥammad al-Ḥilw and Maḥmūd Muḥammad al-Ṭanāḥī. Cairo: ʿĪsā ʾl-Bābī ʾl-Ḥalabī, 1964–76.
al-Suyūṭī, Jalāl al-Dīn. *Taʾrīkh al-khulafāʾ*. Beirut: Dār al-Turāth, 1969.
Syriac Apocalypse of Daniel. Edited and translated by Matthias Henze. Tübingen: Mohr Siebeck, 2001.
al-Ṭabarī, Abū Jaʿfar Muḥammad b. Jarīr. *The History of al-Ṭabarī*. Vol. 14: *The Conquest of Iran*. Translated by Gerald Rex Smith. Albany: State University of New York Press, 1994.
———. *The History of al-Ṭabarī*. Vol. 34: *The Incipient Decline*. Translated by Joel Kraemer. Albany: State University of New York Press, 1989.
al-Ṭabarī, ʿAlī b. Sahl Rabbān. *Firdaws al-ḥikma fī ʾl-ṭibb*. Edited by Muḥammad Zubayr al-Ṣiddīqī. Berlin: Sonne, 1928.
al-Tawḥīdī, Abū Ḥayyān. *Kitāb al-imtāʿ wa ʾl-muʾānasa*. Edited by Aḥmad al-Zayn and Aḥmad Amīn. Beirut: al-Maktabat al-ʿAṣriyya, 1953.
al-Thaʿālibī, ʿAbd al-Malik. *Laṭāʾif al-maʿārif*. Edited by Ibrāhīm al-Abyārī and Ḥasan Kāmil al-Ṣayrafī. Cairo: Dār Iḥyāʾ al-Kutub al-ʿArabiyya, 1960.
al-Thaʿlabī, Aḥmad b. Muḥammad. *ʿArāʾis al-majālis fī qiṣaṣ al-anbiyāʾ*. Cairo: al-Maktaba al-ʿAlāmiyya, 1929.

——. *ʿArāʾis al-majālis fī qiṣaṣ al-anbiyāʾ = Lives of the Prophets*. Translated by William M. Brinner. Leiden: Brill, 2002.
——. *al-Kashf wa 'l-bayān*. Edited by Abū Muḥammad b. ʿĀshūr. Beirut: Dār Iḥyāʾ al-Turāth al-ʿArabī, 2002.
al-Tirmidhī, Abū ʿĪsā. See under *Mawsūʿat al-ḥadīth*.
al-Ṭūsī, Muḥammad b. Maḥmūd. *ʿAjāʾib-nāma*. Edited by Manūchir Sutūda. Tehran: Nashr-i Kitāb, 1966.
al-ʿUmarī, Ibn Faḍl Allāh. *Masālik al-abṣār*. Edited by Kāmil Salmān al-Jubūrī. Beirut: Dār al-Kutub al-ʿIlmiyya, 2010.
Voltaire, *Correspondence*. Edited by Theodore Besterman. Geneva: Institut et musée Voltaire, 1953–65.
Ximénez de Rada, Rodrigo. *Historia de rebus hispanie*. Edited by Juan Fernández Valverde. Turnhout, Belgium: Brepols, 1987.
al-Zabīdī, Murtaḍā. *Tāj al-ʿarūs min jawāhir al-qāmūs*. Edited by ʿAlī Shīrī. Beirut: Dār al-Fikr, 1994.
Zand-Ākāsīh, Iranian or Greater Bundahisn. Translated by Behramgore T. Anklesaria. Bombay: Rahnumae Mazdayasnan Sabha, 1956.
al-Zarkashī, Muḥammad b. Bahādur. *al-Burhān fī ʿulūm al-Qurʾān*. Edited by Muḥammad Abū 'l-Faḍl Ibrāhīm. Cairo: Dār Iḥyāʾ al-Kutub al-ʿArabiyya, 1957.
al-Zayyānī, Abū 'l-Qāsim b. Aḥmad. *al-Tarjumāna al-kubrā*. Edited by ʿAbd al-Karīm al-Fīlālī. Rabat: Wizārat al-Anbāʾ, 1967.
al-Zayyāt, Isḥāq b. al-Ḥasan. *Dhikr al-aqālīm*. Edited by Francisco Castelló. Barcelona: CSIC, 1989.

Secondary Literature

Abbott, Nabia. *Studies in Arabic Literary Papyri*. Chicago: University of Chicago Press, 1957–72.
Ahmad, Sayyid Maqbul. *A History of Arab-Islamic Geography*. Amman: al-Bayt University, 1995.
Alemany, Agustí. *Sources on the Alans: A Critical Compilation*. Leiden: Brill, 2000.
Al-Alwan, Muna. "The Orient 'Made Oriental': A Study of William Beckford's *Vathek*." *Arab Studies Quarterly* 30 (2008): 43–52.
Anderson, Andrew Runni. "Alexander at the Caspian Gates." *Transactions and Proceedings of the American Philological Association* 59 (1928): 130–63.
——. *Alexander's Gate, Gog and Magog, and the Enclosed Nations*. Cambridge: Mediaeval Academy of America, 1932.
——. "Alexander's Horns." *Transactions and Proceedings of the American Philological Association* 58 (1927): 100–22.
——. "The Arabic History of Dulcarnain and the Ethiopian History of Alexander." *Speculum: A Journal of Medieval Studies* 6 (1931): 434–45.
Arberry, A. J. *Classical Persian Literature*. London: G. Allen and Unwin, 1958.
Arkoun, Mohammed. "Peut-on parler de merveilleux dans le Coran?" *L'Etrange et le merveilleux dans l'islam médiéval*. Edited by Mohammed Arkoun, et al.,

1–24. Paris: Editions J. A., 1978.
Ashtor, Eliyahu. *A Social and Economic History of the Near East in the Middle Ages.* London: Collins, 1976.
Badiee, Julie Anne Oeming. "An Islamic Cosmography: The Illustrations of the Sarre Qazwīnī." Ph.D. dissertation. University of Michigan, Ann Arbor, 1978.
Bailey, H. W. *Indo-Scythian Studies, Being Khotanese Texts.* Cambridge: Cambridge University Press, 1985.
———. "The Staël-Holstein Miscellany." *Asia Major* 2 (1951): 1–45.
Baron, Salo Wittmayer. *Social and Religious History of the Jews.* New York: Columbia University Press, 1952–83.
Barthold, V. V. *Four Studies on the History of Central Asia.* Translated by Vladimir and Tatiana Minorsky. Leiden: Brill, 1956.
———. *Zwölf Vorlesungen über die Geschichte der Türken Mittelasiens.* Berlin: Deutsche Gesellschaft für Islamkunde, 1935.
Basset, René. *Mille et un contes, récits et légendes arabes.* Paris: Maisonneuve Frères, 1924.
Bayer, T. S. "De Muro Caucaseo." *Commentarii Academiae Scientiarum Imperialis Petropolitanae* 1 (1726): 425–63.
Beckwith, Christopher. *The Tibetan Empire in Central Asia.* Princeton: Princeton University Press, 1987.
Bendefy, László. *Szallam tolmács küldetése Nagy Sándor falához (Góg és Magóg fala).* Budapest: Szentföldi Ferencrendi Zárda, 1941.
Beveridge, H. "The Garden of Climes." *Asiatic Quarterly Review* (January 1900): 145–62.
Biran, Michal. *The Empire of the Qara Khitai in Eurasian History.* Cambridge: Cambridge University Press, 2005.
Blair, Sheila. *The Monumental Inscriptions from Early Islamic Iran and Transoxiana.* Leiden: Brill, 1992.
Bonebakker, Seeger. "*Nihil Obstat* in Storytelling?" In *The Thousand and One Nights in Arabic Literature and Society*, edited by Richard Hovannisian and Georges Sabagh, 56–77. Cambridge: Cambridge University Press, 1997.
———. "Some Medieval Views on Fantastic Stories." *Quaderni di studi arabi* 10 (1992): 21–42.
Bosworth, Clifford Edmund. *The Mediaeval Islamic Underworld: The Bānū Sāsān in Arabic Society.* Leiden: Brill, 1976.
———. "The Persian Impact on Arabic Literature." In *The Cambridge History of Arabic Literature.* Vol 1: *Arabic Literature to the End of the Umayyad Period*, edited by A. F. L. Beeston et al., 483–96. Cambridge: Cambridge University Press, 1983.
Boustany, Said. *Ibn ar-Rūmī: sa vie et son œuvre.* Beirut: Publications de l'Université Libanaise, 1967.
Bouvat, Lucien. *Les Barmécides d'après les historiens arabes et persans.* Paris: E. Leroux, 1912.

Bovill, E. W. "The Silent Trade of Wangara." *Journal of the Royal African Society* 29 (1929): 27–38.
Boyle, John. "The Alexander Legend in Central Asia." *Folklore* 85 (1974): 217–28.
———. "Alexander and the Mongols." *JRAS* 2 (1979): 123–36.
Brady, John. *Varieties of Literature*. London: G. B. Whittaker, 1826.
Brauer, Ralph. "Boundaries and Frontiers in Medieval Muslim Geography." *Transactions of the American Philosophical Society* 85, no. 6 (1995): 1–73.
Brockelmann, Carl. *Lexicon Syriacum*. Berlin: Reuther & Reichard, 1895.
Brunner, Christopher. "Geographical and Administrative Divisions: Settlements and Economy." In *The Cambridge History of Iran*, edited by Ehsan Yar-Shater. Vol. 3, part 2, *The Seleucid, Parthian and Sasanid Periods*, 747–77. Cambridge: University of Cambridge Press, 1983.
Buell, Paul. "The Role of the Sino-Mongolian Frontier Zone in the Rise of Chinggis-Qan." *Studies on Mongolia*. Bellingham: Western Washington University, 1979.
Bulgakov, Pavel Georgievich. "'*Kniga putei i gosudarstv*' Ibn Xordāḏbeha (K izucheniiu i datirovke redaktsii)." *Palestinskii Sbornik*, vol. 66 = vol. 3 (1958), 127–36.
Bulliet, Richard. *Conversion to Islam in the Medieval Period: An Essay in Quantitative History*. Cambridge: Harvard University Press, 1979.
Burton, Richard, trans. *The Book of the Thousand Nights and a Night*. Benares: Kamashastra Society, 1885–6.
Bynum, Caroline Walker. "Wonder." *American Historical Review* 102 (1997): 1–26.
Canard, Marius. *Histoire de la dynastie des H'amdanides de Jazîra et de Syrie*. Paris: Presses universitaires de France, 1953.
Carter, Michael. "The Kātib in Fact and Fiction." *Abr-Nahrain* 11 (1971): 42–55.
A Catalogue of the Provincial Capitals of Ērānshahr. Edited by Giuseppe Messina with commentary by Josef Marquart. Rome: Pontificio Istituto Biblico, 1931.
Cereti, Carlo. "Middle Persian Geographical Literature." In *Contributions à l'histoire et la géographie historique de l'empire sassanide*, edited by Rika Gyselen, 11–36. Leuven: Peeters, 2004.
Chang, Sen-Dou. "Some Observations on the Morphology of Chinese Walled Cities." *Annals of the Association of American Geographers* 60 (1970): 63–91.
Ciancaglini, Claudia. "The Syriac Version of the Alexander *Romance*." *Le Muséon* 114 (2001): 120–40.
Clayton, Peter, and Martin Price, eds. *The Seven Wonders of the Ancient World*. London: Routledge, 1989.
Cook, Albert S. "Ibn Fadlān's Account of Scandinavian Merchants on the Volga in 922." *Journal of English and Germanic Philology* 22 (1923): 54–63.
Cook, David. *Studies in Muslim Apocalyptic*. Princeton: Darwin Press, 2002.
Cook, Michael. "Pharaonic History in Medieval Egypt." *Studia Islamica* 57 (1983): 67–103.
Cooperson, Michael. "Al-Maʾmūn, the Pyramids, and the Hieroglyphs." In *ʿAbbāsid Studies II. Occasional Papers of the School of ʿAbbāsid Studies,* edited by John Nawas. Leuven: Peeters, forthcoming.

———. "Probability, Plausibility, and 'Spiritual Communication' in Classical Arabic Biography." In *On Fiction and Adab in Medieval Arabic Literature*, edited by Philip Kennedy, 69–71. Wiesbaden: Harrassowitz, 2005.

Crone, Patricia. *Slaves on Horses: The Evolution of the Islamic Polity*. Cambridge: Cambridge University Press, 1980.

Crone, Patricia, and Martin Hinds. *God's Caliph: Religious Authority in the First Centuries of Islam*. Cambridge: Cambridge University Press, 1986.

Czeglédy, Károly. "The Syriac Legend Concerning Alexander the Great." *AOASH* 7 (1957): 231–49.

Daston, Lorraine, and Katharine Park. *Wonders and the Order of Nature, 1150–1750*. New York: Zone Books, 1998.

Delitzsch, Frederic. *The Hebrew Language Viewed in the Light of Assyrian Research*. London: Williams and Norgate, 1883.

Demiéville, Paul. *Le concile de Lhasa*. Paris: Imprimerie nationale, 1952.

Dennett, Daniel Clement. *Conversion and the Poll Tax in Early Islam*. Cambridge: Harvard University Press, 1950.

Dew, Nicholas. "The Order of Oriental Knowledge: The Making of d'Herbelot's *Bibliothèque Orientale*." In *Debating World Literature*, edited by Christopher Prendergast, 233–52. London: Verso, 2004.

Doerfer, Gerhard. *Türkische und mongolische Elemente im Neupersischen*. Wiesbaden: F. Steiner, 1963–75.

Donkin, R. A. *Dragon's Brain Perfume: An Historical Geography of Camphor.* Leiden: Brill, 1999.

Doufikar-Aerts, Faustina. "Alexander the Flexible Friend, Some Reflections on the Representation of Alexander the Great in the Arabic Alexander Romance." *Journal of Eastern Christian Studies* 55 (2002): 195–210.

———. "Alexander Magnus Arabicus, Zeven eeuwen Arabische Alexandertraditie." Ph.D. dissertation. Leiden University, 2003.

———. "*Sīrat al-Iskandar*: An Arabic Popular Romance of Alexander." *Oriente Moderno* 22 (2003): 505–20.

Drompp, Michael. *Tang China and the Collapse of the Uighur Empire*. Leiden: Brill, 2005.

Drory, Rina. *Models and Contacts: Arabic Literature and Its Impact on Medieval Jewish Culture*. Leiden: Brill, 2000.

Dubler, César E. *Abū Ḥāmid el Granadino y su relación de viaje por tierras eurasiáticas*. Madrid: Editorial Maestre, 1953.

Dunbar, James. *Essays on the History of Mankind in Rude and Cultivated Ages*. London: W. Strahan, 1780.

Dunlop, D. M. *Arab Civilization to A.D. 1500*. London: Longman, 1971.

———. *The History of the Jewish Khazars*. Princeton: Princeton University Press, 1954.

———. "Muḥammad b. Mūsā al-Khwārizmī." *JRAS* (1943): 248–50.

Dunlop, John. *The History of Fiction*. London: Longman, 1814.

Fahd, Toufic. *La divination arabe*. Leiden: Brill, 1966.

———. "The Dream in Medieval Islamic Society." In *The Dream and Human Societies*, edited by G. E. von Grunebaum and Roger Caillois, 351–363. Berkeley: University of California Press, 1966.

Fairholt, Frederick. *Gog and Magog: The Giants in Guildhall, Their Real and Legendary History*. London: J. C. Hotten, 1859.

Fodor, A. "The Origins of the Arabic legends of the Pyramids." *AOASH* 23 (1970): 335–63.

Foucault, Michel. *The Order of Things: An Archaeology of the Human Sciences*. New York: Vintage Books, 1994.

Fowden, Garth. *Quṣayr ʿAmra, Art and the Umayyad Elite in Late Antique Syria*. Berkeley: University of California Press, 2004.

Frazer, J. G. "The Killing of the Khazar Kings." *Folklore* 28 (1917): 382–407.

Freedman, Paul. "The Medieval Other: The Middle Ages as Other." In *Marvels, Monsters, and Miracles: Studies in the Medieval and Early Modern Imaginations*, edited by Timothy Jones and David Sprunger, 1–24. Kalamazoo, MI: Medieval Institute Publications, 2002.

Friedländer, Israel. *Die Chadhirlegende und der Alexanderroman*. Leipzig: Teubner, 1913.

Friedman, John. *The Monstrous Races in Medieval Art and Thought*. Cambridge: Harvard University Press, 1981.

Frye, Richard. *The History of Ancient Iran*. München: Beck, 1984.

———. "Two Iranian Notes." In *Papers in Honour of Professor Mary Boyce*, edited by Jacques Duchesne-Guillemin and Pierre Lecoq, 185–90. Leiden: Brill, 1985.

Gaudefroy-Demombynes, Maurice. *Le pèlerinage à la Mekke, étude d'histoire religieuse*. Paris: P. Geuthner, 1923.

Geary, Patrick. *Furta Sacra: Thefts of Relics in the Central Middle Ages*. Princeton: Princeton University Press, 1978.

Geertz, Clifford. *The Interpretation of Cultures: Selected Essays*. New York: Basic Books, 1973.

Gibb, H. A. R. "Chinese Records of the Arabs in Central Asia." *BSOS* 2 (1923): 613–22.

Gibbon, Edward. *The History of the Decline and Fall of the Roman Empire*. London: A. Strahan and T. Cadell, 1791–2.

Gignoux, Philippe. *Noms propres sassanides en moyen-perse épigraphique*. Vol. 2: *Iranisches Personennamenbuch*. Vienna: Österreichische Akademie der Wissenschaften, 1986.

Gignoux, Philippe, and Aḥmad Tafażżole. "Some Middle-Persian Quotations in Classical Arabic and Persian Texts." In *Mémorial Jean de Menasce*, edited by P. Gignoux and Aḥmad Tafażżole, 337–49. Leuven: Imprimerie Orientaliste, 1974.

Giles, Lionel. "A Chinese Geographical Text of the Ninth Century." *BSOS* 6 (1932): 825–46.

Grierson, Philip. *The Silent Trade*. Edinburgh: W. Green, 1903.

Göckenjan, Hansgerd, and István Zimonyi. *Orientalische Berichte über die Völker Osteuropas und Zentralasiens im Mittelalter: die Ǧayhani-Tradition*. Wiesbaden:

Harrassowitz in Kommission, 2001.
Goeje, Michael Jan de. "De Muur van Gog en Magog." *Verslagen en Mededeelingen der Koninklijke Akademie van Wetenschappen*, ser. 3, vol. 5 (1888): 87–124.
Goitein, S. D. *Studies in Islamic History and Institutions*. Leiden: Brill, 1966.
Golden, Peter. "The Conversion of the Khazars to Judaism." In *The World of the Khazars: New Perspectives*, edited by Peter Golden, Haggai Ben-Shammai, and András Róna-Tas, 123–62. Leiden: Brill, 2007.
———. "The Khazar Sacral Kingship." In *Pre-modern Russia and its World*, edited by Kathryn L. Reyersen, Theofanis G. Stavrou, and James D. Tracy, 79–102. Wiesbaden: Harrassowitz, 2006.
———. *Khazar Studies*. Budapest: Akadémiai Kiadó, 1980.
———. "The Migrations of the *Oğuz*." *Archivum Ottomanicum* 4 (1972): 45–84.
———. "The Peoples of the Russian Forest Belt." In Vol. 1, *The Cambridge History of Early Inner Asia*, edited by Danis Sinor, et al., 229–55. Cambridge: Cambridge University Press, 1990.
———. "The Question of the Rus' Qağanate." *AEMA* 2 (1982): 77–97.
Gordon, Matthew. *A Breaking of a Thousand Swords: A History of the Turkish Military of Samarra*. Albany: State University of New York Press, 2001.
Greenblatt, Stephen. *Marvelous Possessions: The Wonder of the New World*. Chicago: University of Chicago Press, 1991.
Gutas, Dimitri. *Greek Thought, Arabic Culture: The Graeco-Arabic Translation Movement in Baghdad and Early ʿAbbāsid Society (2nd-4th/8th-10th centuries)*. New York: Routledge, 1998.
Haarmann, Ulrich. "Muslim Medieval Perceptions of Pharaonic Egypt." In *Ancient Egyptian Literature*, edited by Antonio Loprieno. Leiden: Brill, 1996.
Hamilton, James Russell. "Autour du Manuscrit Staël-Holstein." *T'oung Pao* 46 (1958): 115–53.
———. *Les Ouïghours à l'époque des cinq dynasties d'après les documents chinois*. Paris: Imprimerie national, 1955.
Haneda, Tôru. "A propos d'un text fragmentaire de prière manichéenne en ouigour provenant de Turfan." *Memoirs of the Research Department of the Toyo Bunko* 6 (1932): 1–21.
Harvey, L. P. *Muslims in Spain, 1500 to 1614*. Chicago: University of Chicago Press, 2005.
Hawting, Gerald R. *The First Dynasty of Islam: The Umayyad Caliphate A.D. 661–750*. London: Croom Helm, 1986.
———. "The 'Sacred Offices' of Mecca from Jāhiliyya to Islam." *Jerusalem Studies in Arabic and Islam* 13 (1990): 62–84.
Heck, Paul. *The Construction of Knowledge in Islamic Civilization: Qudāma b. Jaʿfar and his Kitāb al-Kharāj wa-ṣināʿat al-kitāba*. Leiden: Brill, 2002.
Hees, Syrinx von. "The Astonishing: A Critique and Re-reading of ʿAǧāʾib Literature." *MEL* 7 (2005): 101–20.
Hennig, Richard. *Terrae incognitae*. Leiden: Brill, 1936–9.

Henning, Walter Bruno. "The Date of the Sogdian Ancient Letters." *BSOAS* 12 (1948): 601–15.
Hinz, Walther. *Islamische Masse und Gewichte; Umgerechnet ins metrische System*. Leiden: Brill, 1955.
Husaini, Saiyid Abdul Qadir. *Arab Administration*. Madras: M. Abdur Rahman, 1949.
Jackson, Sherman. "Al-Jahiz on Translation." *Alif: Journal of Comparative Poetics* 4 (1984): 99–107.
Karamustafa, Ahmet. "Introduction to Islamic Maps." In *Cartography in the Traditional Islamic and South Asian Societies*, edited by J. B. Harley and D. Woodward, 3–11. Chicago: University of Chicago Press, 1992.
Kennedy, Philip, ed. *On Fiction and Adab in Medieval Arabic Literature*. Wiesbaden: Harrassowitz, 2005.
Khan, Gulfishan. *Indian Muslim Perceptions of the West During the Eighteenth Century*. Karachi: Oxford University Press, 1998.
Kilpatrick, Hilary. *Making the Great Book of Songs: Compilation and the Author's Craft in Abū l-Faraj al-Iṣbahānī's Kitāb al-Aghānī*. London: Routledge, 2003.
Kimber, Richard. "The Early Abbasid Vizierate." *Journal of Semitic Studies* 37 (1992): 65–85.
Kohlberg, Etan. *A Medieval Muslim Scholar at Work: Ibn Ṭāwūs and his Library*. Leiden: Brill, 1992.
Konow, Sten. "The Khotanese Text of the Staël-Holstein Scroll." *Acta Orientalia* 20 (1947): 131–60.
Krachkovskii, Ignatii. *Istoria arabskoi geograficheskoi literatury*. Moscow, 1957. Translated by Ṣalāḥ al-Dīn ʿUthmān Hāshim, as *Taʾrīkh al-adab al-jughrāfī 'l-ʿarabī*. Cairo: Lajnat al-Taʾlīf wa 'l-Tarjuma wa 'l-Nashr, 1963–5.
Kramers, Johannes. "L'influence de la tradition iranienne dans la géographie arabe." *Analecta Orientalia: Posthumous Writings and Selected Minor Works*. Leiden: Brill, 1954–6.
Krieger, Murray. *Ekphrasis: The Illusion of the Natural Sign*. Baltimore: Johns Hopkins University Press, 1992.
Kruk, Remke. "Gog and Magog in Modern Garb." In *Gog and Magog: The Clans of Chaos in World Literature*, edited by A. A. Seyed-Gohrab, 53–68. Amsterdam: Rozenberg Publishers, 2007.
Kugel, James L. *Traditions of the Bible: A Guide to the Bible as it was at the Start of the Common Era*. Cambridge: Harvard University Press, 1998.
Lamoreaux, John. *The Early Muslim Tradition of Dream Interpretation*. Albany: State University of New York Press, 2002.
Lane, Edward. *An Arabic-English Lexicon*. London and Edinburgh: Williams and Norgate, 1863–93.
Laufer, Berthold. *The Diamond: A Study in Chinese and Hellenistic Folk-lore*. Chicago: Field Museum of Natural History, 1915.
La Vaissière, Étienne de. *Samarcande et Samarra: élites d'Asie centrale dans l'empire abbasside*. Paris: Association pour l'avancement des études iraniennes, 2007.

———. *Sogdian Traders: A History*. Translated by James Ward. Leiden: Brill, 2005.

Lazard, Gilbert. "The Rise of the New Persian Language." In *The Cambridge History of Iran*. Vol. 4: *From the Arab Invasion to the Saljuqs*, 595–632. Cambridge: Cambridge University Press, 1975.

Leder, Stefan, ed. *Story-telling in the Framework of non-Fictional Arabic Literature*. Wiesbaden: Harrassowitz, 1998.

———. "The Use of Composite Form in the Making of the Islamic Historical Tradition." In *On Fiction and Adab in Medieval Arabic Literature*, edited by Philip Kennedy, 125–48. Wiesbaden: Harrassowitz, 2005.

Levy, Reuben. *The Social Structure of Islam: Being the Second Edition of the Sociology of Islam*. Cambridge: Cambridge University Press, 1957.

Lewicki, Tadeusz. *Źródła arabskie do dziejów słowiańszczyzny*. Warsaw: Zakład imienia Ossolińskich, 1956–88.

Lidzbarski, Mark. "Zu den arabischen Alexandergeschichten." *Zeitschrift für Assyriologie* 8 (1893): 263–312.

Lindesay, William. *The Great Wall Revisited: From the Jade Gate to Old Dragon's Head*. Cambridge: Harvard University Press, 2008.

Lippert, Julius. "Abū Maʿshar's *Kitāb al-Ulūf*." *Wiener Zeitschrift für die Kunde des Morgenlandes* 11 (1895): 351–8.

Loebenstein, Helene. *Katalog der arabischen Handschriften der Österreichischen Nationalbibliothek Neuerwerbungen 1868–1968 1: Codices mixti ab Nr 744*. Vienna: Hollinek, 1970.

Løkkegaard, Frede. *Islamic Taxation in the Classic Period, with Special Reference to Circumstances in Iraq*. Copenhagen: Branner and Korch, 1950.

Lundbæk, Knud. *T. S. Bayer (1694–1738), Pioneer Sinologist*. Copenhagen: Curzon Press, 1986.

Madelung, Wilferd. "Apocalyptic Prophecies in Ḥimṣ in the Umayyad Age." *Journal of Semitic Studies* 31 (1986): 141–85.

———. *Der Imam al-Qāsim ibn Ibrāhīm und die Glaubenslehre der Zaiditen*. Berlin: de Gruyter, 1965.

Mahdi, Muhsin. "Language and Logic in Classical Islam." In *Logic in Classical Islamic Culture*, edited by G. E. von Grunebaum, 51–83. Wiesbaden: Harrassowitz, 1970.

———. *The Thousand and One Nights*. Leiden: Brill, 1995.

Makkī, M. "Egipto y los orígenes de la historiografía arábigo-española." *Revista del Instituto de Estudios Islámicos en Madrid* 5 (1957): 157–248.

Margoliouth, D. S. "The Discussion between Abū Bishr Mattā and Abū Saʿīd al-Sīrāfī on the Merits of Logic and Grammar." *JRAS* (1905): 79–129.

Marquart, Josef. *Osteuropäische und ostasiatische Streifzüge; ethnologische und historisch-topographische Studien zur Geschichte des 9. und 10. Jahrhunderts (ca. 840–940)*. Leipzig: Dieterich'sche Verlagsbuchhandlung, 1903.

———. "Skizzen zur geschichtlichen Völkerkunde von Mittelasien und Sibirien." In *Festschrift für Friedrich Hirth*, 289–93. Berlin: Oesterheld and Co., 1920.

Mason, Richard. "The Religious Beliefs of the Khazars." *Ukrainian Quarterly* 51 (1995): 383–415.

Mathews, R. H. *Chinese-English Dictionary*. Cambridge: Harvard University Press, 1941.

Mavroudi, Maria V. *A Byzantine Book on Dream Interpretation: The Oneirocriticon of Achmet and its Arabic Sources*. Leiden: Brill, 2002.

McCrindle, J. W. *Ancient India as Described by Ktêsias the Knidian*. London: Trübner and Co., 1882.

McGann, Jerome. *The Textual Condition*. Princeton: Princeton University Press, 1991.

McKinney, Robert. *The Case of Rhyme Versus Reason: Ibn al-Rūmī and his Poetics in Context*. Leiden: Brill, 2004.

Meyendorff, John. "Byzantine Views of Islam." *Dumbarton Oaks Papers* 18 (1964): 113–32.

Meyerhof, Max. "ʿAlī aṭ-Ṭabarī's 'Paradise of Wisdom,' One of the Oldest Arabic Compendiums of Medicine." *Isis* 16 (1931): 6–54.

Mez, Adam. *Die Renaissance des Islâms*. Heidelberg: C. Winter, 1922.

Miller, Konrad. *Charta Rogeriana: Weltkarte des Idrisi*. Stuttgart: Konrad Miller, 1928.

Milstein, Rachel, Karin Rührdanz, and Barbara Schmitz. *Stories of the Prophets: Illustrated Manuscripts of Qiṣaṣ al-Anbiyāʾ*. Costa Mesa, CA: Mazda Publishers, 1999.

Minorsky, Vladimir. *A History of Sharvān and Darband in the 10th-11th Centuries*. Cambridge: W. Heffer and Sons, 1958.

———. "The Older Preface to the *Shāh-nāma*." *Studi Orientalistici in onore di Giorgio Levi Della Vida* 2 (1956): 159–79.

———. "Tamīm ibn Baḥr's Journey to the Uyghurs." *BSOAS* 12 (1948): 275–305.

Miquel, André. *La Géographie humaine du monde musulman jusqu'au milieu du 11e siècle*. Paris: Mouton, 1967–87.

Montgomery, James. "Serendipity, Resistance, and Multivalency: Ibn Khurradādhbih and his *Kitāb al-Masālik wa-l-mamālik*." In *On Fiction and Adab in Medieval Arabic Literature*, edited by Philip Kennedy, 177–232. Wiesbaden: Harrassowitz, 2005.

———. "Travelling Autopsies: Ibn Faḍlān and the Bulghār." *MEL* 7 (2004): 3–32.

Morgan, David. "Prester John and the Mongols." In *Prester John, the Mongols, and the Ten Lost Tribes*, edited by Charles Beckingham and Bernard Hamilton, 159–70. Aldershot: Variorum, 1996.

Morony, Michael. "Continuity and Change in the Administrative Geography of Late Sasanian and Early Islamic al-ʿIrāq." *Iran: Journal of the British Institute of Persian Studies* 20 (1982): 1–49.

———. *Iraq after the Muslim Conquest*. Princeton: Princeton University Press, 1984.

Morrison, Robert. "Reasons for a Scientific Portrayal of Nature in Medieval Commentaries on the Qurʾān." *Arabica* 52 (2005): 182–203.

Mottahedeh, Roy. "The ʿAbbāsid Caliphate in Iran." In *The Cambridge History of Iran*, edited by R. Frye. Vol. 4: *From the Arab Invasion to the Saljuqs*, 57–89. Cambridge: Cambridge University Press, 1975.

———. "ʿAjāʾib in *The Thousand and One Nights*." In *The Thousand and One Nights in Arabic Literature and Society*, edited by Richard Hovannisian and Georges Sabagh, 29–39. Cambridge: Cambridge University Press, 1997.

Muss-Arnolt, William. *Assyrisch-English-Deutsches Handwörterbuch*. Berlin: Reuther und Reichard, 1905.

Nallino, C. A. "Al-Khuwārizmī e il suo rifacimento della Geografia di Tolomeo." *Raccolta di scritti editi e inediti* 5 (1944): 458–532.

Nāẓim, Muḥammad. *The Life and Times of Sulṭān Maḥmūd of Ghazna*. Cambridge: Cambridge University Press, 1931.

Needham, Joseph, et al. *Science and Civilisation in China*. Vol. 4, part 3: *Civil Engineering and Nautics*. Cambridge: Cambridge University Press, 1971.

Niẓām al-Dīn, Muḥammad. *Introduction to the Jawāmiʿu ʾl-ḥikāyāt wa lawāmiʿu ʾr-riwāyāt of Sadīdu ʾd-Dīn Muḥammad al-ʿAwfī*. London: Luzac and Co., 1929.

Nöldeke, Theodor. "Beiträge zur Geschichte des Alexanderromans." *Denkschriften der Kaiserlichen Akademie der Wissenschaften, Philosophische-historische Classe* 38 (1890): 1–56.

Noonan, Thomas. "Fluctuations in Islamic Trade with Eastern Europe during the Viking Age." *Harvard Ukrainian Studies* 16, nos. 3–4 (1992): 237–59.

———. "Some Observations on the Economy of the Khazar Khaganate." In *The World of the Khazar: New Perspectives*, edited by Peter Golden, Haggai Ben-Shammai, and András Róna-Tas, 207–44. Leiden: Brill, 2007.

———. "When did Rūs/Rus' Merchants first visit Khazaria and Baghdad?" *AEMA* 7 (1987–91): 213–9.

———. "Why Dirhams First Reached Russia: The Role of Arab-Khazar Relations in the Development of the Earliest Islamic Trade with Eastern Europe." *AEMA* 4 (1984): 151–282.

Northedge, Alastair. *The Historical Topography of Samarra*. London: British School of Archaeology in Iraq, 2005.

———. "The Racecourses at Sāmarrāʾ." *BSOAS* 53 (1990): 31–56.

Ohsson, Constantin Mouradgea d'. *Des peuples du Caucase et des pays au nord de la mer Noire et de la mer Caspienne, dans le dixième siècle, ou Voyage d'Abou-el-Cassim*. Paris: Firmin Didot, 1828.

Ormsby, Eric. *Theodicy in Islamic Thought: The Dispute over al-Ghazālī's "Best of all Possible Worlds."* Princeton: Princeton University Press, 1984.

Patton, Walter Melville. *Aḥmed ibn Ḥanbal and the Miḥna*. Leiden: Brill, 1897.

Pellat, Charles. "Ǧāḥiziana i. Le *Kitāb al-tabaṣṣur bi ʾl-tijāra* attribué à Ǧāḥiẓ." *Arabica* 1 (1954): 153–65.

Pelliot, Paul. "Chrétiens d'Asie centrale et d'Extrême-Orient." *T'oung Pao* 15 (1914): 623–44.

———. *Notes on Marco Polo*. Paris: Imprimerie nationale, 1959–63.

Perkins, Justin. "Notice of the Life of Alexander the Great." *JAOS* 4 (1854): 359–440.

Pettigrew, Mark. "The Wonders of the Ancients: Arab-Islamic Representations of Ancient Egypt." Ph.D. dissertation. University of California at Berkeley, 2004.

Pingree, David. *The Thousands of Abū Maʿshar*. London: Warburg Institute, 1968.
Pistor-Hatam, Anja. "Übersetzungen innerhalb des islamischen Kulturraums." Vol. 2: *Übersetzung: ein internationales Handbuch zur Übersetzungsforschung*, edited by Harald Kittel, et al., 1220–30. Berlin: Walter de Gruyter, 2007.
Popović, Alexandre. *Revolt of African Slaves in Iraq in the Third/Ninth Century*. Translated by Léon King. Princeton: Markus Wiener Publishers, 1999.
Pourshariati, Parvaneh. *Decline and Fall of the Sasanian Empire*. London: I.B.Tauris, 2008.
Prier, Raymond. *Thauma idesthai: The Phenomenology of Sight and Appearance in Archaic Greek*. Tallahassee: Florida State University Press, 1989.
Pritsak, Omeljan. "An Arabic Text on the Trade Route of the Corporation of Ar-Rūs in the Second Half of the Ninth Century." *Folia Orientalia* 12 (1970): 241–59.
———. *The Origin of Rus'*. Cambridge: Harvard University Press, 1981.
Rachewiltz, Igor de. "Marco Polo went to China." *Zentralasiatische Studien* 27 (1997): 34–92.
Rehman, Abdur. "Ethnicity of the Hindu Shahis." *Journal of the Pakistan Historical Society* 51, no. 3 (2003): 3–10.
Reichelt, Hans. *Die soghdischen Handschriftenreste des Britischen museums*. Heidelberg: C. Winter's Universitätsbuchhandlung, 1928.
Reinink, Gerrit J. *Syriac Christianity under Late Sasanian and Early Islamic Rule*. Aldershot: Ashgate, 2005.
Rennell, James. *The Geographical System of Herodotus, Examined, and Explained*. London: W. Bulmer, 1800.
Reynolds, Dwight, and Kristen Brustad, eds. *Interpreting the Self, Autobiography in the Arabic Literary Tradition*. Berkeley: University of California, 2001.
Roggema, Barbara. *The Legend of Sergius Baḥīrā: Eastern Christian Apologetics and Apocalyptic in Response to Islam*. Leiden: Brill, 2009.
Romm, James. *The Edges of the Earth in Ancient Thought: Geography, Exploration, and Fiction*. Princeton: Princeton University Press, 1992.
Rosenthal, Franz. *Aḥmad b. aṭ-Ṭayyib as-Saraḫsī*. New Haven: American Oriental Society, 1943.
———. "From Arabic Books and Manuscripts III: The Author of the *Ġurar as-siyar*." *JAOS* 70 (1950): 181–2.
Ruska, Julius. *Das Steinbuch des Aristoteles*. Heidelberg: C. Winter, 1912.
Sabra, A. I. "The Appropriation and Subsequent Naturalization of Greek Science in Medieval Islam: A Preliminary Statement." *History of Science* 25 (1987): 223–43.
Sadek, Mahmoud Mohamed. *The Arabic Materia Medica of Dioscorides*. St-Jean-Chrysostome, Québec: Les Éditions du Sphinx, 1983.
Ṣafā, Dhabīḥ Allāh. *Tārīkh-i adabiyyāt dar Īrān*. Tehran: Ibn Sīnā, 1956–7.
Saʿfī, Waḥīd. *al-ʿAjīb wa 'l-gharīb fī kutub tafsīr al-Qurʾān*. Tunis: Tibr al-Zamān, 2001.
Said, Edward. *Orientalism*. New York: Pantheon Books, 1978.
Salama-Carr, Myriam. "Translation as seen by al-Jahiz and by Hunayn Ibn Ishaq—Observer versus Practitioner." In *International Medieval Research I, Across*

the Mediterranean Frontiers: Trade, Politics and Religion 650–1450, edited by Dionisius Agius and Ian Netton, 386–93. Turnhout, Belgium: Brepols, 1997.
Savant, Sarah. "Finding Our Place in the Past: Genealogy and Ethnicity in Islam." Ph.D. dissertation. Harvard University, 2006.
Schoeler, Gregor. "Schreiben und Veröffentlichen. Zu Verwendung und Funktion der Schrift in den ersten islamischen Jahrhunderten." *Der Islam* 69 (1992): 1–43.
Serruys, Henry. "Mongol Altan 'gold' = 'imperial.'" *Monumenta Serica* 21 (1962): 357–78.
Sezgin, Fuat. *The Contribution of the Arabic-Islamic Geographers to the Formation of the World Map*. Frankfurt: Johann Wolfgang Goethe-Universität, 1987.
Shafīʿī Kadkanī, Muḥammad Riḍā, "Kuhantarīn namūna-i shiʿr-i fārsī: yakī az khusrūwānīhā-i Bārbad." *Ārash* 6 (1963): 18–28.
Silverstein, Adam. *Postal Systems in the Pre-Modern Islamic World*. Cambridge: Cambridge University Press, 2007.
Slane, William MacGuckin, baron de. *Catalogue des manuscrits arabes*. Paris: Imprimerie nationale, 1883–95.
Smith, Robert Payne. *A Compendious Syriac Dictionary*. Edited by Jessie Payne Smith. Oxford: Clarendon Press, 1903.
Smith, William. *Dictionary of Greek and Roman Geography*. London: Walton and Maberly, 1854.
Sourdel, Dominique. "Questions de cérémonial 'abbaside." *Revue des études islamiques* 28 (1960): 121–48.
——. *Le vizirat ʿabbāside de 749 à 936 (132 à 324 de l'hégire)*. Damascus: Institut français, 1959–60.
Sourdel-Thomine, Janine. "Clefs et serrures de la Kaʿba, notes d'épigraphie arabe." *Revue des études islamiques* 39 (1971): 29–86.
Sprenger, Aloys. *Die Post- und Reiserouten des Orients*. Leipzig: F. A. Brockhaus, 1864.
Sprengling, M. "From Persian to Arabic." *American Journal of Semitic Languages and Literatures* 56–7 (1939/40): 175–224, 325–36/302–5.
Stein, Aurel. *On Alexander's Track to the Indus*. London: Macmillan and Co., 1929.
——. *Ruins of Desert Cathay*. London: Macmillan and Co., 1912.
——. *Serindia: Detailed Report of Explorations in Central Asia and Westernmost China*. Oxford: Clarendon Press, 1921.
Steiner, George. *After Babel: Aspects of Language and Translation*. New York: Oxford University Press, 1975.
Stetkevych, Suzanne. *The Poetics of Islamic Legitimacy*. Bloomington: Indiana University Press, 2002.
Storey, C. A., and François de Blois. *Persian Literature: A Bio-Bibliographical Survey*. London: Luzac and Co., 1970.
Sumi, Akiko Motoyoshi. *Description in Classical Arabic Poetry: Waṣf, Ekphrasis, and Interarts Theory*. Leiden: Brill, 2004.
Thomas, F. W. "Tibetan Documents Concerning Chinese Turkestan." *JRAS* (1927): 51–86, 807–844.
Tibawi, A. L. "Is the Qurʾān Translatable?" *Moslem World* 52 (1962): 4–16.

Togan, İsenbike. *Flexibility and Limitation in Steppe Formations*. Leiden: Brill, 1998.
Tolmacheva, Marina. "The Medieval Arabic Geographers and the Beginnings of Modern Orientalism." *IJMES* 27 (1995): 141–56.
Tomaschek, Wilhelm. "De Muur van Gog en Magog." *Vienna Oriental Journal* 3 (1889): 103–8.
Toorawa, Shawkat. *Ibn Abī Ṭāhir Ṭayfur and Arabic Writerly Culture, A Ninth-Century Bookman in Baghdād*. London: Routledge Curzon, 2005.
———. "Proximity, Resemblance, Sidebars and Clusters: Ibn al-Nadīm's Organizational Principles in *Fihrist* 3.3." *Oriens* (forthcoming).
———. "Wāq al-wāq: Fabulous, Fabular, Indian Ocean (?) Island(s)." *Emergences: Journal for the Study of Media and Composite Cultures* 10 (2000): 387–402.
Uray, G. "The Old Tibetan Sources of the History of Central Asia up to 751 A.D.: A Survey." In *Prolegomena to the Sources on the History of Pre-Islamic Central Asia*, edited by J. Harmatta, 275–304. Budapest: Akadémiai Kiadó, 1979.
Uri, Johannes. *Bibliothecae Bodleianae codicum manuscriptorum orientalium*. Oxford: Clarendon, 1787.
Utas, Bo. "Semitic in Iranian: Written, Read and Spoken Language." In *Linguistic Convergence and Areal Diffusion*, edited by Éva Ágnes Csató, Bo Isaksson, and Carina Jahani, 65–78. London: Routledge, 2005.
Vajda, Georges. "Fasting in Islam and Judaism." In *The Development of Islamic Ritual*, edited by Gerald Hawting, 133–149. Aldershot: Ashgate, 2006.
Van Bladel, Kevin. "The Alexander Legend in the Qurʾan 18:83–102." In *The Qurʾan in its Historical Context*, edited by Gabriel Reynolds, 175–203. London: Routledge, 2008.
———. "Heavenly Cords and Prophetic Authority in the Qurʾān and its Late Antique Context." *BSOAS* 70 (2007): 223–46.
Van Donzel, E. J., A. B. Schmidt, and C. Otto. *Gog and Magog in Early Syriac and Islamic Sources: Sallam's Quest for Alexander's Wall*. Leiden: Brill, 2010.
Van Reeth, J. M. F. "Caliph al-Maʾmūn and the Treasure of the Pyramids." *Orientalia Lovaniensia Periodica* 25 (1994): 221–36.
Vasilev, A. A. *Byzance et les Arabes*. Brussels: Institut de philologie et d'histoire orientales, 1935.
Versteegh, C. H. M. "Logique et grammaire au dixième siècle." *Histoire Épistémologie Langue* 2 (1980): 39–52.
von Grunebaum, G. E. "Observations on the Muslim Concept of Evil." *Studia Islamica* 31 (1970): 117–34.
Waldron, Arthur N. *The Great Wall of China: From History to Myth*. Cambridge: Cambridge University Press, 1992.
———. "The Problem of the Great Wall of China." *Harvard Journal of Asiatic Studies* 43 (1983): 643–63.
Warton, Thomas. *The History of English Poetry*. London: J. Dodsley, 1774–81.
Webb, Ruth. "Ekphrasis Ancient and Modern: The Invention of a Genre." *Word and Image* 15 (1999): 7–18.

Wessels, C. *Early Jesuit Travellers in Central Asia, 1603–1721*. The Hague: Nijhoff, 1924.
Wheatley, Paul. *The Places Where Men Pray Together: Cities in Islamic Lands Seventh Through the Tenth Centuries*. Chicago: Chicago University Press, 2001.
Wheeler, Brannon. *Mecca and Eden, Ritual, Relics, and Territory in Islam*. Chicago: University of Chicago, 2006.
———. "Moses or Alexander? Early Islamic Exegesis of Qurʾan 18:60–65." *Journal of Near Eastern Studies* 57 (1998): 191–215.
Widengren, Geo. "Recherches sur le féodalisme iranien." *Orientalia Suecana* 5 (1956): 79–182.
Wilson, C. E. "The Wall of Alexander against Gog and Magog; and the Expedition sent out to find it by the Khalif Wāthiq." In *Hirth Anniversary Volume*, edited by Bruno Schindler, 575–612. London: Probsthain, 1923.
Witkam, Jan Just. "Manuscripts and Manuscripts." *Manuscripts of the Middle East* 1 (1986): 111–7.
Wittkower, Rudolf. "Marvels of the East. A Study in the History of Monsters." *JWCI* 5 (1942): 159–97.
Witzel, Michael. "The Home of the Aryans." In *Anusantatyai: Festschrift für Johanna Narten zum 70. Geburtstag*, edited by Almut Hintze and Eva Tichy, 283–338. Dettelbach: J. H. Röll, 2000.
Yücesoy, Hayrettın. *Messianic Beliefs and Imperial Politics in Medieval Islam: The ʿAbbāsid Caliphate in the Early Ninth Century*. Columbia: University of South Carolina Press, 2009.
———. "Translation as Self-Consciousness: Ancient Sciences, Antediluvian Wisdom, and the ʿAbbāsid Translation Movement." *Journal of World History* 20 (2009): 523–57.
Yule, Henry. *Cathay and the Way Thither*. London: The Hakluyt Society, 1866.
Zadeh, Travis. "Translation, Geography, and the Divine Word: Mediating Frontiers in pre-modern Islam." Ph.D. dissertation. Harvard University, 2007.
———. "The Wiles of Creation: Philosophy, Fiction, and the *ʿAjāʾib* Tradition." *MEL* 13 (2010): 21–48.
Zakeri, Mohsen. "Translation from Middle Persian (Pahlavi) into Arabic to the Early Abbasid Period." Vol. 2: *Übersetzung: ein internationales Handbuch zur Übersetzungsforschung*, edited by Harald Kittel, et al., 1199–1205. Berlin: Walter de Gruyter, 2007.
Zhewen, Luo, and Zhao Luo. *The Great Wall of China in History and Legend*. Beijing: Foreign Languages Press, 1986.
Zichy, Étienne. "Le voyage de Sallām, l'interprète, à la muraille de Gog et de Magog." *Kőrösi Csoma-Archivum* 1, part 3 (1922): 190–204.
Zimonyi, István. *The Origins of the Volga Bulghars*. Szeged: Universitas Szegediensis de Attila József Nominata, 1990.
Zuwiyya, Zachary David. *Islamic Legends Concerning Alexander the Great*. New York: Global Publications, 2001.

INDEX OF PEOPLE

ᶜAbbās b. ᶜAbd al-Muṭṭalib (d. ca 32/653), 114
ᶜAbbās b. Ṭarkhān (fl. 225/840), 30, 219n96
ᶜAbd Allāh b. Ṭāhir (d. 230/844), 121, 124–5, 172
ᶜAbd al-Raḥmān b. Rabīᶜa, 78
ᶜAbd al-Razzāq (d. 211/827), 101
ᶜAbdūn b. Makhlad (d. 310/922–3), 182, 214n17
Abraham, 119. *See also* Ibrāhīm
Abū Bishr Mattā b. Yūnus (d. 328/940), 55–6, 105
Abū Dulaf (fl. 375/985), 9, 163, 256n88
Abū Isḥāq Ibrāhīm b. Alptakīn (d. 356/967), 145
Abū 'l-Fidāʾ (d. 732/1331), 154
Abū Maᶜshar (d. 272/886), 44, 104–5, 224n43
Abū Nuwās (d. ca 198/813), 32
Abū Tammām (d. 231/845), 220n107
Abū ᶜUbayd al-Bakrī (d. 487/1094), 81, 130, 174
Adam, 25–6, 106, 116
ᶜAḍud al-Dawla (r. 338–72/949–83), 9, 134, 188–90
Aḥmad b. al-Ḥārith al-Kharrāz (d. ca 258/872), 214n8
Alexander the Great (356–323 B.C.E.). *See also* Dhū 'l-Qarnayn; Subjects: Alexander Romance; Pseudo-Callisthenes cycle
- in Arabic sources, 99, 100, 116, 123, 161, 135, 138–9, 186, 237n1
- Brahmans and, 120
- destruction of Persepolis, 188
- as Dhū 'l-Qarnayn, 5, 93, 98, 100
- diving bell, 232n54
- fountain of life and speaking trees, 242n57
- in Ibn Khurradādhbih, 29
- Indian campaign of, 167–8
- in Middle Persian sources, 111–2, 237n1, 242n58
- in New Persian sources, 100
- secret Persian identity of, 112
- in Syriac sources, 42–3, 107–10, 116, 118, 120, 240n46
- wall of. *See* Subjects: wall against Gog and Magog

ᶜAmr b. al-ᶜĀṣ (d. 42/663), 47
Anderson, Andrew, 165, 257n106
Anūshirwān, Khusraw I (r. 531–78 C.E.), 72–3, 76–7, 83, 153, 218n76; Plate 3
Ardashīr I (d. 242 C.E.), 23
Aristotle
- in Alexander Romance, 100, 139
- in Arabic, 53–6, 57, 105
- on Gog and Magog, 93
- on pygmies and cranes, 99

on wonder, 3
Arrian of Nicomedia (d. ca 160 C.E.), 167
Artemidorus (fl. second century C.E.), 51, 62, 63
Ashinās, Abū Jaʿfar (d. 230/844), 51, 67, 71, 124, 195
ʿAskarī, Abū Hilāl (fl. 395/1005), 105
ʿAṭāʾ al-Khurāsānī, 230n9
ʿAwfī, Sadīd al-Dīn (fl. 625/1228), 146

Bahādur Khān, Abū ʿl-Ghāzī (d. 1074/1663), 159
Bahrām V / Bahrām Gūr (r. 420–38 C.E.), 29, 31, 72, 219nn94–95
Balādhurī, Aḥmad b. Yaḥyā (d. ca 279/892), 72, 73, 88
Balʿamī, Abū ʿAlī (d. 363/974), 81
Balkhī, Abū Zayd (d. 322/934), 131, 145, 170
Balkhī, Muḥammad b. Darwīsh, 249n80
Bāris, 38–9, 222n17
Baron, Salo Wittmayer, 166
Baṣrī, Abū Zayd (fl. 303/915), 8
Bayer, Theophilus (Gottlieb) Siegfried (d. 1738), 149–51, 159, 251n17
Beckford, William (d. 1844), 148
Bendefy, László, 167–8, 257n22
Bilgrāmī, Murtaḍā Ḥusayn (d. ca 1210/1795), 143
Bilqīs. *See* Sulaymān, and Bilqīs
Biqāʿī, Burhān al-Dīn (d. 885/1480), 139
Bīrūnī, Abū ʿl-Rayḥān (d. ca 442/1050), 84–5, 90–1, 136–8, 180, 221n12
Bughā al-Kabīr (d. 248/862), 71
Bughrān Shāh, 73
Buḥturī, Abū ʿUbāda (d. 284/897), 18, 77, 182–3, 185, 214n17
Bukhārī, Muḥammad b. Ismāʿīl (d. 256/870), 101
Bukhtīshūʿ (d. 256/870), 52, 226n15
Burton, Richard (d. 1890), 161

Charles V (r. 1516–58), Holy Roman Emperor, 6
Ctesias, 252n26

Darius (d. 330 B.C.E.), 112, 188
Decius, Emperor (r. 249–51 C.E.), 36
Dhahabī, Shams al-Dīn (d. 748/1348), 81, 135
d'Herbelot, Barthélemy (d. 1695), 148–9, 151, 154
Dhū ʿl-Qarnayn, 42–3, 97–100, 116, 118–9, 138. *See also* Alexander the Great
in Arabic poetry, 82–3
Brahmans and, 120
cave of darkness and, 233n72
construction of wall, 102–3
epithet, 43, 104, 147, 223n36, 224n38, 241n53
Greek origins of, 238n9
Khiḍr and, 82, 98
as pious king, 82–3
prophethood of, 43, 224n38
in the Qurʾān, 5, 42, 93, 99–100, 103, 109, 113, 118, 152, 181–2
in Qurʾānic exegesis, 43, 113, 118
in *The Thousand and One Nights*, 161
Dīnawarī, Abū Ḥanīfa (d. ca 282/895), 100, 112
Dioscorides, 59, 158
d'Ohsson, Constantin Mouradgea (d. 1851), 151–4, 252n21
Dunbar, James (d. 1798), 161
Dunlop, D. M., 166, 221n10

Efendī, ʿAbd al-Raḥmān, 16

al-Faḍl b. Marwān (d. 250/864), 219n96
Fārābī, Abū Naṣr (d. 339/950), 55, 56–7, 105
Farghānī, Muḥammad b. Kathīr (fl. 247/861), 136, 153, 247n58
Farīda, 50
Farīdūn, 28

Fīlān Shāh, 73–5, 95, 196, 201, 206, 231n34
Firdawsī, Abū 'l-Qāsim (d. 411/1020), 28–9, 100; Plate 5
Flavius Josephus (fl. 93 C.E.), 42
Foucault, Michel, 4

Gagnier, Jean (d. 1740), 239n33
Galen (d. ca 216 C.E.), 4, 22, 51, 52, 55, 59–60, 82
Galland, Antoine (d. 1715), 148
Gardīzī, Abū Saʿīd (fl. 440/1049), 145, 254n58
Geoffrey of Monmouth (d. ca 1155), 149
Gharnāṭī, Abū Ḥāmid (d. 565/1169–70), 139, 141, 249n86
Ghazālī, Abū Ḥāmid (d. 505/1111), 4
Gibbon, Edward (d. 1794), 159
Goeje, Michael Jan de, 16, 121, 155–62, 163–5, 167–74, 176–7

Ḥājjī Khalīfa (d. 1067/1657), 131, 232n36, 238n9, 248n66, 259n147
Ḥakīmī, Abū ʿAbd Allāh al-Kātib (d. 336/948), 133
Ḥām, 92
Hamdānī, al-Ḥasan b. Aḥmad (d. 334/945), 86, 90, 93–4
Ḥarrānī, Aḥmad b. Ḥamdān (fl. 732/1332), 248n79
Hārūn al-Rashīd (r. 140–93/786–809), 30, 50, 83, 234n74
Ḥassān b. Thābit (d. ca 40/659), 31, 98
Hastings, Warren (d. 1818), 143
Henning, Richard, 163–4
Heraclius (r. 610-41 C.E.), 108
Herodotus, 92, 236n133, 252n26
Hesronita, Joannes, 146
Ḥimyarī, Ibn ʿAbd al-Munʿim (d. 900/1494), 81, 130
Hippocrates, 51, 52
Hishām b. ʿAbd al-Malik (r. 105–25/724–43), 38
Homer, 51
Ḥunayn b. Isḥāq (d. 260/873)
  the Nasnās and, 48
  as polymath, 51, 226n17
  on translation, 55, 57, 60, 227n42
  as translator, 51, 59–60, 62, 109, 158, 226n14, 228n50, 229n69, 236n114
  al-Wāthiq and, 51–2
Ḥusayn b. al-Ḍaḥḥāk (d. ca 250/864), 32
Hyde, Thomas (d. 1703), 159

Ibn ʿAbbās (d. 68/687–8), 97, 230n9
Ibn ʿAbd al-Ḥakam (d. 257/871), 99
Ibn Abī Ṭāhir (d. 280/893), 184
Ibn Abī Uṣaybiʿa (d. 668/1270), 59
Ibn al-Athīr, 175, 194
Ibn al-ʿArabī (d. 638/1240), 58, 228n48
Ibn Baṭṭūṭa (d. ca 779/1377), 160–1
Ibn Faḍlān (fl. 310/922), 38–9, 145, 166, 252
  on Gog and Magog, 144–5, 186–7; Plate 14
  on Rūs funeral rites, 236n128
Ibn al-Faqīh (fl. 289/902)
  on Caucasus, 69, 75–6
  on the composition of geography, 173, 259n157
  on divisions of land, 23, 90
  on Gospels, 239n24
  interpreters and, 38
  al-Muʿtaṣim and, 82–3
  on pyramids, 44
  Sallām in, 130, 170, 173, 175
  Sulaymān the Merchant and, 8
Ibn Furāt, Abū 'l-Fatḥ (d. 327/938), 55
Ibn Ḥawqal (fl. 378/988)
  on Caucasus, 75
  on divisions of land, 88, 235n95
  empiricism of, 9
  on Gog and Magog, 131, 144–5, 250n108
  on Ibn Khurradādhbih, 18
  Sallām's account and, 131, 170, 174, 194

Ibn Ḥazm (d. 456/1064), 93–4, 137–8, 142, 194, 245n7
Ibn Hishām (d. ca 218/833), 97–9, 119
Ibn Iyās (d. ca 930/1524), 141, 146, 248n66
Ibn al-Jawzī (d. 597/1200), 111, 135, 138, 242n60, 246n30
Ibn Jinnī (d. 392/1002), 7
Ibn Juljul (d. ca 384/994), 59
Ibn Kathīr (d. 774/1373), 139
Ibn Khaldūn (d. 808/1406), 137
Ibn Khurradādhbih, Abū 'l-Qāsim (fl. 269/882)
  Arabic poetry in, 28, 32–3, 77
  on Caucasus, 69–70, 72
  composition of *Masālik* and, 171–3, 213n2, 220n3
  on Dead Sea, 237n140
  on divisions of land, 25, 88, 90–2, 230n11
  on exotica and wonders, 39, 43, 46–8, 102
  humoral geography and, 91–2
  identification of, 100
  Jayhānī and, 123, 134, 164, 237n137, 246n24
  on Khāqān, 231n35
  life and career of, 17–20
  as *nadīm* and court official, 17, 30, 34, 50, 131–2, 172, 182–6, 214nn17–8, 241n54
  on People of the Cave, 35–7, 138, 182
  on Persian history, 28–9, 77, 136
  Persian language and poetry in, 24–7, 31, 111, 219n96
  on Prophet Muḥammad, 26
  Ptolemy and, 23, 91, 94, 216n48
  on pyramids, 44–6, 224n43, 224n45
  reliability of, 18, 51, 136, 167, 173, 215n19, 220n100
  on Sallām, 16, 50–1, 67–8, 83, 111, 125–6, 130, 132–3, 136, 140, 170, 173–4, 189, 194, 201, 205, 246nn29–30
  on Tamīm b. Baḥr, 101
  translation and, 22–4, 43
  on Turks, 49
  use of Sāsānian models, 24–5, 27, 29–30
  vocalization of name, 213n2
  works by, 18, 28, 30, 182, 186
Ibn Manẓūr (d. 711/1311–12), 57
Ibn al-Marzubān (d. 309/920), 184
Ibn Māsawayh (d. 243/857), 52, 226n15
Ibn al-Munādī (d. 333/944), 111–3, 174–5, 194, 246n30
Ibn al-Muqaffaʿ (d. ca 142/759), 73
Ibn al-Nadīm (d. ca 385/995), 8, 17, 62, 184–5, 213n8, 245n7, 259n153
Ibn al-Qāṣṣ (d. 335/946), 84, 130, 132–3, 174–5, 194, 253n53
Ibn Qutayba (b. 276/889), 61–3, 100, 116
Ibn al-Rūmī (d. 283/896), 182
Ibn Rusta (fl. 300/912), 51, 72–3, 91, 130, 136, 173, 175, 180, 194
Ibn Ṣāʿid (d. 462/1070), 86
Ibn Sīnā (d. 428/1037), 55
Ibn Sīrīn, Muḥammad (d. 110/728), 61–3
Ibn Taghrībirdī (d. 874/1470), 135
Ibn Ṭūlūn (d. 270/884), 44–5, 171, 183–4, 224n46
Ibn al-Wardī (d. 861/1457), 140, 141, 143, 180, 248n79, 252n19
Ibn ʿUfayr, Saʿīd (d. 226/840), 81–2
Ibrāhīm, 26
Ibshīhī, Abū 'l-Fatḥ (d. ca 850/1446), 249n86
Idrīsī, Abū ʿAbd Allāh (d. 560/1165)
  on Adhkish, 101, 123, 167, 176, 244n113, 259n162
  commissioned by Roger II, 146
  French translation of, 154
  Latin translation of, 146–7, 150
  maps of, 123, 135, 165; Plates 6–7

Medici edition of, 146
on Sallām, 94, 101, 102, 123–4, 129, 130, 155, 163–5, 167, 170, 175, 181, 205–7
use of Jayhānī and Ibn Khurradādhbih, 123, 134, 174–5, 194, 237n139, 248n79
use of Turkish informant, 123, 134, 247n40
Īliyā b. Shīnā (d. 439/1047–8), 228n42
Imruʾ al-Qays b. Ḥujr (d. ca 550 C.E.), 31–2, 98
Īrān, son of Farīdūn, 28
ʿĪsā (Jesus), 45
Iṣfahānī, Abū 'l-Faraj (d. 356/967), 18, 30, 47, 50, 173, 185, 189
Iṣfahānī, Ḥamza (d. ca 350/961), 73
Isfandiyār, 73
Isḥāq b. Ismāʿīl (d. 238/852), 70–1, 196, 201, 205
Isḥāq b. Kundajīq, 183–4, 260n10
Isḥāq al-Mawṣilī (d. 235/850), 50, 185
Ismāʿīl (Ishmael), 26
Iṣṭakhrī, Abū Isḥāq (fl. 324/936), 72, 88, 131, 170, 234n89, 234n95
Iṣṭifan b. Basīl, 59–60

Jacob of Sarug (d. 521 C.E.), 42, 107, 109
Jāḥiẓ, Abū ʿUthmān (d. 255/868–9), x, 3–4, 9–10, 22, 130
Jahshiyārī, Abū ʿAbd Allāh (d. 331/942), 27
Jarmī, Muslim b. Abī Muslim, 35, 220n3
Jayhānī, Abū ʿAbd Allāh (fl. 309/922), 18, 220n2, 246n24
account of the wall in, 123, 130, 164, 174, 175, 194, 205, 237n139
Ibn Khurradādhbih's *Masālik* and, 134
Jeremiah, 108
Jūzjānī, Minhāj al-Dīn (fl. 658/1260), 138

Kāshgharī, Maḥmūd (fl. 476/1094), 144, 166
Kawkabī 'l-Kātib, Abū ʿAlī (d. 327/939), 133
Khiḍr, 26, 69, 82, 98
Khusraw, Amīr (d. 725/1325), 29
Khusraw II Parwīz (r. 591–628 C.E.), 31
Khwārazmī, Muḥammad b. Mūsā (d. ca 232/847), 24, 217n53, 221n10, 232n36, 235n105
on location of Gog and Magog, 237n138
on mission to Cave, 36–7, 182, 221n12
on mission to Khazar, 50, 74
translation movement and, 60
Kindī, Abū Yūsuf (d. ca 260/874), 24, 214n8; Plate 12

Landberg, Count Carlo de (d. 1924), 169
al-Lub (al-L.b), 121, 156, 200, 260n163
Luʾluʾ (d. 304/916–7), 44, 183, 225n49

Maʿarrī, Abū 'l-ʿAlāʾ (d. 449/1058), 215n19
al-Mahdī (r. 158–69/775–85), 114–5
al-Maʾmūn (r. 198–218/813–33), 17, 115, 154, 219n96
miḥna and, 49, 117
pyramids and, 46, 225n52
translation movement and, 229n66
Turkish slaves and, 172
world map and, 24, 217nn53–4
al-Manṣūr (r. 136–58/754–75), 52, 114
Baghdad and, 21–2
translation movement and, 20
Maqdisī, al-Muṭahhar b. Ṭāhir (fl. 355/966), 84
Marco Polo (d. 1324), 160
Marinos, 217n54
Marquart, Josef (d. 1930), 163
Marwazī, Abū 'l-ʿAbbās (d. 274/887–8), 213n8, 259n153
Marwazī, Ṭāhir (fl. 483/1090)
humoral geography and, 91–2

silent trade and, 39–40, 222n26
Maslama b. ʿAbd al-Malik, Abū ʿAlī (d. 122/740), 233n72
Masʿūdī, Abū 'l-Ḥasan (d. 345/956), 8, 35, 48, 88, 152, 221n12, 225n55
Alexander Romance and, 100, 233n54
on Caucasus, 70, 72, 73, 76
early maps and, 135, 217n54, 235n105
famous buildings and, 44, 104–5
on first language, 116–7
Ibn Khurradādhbih and, 18, 28, 30
on Khazar conversion, 232n37
Persian verse in, 218n86
Ptolemy and, 216n46, 216n48
on wall of Gog and Magog, 135, 136
Wāthiq and Ḥunayn and, 51–2
Maṭar b. Thalj al-Tamīmī, 80
Mazdak, 29
Meynard, Charles Barbier de (d. 1908), 16, 154–5, 169–70
Miller, Konrad (d. 1933), 165
Minorsky, Vladimir, 166, 172, 222n26, 232n35, 239n22
Mīr Khwānd, Muḥammad b. Khāwandshāh (d. 903/1498), 152–3, 247n58; Plate 10
Montgomery, James, 10, 171, 183, 221n8, 259n147
Moses, 26, 69, 119, 130, 180
Muʿāwiya b. Abī Sufyān (r. 41–60/661–80), 80
mission to wall and, 81–2, 113, 181
Muhallabī, Ḥasan b. Aḥmad (d. 380/990), 232n45
Muhallabī, Ismāʿīl b. Yazīd, 44–6, 225n49
Muḥammad b. ʿAbd al-Ṣamad, 47
Muḥammad b. Mūsā. *See* Khwārazmī, Muḥammad b. Mūsā
Muḥammad b. Najīb Bakrān (fl. 604/1208), 37, 130, 246n18
Muḥammad (Prophet), 45, 58, 139, 150
ʿAbbāsids and, 21, 52, 114
dream interpretation and, 61–2
Gog and Magog and, 5, 62, 99, 152
Ibn Khurradādhbih and, 25–6, 186
Qurʾān and, 38, 43, 54, 58, 117, 130
Muqaddasī, Abū ʿAbd Allāh (fl. 375/985)
on archives, 11, 74, 132, 133, 216n42, 233n72
on divisions of land, 88, 235n97
on empiricism, 9–10
Ibn Khurradādhbih and, 133–4, 214n11, 214n14, 246n24
on location of Gog and Magog, 145
maps and, 134–5
on Sallām's adventure, 130, 131–2, 174–5, 228n50
Muqātil b. Sulaymān (d. 150/767), 100
al-Muqtadir (r. 295–320/908–32), 38
Mustawfī, Ḥamd Allāh (d. ca 741/1340), 130, 144, 149
al-Muʿtaḍid (r. 279–89/892–902)
as future caliph, 183
Ibn al-Faqīh on, 173, 259n157
music and, 185
Sarakhsī and, 182, 214n8
al-Muʿtamid (r. 255–79/870–92)
Ibn Khurradādhbih and, 17, 20, 50, 172, 182–3, 186, 214n12
imprisonment of, 183–4, 215n18
Ṣāʿid b. Makhlad and, 183, 214n17
Ṣaymarī and, 185
Turkish guard of, 49
al-Muʿtaṣim (r. 218–27/833–42), 115, 117
military conquests of, 32–3, 82, 220n107
Turkish guard of, 49, 67, 124
al-Mutawakkil (r. 232–47/847–61), 59, 71, 185
Ḥunayn and, 48, 51
translation during reign of, 59
al-Muwaffaq (d. 278/891)
Ibn Khurradādhbih and, 183–4
imprisonment of al-Muʿtaṣim, 183,

214n17
Lu'lu' and, 44, 225n49
Ṣā'id b. Makhlad and, 182–3

Nashwān b. Sa'īd al-Ḥimyarī (d. 573/1178), 98
Needham, Joseph, 162
Nimrod, 116
Nīsābūrī, Niẓām al-Dīn (d. 730/1330), 138–9
Niẓāmī Ganjawī (d. ca 600/1203), 29, 100
Noah, 92, 116, 144
Nöldeke, Theodore (d. 1930), 163, 237n1, 241n52, 242n58

Pīr Muḥammad Khān (r. 963–75/1556–67), 249n80
Plato, 54, 57
Prester John, 160
Pseudo-Ephraem, 43
Pseudo-Methodius, 43, 241n53
Ptolemy (fl. 141 C.E.), 24, 41, 86, 216n48
humoral geography of, 90–4
Ibn Khurradādhbih and, 22–3, 216n46

Qaramānī, Aḥmad b. Yūsuf (d. 1019/1611), 141
Qarāṭīs, 50
Qazwīnī, Zakariyyā' (d. 682/1283)
on marvels, 3, 76, 142, 211n4, 249n91; Plates 2–3
popularity of, 246n20, 249n88
qibla map, Plate 4
on Sallām, 130, 140–1, 149; Plate 9
Qubādh I (r. 488-531 C.E.), 27, 72
Qudāma b. Ja'far (d. 337/948), 8, 18–20, 23, 55, 88, 145
Qutayba b. Muslim (d. 96/715), 47

Rabghūzī, Nāṣir al-Dīn (d. after 710/1310), 138, 248n68
al-Rāḍī (r. 322–9/934–40), 132
Rashīd al-Dīn (d. 718/1318), 144, 176–7
Rāzī, Amīn Aḥmad (fl. 1002/1594), 143
Rāzī, Fakhr al-Dīn (d. 606/1209), 81, 138
Reinaud, Joseph Toussaint (d. 1867), 154
Rennell, James (d. 1830), 159
Riḍā, Muḥammad Rashīd (d. 1935), 5
Roderick (Ludhrīq), 46
Roger II (d. 1154), 146

Ṣa'b b. Dhī Marāthid, 97
Sahl b. Hārūn (d. 215/830), 106
Ṣā'id b. Makhlad (d. 276/889), 182–3, 214n17
Sallām al-Tarjumān, 16–7, 49–51, 118, 140, 166, 248n68, 249n80
'Abd Allāh b. Ṭāhir and, 121, 124–5, 200, 204, 207
Alexander the Great and, 97, 100, 123, 181
among the Bashjirt, 164–5, 167, 175, 206, 237n139
in the Caucasus, 68–74, 83, 196, 201, 205
description of the wall, 102, 104–5, 106, 110, 112, 135, 197–9, 202–3, 206–7
empire and, 49, 181
empiricism of, 43, 68, 95, 112–3, 131, 181, 199
first language and, 116–7, 120
on inhabitants before the wall, 100–2, 113, 196, 202, 206
Island of Sheep and, 140–2
journey of, 42, 84, 94, 100, 121
with the Khazar, 74, 94, 140–1, 196, 205; Plate 9
the maidservant and, 140–2, 249n86; Plate 9
marvelous buildings and, 44, 102
as narrator, 68, 125, 195, 201, 205
number of languages spoken by, 67–8, 195

payment received, 125, 200, 204, 207
in putrid land, 94–5, 100, 196, 202, 206; Plate 6
Qurʾān and, 42, 103
recommended by Ashinās, 51, 67, 71, 195
on ruined cities, 95, 100
in *terra incognita*, 94–6, 120, 181, 186, 196
translation of inscription, 115–7, 199
as translator, 51, 60, 67–8, 76, 147, 228n50
in Transoxiana and Khurāsān, 121–4, 200, 204, 244n107
use of Persian, 68, 110–1
visual representations of, Plates 9–10
Salm, son of Farīdūn, 28
Sām, son of Noah, 92
Samʿānī, ʿAbd al-Karīm (d. 562/1166), 132
Sarakhsī (d. 285/899), 130, 182, 214n8, 221n12, 245n7; Plate 12
Ṣaymarī, Abū 'l-ʿAnbas (d. 275/888), 185, 194
Scott, Jonathan (d. 1829), 143
Shāfiʿī, Muḥammad b. Idrīs (d. 204/820), 54
Shahmardān b. Abī 'l-Khayr (fl. 476/1083), 145, 235n101; Plate 1
Shahrbarāz, 78–82
envoy of, 78–81, 138, 155
parallels with Sallām's mission, 112, 113, 136, 181
Shāh ʿĀlam Bahādūr Shāh I (d. 1124/1712), 143
Sharwān Shāh, 73
Shaybanī, Muḥammad b. al-Ḥasan (d. 189/805), 87
Sionita, Gabriel, 146
Sīrāfī, Abū Saʿīd (d. 368/979), 55–6
Sprenger, Aloys (d. 1893), 154, 166
Stein, Sir Aurel (d. 1943), 167–8
St. Epiphanius (d. 403 C.E.), 79
Strabo (d. ca 23 C.E.), 7, 153, 252n26
Sukkarī, Abū Saʿīd (d. 275/888), 224n45
Sulaymān, and Bilqīs, 26
Sulaymān the Merchant (fl. 237/851), 8
Suyūṭī, Jalāl al-Dīn (d. 911/1505), 138, 248n66

Tabānūyan (Ṭ.ā.ū.n), 121, 156–7, 200, 253n51
Ṭabarī, Muḥammad b. Jarīr (d. 310/923), 29, 50, 71, 116–7, 99, 152, 183, 233n61, 243n94, 260n5
account of Dhū 'l-Qarnayn, 119, 243n94
on Gog and Magog, 223n31, 230n9, 233n61
on Shahrbarāz, 78, 80–1, 138
Takīn, 38–9, 222n17
Tamīm b. Baḥr (fl. 206/821), 101, 172, 239n22
Tawḥīdī, Abū Ḥayyān (d. ca 414/1023), 55
Thaʿālibī, ʿAbd al-Malik (d. 429/1038), 9, 29, 77, 219n88
on Sallām, 136–7, 180
Thābit b. Qurra (d. 288/901), 24
Thaʿlabī, Aḥmad b. Muḥammad (d. 427/1036), 138, 180, 248n64
Theodosius, Emperor (d. 395 C.E.), 36
Togan, Zeki Validi, 166
Tomaschek, Wilhelm, 163
Ṭūj, son of Farīdūn, 28
Ṭūsī, Muḥammad b. Maḥmūd (fl. 555/1160), 139; Plate 14

ʿUmar b. al-Khaṭṭāb (r. 13–23/634–44), 27, 185, 225n55
ʿUqba b. ʿĀmir (fl. first/seventh century), 99

van Donzel, E. J., 168–9, 252n34, 253n46, 254n53, 256n104
Vasco da Gama, 146

Vasiliev, A. A., 166
Voltaire (d. 1778), 148

Wahb b. Munabbih (d. ca 102/720), 97, 116, 119–20
Warton, Thomas (d. 1790), 149
Wāsiṭī, Abū ʿAbd Allāh, 45
al-Wāthiq biʾllāh (r. 227–32/842–7), 35, 37, 48, 50, 70, 83, 115, 125, 135, 171, 219n96, 220n3, 226n15
  court of, 24, 30, 49–52, 172, 185, 189
  death of, 50, 226n7
  dispatch of Sallām, 43, 44, 195–6, 201, 205
  dream of, 15, 43, 60–3, 123, 195, 201, 205
  empiricism and, 51–2, 113, 125, 129, 199, 200
  Ḥunayn and, 51–2
  Kitāb al-aghānī and, 50, 185
  miḥna and, 49–50, 117
  mission to Cave and, 36–7, 182
  in Orientalist literature, 148–9, 150, 252n18
  rebellion of Isḥāq b. Ismāʿīl and, 70–1
  Turkish guard and, 49, 51, 67
Wilson, C. E., 164–5

Yāfith (Japheth), 92, 144
Yaʿqūbī (fl. 278/891), 70–1, 88
Yāqūt al-Rūmī (d. 626/1229), 76, 152, 184
  on divisions of land, 89, 90
  on Ibn Khurradādhbih, 18, 215n19
  on Sallām, 130, 134, 175
Yazdagird III (d. 31/651), 72
Yūḥannā b. al-Baṭrīq (d. ca 200/815), 93, 236n135
Yule, Sir Henry (d. 1889), 160–1
Yūsuf (Prophet), 130, 229n59

Zayyānī, Abū ʾl-Qāsim (d. 1249/1833), 142; Plate 11
Zichy, Étienne, 164–6
Zoroaster, 29

INDEX OF PLACES

Afghanistan, 167
Alexandria (Iskandariyya), 47, 99, 232n54
lighthouse (*manāra*) of, 47, 97, 99
Altai mountains, 123, 154, 165
America(s), 6, 143
ʿAmmūriya (Amorium), 32–3
Anatolia, 84
al-Andalus, 87, 166
Anqira (Ankara), 32–3
Arabian Peninsula, 25–6, 32, 35, 67
Aral Sea, 124
Ardashīr-Khurra, 27
Arrajān, 27
Armenia
location of Gog and Magog and, 230n9
location of Scythia and, 92
and the Qurʾān, 26
rebellion of, 70–1, 84
region of, 25, 84, 230n11
Sallām's journey and, 70, 95, 150, 154, 196, 201, 205, 230n9
Asia (*āsiyā*), 90–1, 163
Azerbaijan, 25, 84, 146, 230n9, 233n72

Bāb al-Abwāb, 70, 85, 233n72. *See also* Darband
Badakhshān, 167
Baghdad, 21–2, 35, 88, 213n8, 216n42
Ibn Khurradādhbih and, 17, 88, 214n11
intellectuals of, 111, 133
translation movement in, 59, 88
Balanjar, 183
Balkh, 17, 63, 84, 121, 200, 244n107
Barskhān, 123, 244n111
Basra, 21
Black Sea, 69
Bukhārā, 121, 200, 244n107
Byzantium, 25, 28, 85
frontiers of, 32, 35, 67, 84
relations with, 21, 35, 37, 84, 87, 89, 234n74, 235n96
wonders of, 9, 35–7, 89, 182

Canton (Kalān), 160, 161
Caspian Sea, 35, 71–2
fountain of life and, 69
in Greek sources, 92
Russian expansion into, 150
Sallām's journey and, 120, 124, 140, 154
wall of Gog and Magog and, 42, 70, 161
wonders of, 76, 140, 142; Plate 3
Caucasus, 74–6, 92, 123, 149–50, 159
fountain of life and, 26, 69
Sallām's journey and, 50, 68, 70, 74, 76, 83, 93, 120–1, 125, 154, 164, 166, 169

Sāsānian relations with, 72–3, 76, 78–9
wall of Gog and Magog and, 70, 79, 93, 165
Central Asia, 30, 123, 158, 162, 177
mercantile networks of, 73, 101, 124, 179. *See also* Subjects: Silk Road
Mongol invasion of, 177
Sallām's travels in, 167, 176
Turks of, 49, 93, 101, 123, 144
China, 9, 25, 28, 85, 157, 158, 234n95
location of wall of Gog and Magog, 142, 145, 159, 175
mercantile networks and, 35, 124, 160
Muslims in, 101, 168–9, 256n88
Constantinople, 47. *See also* Byzantium
Ctesiphon, 21, 31, 77, 102
Cyprus, 79

Dāghistān, 71, 231n23
Damascus, 21, 63
Damāwand, 29
Dārābjird, 27, 218n77
Darband, 70, 73, 75–7, 78–9, 81, 83, 161. *See also* Caucasus
Darial pass (Bāb al-Lān), 73
Daylam, 17
Dead Sea, 237n139

Egypt, 23, 44–5, 47, 67, 85, 99, 146, 216n48
Ephesus, 36, 50
Ethiopia (*ityūfiyā*), 90–1
Europe (*arūfā*), 74, 90–1, 143, 149

Fārs, 27, 85. *See also* Iran
Fasā, 218n77
Fertile Crescent, 20

Gaochang, 156
Georgia, 70, 154, 230n11
Giza, pyramids of, 10, 44–6, 102, 171, 183–4, 224nn44–6
Great Wall of China, 5, 155, 157–62, 164–5, 167–9

Hami, 156–7, 164, 169, 254n60
Hind, 85. *See also* India
Hindū Kush, 167, 176

Iberia, 20, 25, 35, 46, 145
Igu, Īkka, or Īkku, 155–7, 164, 166–9, 176, 257n122, 260n163
Iki-Ögüz, 166
Ili River, 166
India, 9, 20, 40, 68, 84, 85, 119–20, 158, 234n95, 256n88
Indian Ocean, 25, 39, 40, 146
Indus River, 167
Iran, 17, 28–9, 84, 92, 150, 158, 186. *See also* Fārs
Īrānshahr, 21, 89, 91
Iraq
as *axis mundi*, 22, 24, 25, 216
exegetes of, 223
Mongol destruction of, 146
region of, 67, 85, 183
in Sallām's journey, 100–1, 196, 202
Iron Gate (Tiemenguan), 166
Irtysh River, 165
Isbījāb (Isbīshāb), 121, 200, 244n107
Iskandariyya, 99. *See also* Alexandria
Iṣṭakhr, 27. *See also* Persepolis

Jabal (district of), 17, 85, 214n11
Jade Gate, 155–8, 162, 164, 167–8, 169, 253nn52–3

Kaʿba, 10, 22, 25–6, 89, 115, 132, 243n81; Plate 4
Kazakhstan, 123, 156, 166
Khamil, 156. *See also* Hami; Qomul; Yizhou
Khamlīj, 183
Khazaria, 145, 179. *See also* Subjects: Khazar(s)
Khawarnaq, 31

Khotan, 85, 157
Khurāsān, 25, 30, 83–5, 146
  Alexander's journey in, 123
  as location of Scythia, 92, 236n135
  Persian singers from, 30
  Sallām's journey in, 120–1, 124, 200, 204, 207
Khwārazm, 138, 145, 246n18
Krak des Chevaliers, 170
Kufa, 21, 31
Kyrgyzstan, 123

Lake Baikal, 164
Lake Balkhash, 123, 156, 158, 166
Lake Issyk-Kol, 123
Lake Lop-nor, 156
Levant, 25, 28, 85
Libya (*lūbiya*), 90–1

Madīnat al-Salām (the City of Peace), 21. *See also* Baghdad
Maghrib. *See* North Africa
Mecca, 10, 22, 25–6, 32, 45, 89, 114–5, 186, 216n42
Medina, 26, 114, 186, 237n141
Mediterranean, 25, 47, 97, 146
Mesopotamia, 20–2, 23, 25–7, 74, 84, 87, 108, 112, 233n72
Mongolia, 101, 123, 156, 165, 176–7, 255n72
al-Mukhtār, 189. *See also* Sāmarrā᾿

Nīsābūr, 9, 121, 134, 138, 200, 246n24
North Africa, 25, 67–8

Orkhon Valley, 101, 123, 156, 172, 239n22
Oxus River, 20, 121, 244n107

Palmyra, 102
Persepolis, 112, 188–9. *See also* Iṣṭakhr
Persian Gulf (Baḥr al-Ḥijāz), 146

Qāf (mountain), 69, 100
Qocho, 156, 168
Qomul, 156–8, 168–9, 254nn57–58
Qoy-su River, 71

Rāja Girā, 167, 257n122
Rayy, 200, 204, 207
Rūm, 85. *See also* Byzantium

Sacred Mosque of Mecca (*al-masjid al-ḥarām*), 26, 115
Samandar, 83, 201
Samarqand, 30, 121, 123, 124, 172, 200, 204, 207, 219n96, 231n35, 244n107
Sāmarrā᾿, 48, 67, 92, 183, 215n18, 242n65
  as ʿAbbāsid capital, 100, 114, 124
  and Ibn Khurradādhbih, 17, 214n11, 214n17
  minaret of, 48
  Sallām's journey, 68, 121, 125, 196, 200, 201–2, 204, 205, 207
  and Turkish guard, 49, 51, 124
  and al-Wāthiq, 49, 189
Sawād, 25, 26–7, 214n10
Scythia (*isqūtiyā*), 79, 90–3, 94, 236n135
Shābūr, 27
Shalanba, 29
Sharwān, 26
Siberia, 39, 144, 164
Sijistān, 85
Sind, 35, 85
Sri Lanka (Sarandīb), 25
Sumatra, 9
Swāt Valley, 167–8, 176, 247n122
Syria, 44, 67, 84, 87

Ṭabaristān, 17
Taklamakan Desert, 166, 176
Ṭarāz, 123, 207
Tarim Basin, 156–7, 169
Tian Shan mountains, 166
Tibet, 85, 101, 163

Tiemenguan, 166
Tiflīs, 70–1, 75, 196, 201, 205, 230n11
Tirmidh, 121, 200, 244n107
Toledo, 46
Transoxiana, 47, 49, 85, 87, 120–1, 123–5, 146, 155
Ṭukhāristān, 85
Turkistān, 145

Urals, 154, 164, 166, 176
Ushrūsana (Sharūsana), 121, 200, 224n107

Volga River, 38–9, 74, 101, 152, 164, 252n21, 253n53
Wāsiṭ, 21

Xinjiang province, 156, 158, 164, 168

Yablonoi mountains, 164
Yemen, 26, 32, 35, 85, 97, 99–100
Yiwu / Yiwulu, 155, 253n38
Yizhou, 155–8, 166, 168–9, 177, 253n38, 254nn58–60
Yumenguan Pass, 156. *See also* Jade Gate

Zābulistān, 185
Zamzam, 114–5

INDEX OF SUBJECTS AND TERMS

ʿAbbāsid(s), 185
administration, 15, 18–9, 21–2, 24–5, 67, 70, 87, 109
as *axis mundi*, 24–5, 186. *See also* dil-i Īrānshahr
court and literary culture of, 17–8, 29–33, 34, 51–3, 109, 111, 117, 184–6, 220n108, 221n10, 259n147
empire of, 1, 24, 34, 49, 121, 124
expansion, 17, 68, 83
foreign relations of, 35, 50, 67, 70, 72, 75, 87, 124–5, 179
fragmentation of, 87, 186
frontiers of, 70, 72, 74, 76, 123, 177, 183, 191
intellectual history of, 155
legitimacy of, 52–3, 60–3, 83, 92, 114–5, 179–80, 186, 235n102
marvels and, 47
mercantile networks of, 35, 39, 47, 74
messianism and, 60–1
reception of Sallām's adventure among, 112, 184–5, 187
revolution, 20–1
Sāsānian models for, 17, 21–2, 24–5, 27, 62, 216n40, 218n75, 219n95
translations and, 20
Abou-el-Cassim, 152–3. *See also* People: d'Ohsson, Constantin Mouradgea
abwāb (mountain passes), 69
account (*khabar*, pl. *akhbār*), 37, 100
Adhkish, 101, 123, 134, 164, 167, 175–6, 206, 244n113, 256n95, 259n122; Plates, 6–8, 12
adīb, pl. *udabāʾ* (littérateurs), 18–9, 182
ʿajab, pl. *ʿajāʾib*, 1, 3, 23, 93, 100, 181. *See also* marvelous, [the]; wonder(s)
ʿajāʾib al-bunyān (marvels of architecture), 44. *See also* wonder(s): buildings and places as
al-arḍ (of the world), 46
al-makhlūqāt (of creation), 139
ʿajāʾib [literature], 93, 191. *See also* marvel-writing
ʿajam (non-Arabs), 21, 22, 53, 98
ʿajīb, 7, 44, 140, 189, 237n141. *See also* marvelous, [the]
akhbār. *See* account
ākhir (boundary). *See* frontier(s): Arabic terminology of
Alāns (al-Lān), 43, 73, 75–7, 86, 95, 196, 201, 206
Alexander Romance, 43, 80, 97, 99, 110, 112, 116, 163, 237n1. *See also* Pseudo-Callisthenes cycle
aljamiado, 120, 237n1
anecdote(s). *See also* fable(s); *khabar*, pl. *akhbār*; narrative(s); *qiṣṣa*, pl. *qiṣaṣ*
collection of, x, 139, 146, 184
comprehension of, 187

encyclopedism and, 135
khabar as, 129
as a means of engaging with difference, 34, 191
narrative form of, 2, 177
ontology and, 2, 33, 179, 187, 189
relation to history, 37–8, 41, 48, 162–3, 179
structure of, 2, 15, 37, 189, 191
translation and, 59, 190
transmission / translation of, 15, 41, 130–2, 164, 179, 191
wonder and, 43, 153, 172, 180, 186, 191
angels, 4, 180
apocalypse / apocalyptic, 1, 5, 15, 42, 61, 103, 111, 181, 230n77, 239n34, 252n34
destruction of the Kaʿba during, 115, 243n81
discourse of, 5, 82, 101
landscape of, 94–5
the marvelous and, 70, 181
in the Qurʾān, 93, 95
races, 94, 145
in Syriac writings, 43, 106–9
visions of, 60, 63, 230n77, 239n24
wall of Gog and Magog as holding back, 74, 78, 114, 161
aqālīm. *See* clime(s)
Arabic [language]
Alexander Romance, 99–100, 110, 112, 116, 237n1, 241n51
authority of, 27, 29–30
knowledge of, 35, 51, 100–1, 137, 157, 196, 202, 206
literary culture, 19, 31, 190
the Qurʾān and, 54, 117–8
relationship to Persian, 26–7, 29–30
script, 29, 31, 120, 158
transformation of, 22
translation and, 21–2, 24, 41, 53–61, 63, 73, 88, 90–3, 97, 105, 184, 227n42, 230n77, 242n55, 246n20
Arab(s), 49, 54, 61, 84, 92, 132
battle days (*ayyām*) of, 31
conquests and, 20–1, 27, 29, 43, 46, 75, 78–80, 98
Great Wall of China and, 161
relation to the Persians, 219n95, 220n103
Umayyads and, 21, 70
arḍ al-islām (land of Islam), 88, 234n94. *See also dār al-ḥarb/al-islām*
al-arḍ al-maʿmūra (inhabited world), 35, 90. *See also* inhabited world
Armenian(s), 22, 70, 97, 151
asafœtida (*ḥiltīt*, *angudān*, *hing*), 156, 158. *See also* putrid land
aṣḥāb al-kahf. *See* People of the Cave
Ashʿarī theology, 4
asmār, 8, 184. *See also* anecdote(s); authenticity; fable(s); narrative(s)
Assyrian, 116
astonishment, 7, 48, 53, 81, 145, 181, 192, 196, 202
astrologer (*munajjim*), 23, 36, 37, 61–2, 104, 136, 153
astrology, 23, 44, 61–2, 86–7, 94, 185
astronomy, 51, 85, 132, 136
authenticity
of Byzantine relics, 37
codicology and, 11, 169–70
epistemology and, 9–10
of the marvelous, 7–8, 31, 80–2, 153, 179, 185, 191
of merchant tales, 8–9
narrative strategies of, 129
of Sallām's narrative, 2, 68, 131–2, 135–7, 142, 152–3, 164, 168, 173, 180
of travel literature, 160, 163, 256n88
authorship
of *Adab al-ghurabāʾ*, 255n58
of Arabic translation of Artemidorus, 229n69
concept of, 172–3

of *Ghurar*, 219n88
Ibn Khurradādhbih and, 111, 172
of *Mulūk Ḥimyar*, 238n9
autopsia, 239n31. *See also* empiricism; eyewitness; *ʿiyān*
Avars, 76, 231n23
ʿawāṣim (inner fortifications). *See* frontier(s): Arabic terminology of

Babel, tower of, 116
Baḥīrā, apocalypse of, 252n34
barīd (communication / post service), 17, 19–20, 22, 34, , 214n11, 216n40
Barmakids, 17
barrier. *See* wall against Gog and Magog
Bashjirt, 164–5, 167, 175, 206, 237n237
bayān (exposition), 105–6. *See also* ekphrasis
baydar (threshing-floor), 27
bayt al-ḥikma (caliphal library), 51
Brahmans, 62, 120
Buddhist(s), 17, 158
Bulghār(s)
in d'Ohsson, 152–3
Ibn Faḍlān and, 38–9, 86, 144, 166, 186–7, 252n21; Plate 14
as Muslims, 137
Sallām's journey and, 164
trade and, 9, 40
Būyid ruler(s), 9, 134, 188–9
Byzantine(s), and empire, 20, 35, 37, 84, 87, 98, 108, 132, 182, 186

camphor. *See* commodities
cannibals / cannibalism, 39–40, 89, 92, 160
cantons. *See* *ṭassūj / tasūg*
cartography, 10. *See also* map(s)
European, 147, 159, 225n72
mimesis and, 41, 134–5, 142
relation to descriptive geography, 134
cauldrons (*qudūr*), at the barrier, 110–1, 198, 203
cave of darkness, 233n72
Cave of the Sleepers, 36–7. *See also* People of the Cave
chākar, 226n6
Chief of the Mountain (*khāqān al-jabal*), 72
Chin dynasty (1115–1234), 176–7
Chinese, 84, 86, 145, 149, 175
sources, 79, 223n29
wall building and, 158–9, 162
Christian(s), 35, 40, 46, 146, 150
in the ʿAbbāsid court, 51–2, 53, 182, 214n17, 241n54
Alexander Romance and, 98, 106–9, 240n46
in the Caucasus, 72–4
relics, 46
on Seven Sleepers of Ephesus, 36–7
traditions on Gog and Magog, 2, 42–3, 93, 94, 106–7, 163
City of Brass, Plate 8
civilization(s), 2, 20, 86, 95, 101, 115
construction of, 1, 77, 92, 104
geographical demarcations of, 34, 76, 92, 137, 161
civilized, 35, 39–41, 43, 191
client (*mawlā*, pl. *mawālī*), 19, 21. *See also* patronage
climate. *See* geography: humoral
clime(s) (*iqlīm*, pl. *aqālīm*), 23–4, 84, 89, 94, 136, 140, 143
location of Gog and Magog in, 94, 136–7, 144, 237
Ptolemaic system of, 89, 143
seven climes, 3, 23, 84–5, 91
clothing. *See also* nudity
brocade robes, 50, 73
buried in, 124, 200
as commodity, 40
covering corpses, 45
covering genitalia, 141
fashioned out of human skin, 92
necessity of, 118

codicological (evidence, record), 12, 133, 169–74, 181, 182, 184. *See also* recension(s)
coins and currency, 27, 39, 68, 74, 113, 118, 125, 150, 195, 199, 200, 201, 204, 205, 207. *See also* taxation
comedy, 56, 185, 227n41
commerce, 35, 39–41, 74, 89. *See also* Silk Road; trade
  trade routes and, 9, 19
commodities, 9, 35, 39–40, 68, 118, 158
communication, 2, 29, 68, 118
  administration and, 19, 34, 68
  deixis and, 7, 39, 192
  knowledge and, 15, 67, 133
  revelatory power of, 106, 228n48
  translation and, 22, 35, 38, 54, 57–8, 60, 101, 206
communities, 2, 61, 87, 113
  isolated, 100–2, 117–8, 137
  religious (*milal*), 91
conquests, Muslim (*futūḥāt*), 46, 82
conversion
  to Christianity, 73, 160
  to Islam, 17, 20, 38, 78–9, 80, 100–1, 109, 118, 119, 137, 176, 206, 218n74
  to Judaism, 74, 232n37
copper, 103, 107, 109–10, 162, 197, 199, 202, 207, 241n53
Coptic, 97
cosmography, 5, 46, 69, 104
  humoral geography and, 86–7, 237n141
  in Ibn Khurradādhbih, 23, 44, 186
  the marvelous and, 7, 139, 163, 180
cosmopolitanism. *See also* ʿAbbāsid(s): court and literary culture of
  belles-lettres and, 33
  empire and, 21–2, 49, 186
  Ibn Khurradādhbih and, 31, 184
cosmos, 3–4, 24, 85, 89
courtier(s), 9, 18, 185
cranes (*gharānīq*), 93, 99, 236n133
cubit(s), 25, 44–5, 119
  black cubit (*sūdāʾ*), 112, 242n64
  greater cubit (*aʿẓam*), 112–3
  height of Gog and Magog in, 93, 113, 197
  in Sallām's description of the wall, 103–4, 110–1, 113, 133, 197–8, 202–3, 206–7
  in Syriac accounts, 107, 240n51
Cynocephali, 142

dandānka (teeth), 104, 110, 136
dār al-ʿāmma (public audience chamber), 114
dār al-ḥarb/al-islām (realm of strife/Islam), 87–9, 234n89, 234n95, 235n95, 235n97, 235n99
Dari, 29. *See also* Middle Persian; Persian [language]
deixis, 7, 87, 192
demons (*shayāṭīn*), 26
descriptive notes (*ṣifāt*), 102, 207
Dhū ʾl-Suwayqatayn, 243n81
diegesis, 68, 129, 187
difference, 55, 75, 85–7
  geographical demarcations of, 28, 84
  between interpreter and translator, 58–60
  linguistic, 35, 75–6, 85–6
  mediation of / engagement with, 1–2, 7, 38–42; Plates 1–3, 9–10, 14
dil-i Īrānshahr, 25, 186, 235n102
dirham(s). *See* coins and currency
districts. *See kūra*, pl. *kuwar*
diversity, 181, 191
  of existence, 5, 48, 87, 180
  of people / regions, 22, 75–6, 89
diviner / divination, 61–2
dīwān (office), 215
  al-barīd (of communication), 19, 34
  al-kharāj (of taxation), 19
dog-headed people, 3, 6, 10, 99, 142, 249n91

dragoman, 15–6, 58. *See also tarjumān*
dream(s), 60, 151, 230n77
of ʿAbd al-Muṭṭalib, 114
of Alexander, 232n54
of Anushirwān, 76
interpretation of (*taʿbīr al-ruʾyā*), 61–3, 187
of al-Maʾmūn, 229n66
of al-Wāthiq, 15, 43, 63, 123, 195, 201, 205
Yūsuf and, 229n59

eagle-stone, 79–80. *See also* gems, and jewels
east (*mashriq*), 25, 101, 257n106
ekphrasis, 10, 45, 77, 102, 105, 107, 115, 129, 135
embassies / missions, caliphal, 34, 88. *See also* al-Wāthiq, mission to the wall
empiricism, 6–8, 10, 52, 102, 104, 131, 137, 180
encyclopedias / encyclopedism, 2, 3, 22, 30, 41, 51–2, 53, 76, 84, 135, 139, 142, 143, 148–9, 152, 168, 189, 191
Ibn Khurradādhbih and, 18, 33, 48
Masʿūdī and, 8, 70, 104–5
Orientalism and, 148–9, 152
Enlightenment, 6, 150, 155, 159, 180
epistemology, 40, 92, 179
codicology and, 11, 172–3
the Enlightenment and, 6, 150, 180
frontiers and, 15, 102, 192
Orientalism, 143, 148, 150–1, 160
translation and, 1, 15, 20, 57, 211n2
wonder(s) and, 6, 9
eschatology, 2, 42, 58, 61, 63, 79, 99, 109, 113, 241n53
empire and, 115, 123
geography and, 190–1
the marvelous and, 260n3
in the Qurʾān, 26, 42, 95, 101, 115–6, 223, 237n142
time and, 43, 187
espionage, 34, 75, 182
Ethiopic, 97, 237n1, 241n51
European. *See also* al-Wāthiq, mission to the wall: European reception of
construct of Orient, 159–60
epistemology, 6, 143, 150
geography, 147, 159
Gog and Magog as, 146
languages, 97
reception, of *Thousand and One Nights*, 148–9
exegesis, Qurʾānic, 36, 43, 53, 97, 99, 139
exotica, 9
eyewitness, 91, 95, 100, 112, 131, 153
authority of, 7–8, 36, 43, 45, 52, 110, 129, 138, 139, 141, 180, 187
epistemology and, 7, 10, 102, 135
as trope, 60, 187

fable(s), 53, 149–51, 163, 185
fabula, 150–1, 179
*farsakh*s, 102, 136, 196, 199, 203, 206
fetid sea (*yammā saryā*), 107, 237n140. *See also* putrid land
fiction, 7, 129, 162, 163, 191
the marvelous as, 162, 180
as narrative conceit, 151–4
Oriental origin of, 149, 161
Finnish Veps (Wīsū), 144, 187; Plate 14
fortification(s), 84, 162, 165, 167, 177, 180, 196–7, 199, 203
of Caucasus, 69–73, 75–7, 83–4, 149, 231n34
near cave of darkness, 233n72
of Central Asia, 162
Chinese, 156, 158, 162, 175–7
in Sallām's narrative, 95, 100, 102, 110, 165, 175, 180, 196–7, 202, 206–7
colossal size of, 102, 198, 203
guardians of, 113–4, 198–200, 203–4, 206
fountain, of life, 26, 69, 82, 98, 242n57

Franj / Frank(s), 35, 85, 146. *See also* European
frontier(s), 34, 41, 42, 60, 70, 84, 88, 113, 131
ʿAbbāsid relations with, 50, 62, 70–1, 74–5, 101, 123–4, 179, 183, 191
apocalypse and, 103, 108
Arabic terminology of, 67, 87, 166, 235nn97–8
with Byzantium, 67, 84, 87
China and, 156, 163, 168
empire and, 2, 22, 82, 131, 187
engaging with, 2, 34, 40–1
epistemology and, 15, 102, 177, 192
knowledge of, 5, 9, 34–5, 131
Sāsānian relations with, 73–4, 76, 78–9
savages and, 2, 34, 76
furta sacra, 46. *See also* relics

gems, and jewels, 9, 39, 46, 50, 78–81, 115, 181
geographical divisions, 23–4, 84–5, 87–8, 90–2
geography, 41–2, 132. *See also* translation: geography and
administrative, 16–20, 24–5, 27, 55, 68, 88, 186, 187, 191
economy and, 9, 68
empire and, 22, 46–8, 82–3, 179, 182, 184, 186, 225n55
empiricism and, 7–8, 10, 40, 91–2, 104, 131–2, 212n20, 220n2, 239n31
European, 146–7, 155, 159–62, 255n72
humoral, 23, 85–7, 90–2, 94
Islamic, 11, 17, 26, 82, 88–9, 170
Ptolemaic, 22–4, 86, 89, 90–2, 94, 217n45, 217n56
mimesis and, 41–2, 102, 135, 159, 180
relation to belles-lettres, 19, 28–33, 143, 171, 184–5, 187, 190–1
sacred, 82, 89, 101–2, 120, 124, 132, 190–1
Sāsānian / Persian, 24–5, 27, 84–5, 89
wonders and, 23, 34, 43, 44–48, 182, 184–5
ghayb, 9–10, 35, 57, 62
Ghuzz Turks, 39, 85, 172
giants, 47, 144, 149, 187; Plate 14
giant serpents, 39
Gog and Magog, 2, 5, 42, 78, 92, 131, 133, 144, 146, 161, 190
description of
as giants, 187; Plate 14
as hairless, 145
long ears of, 142
small stature of, 92–3, 112–3, 142, 197, 199, 203, 236nn135–6
as swarm, 42, 81, 114, 198
destruction caused by, 43, 95, 100, 103, 115, 123, 176, 196, 202, 206–7
dreams of, 230n77
enclosure of, 5, 42, 76, 82, 93, 98–9, 100, 107–8, 118–9, 123, 134, 143–4, 161, 230n9; Plate 5
identification of, 43, 77, 83, 133, 144–6
as Mongols, 146, 160, 255n72
as Scythians, 93–4
as Turks, 43, 92, 123, 144–5, 166, 175
in Islamic apocalyptic thought, 5, 62–3, 82, 98–9
Jewish and Christian traditions of, 2, 42–3, 107–8
language / sound of, 114, 118, 144, 203, 207
location / lands of, 5, 25, 78, 86, 93–4, 108, 123, 133–6, 142–6, 159–60, 164, 179, 206, 217n54, 250n100, 250n108, 255n72; Plates 6–8, 11–2
Orientalist treatment of, 149, 150, 159–60, 166
pictorial representations of, 236n136; Plates 1, 5, 14
Qurʾānic treatment of, 2, 5, 42, 69–70, 77, 78–9, 82, 93, 95, 103, 109, 115–8, 134, 136–7, 143, 150, 152, 155, 181–2, 223n31, 241n52

reality of, 134, 136, 144, 180
graffiti, 33, 47, 188–91
Greek, 35, 51, 53, 56, 149–50, 251n17
Alexander / Dhū 'l-Qarnayn and, 82, 97–9, 106, 112, 120, 167, 238n9, 241n53
geography and, 7, 24, 41, 90–4, 153, 235n104, 236n135, 249n91
learning / philosophy, 4, 53–5, 77
marvels / marvel-writing, 2–3, 7–8, 42, 142, 236n133
translation and, 20, 22–4, 27, 51–60, 88, 142, 218n78
Greeks, 22, 34, 50, 53
guan (gate, fortified pass), 168
guide(s), 15–6, 38, 39, 44
to People of the Cave, 36–8
Sallām's journey and, 94, 118, 120–1, 187, 196, 200, 201, 204, 206–7
for Shahrbarāz's mission, 78
as translator, 35, 38–9, 41, 51, 58

ḥadd, pl. *ḥudūd* (frontiers). *See* frontier(s): Arabic terminology of
ḥadīth, 58, 61–3, 98–9, 101, 114–5, 133, 144, 154, 228n47
Han dynasty (206 B.C.E.–220 C.E.), 155–6, 158, 162
ḥāshiya (periphery). *See* frontier(s): Arabic terminology of
hermeneutics, 1, 45, 58, 61–2, 138
Hermes, 44, 224n44
hieroglyphics, 44–5, 115–6, 224n45
ḥikāya (story, narrative), 137, 138, 141, 179
Ḥimyarī king, of South Arabia, 97–8, 100
horns, 5, 43, 241n53
on wall, 104, 197, 207, 239n33
hudhud (hoopoe), 180
humor, 185
humors, four, 86, 91. *See also* geography: humoral; nature(s)
Huns, 43, 83, 93, 108–9
hypomnemata, 133

Idrīsids, 87, 186
infidels, 88, 101, 152. *See also kāfir*, pl. *kuffār*; pagan(s)
inhabited world, 8, 23, 39, 42, 84, 86, 89–91, 94, 101, 135, 138, 217n54
inscription(s), 115–8, 175, 188–90, 199. *See also* graffiti
insects, 3, 4–5
intercession (*shafāʿa*), 58
interpreter(s), 106, 191, 228n47
of dreams (*muʿabbir*), 62–3
Sallām as, 15–6, 76, 125, 140–1, 195, 200, 201, 204, 205, 207
intertextuality, 33, 60
iron, 113, 125, 181, 199, 200, 241n53
ḥadīd, 103, 241n53
parzlā / firzil, 107, 108–9, 241n53
of wall, 81, 102, 104, 110–1, 115, 144, 196–200, 202–3, 206–7
ishāra, pl. *ishārāt*, 7, 40, 192
Islam, 38, 43, 46, 79, 101, 115, 168. *See also* conversion: to Islam; salvation history
as geographical category, 72, 87–9, 131, 186, 234n89, 234nn94–5, 235nn97–99, 235n102
Island of Sheep, 140–2
isnād (transmission), 132–3, 174, 246nn29–30
ʿiyān (eyewitness), 7–10, 45, 91, 102, 212n20, 239n31

jāhiliyya, 31
Jewish
Khazar, 38, 74
merchants, 35, 41, 186, 221n4
traditions, 2, 42–3, 116
Jew(s), 22, 74, 138, 166
jinn, 4, 8, 26, 40, 77, 180
Judgment, Day of, 61, 124

kāfir, pl. *kuffār* (infidels), 72–3, 88
kāhin, pl. *kuhhān* (soothsayer), 61
kalām (theology / speech), 54, 57, 117
kātib, pl. *kuttāb*. *See* secretary(ies)
key(s), 104, 109–12, 114–5, 136, 150, 198, 203, 240n51, 248n68
khabar, pl. *akhbār* (account / report), 8, 37, 43, 100, 129, 179, 195
Khāqān, 31, 231n35, 247n40
khaqanate, 74
khāqān al-jabal (Chief of the Mountain), 72
khāqān, of the Adhkish, 175, 206, 259n162. *See also* Adhkish
Khazar(s), 49, 74, 137, 183
  conversion to Judaism, 74, 232n37
  double kingship of, 74, 231n35
  neighbors of, 38, 74–6, 82, 167
  region of, 35, 72, 77, 83, 85, 92, 183
  Sallām's journey in, 49, 74–5, 83, 94, 95, 140–1, 154, 157, 166, 173, 196, 201, 252n27
  ruler of, 74, 81, 94, 140–1, 166, 196, 201, 231n35, 237n139
  wall / land of Gog and Magog and, 25, 43, 81, 86, 94, 101, 132–3, 138, 144–5, 164, 174–5, 186, 253n53, 258n142
Khotanese, 157
khurāfāt (fables), 8, 184–5
Kīmāk, 39–40, 85, 144, 222n24, 244n112, 247n40
kishwar divisions, 84–5, 89, 234n79, 235n101. *See also* clime(s); geographical divisions
knowledge. *See also* epistemology
  acquisition of, 9–10, 42, 52, 60, 78, 82
  archives and, 10, 17, 131
  construction of, 2, 52, 143, 148
  empire and, 27, 131, 182
  experience and, 9, 102, 106
  frontiers and, 5, 60
  geographical, 5, 8, 19–20, 33, 35, 41, 78, 159, 165
  limits of, 3, 6, 8, 10, 12, 35, 103, 179–81
  religious, 61, 132, 182
  transmission of, 10, 15, 38, 42, 52, 53, 60, 106, 130, 133, 142, 143, 187
kufr, 88, 234n89, 235n95, 235n99. *See also* infidels; *kāfir*, pl. *kuffār*
kūra, pl. *kuwar* (districts), 26–7, 218n78

lafẓ, pl. *alfāẓ* (words, expressions), 56
land of darkness, 100, 107
language, first (*al-lisān al-awwal*), 115–8, 120, 175, 199
language(s), 7, 23, 37, 39, 76
  diversity of, 75–6, 85–6, 118
  foreign, 23, 37
  mastery of multiple, 35, 41, 67–8, 77, 119, 195
  mimesis and, 41, 102
  ontology and, 9–10, 104, 191
  power of, 96, 105, 189
  revelation and, 55, 106, 118
  translation and, 15–6, 38, 53–6, 57–9, 101, 206
  visual quality of, 105–6, 108
Latin, 77, 97, 149–50, 251n17
  marvels and, 7, 252n19
  translation and, 16, 58
  translation of Idrīsī, 146–7, 150, 251n18
learning, 6, 22, 24, 138
  ʿAbbāsids and, 51–3, 57
  religious, 61, 100, 132, 142
  transmission of, 133, 143, 173
lighthouse (*manāra*), 47, 97, 99
lisān al-awwal. *See* language, first
Lord of the Throne (*ṣāḥib al-sarīr*), 71–3, 196, 201, 206, 231n19

maghrib (west), 25
Magyars, 43
maidservant, and the fish, 140–2, 149, 151, 153, 249n86, 252n27; Plate 9

*majma*ʿ *al-baḥrayn* (meeting of two oceans), 26
Manicheans, 158
map(s)
of Bīrūnī, 84–5
Genoese map of 1457, 236n136
of Ibn Ḥawqal, 144, 250n108
Ibn Khurradādhbih and, 91
of Idrīsī, 123, 135, 147, 165; Plates 6–7
of the *Kitāb gharāʾib al-funūn*, Plate 8
knowledge and, 48, 94, 120, 131, 174
of al-Maʾmūn, 24, 217nn53–4
mimesis and, 10, 41, 134–5
of Muqaddasī, 134–5
of Nicolas Sanson, 255n72
Ptolemy and, 24, 235n105; Plate 12
qibla, 89; Plate 4
of the world (*ṣūrat al-arḍ / mappa mundi*), 24, 135, 165; Plates, 6, 8, 11–2
of Zayyānī, Plate 11
marvelous, [the], 7, 45–8, 79
accounts of, 143, 149, 182, 185–6, 191
ʿajab / ʿajīb, 1, 2, 44, 181–2
the apocalypse and, 70, 180, 260n4
authenticity of, 6–7, 10, 68
in cosmography, 1, 3, 139
epistemology and, 3, 6, 150
observation of, 7, 10, 192
ontology of, 6–7, 9–10
possession of, 39, 44–8
the savage and, 7, 40–1
theodicy and, 3–4, 10, 139
marvel(s). *See* wonder(s)
marvel-writing, 2–3, 7–9, 39, 93, 102, 139–42, 153, 181, 187
mawlā, pl. *mawālī* (client), 19, 21. *See also* patronage
measurement
as discursive strategy, 102, 107–8, 118
geography and, 8, 104
taxation and, 27
merchants, 8–9, 22, 35, 39–41, 68, 74, 101, 124, 146, 186, 221n4
tales of, 8, 141, 144–5
mermaid, 151
microcosmic, and macrocosm, 3–4
Middle Persian, 20, 22, 23, 27, 29, 213n2, 218n76
Alexander Romance and, 111–2, 242n58
miḥna (inquisition), 49, 117
mimesis, 10, 44, 47, 102, 105, 135, 159, 180, 190, 213n33
Ming dynasty (1368–1644), 158
mirabile visu, 7, 102. *See also* eyewitness
mirabilia, 7. *See also* wonder(s)
misāḥa (cadastral land survey), 27
Modernity, 6
Mongol(s), 43, 146, 158, 160, 176–7, 255n72
origin myth of, 144
monsters, 2–3, 10, 34, 48, 62, 93, 99, 144, 161, 180
monstrous, [the], 1–4, 5, 15, 89, 92, 99
tribes / races, 2, 5, 43, 63, 134, 138, 143–5, 180, 187. *See also* Gog and Magog
muʿāyana (direct or mutual observation), 8, 10, 40, 102, 222n26
mughāyaba, 40, 222n26, 223n29. *See also* commerce
multiplicity, 9, 43, 179
linguistic, 38, 41, 55, 116
textual, 11, 133, 169–71, 174–5, 184, 194
mummies, 36–7, 44–6
mushāhada (direct witnessing), 8
music, 18, 30, 50, 172, 185–6
mutarjim (translator), 59–60, 118, 228n50. *See also tarjumān*
mutawaḥḥish. *See* savage(s)
Muʿtazilī theology, 4, 50, 117, 155. *See also miḥna*

nadīm, pl. *nudamā*ʾ (boon companion), 17, 182, 185, 189, 214n12
nāḥiya (region or district), 26
nāqil, 58–9, 228n50. *See also* translator(s): terminology for
narrative(s) 89, 116, 179, 190
  Arabic categories for, 129–30
  authenticity of, 80–1, 134, 155, 163–4, 168, 179–80
  coherence of, 2, 63, 153, 187
  conversion, 101, 176, 206
  emplotment, 9, 92, 108, 179, 187
  generic expectations of, 106, 179
  logic of, 60, 118
  pleasure and, 8, 10, 150, 154
  techniques of, 32–3, 68, 74, 95, 102, 107, 125, 132, 153, 162, 171, 177, 189, 218n74, 241n53
  transmission of, 125–6, 130–1, 189
narrator(s), 44, 80, 141, 172
Nasnās, 48
nature(s), 61
  construction of, 4, 187
  disposition and, 85–6, 91–3, 47, 237n141
naẓar (investigation), 3, 9, 52
north (*jarbī*), 25
nudity, 39, 120

obscenity, 185
ocean, encircling (*al-baḥr al-mudīr* / *al-muḥīṭ*), 89–90, 99, 107, 235nn104–5; Plate 2
ocular (perception), 7, 10, 60, 91, 95, 102, 112, 135, 139, 180, 187
oecumene, 34, 90–2. *See also* inhabited world
oneiromancy, 51, 61–3, 185
Önggüt (Önggüd, Ong), 160, 176–7
öngü, 177, 260n167
Orientalism, 148, 150–1
Orientalist(s), 11, 42, 148–52, 154–5, 159, 162–3, 169
Oriental(s), 6, 148–51, 159, 161
  imagination of, 149, 161
Orient, constructions of, 148, 159–60
Ottoman(s), 131, 146, 238n9

pagan(s), 38, 98. *See also* infidels; *kāfir*, pl. *kuffār*
Pahlavi, 29. *See also* Middle Persian
patronage, 20, 22, 44, 51, 53, 60, 125, 183, 186, 200, 204
peace treaties (*hudna* / *ṣulḥ*), 87
People of the Book, 99
People of the Cave (*aṣḥāb al-kahf*)
  in the Qurʾān, 74, 180, 181, 252n34
  al-Wāthiq's mission to, 35–7, 44, 50, 138, 154, 166, 221n12
People of the Throne, 72, 231n23. *See also* Lord of the Throne; Sarīr
Persian [language], 27, 29
  knowledge of, 35, 100–1, 157, 196, 202, 206
  literature, 28–31, 53, 73, 77
  relation to Arabic, 30
  terminology, 7, 21, 24–5, 26–7, 68, 110–2, 218n75, 235n101
  translation and, 43, 53, 142
Persian(s), 92
  history, pre-Islamic, 25–9, 72–3, 76, 112, 136
  kings, 25, 28–9, 73, 76–7, 84, 111–2, 136, 189, 216n40, 219n95
pilgrimage (*ḥajj*), 25, 33, 114–5, 132
pleasure
  literary, 33, 50, 186
  of the marvelous, 10, 153, 187
  relation to horror, 39
poetry
  in ʿAbbāsid court, 50, 82–3
  Alexander Romance and, 100
  Arabic, 19, 28, 30–3, 47, 56, 98, 105
  challenges of translating, 53, 56
  ekphrasis and, 102, 105
  as graffiti, 47, 190

Ibn Khurradādhbih's use of, 18, 23, 28–33, 171, 182–6, 191, 220n103, 258n142, 259n153
Latin, 151
melancholy and, 190
Persian, 29–31, 100, 218n86, 219n96, 220n101
postal routes (*sikāk*), 34, 68, 157. *See also barīd*
pragmatism, 68, 118, 125
Prophet. *See* People: Muḥammad (Prophet)
prophetic tales. *See qiṣaṣ al-anbiyā*ʾ
Pseudo-Callisthenes cycle, 97–8, 106, 110, 120, 145, 155. *See also* Alexander Romance
in Arabic, 100, 110
in Middle Persian, 242n58
in Persian, 100
in Syriac, 240n46, 242n55, 242n58
Ptolemaic (division), 23–4, 89, 143
putrid land (*al-muntina*), 94–6, 100, 181, 196, 202
caused by asafœtida 156, 158
caused by rotting carcasses, 175–6
doubts over, 137
on maps, 135; Plate 6
relation to fetid sea and land of darkness, 107–8, 111
pygmies, 3, 39, 93, 99, 142, 236n133. *See also* Gog and Magog
pyramids. *See* Places: Giza, pyramids of

qalawūz, 37–8. *See also* guide(s)
Qarluq, 123, 244n113
qibla, 25, 45, 84, 89, 132; Plate 4
Qirghiz, 123, 156, 165
*qiṣaṣ al-anbiyā*ʾ (stories of the prophets), 99, 129, 132, 138, 142
qiṣṣa, pl. *qiṣaṣ* (edifying tale), 36, 130, 260n5
Sallām's account as, 125, 129, 132, 179, 245n122
Qūfāyā, 165, 257n106. *See also* Places: Caucasus
Qurʾān, 5, 61, 69, 105–6, 130, 180
createdness and, 50, 117. *See also miḥna*
discourse of wonder and, 3, 4–5, 181–2
exegesis of / exegetes, 26, 36, 43, 53, 97, 100, 111, 125, 138–9, 142, 184, 248n68
in geographical discourse, 25–6, 69–70, 154, 191, 237n142
inscription of, 115–7, 162, 175, 241n52
learned by people at wall, 100–1, 117–8, 157, 176, 196, 202, 206
Moses in, 69, 130, 180
parallels with Syriac sources, 241nn52–3
People of the Cave in, 35–7, 252n34
presented as superstition, 150–1
revelation of, 5
self-image of, 105–6
translation of, 38, 54. *See also* Gog and Magog: Qurʾānic treatment of
Qurʾānic schools, 100, 157, 196, 202, 206

rādhāniyya (Jewish merchants), 35, 221n4. *See also* Jewish: merchants
recension(s), 11, 74, 121, 169–72, 193, 237n1, 244n112, 259n153
Bodleian (Hunt 433), 16, 25, 91, 170–3, 201–4, 220n3, 253n53
marginalia in, 136, 247n57
notable divergences in, 123–4, 175, 184, 213n1, 224n45, 239n33
placement of account, 83, 133, 201
poetry in, 183, 258n142
wide circulation of, 169, 175, 194
Bodleian (Hunt 538), 170–1, 203, 258n142
Idrīsī, 102, 123, 150, 163, 175–6, 205–7
Muqaddasī, 74, 246n24
Paris (Supplément arabe 895), 16, 170, 201–4, 239n33

of Sallām's adventure, 123–5, 171, 181, 194
Vienna (Mixt. 783), 16, 19, 83, 129, 155, 157, 170–4, 195–200, 220n3, 230n5, 239n33, 253n53
addendum to, 172, 184
corrections to, 169
date of, 177
dedication of, 171, 183, 259n147
limited circulation of, 156, 175, 184, 194, 224n46
notable divergences in, 102, 121, 123–4, 156, 158, 169–70, 174–5 225n49, 230n5, 259n162
placement of account, 44, 83, 121, 133
poetry in, 183–4, 219n96, 258n142
problems with, 121, 133, 158, 169, 171–2, 174; Plate 13
treatment of guardians, 113–4
reception history, 11–2, 170, 179
of the *Masālik*, 16, 171–6, 182, 184, 193. *See also* recension(s); al-Wāthiq, mission to the wall: early reception
redaction, process of, 11, 16, 59, 68, 111, 133–4, 172
authorial, 102, 105, 133, 171
relics, 25, 36–7, 46–7, 182
Renaissance, 6
Resurrection, Day of, 42, 58, 62–3
ruins. *See also* wonder(s): buildings and places as
Alexander the Great and, 167–8
of Ctesiphon, 21, 77
melancholy and, 190
of Palmyra, 102
of Persepolis, 188–9
in the Qur'ān, 95
seen by Sallām, 100, 162, 168, 181, 196, 202, 206
Rūs, 35, 39, 86, 186, 221n6, 236n128
Rustamids, 186
rustāq (village district), 27
ṣāḥib al-barīd. *See barīd*
ṣāḥib al-sarīr. *See* Lord of the Throne
salvation history, 4, 26, 46, 63, 82
ᶜAbbāsids and, 44, 179
geography and, 5, 25–6, 101–2, 190–1
wall of Gog and Magog as testament to, 181
Sāmānid(s), 87, 131, 133–4
Ṣaqāliba (Slavs), 35, 86, 144
Sarīr, 75, 86, 231n23. *See also* Avars; Lord of the Throne
Sāsānian(s) (r. 224–651 C.E.), 20–1, 24, 29, 75–6, 188
administrative traditions / models, 21–2, 24–5, 27, 62, 89, 186, 218n75, 230n11
history, 28, 72, 78–9, 83
kings / emperors, 17, 29, 31, 72–3, 77
poetry, 31, 219n93
Shahrbarāz and, 78–81, 191
savage(s), 42, 89, 94
enclosure of, 6, 39
engaging with, 7, 39–40
on frontiers, 33, 38, 109
vs. civilized, 1, 7, 33, 39, 43, 86, 94, 118, 145, 153, 191
Sawār, 137
ṣawm al-taṭawwuᶜ (supererogatory fast), 114
science(s), 24, 44, 51–2, 55, 150, 186
religious (*al-ᶜulūm al-sharᶜiyya*), 61–3
translation and, 53–5
scripts, ancient, 44. *See also* language, first
hieroglyphics, 115–6, 224n45
scrolls (*ṣuḥuf*) of Abraham, 119
Scythians, 34, 42–3, 92–3
secretariat, 21, 23, 27, 133, 172, 182, 220n3
secretary(ies) (*kātib*, pl. *kuttāb*), 19, 27, 44–5, 88, 133, 215n23
Seven Sleepers of Ephesus, 36, 50. *See also* People of the Cave

Shahrāzād, 8
sharīʿa, pl. *sharāʾiʿ* (religious precepts / laws), 38, 61–3, 86, 101, 206
Shato Turks. *See* Önggüt (Önggüd, Ong)
shnānāṯā (grooves), 109, 240n51
shuʿūbiyya, 219n86, 219n95, 220n103
ṣifa, pl. *ṣifāt* (description), 23, 102, 207
signs, 26, 39–40, 56, 60, 106, 110, 118
  of dreams, 62–3
  God and, 5, 105
signs, of the Hour (*āyāt al-sāʿa*), 42, 61, 63, 101, 239n24
Silk Road, 156, 176
siqāya, 114–5, 243n74
Sirens, 149
slaves, 35, 36, 124, 222n17
Slavs, 35, 86, 144
Sogdian(s), 47, 49, 124, 157–8, 226n6, 253n41, 254n60
  trade routes, 179
south (*tayman*), 25
specialities (*khawāʾiṣṣ*), 9. *See also* commodities
speech, 105, 117
  as *bayān*, 106
  incomprehensible, 39, 76, 119–20
  trade without, 39–40
spices. *See* commodities
spies. *See* espionage
stories (qiṣaṣ). *See qiṣṣa*, pl. *qiṣaṣ*
storytelling, 7, 48, 129–30, 179, 184–5, 187
supernatural, 4, 6, 77, 149. *See also* nature(s)
superstition(s), 6, 149–50
ṣūrat al-arḍ (image / map of the earth), 41, 135
Sūrat al-Kahf, 35, 42, 69, 130, 138
surrat al-arḍ (navel of the world), 22, 23, 88, 216n42
suryāniyya, 116–7
Syriac, 23, 51, 53, 60, 93–4, 149
  Alexander Romance and, 42–3, 97, 110, 120, 237n1, 240n46
  traditions of the wall, 106–12, 116, 181, 191, 240n51, 241nn52–3

taʿajjub (astonishment), 7, 53, 192
ṭabīʿa (nature), 61
tajriba (experimentation), 52
talismans (*taʿāwīdh*), 44, 46, 76, 224n45
Tang dynasty (618–907 C.E.), 155–8, 168, 253n41
tarjama (to translate), 57–9. *See also* translation
tarjumāniyyūn (translators), 119–20
tarjumān (translator / interpreter), 38–9, 57–9, 60, 75, 106, 120, 191, 228n47, 228n50
ṭassūj / *tasūg* (cantons), 23, 25–7, 218n76
Tatars, 160, 176
taxation, 21
  administrative geography and, 24, 27, 218n76
  director of (*ṣāḥib al-kharāj*), 121, 200
  office of (*dīwān al-kharāj*), 19
tayman (south), 25
temples, 17, 44, 46, 104–5, 115, 254n60
Ten Tribes of Israel, 43
thaghr, pl. *thughūr* (outer breaches, or marchlands). *See* frontier(s): Arabic terminology of
thaumata, 7. *See also* marvelous, [the]; wonder(s)
theodicy, 4, 139
theology (*kalām*), 3–4
  translation and, 54–5, 58
  al-Wāthiq and, 51, 154
thughūr (march-lands, outer frontiers). *See* frontier(s)
Tibetan(s), empire of, 149, 156–8, 254n55, 255n61
trade, 35, 39, 74, 87, 124, 146, 179
  absent / silent, 40, 222n26, 223n29
  with Gog and Magog, 144–5
  networks / routes, 19, 35, 37

tragedy, 56, 227n41
translatio. *See furta sacra*
translation(s), 15–7, 41–2, 116, 119, 135, 140
of the Alexander Romance, 97, 237n1, 240n46
of ancient scripts, 44, 115–7, 188–9, 199
from Arabic, 37, 81, 146–7, 148, 154, 155, 161, 166, 174, 195–207, 246n20, 252n18
benefits of, 11, 57, 58
conversion and, 38, 101, 206
dream interpretation and, 62–3
epistemology and, 1–2, 15, 60, 106, 191, 211n2
geography and, 9, 24, 38–9, 41–2, 91–2, 187, 190–1
from Greek, 2, 4, 22–4, 41, 51, 54–7, 59–60, 62, 88, 90–1, 93, 158, 217n56, 226n14, 229n69, 230n77, 236n114, 236n135
as interpretation, 2, 35, 187, 228n48
limits of, 2, 11, 53–7, 58, 120, 190–1, 228n50
mediation and, 1, 38–9, 41, 43, 53–4, 56, 58, 191
from Middle Persian, 22, 26–7, 31, 61, 73, 110–1, 184, 242n58
movement, 2, 20, 22, 24, 43, 53–7, 58–60, 62–3, 187, 229n66
of Qurʾān, 38, 54
from Sanskrit, 20, 22, 53, 77
from Syriac, 2, 20, 23, 51, 55–6, 60, 88, 109, 242n55
transmission / dissemination and, 41, 120, 153, 179
from Turkish, 38–9, 51, 159
translator(s), 15–6, 51
astrologers and, 61
Brahmans as, 119–20
as guide, 35, 38–9, 41, 191
as imperial informants, 48, 51–3, 58–60, 109
invisibility of, 41, 51, 118
proselytization and, 38–9
terminology for, 57–60, 118, 228n50
travelog (*riḥla*), 142, 152, 154
trivet (*dīgdān*), 110–11, 198, 203
trophies, 47–8, 81, 92, 113, 125, 181, 199–200
Tughuzghuz, 101, 123, 145. *See also* Uyghur Khanate
tukhm, pl. *tukhūm* (border). *See* frontier(s): Arabic terminology of
Turkish [language], 16, 37, 38–9, 51, 131, 137, 138, 144, 149, 152, 246n20
Turk, son of Yāfith, 92, 144
Turks / Turkic tribes, 101, 144, 160, 166. *See also* Adhkish; Bashjirt; Ghuzz; Huns; Khazar(s); Kīmāk; Mongol(s); Önggüt; Ottoman(s); Qarluq; Qirghiz; Tughuzghuz; Uyghur Khanate
ʿAbbāsids and, 22, 44, 49, 51, 67, 71, 124
conquest of, 28
conversion of, 38, 101, 176
danger posed by, 76, 84
location of, 84, 85, 92, 101
translators / informants, 38–9, 51, 123, 134, 244n112

Umayyad(s), 20–1, 38, 70, 87, 185, 215n35
of al-Andalus, 87, 186
conquests of, 46–7, 98
exegetical writing, 100
the Khazar and, 75, 81–2, 83
mission to the cave of darkness, 233n72
mission to the wall of Gog and Magog, 81–2, 191
unseen / unknown (*ghayb*), 9–10, 15–6, 35, 57, 62
ustān (municipality), 26

utopian society, 119–20
Uyghur Khanate (744–840 C.E.) / Uyghur(s), 101, 123, 156–8, 168–9, 172, 179, 239n22, 253n41, 253n44, 254nn57–8, 256n89

verse (*āya*), 181

wall against Gog and Magog, 5–6, 95, 97, 100, 112–4, 135, 136, 165, 189, 195, 197–9, 201–3, 205–7, 240n36, 247n58
  apocalypse and, 5, 42, 78, 114–5, 181
  conquests and, 78–9, 233n61
  destruction of, 5, 42, 43, 62, 63, 113, 115–6, 120, 143, 146
  Dhū 'l-Qarnayn's inscription on, 115–8, 199
  dreams of, 15, 43, 60–1, 62–3
  enclosing monstrous races, 5, 42–3, 63, 145, 180–1, 190
  guardians of, 113–4, 198, 203–4, 207
  Kaʿba and, 114–5
  key to, 104, 109–12, 114, 136, 150, 198, 203, 240n51, 248n68
  location of, 5, 70, 73, 76–8, 81, 83, 101, 137–8, 144–5, 161, 165, 173, 201, 230n9, 240n36, 255n72
  in marvel literature, 139–40, 142
  in Middle Persian sources, 111–2
  protecting humankind, 69–70
  in the Qurʾān, 5, 103, 115–6, 150–1, 152
  in Qurʾānic exegesis, 138–9, 230n9
  reality of, 5, 94, 138, 143, 153, 154, 179–81, 252n34
  in sacred cosmography, 132, 186
  salvation history and, 44
  Syriac tradition on, 42–3, 106–10, 112, 116, 240n51, 241nn52–3
  visual / cartographic representations of, 135, 138, 240n43, 255n72; Plates 5–8, 10–2
  as Wall of China, 5, 155–63, 168–9
  [not] Wall of China, 163–5, 167, 176–7, 254n53, 254nn58–9
  likened to wall of Golden Emperor, 176–7
Wāqwāq islands, 6, 89, 163
waṣf (description), 105
al-Wāthiq, mission to the wall, 44, 48, 49, 83, 181, 185–6
  casualties of, 15, 124, 175, 200
  as confirmation of the Qurʾān, 103–4, 191
  date of, 70–1, 125
  distance and time covered, 174–5, 254n53
  early reception of, 51, 120–1, 129, 180
    in *ʿajāʾib*-writing 139–42
    in geographies, 130–5, 142, 171–6, 194
    in histories and encyclopedias, 135–6, 143
    in maps, 134–5; Plates 6–8
    in Qurʾānic exegesis, 138–9
  European reception of, 149–69, 173–4, 176–7, 232n35, 252n34, 253n46, 254n53, 256n104
  historicity of, 118, 121–3, 125, 135–8, 179–81, 187, 247n58
  manuscript divergences of, 44, 83, 102, 114, 121, 123–4, 129, 133, 156–8, 169–75, 184, 194–207; Plate 13
  Middle Persian material and, 111–2, 191
  mission to cave and, 50, 182
  motivations for, 43, 123, 154, 195, 201, 205, 256n89
  Muʿāwiya's mission and, 81–2, 113, 191
  parallels with Ibn Faḍlān, 186–7
  preparations for, 68, 196, 201, 205, 206
  as *qiṣṣa* / *khabar*, 125, 129–30, 179–80, 200, 204
  return to Sāmarrāʾ, 125, 200, 204, 207
  Shahrbarāz's mission and, 79–80, 113,

191
Syriac sources and, 106–10, 112, 191
Wahrārzān, 72, 231n22
wazīr, pl. *wuzarā*ʾ, 17–8, 21, 55, 123, 134, 182–3, 214n11, 214n14, 216n38, 220n2
west (*maghrib*), 25
White Tatars. *See* Önggüt
wonder(s)
Alexander the Great and, 99, 188
in antiquity, 2–3, 7, 42, 142, 236n133
authenticity of, 7, 9–10
beholding of, 10, 48, 102. *See also* eyewitness
buildings and places as, 44, 46, 77, 102, 105, 107, 139
temples, 44
valley of serpents, 80, 99
conquest and, 47
demystification of, 147, 149, 166
entertainment and, 7–8
enumeration of, 47, 102, 139
experience of, 3, 7, 48, 53
on frontiers, 188, 191
gestures of, 7, 192; Plates 1–3, 9–10, 14
in Gharnāṭī, 139–40, 141
in Ibn Khurradādhbih, 23, 34, 39, 43, 46–8
in Ibn al-Wardī, 141, 180, 260n3
in Qazwīnī, 76, 140–2
organization of, 139
possession of, 38, 44–8
production of, 6–7, 39, 53
in the Qurʾān, 4–5, 181–2
The Thousand and One Nights and, 48
in Ṭūsī, 139
of the world, 1, 76, 139
in Zayyānī, 142

Yājūj and Mājūj, 2, 42. *See also* Gog and Magog
vocalization of, 223n31
yāqūt. *See* gems, and jewels
Yūra, 40, 222n16, 252n27

Zanj, 45, 85, 86
zhou (frontier prefecture), 157–8, 254n55
zodiac, 86, 90–2
Zoroastrian
astrological material, 62
Ibn Khurradādhbih and, 17, 213n2
priest, 188

INDEX OF SCRIPTURAL CITATIONS

Biblical Verses

Genesis 10:2, 42
Genesis 11:1–9, 116
Exodus 3:11–21, 119
Exodus 4:1–14, 119
1 Chronicles 1:5, 5:4, 42
Jer. 1:14, 108
Ezekiel 38–9, 42
Ezekiel 40:5–42:20, 115
Revelation 20:7–10, 42

Qurʾānic Verses

2:31, 106
2:242, 105
3:137, 237
6:11, 237
12:3, 130
12:4–6, 229
12:6, 12, 101, 229
12:109, 237
14:4, 227
16:26, 116
16:36, 237
16:68-9, 211
16:105, 227
18:9, 182
18:9–26, 35–6
18:22, 26, 35, 228
18:58, 237
18:60, 26
18:63, 26
18:64, 130
18:83, 99, 152
18:83–100, 5
18:92–7, 103
18:93, 118, 230
18:96, 241
18:98, 116
21:95–6, 95
28:69, 237
30:9, 237
30:42, 237
35:44, 237
39:29, 227
40:21, 237
40:82, 95
41:44, 227
43:1–2, 227
43:3, 117
55:2–3, 106
55:35, 241
72:1, 181
92:5, 227

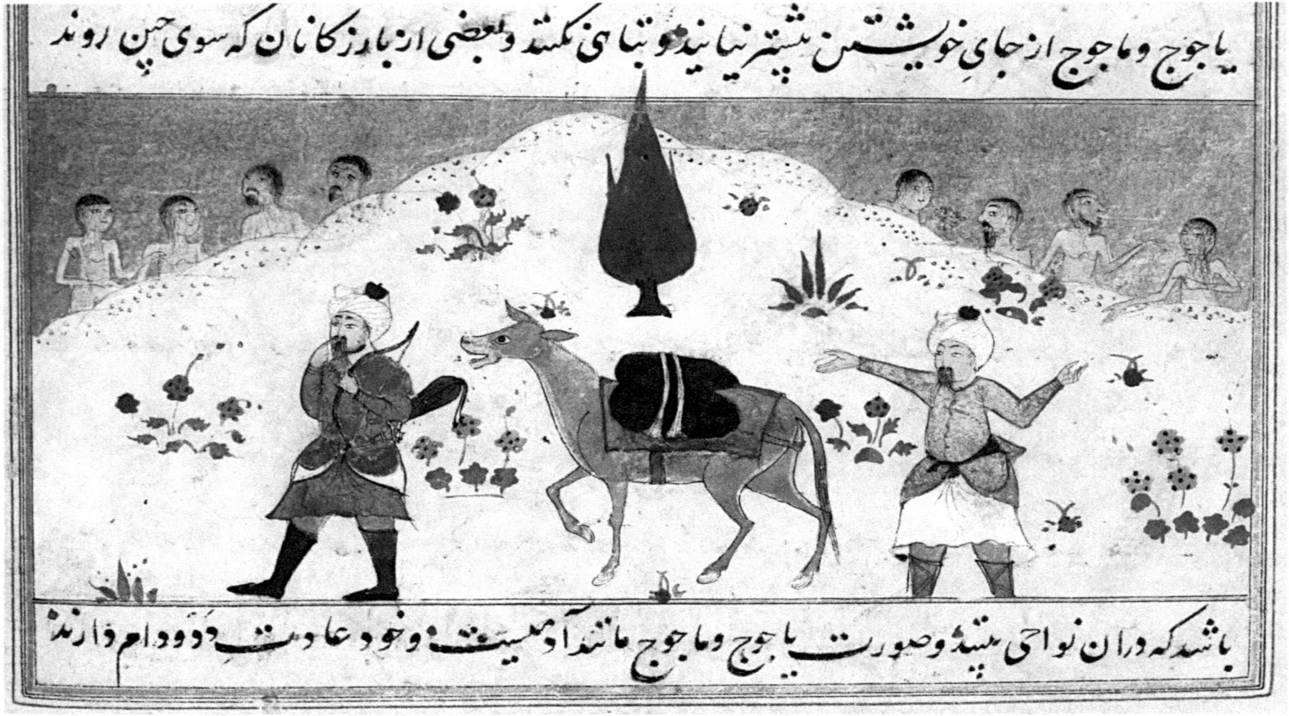

Plate 1: People of Gog and Magog sighted by merchants, Shahmardān b. Abī ʾl-Khayr, *Nuzhat-nāma-i ʿalāʾī*, dated 933/1526. Courtesy of the New York Public Library, Spencer, Persian MS 50, fol. 74b.

Plate 2: The expedition of Alexander the Great in the Encircling Ocean, Zakariyyā᾽ al-Qazwīnī, *ʿAjā᾽ib al-makhlūqāt*, dated 1041/1632. Courtesy of the John Rylands Library, Persian MS 3, fol. 61a.

Plate 3: Khusraw Anūshirwān's dream of the creature from the Caspian Sea, Zakariyyā᾿ al-Qazwīnī, *ʿAjā᾿ib al-makhlūqāt,* twelfth/eighteenth-century Indian MS. Courtesy of the Sackler Museum, Harvard University, MS 1972.33, fol. 91b.

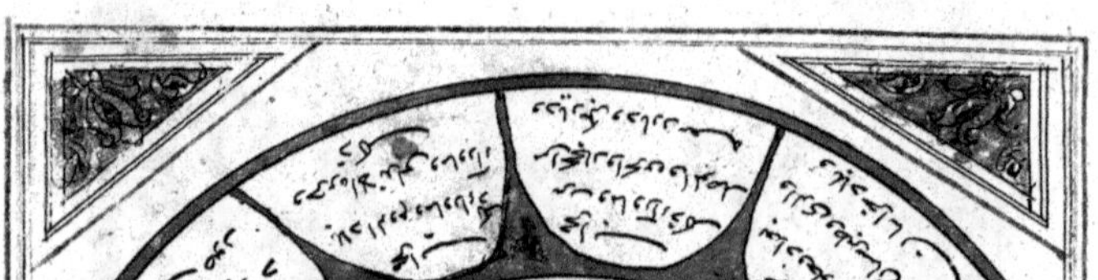

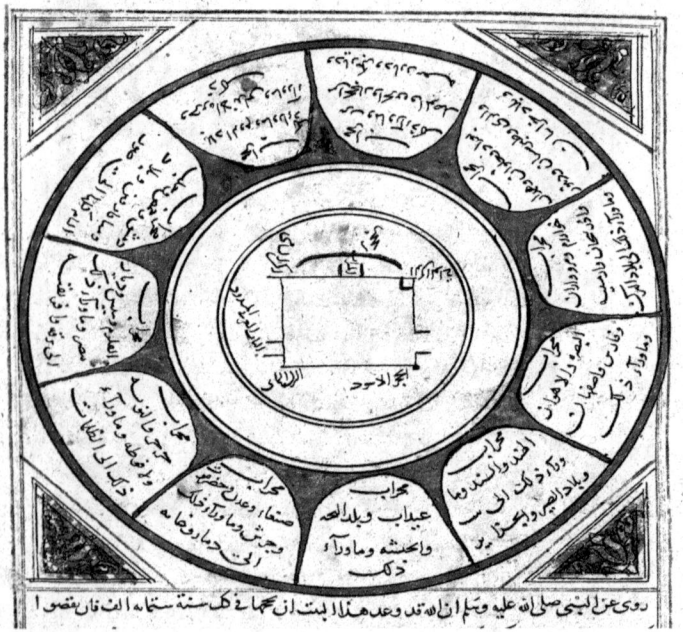

Plate 4: *Qibla* map from Zakariyyā᾿ al-Qazwīnī, *Āthār al-bilād*, dated 729/1329. © British Library Board, MS Or. 3623, fol. 33a.

Plate 5: Iskandar builds a wall against the people of Gog and Magog, with details of the construction materials, Abū ʿl-Qāsim al-Firdawsī, *Shāh-nāma*, ca. 735/1335. Courtesy of the Arthur Sackler Museum, Smithsonian Institution, MS S1986.104.

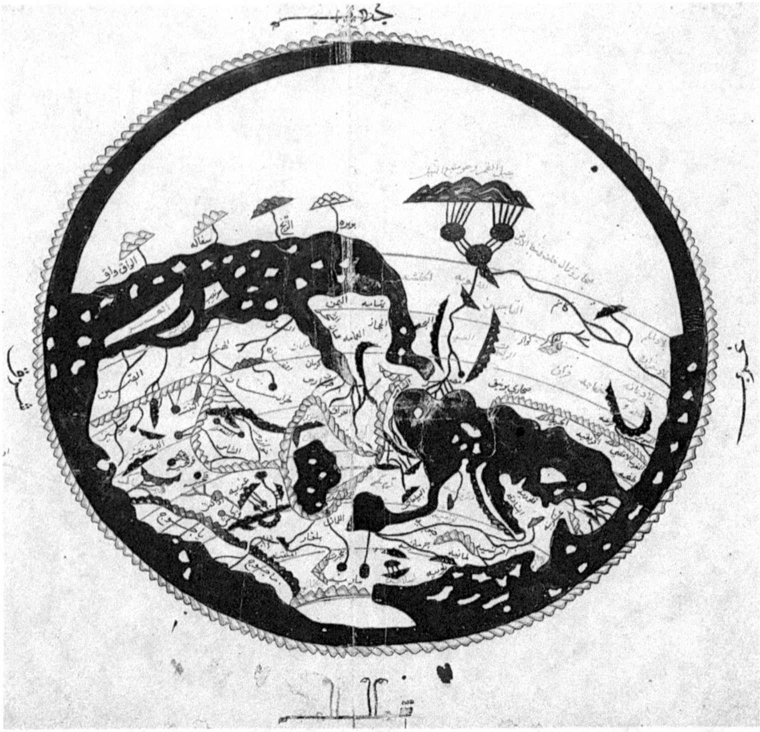

Plate 6a: *Mappa mundi*, Abū ʿAbd Allāh al-Idrīsī, *Nuzhat al-mushtāq*, dated 960/1553. Courtesy of the Bodleian Library, Oxford University, MS Pococke 375, fols. 3a–4b.

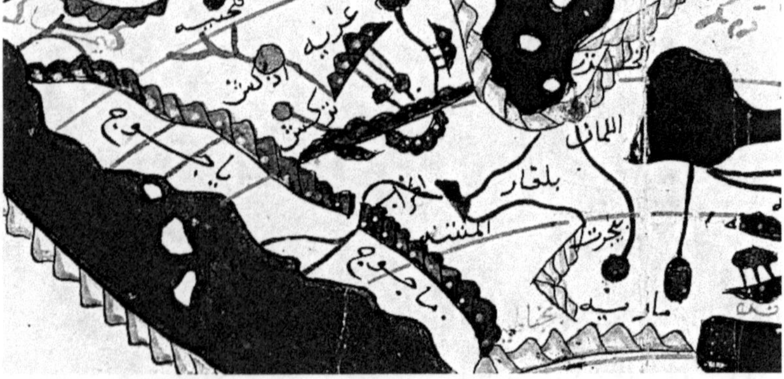

Plate 6b: Detail of *mappa mundi* with the putrid land (*muntina*), the barrier against Gog and Magog, and the Adhkish Turks, Idrīsī, *Nuzhat al-mushtāq*, dated 960/1553. Courtesy of the Bodleian Library, Oxford University, MS Pococke 375, fols. 3a–4b.

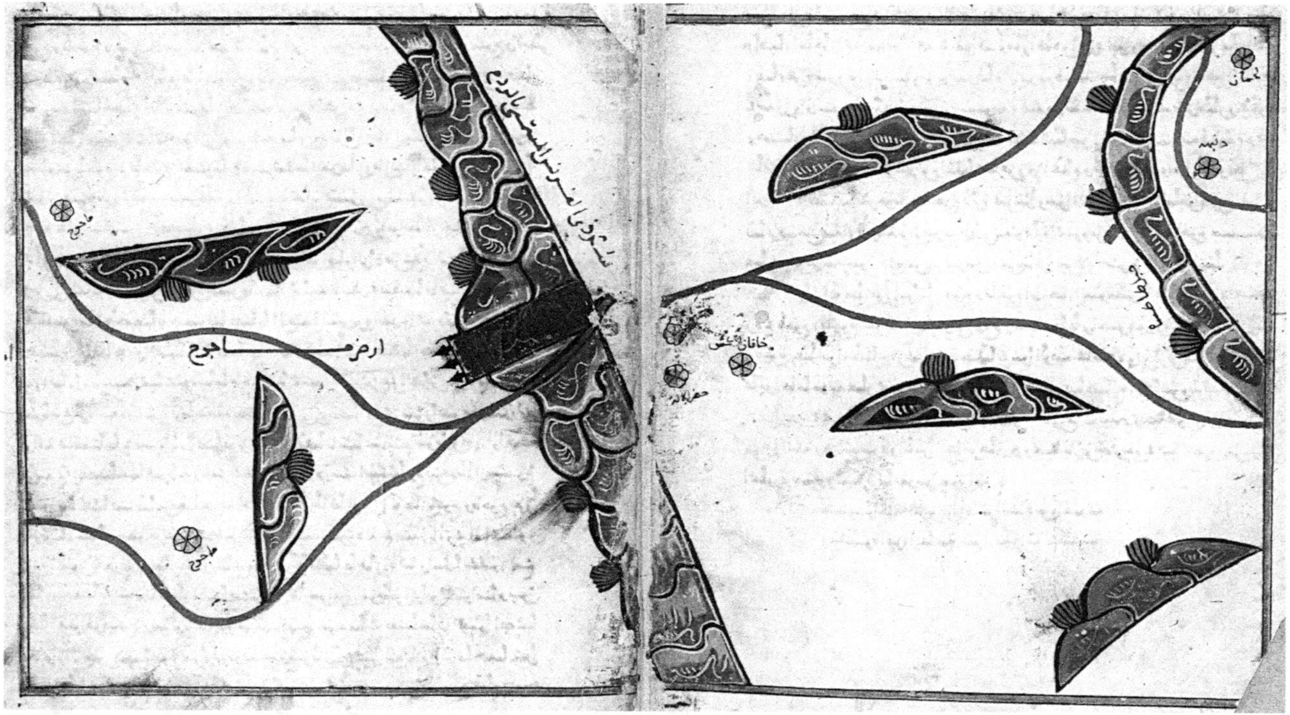

Plate 7: Magnified view of the gate to Dhū 'l-Qarnayn's wall, located before the Khāqān of the Adhkish Turks, Idrīsī, *Nuzhat al-mushtāq*, eighth/fourteenth-century MS. Courtesy of the Bibliothèque nationale de France, MS Supplément arabe 892 (MS arabe 2221), clime 6.9, fols. 33b–34a.

Plate 8: Detail of Dhū 'l-Qarnayn's gate in a *mappa mundi*, near the legendary City of Brass (*madīnat al-nuḥās*), from an anonymous Egyptian manuscript, entitled *Kitāb gharā'ib al-funūn wa mulaḥ al-ʿuyūn*, eighth/fourteenth-century MS. Courtesy of the Bodleian Library, Oxford University, MS Arab c. 90, fols. 23b–24a.

Plate 9: Sallām al-Tarjumān observing a maiden pulled from the belly of a fish by Khazar sailors in the Caspian Sea, Zakariyyāʾ al-Qazwīnī, *ʿAjāʾib al-makhlūqāt*, ca. 710/1310. © British Library Board, MS Or. 14140, fol. 46b.

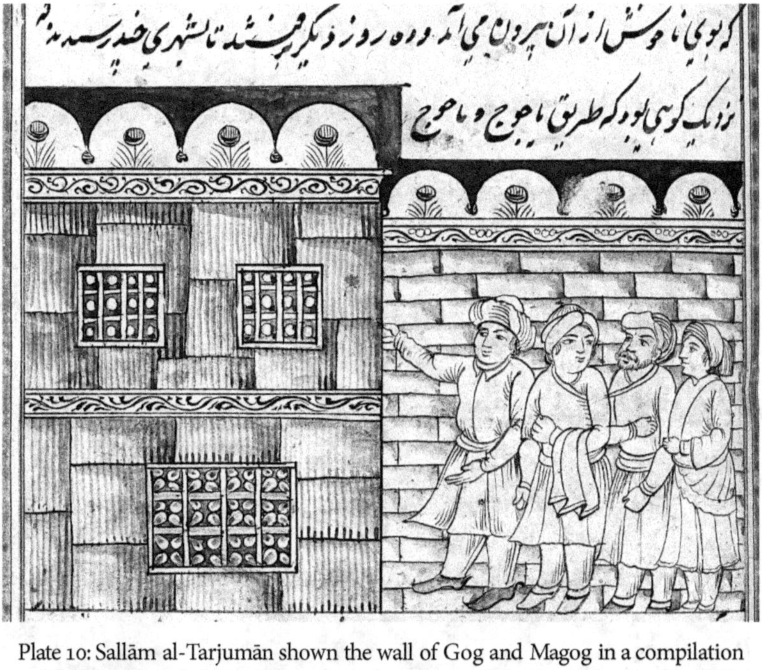

Plate 10: Sallām al-Tarjumān shown the wall of Gog and Magog in a compilation entitled *ʿAjāʾib al-buldān*, from selected passages of the *Rawḍat al-ṣafāʾ* of Mīr Khwānd on the marvels of the world, compiled for the wazīr of Bisṭām in 1240/1824. © British Library Board, MS Or. 12995, fol. 75a.

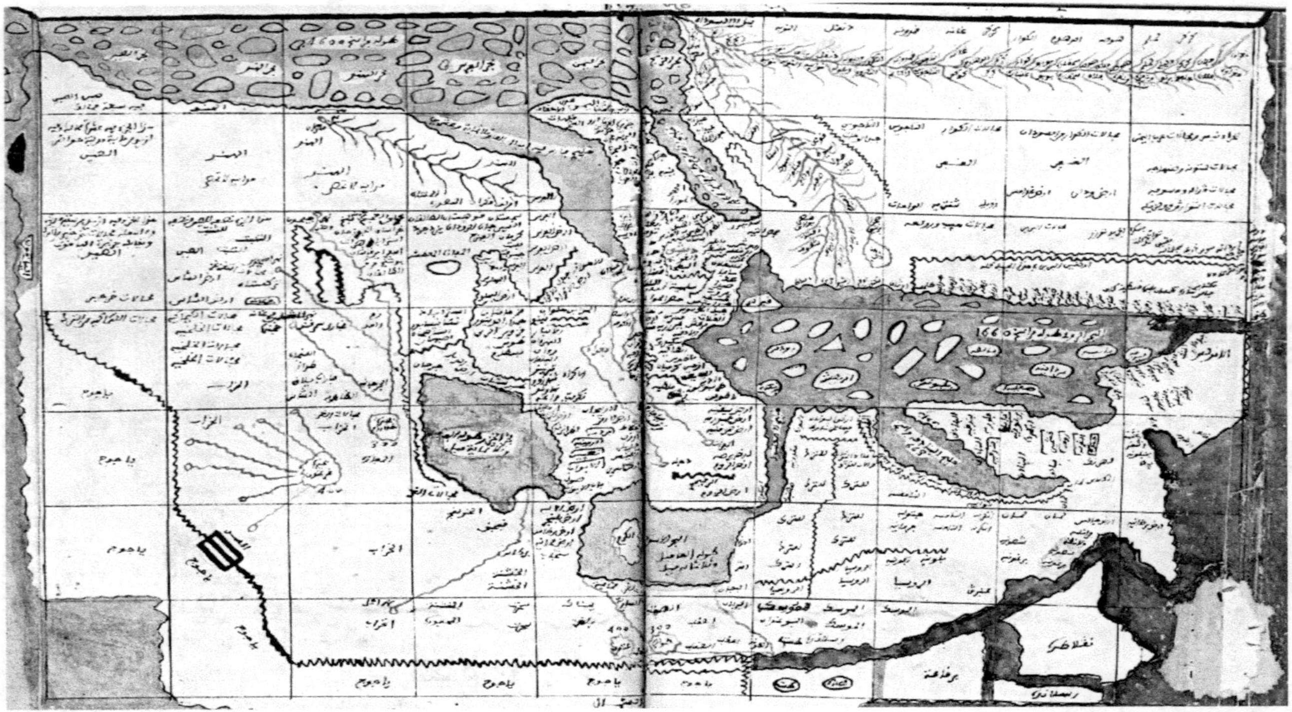

Plate 11: *Mappa mundi*, with the gate and wall of Gog and Magog occupying the bottom quarter of the map, Abū ʿl-Qāsim al-Zayyānī, *Riḥlat al-ḥudhdhāq*, thirteenth/nineteenth-century MS. Courtesy of al-Khizāna al-Ḥasaniyya, Rabat, MS 2470.

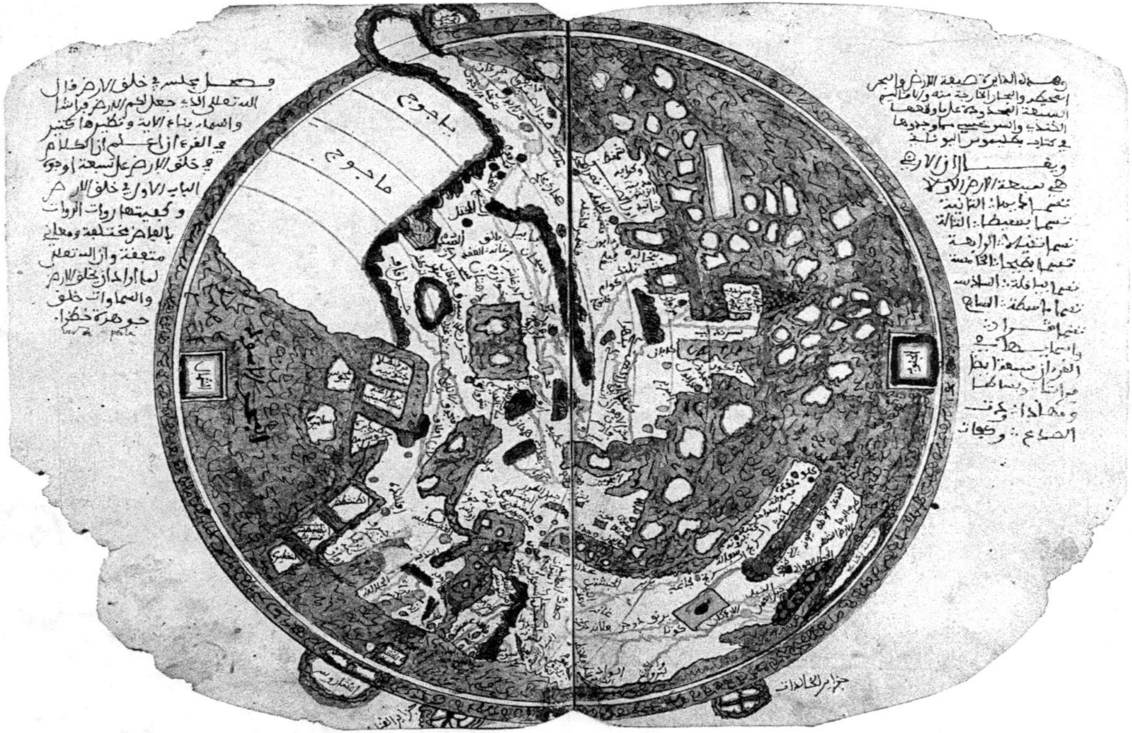

Plate 12: *Mappa mundi* attributed to Abū Yūsuf al-Kindī and Aḥmad b. al-Ṭayyib al-Sarakhsī, and said to have been derived from Ptolemy, with a prominent focus on the *terra incognita* of Gog and Magog; also including a detail of Alexander's gate located in the upper left-hand portion, near the Adhkish Turks and the Mountain of Qāf, dated 977/1570. Courtesy of the Bodleian Library, Oxford University, MS Laud. Or. 317, fols. 10b–11a.

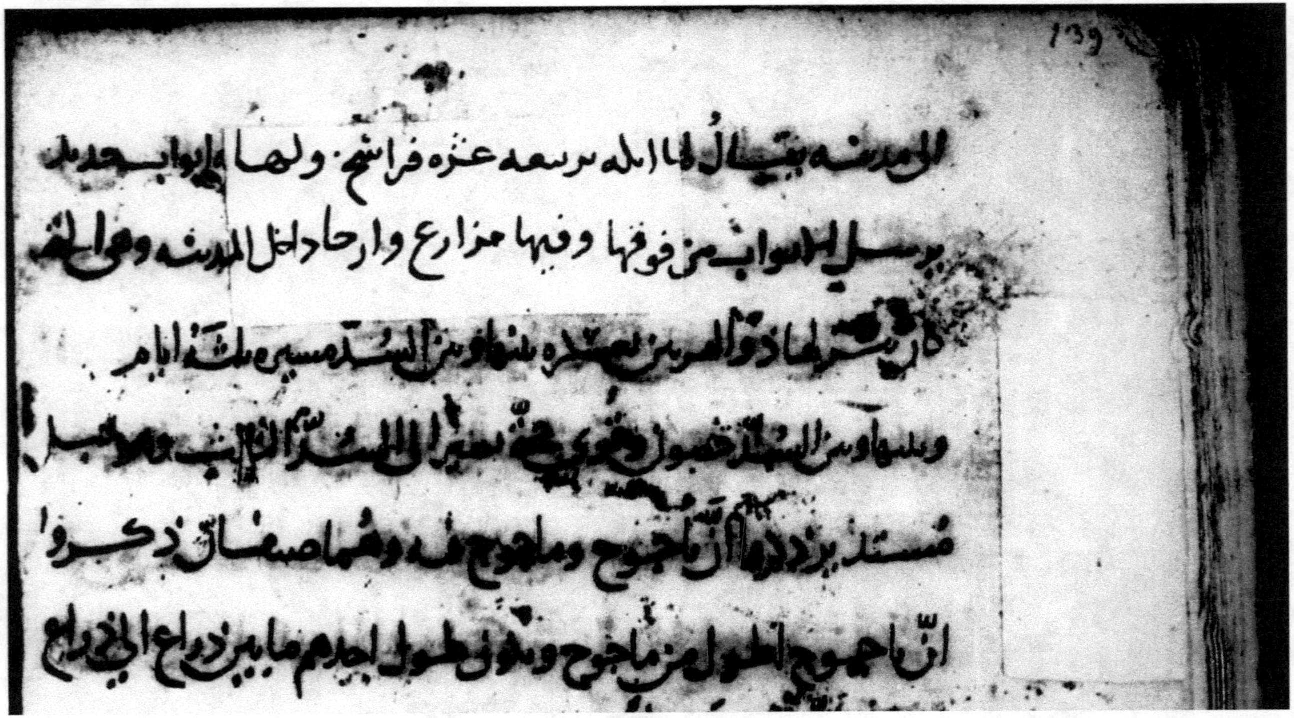

Plate 13: Detail of emended section of Ibn Khurradādhbih, *al-Masālik wa ʾl-mamālik*. Courtesy of the Österreichische Nationalbibliothek of Vienna, MS Mixt. 783, fol. 69b.

Plate 14: Ibn Faḍlān shown a dead giant from the people of Gog and Magog, Muḥammad b. Maḥmūd al-Ṭūsī, *ʿAjāʾib-nāma*, dated 790/1388. Courtesy of the Bibliothèque nationale de France, MS Supplément persane 332, fol. 193b.

www.ingramcontent.com/pod-product-compliance
Lightning Source LLC
Chambersburg PA
CBHW050134240426
43673CB00043B/1670
* 9 7 8 1 7 8 4 5 3 7 3 9 5 *